מסורה

ArtScroll Judaiscope Series

OF HOME

Collected from the pages of
The Jewish Observer
Rabbi Nisson Wolpin, Editor

Mesorah Publications, ltd

Son
4/11/04

AND HEART

REFLECTIONS ON THE WORLD OF THE JEWISH WOMAN

EDITED BY SARAH SHAPIRO

FIRST EDITION
First Impression . . . February 1993

SECOND EDITION
First Impression . . . May 1995

Published and Distributed by
MESORAH PUBLICATIONS, Ltd.
4401 Second Avenue
Brooklyn, New York 11232

Distributed in Europe by
J. LEHMANN HEBREW BOOKSELLERS
20 Cambridge Terrace
Gateshead, Tyne and Wear
England NE8 1RP

Distributed in Israel by
SIFRIATI / A. GITLER—BOOKS
4 Bilu Street
P.O.B. 14075
Tel Aviv 61140

Distributed in Australia & New Zealand by
GOLDS BOOK & GIFT CO.
36 William Street
Balaclava 3183, Vic., Australia

Distributed in South Africa by
KOLLEL BOOKSHOP
22 Muller Street
Yeoville 2198, Johannesburg, South Africa

ARTSCROLL JUDAISCOPE SERIES ®
OF HOME AND HEART
© *Copyright 1993, by* MESORAH PUBLICATIONS, Ltd.
4401 Second Avenue / Brooklyn, N.Y. 11232 / (718) 921-9000

The essays in this volume have been adapted from articles
that have appeared in the pages of
THE JEWISH OBSERVER
published by Agudath Israel of America. Rabbi Nisson Wolpin, Editor
Copyright and all rights reserved by The Jewish Observer, New York City

No part of this book may be reproduced
in any form *without* **written** *permission from the copyright holder,*
except by a reviewer who wishes to quote brief passages in connection with a review
written for inclusion in magazines or newspapers.

THE RIGHTS OF THE COPYRIGHT HOLDER WILL BE STRICTLY ENFORCED.

ISBN:
0-89906-890-1 (hard cover)
0-89906-891-X (paperback)

Printed in the United States of America by Noble Book Press Corp.
Bound by Sefercraft Quality Bookbinders, Ltd., Brooklyn, N.Y.

Table of Contents

Introduction — Of Home and Heart / *Sarah Shapiro*   13

≈§ Her Housekeeping

Musings on Matchmaking / *Hindy Kviat*   27
A Down-Home Pesach in Philly / *Edith Krohn*   29
Answering the Fifth Question / *Emmy Stark Zitter*   33
Getting Ready for Shabbos / *Hadassah Becker*   37

≈§ Her Soulkeeping

Between the Braids / *Bracha Druss Goetz*   47
Measure for Measure / *Hanoch Teller*   49
"Chevra Kadisha" — A Woman's View / *Betsy Kaplan*   57
The Search / *Ruth Finkelstein*   59
Shadows in the Kitchen / *Sarah Shapiro*   64
Standing Alone / *Yaffa Ganz*   71

≈§ Her Housekeeping vs. Her Soulkeeping

Time for Personal Growth / *Shira Silvers Frank*   77
Housekeeping vs. Soulkeeping / *H.D. Wolpin*   83
Woman's Place in Torah Study / *Fraida Blau*   88
Jewish Women in a Torah Society / *Nisson Wolpin*   92
Letters in Response   106
In the Wake of the Thomas Hearings / *Rabbi Nisson Wolpin*   119
Woman at the Crossroads / *Nechama Bakst*   121
When Feminists Demand, Can Judaism Deliver? / *Rabbi Yisroel Miller*   126
Sanctity and Self-Expression / *Yaakov Amitai*   133
"Where There's a Rabbinic Will, There's a Halachic Way" / *Rabbi Yissocher Frand*   138

Music — By and For a Jewish Woman / *Nama Frenkel*	150
Wonder Woman / *Bracha Druss Goetz*	156

⇜§ She Longs for the Whole Family

High in the Hills of Yerushalayim / *Malky Brailofsky*	159
A Daughter Recalls a Great Father / *Adele Engel*	162
Rebbetzin Henkin and Me — A Story / *Joanne Jackson Yelenik*	166
Avraham's Household / *Fayge Osnat Levy*	168
Letter in Response: Children of Avraham's Household	180
This Side of the Fence / *Miss Anon*	182
Letter to the Editor	189
Love and Marriage / *David Gottlieb*	193
A Private Waterloo / *Libby Lazewnik*	202
The Battle for the Jewish Family / *Rabbi Mattisyahu Solomon*	205
"Sidney (Also Known as Steven)" / *Yaakov Jacobs*	210
Invisible Ledgers / *Libby Lazewnik*	213
Life-styles of the Childless Poor / *Anonymous*	215
Jewish Kids up for Grabs / *Vicki Krausz*	218
My Children's Brother / *Malka Schaps*	224
Reflections of a Parent / *Ephraim Milch*	226
Dear Mom / *Bracha Druss Goetz*	232
An Open Letter to My Questioning Friend	234
Kids on the Fringe	238
Letter From a Mother of "Kids on the Fringe"	244
The Seed of Hope / *Shaindel Weinbach*	248

⇜§ The Mother is the Teacher

"Chinuch" — Whose Responsibility Is It? / *Rabbi Yisroel Reisman*	253
Shabbos: A Time for All Ages / *Dr. Meir Wikler*	261
Training Children Not to Speak Lashon Hara / *Rabbi Zelig Pliskin*	266
How to Raise Children by Really Trying / *Rabbi Chaim Dov Keller*	273
The Critical Parent's Guidebook / *Avi Shulman*	285
Letter in Response to: Critical Parent's Guidebook	296
And He Who Knows Not How to Ask Open for Him / *Shani Perr*	298

... And Vice-Versa

The Teacher Is the Lesson / *Miriam Zakon*	303
Were It Not for Her . . . / *Rabbi Chaim Dov Keller*	314
An Overwhelming View / *Baila bat Rifka*	324
Dear Morah, / *Ita Grinblat*	327
Dear Mother / *Breindy Leizerson*	330
R=I: A Dangerous Equation / *Helene Ribowsky, M.S.*	334
Teaching the Learning Disabled Student / *Rebecca Amster*	340
In Search of Chavie / *Malky Brailofsky*	354

What She Learns From Adversity

Building a Ghetto of Our Own / *Edith Krohn*	363
The Out-of-Towners / *Emmy Stark Zitter*	371
Letters in Response	379
Commuting on the Right Track / *Bat Sheva Menucha*	382
The Call Unanswered / *Bat Sheva Menucha*	384
Of Peace. And Pieces / *Faygie Borchardt*	386
"I Know" / *Aharon Amir*	388

How to Be a Jewish Mother

To the Rabbi's Wife / *Bracha Druss Goetz*	390
Cholent — Food for Thought / *Anna Gotlieb*	392
The Credit Is Yours / *F.H.*	394
A Prayer / *Devorah Gershon*	396
The Oheiv Yisrael: A Profile / *Rabbi Zelig Pliskin*	398

Home Sweet Home

Women at the Wester Wall / *Arleen Naomi Habshush*	407
Post-Blizzard Musings / *Faygie Borchardt*	409
The Road Home / *Leah Kohn*	411
Teshuvah / *Marsha Shine*	419
Three Cheers for Turbulence Le-Shem Shomayim!	420
The Traveler and the Princess / *Libby Lazewnik*	428

Contributors to this volume*
(in alphabetical order)

Aharon Amir is an anti-religious writer for the Israeli daily *Yediot Acharanot.*

Yaacov Amitai wrote his essay as an open letter to his neighbors who are participating in the women's *minyan* described in his piece.

Mrs. Amster, a graduate of the Beth Jacob Seminary of Jerusalem, holds a Masters Degree in Education from Columbia University and has worked as a journalist and teacher. She lives in Rochester, N. Y., where her husband is connected with the Yeshiva Chofetz Chaim Talmudical Institute of upstate New York.

Nechama Bakst (nee Krupenia) lives in Oak Park, Michigan.

Hadassah Becker teaches in a Bais Yaakov High School in the Flatbush section of Brooklyn. She expresses gratitude to her husband for several of the sources for this article.

Fraida Blau, a Monsey housewife, is indebted to her husband, Rabbi Nosson Binyomin Blau, for the sources on which her essay is based.

Faigy Borchardt teaches in a Bais Yaakov High School as well as in a Teachers Seminary in Brooklyn, New York.

Malka Brailofsky lives in Brooklyn, New York. She is the author of the popular children's novel *Flying with Daniel* (Artscroll/Mesorah).

Adele Engel is a daughter of the late *Moreinu* Yaakov Rosenheim. She lives in Far Rockaway, New York.

Rabbi Yissocher Frand says a *shiur* in Yeshivah Ner Israel in Baltimore, as well as a weekly *shiur* in the Agudath Israel of Baltimore. These *shiurim* are available through his highly successful and popular tape series. His essay in this volume is based on a fuller treatment of the topic delivered by Rabbi Frand at a symposium at the 67th National Convention of Agudath Israel of America.

---

* Most of the biographical information was culled from the original Jewish Observer articles.

Shira Silvers Frank CSW lives in the Flatbush section of Brooklyn, and works with Torah Umesorah's Counterforce Program. She also maintains a private practice in counseling.

Nama Frenkel is an independent film maker whose film, *JEWISH MOTHERS*, is an attempt to show the non-verbal and environmental qualities of Jewish homes.

Yaffa Ganz, a much-published author of popular juvenile literature, lives in the Bayit Vegan section of Jerusalem. She is the author of *All Things Considered* (Artscroll/Mesorah).

Devorah Gershon is an American who lives in Bayit Vegan, Jerusalem.

Bracha Druss Goetz, a poet and author of children books, lives in Baltimore, Maryland.

Anna Gotlieb of Spring Valley, New York, writes feature columns for various local newspapers.

Rabbi David Gottlieb is a member of the faculty of Yeshivah Ohr Somayach in Jerusalem. He lectures on Torah topics in Israel as well as virtually every English-speaking country on the globe. He is the author of *The Informed Soul* (Artscroll/Mesorah).

Arleen Naomi Habshush, formerly of Rochester, New York, lives in Jerusalem.

Yaakov Jacobs, served as the editor of the *Jewish Observer* from 1965-1970. He lives in Staten Island, New York.

Betsy Kaplan lives in Atlanta, Georgia, where she is an active member in the *Chevra Kadisha*.

Rabbi Chaim Dov Keller, *Rosh Hayeshivah* of Telshe Yeshivah, Chicago, lectures and writes on Torah topics. He based his essay "Were It Not For Her . . ." on his address to the gathering marking the 50th Yahrzeit of Sarah Schenirer, that took place in New York's Madison Square Garden in March, 1985.

Leah Kohn of Monsey, NY is principal of Netzach Yisrael — Jewish Renaissance Center — a school in New York City that specializes in uniting Jewish women of secular background with their Torah heritage.

Vicki Krausz, of Denver, Colorado, is the founder and director of the Jewish Children's Adoption Network.

Edith Krohn (nee Ackerman) of Kew Gardens, New York, is a popular author of several articles and books, including *The Way It Was* (Artscroll/Mesorah). Among her many accomplishments — she is the proud mother of Rabbi Pesach Krohn, author of *Bris Milah* and the superb *Maggid* series.

Hindy Kviat lives in Brooklyn, New York, and teaches in a Bais Yaakov there.

Libby Lazewnik, a published poet and author of stories for youth, lives in the Har Nof section of Jerusalem.

Breindy Leizerson is a teacher of a pre 1-A class in Yeshiva Torah Temimah of Brooklyn, New York.

Fayge Osnat Levy is an American living in Jerusalem.

Bat Sheva Menucha lives in Toronto.

Ephraim Milch, a *talmid* of Yeshiva Ner Israel, in Baltimore, Maryland lives in Pittsburgh, Pennsylvania where he practices law with the firm of Campbell and Levine. The author acknowledges the contribution of a number of people to the formulation of his essay, most notably, Maier Kutoff of Minneapolis, Minnesota.

Rabbi Yisroel Miller, author of *What's Wrong With Being Human?* (Artscroll/Mesorah) serves as *Rav* of Congregation Poale Zedeck in Pittsburgh, Pennsylvania. His essay in this volume is based on his presentation of the topic at a national convention of Agudath Israel of America.

Shanie Perr is Program Director of Camp Bnos in Liberty, New York, counselor and therapist with Torah Umesorah's Counterforce Program, and is currently in private practice.

Rabbi Zelig Pliskin, well-known author and lecturer, is Director of Aish Hatorah's Counseling Center in Jerusalem. His grandfather, Rabbi Yaakov Yisroel Berger zt"l, was *Rav* in Cleveland, Ohio for many years and authored three *seforim* on the topic of this article: *Ahavas Yisroel, Kol Yisroel Chaverim,* and *She'aris Yaakov.*

Rabbi Yisroel Reisman, well-known lecturer and author, is author of several volumes in the Schottenstein edition of the Talmud published by Mesorah Heritage Foundation, is a member of the Kollel of Mesivta Torah Vodaath, and serves as Rav of Agudath Israel of Madison, in Brooklyn, New York.

Dr. Helene Ribowsky, is an educational consultant in *yeshivos* and

Day Schools and is in private practice as a learning disabilities specialist in Brooklyn, New York.

Dr. Malka Schaps, a professor of mathematics, lives in Bnei Brak.

Sarah Shapiro, well-known author and editor of this volume, lives in Arzei HaBira, Jerusalem.

Marsha Shine lives in Memphis, Tennessee.

Avi Shulman is an author and lecturer on educational themes. He heads Torah Umesorah's S.E.E.D. Program. His essay in this volume is taken from his book, "Getting Children to Respond to Criticism."

Rabbi Mattisyahu Solomon is *mashgiach ruchani* of the Gateshead Yeshivah. His essay in this volume is based on his address to an Agudath Israel of America conference dedicated to "Contemporary Society vs. The Jewish Family" held in Brooklyn in April 1986.

Hanoch Teller, author of a number of popular books of inspiring stories, lives in Jerusalem. His essay, based on information offered by Rebbitzins Sarah Angel and Rivka Plitnick, is excerpted from a chapter in his book, *Hey Taxi!*.

Shaindel Weinbach, is a published poet and author whose works include *The Three Merchants*, *The Friendly Persuader*, *Cartons in The Air*, and other books published by Artscroll/Mesorah. She lives in Kiryat Mattesdorf, Jerusalem.

Dr. Meir Wikler is a psychotherapist and family counselor in private practice in Brooklyn, New York.

Hinda Devora Wolpin (nee Glassman) has a varied background of experience in journalism and teaching. She is the wife of Rabbi Chaim Boruch Wolpin, *Rosh Hayeshivah* of Yeshivah Karlin-Stolin in Brooklyn, New York.

Rabbi Nisson Wolpin is the editor of *The Jewish Observer*, Agudath Israel of America's monthly journal of thought and opinion, where the articles in this volume originally appeared.

Joanne Jackson Yelenik is a teacher and writer living in Washington, D.C.

Miriam Zakon served as translator for the English-language *Tzena U'rena* and the best-selling *Silent Revolution* (Artscroll/Mesorah) and is author of several novels for teenagers.

Emmy Stark Zitter, who lives in Rochester, New York, wrote her essay for this volume on a Sunday that had been reserved for cleaning the attic for Pesach.

Introduction

At some point during my junior high school years, a little volume of humor became a national best-seller across America. In spite of the fact that I never read it, this book had a remarkably long-lasting impact upon the earnestly searching young girl who was then myself: The title alone was enough to keep me wincing for the next decade.

"How to Be a Jewish Mother." I must have come across a copy and briefly skimmed through it, for unless I'm just imagining it, I see that book in my mind's eye. Size: six inches square. Text: scant. Author: forgotten — all I know is, it was something like Dan Goldberg, or Greenberg; not the sort of name there'd be a long list of in our suburban Connecticut telephone book. Illustrations: cleverly executed cartoons. Of what? Or rather, of whom? Of her, of course, our ridiculous Jewish mother. Here she is at the stove, here at the kitchen sink. Here's a shot of J.M. at the supermarket, and here we see her, receiver in one hand, stirring spoon, as usual, in the other, conversing with grown son Marvin, who's a lawyer: "You like the new shirts I sent you? You didn't say anything."

"Oh, yes, Ma, I'm sorry. Thanks a lot. They're very nice."

"They fit all right?"

"Yes, Ma, perfect. I've got the blue one on right now."

"So what's wrong with the other one?"

Ha, ha, no wonder it made the best-seller lists. I couldn't tell if it embarrassed me so keenly to have this woman exhibited before the whole country because the portrait was true or because it was false. A Jewish friend of my sister's got it for her mother's birthday, and how it regaled them all at the family party! These were Jews, evidently, who knew how to take a joke; good-natured ribbing at the hands of a fellow Jew didn't make *them* feel like finding the nearest dark closet and retiring there for the forseeable future, whereas I....

And I wasn't even a Jewish mother!

❦ ❦ ❦

Press the fast-forward button. The earnestly seeking young girl of Fairfield County is now the earnestly seeking young mother on a settlement in the Judean Desert. But though I'd managed magnificently to get out of exile, exile hadn't gotten out of me. Way up there in my mind's attic, among other dim and dusty suburban relics, was none other than Greenberg's, or Goldberg's, anti-heroine, hovering benevolently as if on little angel wings, worry lines on forehead, spoon still in hand, splattered apron forever tied, naively unaware of any malice or condescension on the part of that nice young man whose cute book had once made her a star. Nor all those witty stand-up comedians — they never really meant any harm, did they? And that very intelligent Jewish writer — the one who had really made her famous — what was his name again?

Why did I keep taking a broom and shooing this woman into the corner, wishing she'd take a hint and disappear? How could I, who was so fervently embracing my Jewish identity, be so cold hearted when it came to this well-known mascot of my heritage? Yes that was indeed the case. If I thought about her at all, it was just to hope I wasn't becoming like her. Without consciously setting up an agenda of strategies, I took what steps I could to forestall what I hoped was not an inevitable transformation.

These vaguely conceived preventative measures had as their focus, first and foremost, my physical self. Where she and I came from, society equated self-mastery with control over one's physique, and by this standard, Mrs. Jewish Mother had not fared well; the most visible attribute rendering her vulnerable to ridicule was her waistline. So I resolved (many times) to refrain from baked goods, but this was hard. One day — horror of horrors — would I stop caring about the way I look? There's a wonderful colloquialism for that: "to let yourself go." To let oneself go, according to its other dictionary definitions, connotes relinquishing one's ego or just relaxing and having a good time. But for me as a housewife, it meant one thing and one thing only. By caring so much about my family, I'd forget to "take care of myself."

Secondly, I refused to join in on her aspirations for Marvin. This was easy. *Cheder* wasn't preparing my son for law school, and Bloomingdale's was ever so far away. Third, I tried hard not to push food on my children. This was very difficult. Fourth, I tried to find time to think about something besides my floors and what I was going to make for dinner, another hard one. There was a lot of mud out there on the *yishuv*, and shopping for dinner was the only social event on the housewife's daily calendar. Perhaps my mind's unavoidable fate would be to turn into a fluffy *matzah* ball from having been exposed too long to the mundanities of housekeeping.

Last but not least, (the hardest of the bunch,) I would stay psychologically savvy about myself: I wouldn't advertise my self-sacrifice, nor deny how much I needed to do all this work for the sake of my own identity. I wouldn't inflict my own futile longing for perfection upon my offspring.

So I tried. I would be Jewish, and a mother, but not a Jewish mother.

Nonetheless, in spite of my efforts, I felt it happening. Yet not precisely in the way I had feared. It gradually became apparent that there was a force within me, an irrepressible drive toward something or other, and that there was no way it could be squashed. Something in my personality had been in the works long before my arrival on the Judean Desert, and even before I'd ever set foot in New Canaan Junior High. I simply *was*, eternally, a Jewish mother. But what was it about me that made it so?

This question tugged at me quietly like a mute child wanting some attention. But for ten years I was very busy making dinners and putting small people to bed, and didn't put it into words. All I knew is that whatever it was I feared, I was missing the point if I defined it in terms of the outward signs that had been the easy targets of America's derisive mirth. It was, in truth, something that at its roots was intrinsic to my nature, my Jewish nature, something that the comedians and literati had deprecated because they, too, were scared. And a receptive audience across the land had chimed in, in order to distance themselves from this concealed principle of our culture:

Beware: What an unappreciated fool you'll be, if you give so much you give yourself away.

Introduction / 15

❦ ❦ ❦

Skip ahead another decade, to yesterday afternoon, and you'll find the person who is now myself sequestered in her room, intently opening one desk drawer after another, still earnestly searching — in this case, for a certain statement I was sure I had jotted down somewhere. It had remained in my memory ever since I'd first heard it in a *shiur* given by Rebbetzin Tzippora Heller, a few days before Purim, several years back. And now I needed it to answer my own question, the one presented by this introduction to a collection of *Jewish Observer* articles about the Jewish woman.

I had long since, with many apologies, invited Mrs. J.M. down from the attic. I was ashamed of the way she'd been ostracized, and realized that in any case she was just a figment of imagination: No stereotype could accommodate reality — it would be like trying to get a size eighteen into a tidy little seven. People are just too complicated, life is too complicated. Life itself had smartened me up.

So I had grown tolerant of human foibles, having a front-seat view of my own, but still desired explanations. The doorbell rang. I would have to ignore it. I had just been informed that the deadline for this introduction is this week, my children would arrive at one and lunch wasn't ready. I had no time for solicitations or the *kibbutz* egg salesman this morning. I had to find that line!

Again the bell. Don't answer it. Not this morning. I flipped through old notebooks, beginning to doubt that there was such a line at all when all of a sudden there it was.

We Jews define ourselves by giving.

Hurrah!

Notes from this particular lecture were sandwiched between notes from a *shiur* by Rabbi Zev Leff in February 1989, and others from a class given by Rebbetzin Esther Greenberg, of blessed memory. What I had managed to scribble down, obviously in a hurry to scramble after Rebbetzin Heller's swift mind, was as follows:

> *The reason we send gifts on Purim, especially gifts that people don't really need, is to emphasize the fact that we want to identify ourselves on Purim as Jews, and we Jews define ourselves by giving. A descendent of Avraham is said in the Gemara to to be recognizable by three signs: his mercifulness, his shyness, and his nurturing kindness.*

We tend to feel divided amongst ourselves, both as a nation and as individuals. It is written in the Gemara that the Jews are more quarrelsome than other nations because we care so much about truth. Giving, on the other hand, creates unity. Giving unites Hashem with the world. Giving creates bonding between one another. Mishloach manos, therefore, is about the removal of differences between us.

Don't allow yourself to feel separate or alienated for material reasons. The laws of Ahavas Israel stipulate that you have to care about the other person's material needs, rather than feel jealousy towards those who have more than you, or behave with stinginess or a sense of superiority towards those who have less. We are required as Jews to give according to the other person's genuine need, even if you feel separate. The way to transcend your judgment of the needy is to be helpful towards them.

Why gifts of food? Because sharing the pleasure of food is supposed to make us aware of Hashem's chessed.

We are giving because it's our nature to give. Jews by nature want to use the world for giving, not for taking. The word gemillut, as in gemillut chessed, is the same term used for a nursing mother. The impulse to nurture is a feminine trait.

There aren't any coincidences, Everything has a beginning and everything leads towards something.

The doorbell was buzzing again, followed then by the distinctive knock that identified my visitor: faint, shy, irregular as a little child's but still, somehow, determined. Malka! Not again! She was just here a few days ago!

When I opened the door, there indeed was she, in all her tininess. Four foot something, kerchief knotted beneath the chin. Outfit, as always, a random assortment of mismatched handouts. A sweater in all weather, even in the summer heat; now that it was getting cold, I was pleased to see that someone had given her quite a nice one during the last few days. Her hesitant, hopeful smile of greeting. Blue eyes — two faded gems of old glass. Forehead squinched up in anticipation of her entreaties on behalf of her grandchildren, face creased and recreased with a thousand lines. Her feet not filling the familiar pair of sneakers; they'd been partially amputated as a result of diabetes. From age fifteen to nineteen she had been in Auschwitz. There her mother and sister had died.

"Shalom, Malka!" My thoughts darted to my purse. There was absolutely no money in it this morning. My last change had gone for one of the children's bus tickets. She'd never believe me. And I'd already given her next month's sum in advance, more than the maximum, much more than *maaser*. I couldn't give more! The more I gave, the more she expected. My stomach was already in a knot. How could I say no? but how could I say yes? Maybe I was being a fool, letting myself be taken advantage of.

"Shalom!" She shuffled right in. "Thought you weren't home! No more money," she muttered, holding up two empty palms.

"But I told you I'd only have more on Rosh Chodesh, Malka. Remember?" She nodded and gave a shrug. I went to the stove and put the kettle on. My daughter Mimi, who had stayed home from school with a cold, wandered into the kitchen.

Malka was taking out the *sucrazit* (saccharin) from her purse. "No more money. *Shum devar (Nothing!)!*"

"I can't give more until Rosh Chodesh."

Her face fell into its own shadow, crumpled up like a dry leaf, then the next instant magically reflowered, a thousand new lines appearing as she grinned, nearly toothless. "Another grandchild this week! A boy!"

"Mazel tov! Mazel tov!"

"Mommy," Mimi whispered, even while knowing that Malka doesn't understand English, "You have to give her."

"But I gave her for the month already, and besides, I don't have anything more in my purse this morning."

"So clothes."

"I already showed her what I have left and she's not interested. It's not their sizes. And I don't have anything for infants."

"So food!"

I nodded assent.

As I served Malka coffee, Mimi dashed around the kitchen with a bag, opening all the cabinets. Tuna fish, crackers, spaghetti, rice.... She took note of the fruit bowl. "Do you like bananas?" she inquired. Malka shook her head. "Apples?" No again. Mimi paused, then tried the freezer compartment. Two sweet *challahs* and half a bag of frozen peas dropped into the bag. Mimi, the hamburger meat? That was for tonight's dinner —

When Malka shuffled out to the elevator, face fallen again like a crushed leaf, there it was in the pit of my stomach — ridiculous!

— the familiar self-accusation: *I didn't give enough, I should have given more.* Jewish mother! There you are! Incurable!

And Mimi! Another Jewish mother!

And Malka! Another Jewish mother! Foraging for her little ones!

A rush of joy soared through me for a few seconds like a song in flight. No other joy is quite like it, it's such authentic, solid music, it must be the joy for which we are made. Go on, *let yourself go.* No matter what you lose when you give yourself away — even if it's tonight's dinner — at least what you get in return is this: a self that's been enlarged not in terms of dress size but according to the extent that another person's life thereby merges with your own, and your own small self with the infinitely generous Divine will.

※ ※ ※

So if the Jew defines himself by his desire to give, and if it is the Jewish woman's tendency to be particularly well endowed with this desire; and furthermore, if doing so is a joy that gets her in tune with her own essential nature, then what is the answer to Bracha Goetz's plaintive query in "Between the Braids": "When did simple giving get such a bad name?"

I called Rebbetzin Heller last night to request that she listen to my lecture notes to check for misquotes, and in my own mind resolved to ask, in addition, for her reaction to that question. I wanted to get her reaction to the negative stereotyping of the Jewish mother. But she was too busy with her children to talk, and said that the only time she would be free for a conversation today was the twenty-minute lunch break after her morning classes at Neve Yerushalaim Women's Yeshiva.

At a quarter to one this afternoon in an empty classroom, there sat Rebbetzin Heller with a tray of soup and meat loaf and I with my old notebook. After surveying the notes, she was about to rise when I asked if she had ever seen a little best-seller in the sixties called, "How to Be a Jewish Mother."

She seemed to search her memory a bit and smiled wryly. "Yes."

I told her that it seemed to me that the ridicule was motivated in party by the Jewish mother's having opted for a life of constant giving without being paid or recognized for it by others. Invisible giving without getting something back is not considered a smart move in our American culture, unless you can somehow manage to get credit for being saintly. "But there was also something about that stereotype that rang true, don't you think? And that's why it embarrassed me so."

"What's true about it is that the stereotypical Jewish mother is so concerned with her own need to give that it eclipses any sensitivity on her part towards the other person's genuine needs."

"Why do you think she does that?"

"Because she wants to feel important. Don't forget, we're talking about a society geared to monetary reward and structure. People work between certain designated hours and get compensated accordingly. Being a mother doesn't lend itself to that."

"So she can solve that by getting a nine-to-five job?"

"A nine-to-five job would answer one problem: her need for status and self-expression. But it wouldn't take care of her family's problem — that they still have to get satisfaction for their genuine emotional, intellectual and spiritual needs. There was an article recently in the Israeli magazine *Mishpachah* about a Me'ah She'arim family with twelve children, some of them grown, whose mother died. The father remarried a highly educated professional woman with a respected position in *chinuch*, but the new wife could not handle the way all the older daughters would come over to the parents' house with the grandchildren every afternoon and just spend time together. She complained to the father: 'It's like a wedding here every day!' What was shown in the article was that the first wife hadn't done anything special during those afternoon get-togethers. She had finished all the cooking and cleaning in the morning hours so that the afternoons would be free to do nothing. But for a person who has developed a spiritual self, doing nothing is doing something. Being is doing. She had something of herself to give. The stereotypical Jewish mother, on the other hand, creates duties for herself that, strictly speaking, are unnecessary — all in an effort to bond herself to her family, to make herself indispensable, because she has nothing of herself to give. For her, doing nothing is really doing nothing."

"So the answer is to develop her spiritual self."

"Yes," replied Rebbetzin Heller, regarding me gently with her level gaze. "The answer is to develop her spiritual self."

❦ ❦ ❦

But how? How do you develop a spiritual self when you're peeling potatoes? Washing dishes? How, asks Emmy Zitter, do you clean for Pesach without bleaching out your spirit along with the refrigerator? How, asks Hadassah Becker, do you get ready for *Shabbos* without forgetting that feeling joy is the ultimate preparation? How, asks Bat Sheva Menuchah, do you keep your soul awake while daily riding the subway to and from your nine-to-five job? There's no realm of activity that precludes spiritual growth, but life by force of circumstance is so often under the thumb of mundane routine that a given moment's spiritual potential can go unexploited. The small modification in one's boundaries that we call growth — whether it has been caused by an act of self-restraint or of self-expansion, by reaching out to G-d or by reaching out to one's fellow — does not usually happen automatically but with conscious effort. It's supposed to be this way. Judaism is the path that leads us through the quotidian world to our own spirituality; we are not taught in the Torah to remove ourselves from mundane daily existence but rather to consecrate it.

"Only her hairdresser knows for sure," the hair-coloring ad intoned to untold thousands of females throughout my childhood. *Lehavdil*, only you and your Creator can ever know for sure what you're actually up to at any given moment. No matter how impressive, whatever you're engaged in is empty at its core if it's utterly devoid of relationship to *Hashem*. But the reverse is equally true: No matter how mundane some activity may seem, nothing you do will end up being nothing if in some part of you you're relating through it to G-d.

Women, generally speaking, have a particular potential in this area: the ability to find something heavenly in an earthly form. Because a woman's mobility is so often circumscribed by motherhood, she has no choice but to turn inward and find her freedom by adjusting her perspective. Precisely the same principle applies to a woman who's coping with *not* being circumscribed by motherhood: There's nowhere else to turn but inward, where in any case true freedom lies.

It is a Jew's nature to want to give. Though it's wise to avoid generalities, it's not too farfetched to maintain that a woman is congenitally well equipped to reach out to others, as a mother would, by virtue of the fact that it is in the female nature to nurture. In his article "Reaching Out to the Lonely and the Unattached,"

Rabbi David Cohen speaks of the Torah obligation to help the stranger, the deprived, the unwell — in short, to help those in need of help. My understanding of just whom this category includes was forever broadened when I heard, fifteen years ago, in a *shiur* that the Gemara describes the whiteness of a smile as having more capacity to nourish than the white substance in a cup of milk. I began to realize just how much my soul does respond to a smile. A neighbor's friendly nod on my way to the store can lift my heart. A drop of kindness from the stranger next to me on the bus can redeem my morning and water my faith as if it were a flower. "Our everyday contacts with numerous people," writes Rabbi Zelig Pliskin in "The *Oheiv Yisroel:* A Profile," are all fruitful opportunities for word-charity, for in this respect who is not needy? How amazing that with the slightest exertion, I myself am equally empowered to bestow this extraordinary nourishment upon my neighbor, and that by doing so, writes Devorah Gershon, "open the prison of the lonely self.... Give me strength, lest I remain alone, an imperfect creature forever apart."

Not everyone is privileged in his or her lifetime to perform an act of heroism on a noticeable scale. Not everyone has the experience of passing by a drowning man and marveling later how he (the passerby) jumped in for the rescue without a second thought. But ordinary day-to-day life is more of a challenge in this respect. To be heroic on a small scale, when you don't get human recognition for it: enduring someone's self-aggrandizement at your expense, without condemning him; exercising patience while diapering a baby; listening to someone's problem when you've just gotten yourself a cup of tea and a good book; resisting the impulse to divulge a fascinating detail about someone else's life; resisting the pleasure of listening to some innocent-sounding *lashon hara*.... These small heroisms, unfueled by the bursts of adrenalin that a sudden rescue attempt rushes through our nervous system, are acts of will and of *emunah*. Will, because no one will blame you or even notice that much if you take the course of least resistance and behave "like any normal person." *Emunah*, because you need a sturdy belief that your slightest, least visible deeds are observed and appreciated by One Whose appreciation is infinite.

I've heard it said that life is so short. What a shame to spend it being someone other than yourself. It's my prayer that societal pressures, therefore, should have nothing to do with our choices in life. May we blithely ignore negative stereotyping about us of any kind, and blithely ignore other people's false interpretations of our behavior; learn to transcend false limitations generated by our own false self-images. May we utilize our brief stay here in this world to be constantly becoming ourselves, Jewish women imbued with the general tendencies characteristic of us as Jews, and with the particular tendencies that distinguish us as unique individuals; to resist the sundry magnetic beliefs that each passing generation offers. May the eternal Jewish woman within each one of us blossom. That's heroism.

In *Bereishis*, *Hakadosh Baruch Hu* is shown creating the world and its creatures in an ascending order of spirituality, beginning with the inanimate, continuing to the least complex up through the most intelligent species of animals, then finally, man, and lastly, woman. "According to His will," we're born near the top, with a nature attuned to an awareness of the Creator. In this world, our instinct — often misdirected, sort of like a misappropriation of funds — is to seek perpetually to bond with the Divine. Our desire to give to others makes this bonding with G-d possible, and makes each and every Jewish women, no matter what her particular circumstance, a potential prototype of the *Oheiv Yisroel*.

On some level, we are all, every last one of us, lonely and unattached; on some level, we are all poor people in need of crumbs of bread, and of light.

And on some level, we are all Jewish mothers needing to give according to the other's genuine need.

May we serve each other well.

Sarah Shapiro
Jerusalem, Shevat 5753

❧ Her Housekeeping

Musings on Matchmaking
A Down-Home Pesach in Philly
Answering the Fifth Question
Getting Ready for Shabbos

Hindy Kviat

Musings on Matchmaking

I was obsessed
with matching.
Everything
for my new home had to be
perfect.
Hitting on
just the right shade
wasn't easy — one color too dark
another — a bit light...
and on
   and on....
The relief I felt when I
finally
made up my mind
was shortlived.
I'll never forget
my shock
when I saw my newly furnished kitchen
for the first time...
The freshly hung wallpaper
greeted me boldly,
The linoleum barely one day old
glistened...
but the "browns"
CLASHED!
I blinked hard, stared...

How did I ever think
Those two would blend well together?
Two years since...
The wallpaper is not as white as it used to be,
The linoleum has lost its shine.
And I...
I have also changed.
Now I wonder why the match ever bothered me.

They go so well together.

Time has surely done the trick,
my eyes have been won over.
Wallpaper and linoleum —
Big deal!
But it set me thinking. How many things
That don't match
    my life
new life have my eyes grown accustomed to
with
time.

Edith Krohn

A Down-Home Pesach In Philly

Circa 1920

PESACH — it was the worst of the year, it was the best of the year. The backyard was awash with green. Early weeds, crabgrass, spindly stems of garlic bulbs and an occasional robin picking up an unsuspecting worm. The old apple tree was bursting to wear her yearly bridal gown and the breezes had a velvet touch. It was Pesach time, indeed.

Inside there was a quiet pandemonium. Mother always began to worry about Pesach around Chanukah time. Before the last latke was digested, she had already settled in her mind when to make the "russel" — Don't know what "russel" is? It's fermented beet juice out of which ubiquitous borscht was made. Pounds and pounds of beets were peeled and cubed and steeped in gallons of water. They were left to drown in the liquid for weeks, after which the russel was tasted. If it was sharp enough to scratch your throat into ribbons, it was considered done. It was stored in a cool, dark place, preferably in the cellar, not too far from the coal bin. But the jug was covered with many layers of cloth so the ash and soot never got into it. Cooked with soursalt, lots of sugar and — if the husband like it meaty — a few beef bones, the end result was a brew of a deep, clear, claret color, tasting somewhere between a sweet acid and a tart appetizer. Ladies sampled, smelled and judged the clarity of each other's brew with the deftness and concentration that French winemakers reserve to judge the product of their vineyards. It was one of the rituals of Pesach.

The first Sunday after Purim, the Orthodox men of the community arranged for a matzah baking in the only bakery in Philadelphia that would give them time — Friedman and Son, all the way in South Philadelphia. The men cleaned and scoured the machines, and meticulously supervised as the proper amounts of flour and *mayim shelanu* (guarded water drawn the previous day) were put together, and closely watched as the machines mixed and baked the matzos in less than the prescribed 18 minutes. Not rabbis, teachers or scribes, they were all businessmen, workers, shopkeepers — earnest *baalabatim* of old Philadelphia, who strived to be holy before G-d and man. To them, the *mitzva* of baking their own matzos, in a city where *kashrus* was always a process of elimination, was an act of gentle glory, little spoken about. If you understood and felt the beauty of *zehirus* (caution) in *kashrus*, you were welcomed into the charmed circle. Otherwise the local grocery could supply you with *matzos* ... kosher, no doubt.

Then there was *shemura*. Since no one baked *shemura* in Philadelphia, it was imported from New York. Only your personal rabbi had the *shemura* which you bought with your life's blood in work. One wrapped it ever so gently and carried it home on the trolley, holding it and guarding it so that no one came near to break or even crack it. A father usually took along his eldest child who paid the fare, scouted for a seat, and in general was proud to be the lieutenant who came along to escort the *shemura* home. It was placed on the top of the china closet, away from busy little hands and awkward adolescents.

Cleaning and scrubbing went on relentlessly. Everyone pitched in, from toddlers who could hold the dustpan and bring a diaper for the baby (cloth, please, there were no Pampers yet) to Bubby, who joined us to polish the silver after she did the chores in her own house. Every child was responsible for his or her own drawer.

Then Mother made the food list. When you came right down to it, there was quality, huge quantity — but no variety.

☐ **Milk.** We had no supervised milk, so only children under three had any to drink. Everybody else drank tea or milkless hot water, sweetened with sugar and on occasion honey. Why on occasion? Because not every year did the honey get a *hechsher*. The variables of *hechsheirim* was as unpredictable then as it is today, except that today we hang our *emunah* on symbols, in their infinite variety. Then, most Orthodox women were non-believers. If the local Orthodox rabbi supervised it personally, mother used it. If not — not!

- **Teabags.** Not yet invented. Sweetouchnee Tea came in enchanting little red-and-black metal treasure chests. You had to place an early order with Mother for the metal box when the tea was finished, since everybody wanted it.

- **Coffee.** This was imported. The *Rav* could give no assurance that it was all right for Pesach. He suggested chicory — a distant cousin to the real thing. Coffee drinkers killed the taste with sugar. No milk.

- **Canned foods and candy** were an absolute no-no. As is, Orthodox Jews used practically no canned foods all year long. There was no surety on anything. (Somehow, sardines were an exception. I never figured out why.) For many years candies were also *verboten*. and when by dint of much investigation, we were finally allowed a Hershey bar, paradise had opened its doors. But never on Pesach. The only "confections" we knew then were sweet home-made applesauce and candied orange peel. (Sometimes mother would cajole us into doing some of her endless chores, and in return, she would make a nut brittle. Now, that was candy fit for angels — but not really, because we were no angels. As soon as it was cold enough to handle and break into pieces, we attacked it with glee.)

- **Fish and chicken** were the mainstays of the Pesach diet. There were no freezers, so the week before *Yomtov* was utter hysteria. Mother went to the chicken market on Marshall Street, chose her chickens and bought them to her *shochet*. Then, for a shiny dime, a boy would lug the chickens home, where all the *kashering* was done (naturally). The salt and water ran freely.... Then Mother went to the fish market and chose her catch live from the big tank, and watched as the fishmonger dressed the jumping carp. For another shiny dime, a boy would lug that home, too. Fishmongers did not grind fish, and "fillet" was a French word in the dictionary. Ben-Z and Unger had not been born yet.

A Down-Home Pesach in Philly / 31

☐ In the world of **fruits** and **vegetables,** we knew of potatoes, carrots, onions, apples, oranges, and an occasional pineapple. Things like leeks, artichokes, and rutabaga were eighth grade spelling words, and beets were already accounted for in the "russel." It was too early in the season for cucumbers and tomatoes — no airlifts of produce from California or Florida. Sometimes there were strawberries — "hothouse strawberries," they were called. As much as 50 cents a box (a small fortune), they usually were not sweet, so we dunked them in sugar for a bit of flavor.

Potatoes were in a class by themselves. Mother cooked them, baked them, scraped them, ground them, fried them raw, fried them cooked, made kugels, latkes and hashbrowns out of them. They were served hot, cold, and mixed with carrots. No one was ever hungry, for there was always something made out of potatoes to eat. A hundred pounds of potatoes melted within the week like *schmaltz* on a hot frying pan.

Speaking of *schmaltz* (today it is euphemistically called "shortening"), we must have had a digestive system made out of refined steel. Chicken *schmaltz* is heavy, fat and tolerable. Beef fat, the mainstay of most frying, was processed by rendering the white fat from beef cuts. It takes an hour or more on the fire just to begin the rendering, and when it is completed, about another hour later, it is pure white.

The day before Pesach finally arrived and with it, the kaleidoscope of preparations, cooking, children-ing, once-over-lightly cleaning, chometz-burning, and finally the setting of the Seder Table.

Nothing, absolutely nothing in this world, can match the wonder and the glory and the sanctity of that Seder Table. The days and the work fell away like a wind-swept mist and here before our dazzled eyes was the silver, the lighted crystal candelabra, the beautifully colored cover of the matzah plate, the immaculate settings, the items set out for the Seder Plate that only Father could assemble. It was almost too much to behold. It was the culmination, the goal that had been reached — it was the reward for which we had worked.

This was how we prepared for an old-fashioned, down-home Pesach in Philly — with beauty, sanctity, and simplicity.

Emmy Stark Zitter

Answering the Fifth Question:

How Much Pesach Is too Much Pesach?

❧ The Longest "Eve" on the Calendar

IT IS A frigid Monday morning in Rochester, New York and the wind chimes on the porch outside play wild, tumultuous winter tunes.

The kitchen where I sit with a friend, however, is warm and cozy as we sip hot chocolate together, watch the children outside building a slightly humpbacked snowman, and enjoy an unforseen moment off from our preparations for — for — for — Pesach.

And what has a snowy January morning to do with Pesach, with *Chag HaAviv*, the only one of the *Shelosh Regalim* that the *Chumash* specifically associates with a season — and that, the season of lengthened days, of budding plants, of spring?

The answer clearly is, or rather should be, not much. I remember my mother telling me that, like her mother before her, she would begin preparing for Pesach on the day after Purim. I would be suitably impressed by the obvious importance of a holiday that took four whole weeks to plan and prepare for! Yet now, it seems, the work which it took my grandmother ע״ה four weeks to complete, without benefit of hand vacuum, washing machine, or Sears Carpet Cleaning Service, takes an ordinary woman months to finish adequately.

Some of this obviously has to do with the new roles which women have assumed in our society; things have changed considerably since my grandmother's day. Women who work or go to school will probably need a head start on the admittedly difficult task of cleaning a house for Pesach. But many do have some household help, and as much of the hysteria about Pesach seems to come from those who are primarily homemakers as from those who work outside the house. There are other reasons, ranging from the serious to the just plain silly, for the mass insanity which we call Pesach cleaning.

✥ The Broadest Category in the Dictionary

First of all, we plainly lump together too many unnecessary and demanding jobs into the category of Pesach cleaning. A friend of mine, planning to be with her in-laws for the whole week of Pesach, spent just one week clearing her house of *chometz*. With a new baby in the house and no plans to remain home for the holiday anyway, she didn't bother with all the usual washing and scrubbing, with the emptying and arranging and throwing out which in past years had literally taken her months to complete. Three days before Pesach the baby got sick, and my friend had to make Pesach at home after all. Shopping, cooking, and finishing her work in a *chometz*-free kitchen were obviously her first priorities in making a kosher and festive Pesach on such a short notice. When the *seder* finally came, she found, to her relief and astonishment, that she had managed in less than two weeks of work to rid her house of all *chometz* and to prepare as lovely and kosher a Pesach as ever she had done. True, the carpets were well vacuumed but not shampooed; her closets, though devoid of any *chometz*, were still disorganized; and her curtains (gasp!) had not been freshly washed; but as she sat down to the first *seder* she discovered that much of the work that she had always considered to be crucial to the Pesach process was in reality just "spring cleaning" and could be done as well after Pesach as in the hectic weeks before.

Things have changed for her; she now distinguishes between what is necessary and what is optional, what must be done before *bedikas chometz* and what can be put off until the second Sunday of *Sefiras HaOmer*.

Closet Wars

While most of the women I know share Pesach "war stories" in a spirit of help and camaraderie, there is among some women a measure of competition in their discussions of who has scrubbed more, who has shined harder, who has broken more fingernails and scraped more fingers, who has outdone whom in becoming a martyr to the pail and mop. A woman I once knew was particularly irritating in this respect, regarding her heroic efforts to achieve an immaculate house for Pesach as a reflection not only of her achievement as homemaker but of the cleanliness of her very soul. *Mitzvah Haba'ah l'yadcha al tachmitzenah*, she would quote to us in her lofty way as explanation of why it was necessary for her to re-fold all her linens two months before Pesach. I must admit that I listened with as much glee as pity when I heard that two weeks before the holiday her three-old daughter had sneaked upstairs with a whole box of Cheerios and cheerfully spread *chometz* throughout the bedrooms which had been kosher for Pesach since February. There are enough *mitzvos* at hand that we need not look only to our closets to find them.

Trapped in Anger

I know an older woman who insists with a laugh that Pesach was an evolutionary tool to keep Jewish people strong — it kills off the weak women. All said in good fun, of course, but beneath the laughter I sense an anger that I find truly disturbing. Anger is at husbands who aren't helping enough; at children, who never seem to stop hindering; and sometimes, though we hesitate to admit it, we are angry at Pesach itself, at the holiday which seems to keep us from doing jobs more rewarding and fulfilling than cleaning the cracks in the floor with a Q-tip or scouring the underside of the sink. Our frustration grows as we feel trapped in the dustiest corners of our homes and our lives. All of this comes to a head on the night of the *seder*, when we are too tense, or too angry, or simply too exhausted to participate or even to sit back and enjoy ourselves.

If in the past years we have come down to the *seder* more worn out than last year's Pesach shoes, it is time to take stock and to cut out that cleaning which is not necessary to rid the home of *chometz*. We should look with a piercing and honest stare at those jobs which we do merely to impress our friends or our guests, our in-laws or ourselves, and analyze what must be done, what should be done, what is nice to do, and what we have been doing just for the sake of doing. These "extras" can be dropped.

What, then, should women do about Pesach cleaning? The answer, of course, does not lie in taking fewer pains to clean and clear our homes of the *chometz*, which we are forbidden by Torah law to own or even to have seen on our premises, come Pesach. If we need help in accomplishing this goal, we should seek it — from husbands, from children — from maids and cleaning services where a family can afford them — or even to hire a teenager from a nearby yeshiva.

We must rid ourselves of our anger even as we rid our homes of *chometz*. Pesach in January? Ridiculous. Let's put away the mops and brooms and take out the snowshovels — or, better yet, let's go out with the children and help build the snowman. *Dayenu!*

Hadassah Becker

Getting Ready for Shabbos: Preparing for Moshiach

A search for redeeming spiritual values in the frantic Friday rush

◆§ The Unfinished Prelude

MUCH HAS BEEN spoken and written through the ages about the joy and fulfillment the Jewish Woman experiences through her *Shabbos* preparations. Countless poems have described that hushed exalted moment when, dressed in her *Shabbos* finery, her house in gleaming order, her proud husband and glowing children gathered around her, she steps forward to light the candles and welcome the *Shabbos* to her home.

How remote that picture sometimes seems — a romanticized image, a beautiful dream that has slipped beyond our grasp. How much closer to reality seems the often humorously exaggerated cliche of *The Erev Shabbos Rush* — of the frantic housewife brandishing her pots and brooms, rushing and huffing and puffing as the deadline looms before her bleary eyes. Indeed, in varying degrees, *Erev Shabbos* can often be a harried time of frazzled nerves and short tempers, when the house seems to echo with shouted commands and accusations, when everything seems to go wrong, schedules go awry and no matter how hard you work, little seems to be getting done.

This can be attributed in part to the simple difficulty of meeting a deadline. The very nature of housework is that nothing ever seems to be completed with much finality. The remains of one meal are scarcely cleared away when you must begin to prepare for the next one. Sticky fingerprints reappear as if by magic, moments after they are wiped away. Cups and saucers pile up in the sink almost as fast as they can be washed and put away. And the bottom of the laundry hamper is a rare sight indeed! Since one can't do everything at once, at almost any given moment there is something which is untidy, undone, and for every task completed there are often two waiting. Count in the usual amount of miscellaneous interruptions, emergencies and the normal hustle and bustle of the average household and you can begin to understand why the Torah exempted woman from most time-bound *mitzvos*. You can also understand why the tension that can come from the simple necessity of preparing for *Shabbos*, and having everything ready on time, should not be underestimated.

This is not a twentieth-century problem. The *Gemara* in *Shabbos* cautions men not to leave their home for *shul* on Friday night until they have witnessed that their wives have lit candles at the proper time, "for women are lax in doing so." It is also stated that one should verbally ask his wife whether she has separated *challah* (because this cannot be done on *Shabbos*). He should also verbally remind the members of his household to light candles. However, *Chazal* caution that one must do this gently, and speak with soft words.

While our *chachamim* understood well the need for this reminder, they also understood how it can lead to bitterness and wounded feelings. A woman who is behind in her work on *Erev Shabbos* is working under great pressure. Her feelings of failure, combined with any expressed or implied (or imagined) reproach from her spouse, can create a state of extreme tension where any irritation is greatly magnified. In this state, even a simple reminder of her need to complete a given task may lead to tears or an explosion of tempers.

Indeed, it is on *Erev Shabbos*, more than at any other time, that *Shalom Bayis* (domestic harmony) is vulnerable. We can reach a deeper understanding of this potential for difficulty in our preparations for *Shabbos* by examining the nature of these preparations.

◆§ Preparing — An End Unto Itself

While the preparations for any *mitzva* has great importance, the preparations for *Shabbos* have a special uniqueness, and our *seforim* abound with descriptions of their loftiness. The late Rabbi Yitzchak Hutner צז"ל offers a special insight into this loftiness in his monumental work, *Pachad Yitzchok: Chazal* tell us that *Shabbos* is *me'ein Olam Haba* — a lesson, a taste, a glimpse and a microcosm of the World-to-Come in all its aspects. One fundamental aspect of *Olam Haba* is the requirement that we long for it. We are to seek redemption, hope for it, pray for it, and try with all our strength to bring about the Messianic Era, which is so much more similar to *Olam Haba* in its spirituality than is our current state of affairs. This anticipation and preparation for redemption is a crucial part of redemption itself.

Rabbi Hutner explains that just as *Shabbos* is a microcosm of *Olam Haba*, our preparation for *Shabbos* is a microcosm of "anticipating the Redemption." This casts our preparations for *Shabbos* in an entirely new light. They are not merely a means to an end, they constitute an end in themselves. The dishes that we prepare on *Erev Shabbos* are important not only because we will enjoy them on *Shabbos*. They have an importance in and of themselves, for they are a concrete expression of our longing for *Olam Haba*. The feelings that go into the preparation and the aura that is created by them have a unique significance. For creating an atmosphere of anticipation for *Shabbos* is a goal, no less important, no less deserving of thought and planning than the completion of the physical tasks involved.

◆§ Receiving the Queen

And if the preparations for *Shabbos* are so fraught with significance, the moment of greeting her and of welcoming her presence has a special sanctity. A special emphasis has always been placed upon *Kabbolas Shabbos*, receiving the *Shabbos*. Not content to sit and wait for her, Rabbi Chaninah would wrap himself in his cloak and say: "Come, let us go and greet the *Shabbos* Queen." Rabbi Yannai would don his garment and say: "Enter, O bride!

Enter, O bride!" The 16th-century *mekubalim* (Kabbalists) of Tzfas dressed in white garments and went out to greet the *Shabbos* queen, to receive her with songs of praise. And we, too, recite some of those same words of greeting and praise in *"Lecha Dodi."*

How often do we catapult into *Shabbos*, out of breath, *tichels* askew, shouting last-minute instructions and reminders. *Shabbos* has arrived, but have we received her? One noted *mechaneches* (educator) spoke recently about the frequency with which the members of the household are busy brushing their hats and polishing their shoes even after the women have lit the candles. "The *Shabbos* queen has come," she said, "and you are telling her to wait in the hall while you polish your shoes."

Yet, even if we are not always perfectly ready, it is undeniable that the moment of lighting candles is one of an almost palpable descent of *kedusha*. In the words of a sensitive young *ba'alas teshuva*, "The first time I saw someone lighting candles was an unbelievable moment. I felt" —and she made a fluttering gesture with her hands — "I could feel the *Shechina* coming down."

And this is the heart of the matter. There is an axiom, זה לעומת זה עשה האלוקים (קהלת ז'), that G-d has created opposing forces in the world. Wherever a powerful potential for *kedusha* exists, an equally powerful force opposes its realization. It is precisely because of the great sanctity of preparing for *Shabbos* and receiving her that there exists an increased potential for discord. When we prepare to receive the gift of *Shabbos*, the harmony of our homes is threatened so that we will not merit to experience the true tranquility of *Shabbos*.

How ironic if one lights the *Shabbos* candles, which are a symbol of *Shalom Bayis* — indeed the Sages mandated them for reasons of *Shalom Bayis* — in an atmosphere of tension and unhappiness. And how unfortunate if this *eis ratzon*, this special opportunity for a woman to place her requests before Him, is not utilized because of haste, confusion, or exhaustion.

A Night for the Angels

Two angels — one good, one evil — escort a person home from the synagogue on Friday night. If he arrives home and finds the candles lit, a set table and a made bed, the good angel says: "May it be G-d's will that it also be so next Shabbos." The evil angel is compelled to answer: "Amen."

Why is it that on Friday night — more so than at any other

time — we merit to have angels accompany us? The *Maharal* explains that *Shabbos* itself so elevates us and brings us so much closer to perfection that we are worthy of being visited and escorted by angels. But it is not automatically assumed that they will find order and harmony in every home.

But if he does not find everything in order, then the evil angel says: "May it be G-d's will that it also be so next Sabbath." The good angel is compelled to answer: "Amen."

In the performance of any *mitzva* there is the possibility of failure. Why is it that in regard to Friday night the possibility of not being ready is so explicitly expressed, so openly anticipated? Why is it so strongly voiced?

The very loftiness of the potential to merit the blessing of angels *must* cause the possibility of failure to be so real. The very greatness of this opportunity promotes a counterforce of unusual power aimed at preventing us from reaching its height.

And powerful it is indeed. How often does our very appreciation of the *Shabbos* itself and our desire to honor her properly turn against us and prevent its true attainment. Rabbi Avrohom Pam שליט״א often presents his students with the following scenario: It is close to *Shabbos*. A *bachur* is busy brushing his hat or polishing his shoes. His mother calls from the kitchen with a request for assistance. "I can't," he replies (in annoyance), "I'm getting ready for *Shabbos*." The young fellow thinks that he is occupied with a *mitzva*, but in truth, he has trampled upon a basic precept of the Torah for something that, important as it may be, is only a *hiddur* — an embellishment.

We can certainly appreciate this example from the mother's point of view, but how often are we the ones who, in our desire to prepare for *Shabbos* with perfection, ignore the rudiments of *bein adam le'chaveiro* (interpersonal commands)? How often in pushing ourselves to capacity and beyond, to scrub and polish for *Shabbos*, do we let out our tension on those around us? If so, we are preparing our homes for *Shabbos*, but not our hearts. We are preparing an external welcome, while banishing her spirit from our midst.

The Chofetz Chaim refused to let his wife wash the floors of their simple dwelling, for fear that the many people who came to their door would be afraid to step on a freshly washed floor with their muddy shoes. He even reprimanded his daughter for scrubbing

Getting Ready for Shabbos / 41

the floor on *Erev Shabbos*, telling her to "polish her *neshama* instead," in honor of the *Shabbos*. Certainly when we work on Friday to make our homes sparkle, it should not be at the expense of another person's feelings. For when in the process of causing a house to shine, the glow of *Shalom Bayis* is diminished even slightly, then a family was prevented from attaining the full joy of *kabbolas Shabbos*.

This is not to minimize the importance of our physical preparations themselves. Each dish prepared, each vessel polished in honor of the *Shabbos* has *kedusha*. We are told that the preparation of a person exerting himself for *Shabbos* has a power similar to that of tears in erasing transgressions. If we would but realize the true significance of each act we do in honor of *Shabbos*, perhaps we would find even more to do!

Planning and preparing ahead is one obvious way to make our *Shabbos* preparations proceed more smoothly. The *Shulchan Aruch* tells us to rise early Friday morning to prepare for *Shabbos*, just as our ancestors rose early to collect and prepare the double portion of *manna*. It is considered a *hiddur* to prepare and purchase things on Friday itself.

This does not mean that you must leave everything for Friday. The *Shulchan Aruch* does state that food requiring extensive preparation should be purchased and prepared earlier. Many preliminary preparations can be made, even for things that we will do on Friday itself. Leaving everything for one day tends to result in overwork and fatigue, rendering one vulnerable and susceptible to last-minute rushing and *Shalom Bayis* tensions. Certainly, starting early is essential for working women and mothers of young children, especially on short Fridays.

This is not just a practical suggestion to facilitate our readiness for *Shabbos*. Only if we organize ourselves so that we are not working under pressure can we taste the joy and sweetness of preparing for *Shabbos*. Only then can we have the peace of mind to feel happiness and satisfaction in what we are doing. And only then can we communicate these feelings to our families, and create an atmosphere of anticipation and expectation in our homes.

To a young child, *Erev Shabbos* can be a day of tantalizing sights and sounds. His eyes watch in wonder as his mother cuts, chops, grates, peels and whisks various ingredients into and out of the stove. He tags after her in fascination as she dusts, sprays, scrubs and polishes in honor of the *Shabbos*. If his mother takes the time to show him and comment on what she is doing, and even lets him help a bit, his excitement knows no bounds.

Older children, too, can gain a sense of fulfillment and satisfaction from participating in *Shabbos* preparations. There is no guaranteed formula for motivating them to help, but the spirit in which the request is made has a great impact on the attitude with which their assistance is offered.

"I remember bickering with my sisters about the chore of setting the table for Shabbos," said a young mother, *"but now that I have a home of my own, I get such satisfaction from placing each object on the table and watching the room become transformed. My children are still very young, but I would like to imbue them with that feeling. Even now, I let them place the becher on the table, but I try to present it as a privilege, not a chore."*

But what about those fragile Fridays when, despite our worthy ambitions, despite our careful planning, everything seems to fall apart? What can be done once we have already fallen hopelessly behind schedule, the *kugel* has burnt, the children are bickering, and our reserves of patience have been long depleted? What about those afternoons when we can't complete our basic tasks, never mind imbue our households with *Erev Shabbos* excitement? What happens to our beautiful ideals then?

A mother of a large family became increasingly frustrated at the Erev Shabbos scene in her house. Somehow her tablecloths never came out snowy white, her cakes were never fluffy, her candlesticks never shone the way her neighbors did and her floors just refused to be clean.

The more she struggled for that orderly Erev Shabbos perfection, the more messy and out-of-control things seemed to get, and the more tense she became. This resulted in a vicious cycle of tensions and frustration.

Finally she consulted a Rav. "You have a problem of bitachon," she was told.

"Bitachon? What does that have to do with preparing for Shabbos?" she asked in surprise.

"Much of your tension stems from the fact that you are comparing yourself to others, and berating yourself for not living

up to others, and berating yourself for not living up to their standards," said the Rav. "Self-acceptance is an important factor in bitachon. G-d created each person with his own unique nature and abilities. He did not create you with the nature to be a Super-Balabusta. Accept this fact. Work with the abilities that Hashem has given you and rejoice in them!"

Often, it is the very nature of our high aspirations that causes us to fail, especially, if they are unrealistically based on other peoples' standards that are not commensurate with our own abilities. Setting up an image of the "perfect *Erev Shabbos*" in our minds can be counterproductive if we become frustrated by our failure to live up to this ideal. Because we are human, we will inevitably fall short of perfection. Does that mean that we cannot dream of *Erev Shabbos* tranquility? Is it futile, then, for us to strive for lofty goals?

Not at all. Ironic as it may seem, the realization that we will inevitably fall short of our goals is the first step towards reaching those goals. To the degree that we accept our limitations and human frailties, we will not be demoralized and frustrated by our failures, but we will be able to learn and grow through them.

Our desire for *Erev Shabbos* tranquility must also be tempered with the understanding that success or failure is measured not merely in the tangible results of our efforts.

In *Shomayim*, our intentions and feelings are the crucial measure, not only the physical perfection of our results. If we struggled to remain calm in the face of repeated mishaps — isn't that success? If we lost our tempers, but managed to apologize and regain control — is that not a triumph? If our floors did not receive that gleaming finish, but we did our best — can we say that we have failed?

"ויהיה ביום הששי, והכינו את אשר יביאו." — We are told that on the sixth day of the week, our ancestors brought home their portion of *manna*, and prepared it for *Shabbos*. The ויהי expression, "and it was," always denotes joy. The *Chidushei HaRim* explains that the use of the expression ויהי in this context is to teach us that feeling joy upon the advent of *Shabbos* is the ultimate preparation for *Shabbos*. Let us not forget this as we go about our *Erev Shabbos* tasks. As the hustle and bustle and hum and clatter of *Shabbos* preparations fill our home, let us remember what Rabbi Hutner זצ״ל has taught us: "Anticipation, not readiness, is the crucial goal."

✢ Her Soulkeeping

Between the Braids
Measure for Measure
Chevra Kadisha
The Search
Shadows in the Kitchen
Standing Alone

Bracha Druss Goetz

Between the Braids

What's in the spaces between the braids
Of these new *challahs* I just made?
How much of me is hidden there?
Between the braids my thoughts appear.

First I sifted the flour through
Thinking of what else I could do.
Who wants to be here baking bread?
I could write my first book instead.

I added each ingredient
And wondered why my soul was sent.
I cracked two eggs and then two more.
Is this what I was created for?

"*Shabbos Kodesh, Shabbos Kodesh,*" my lips whisper,
    hands knead the dough.
Let me see my work is holy. Raising high
    what seems so low.

Does the *challah* absorb frustration?
Does the *challah* hear my voice so shrill?
Does the *challah* absorb my confusion
As it rises for hours on the window sill?

I've heard that Sarah, our first mother, once had the
    right recipe.
What happened to it through the years — is there a
    copy left for me?

Stuck here in the kitchen and still longing for fame.
When did simple giving get such a bad name?

"Shabbos Kodesh, Shabbos Kodesh" — Open up my eyes.
Let me see my work is holy. Let me stop chasing lies.

On Friday night my husband makes a *brachah* and I know
Just what's inside those *challahs* — though I wouldn't
    tell him so.
He cuts them up, we eat them and I can't help but smile.
For all that work, I used to think, they last such a short while.
But this time — I see what's left — I know what's hidden there.
In the empty spaces between the braids — that's where my
    thoughts appear.

When every crumb has vanished from the *challahs* that I
    made
What will remain? Just my secret struggles. Offered up
    between the braids.

Hanoch Teller

Measure for Measure

*The last days of
Chedva Silberfarb* ע״ה

"IT WAS A tempestuous storm...." This is how Chedva Silberfarb often began her *shiur*. It was not uncommon for her to seem to be talking to herself as much as to her audience. "...and the wind howled, heaving the flimsy bridge to and fro. High above the churning waters stood a terrified woman, clutching the rail for dear life. All she wanted was to traverse the narrow bridge to her home. But now, as the storm's fury peaked and the wind's velocity increased, the frightened woman realized beyond all hope that in seconds, nature would have its way and she would plunge to her death in the raging, icy waters below. In desperation she began to offer every spiritual commitment imaginable. 'I shall refrain from *lashon hora!*' she vowed. 'I will never get angry again, I shall extend myself for *chessed*, I will pray with fervor —

"After pledging to pursue a life of piety and spiritual endeavor, she felt secure enough to proceed. With each precarious step, the storm began to subside, until it dissipated into a gentle breeze.

"Instead of relief, however, the woman was overwhelmed with consternation. 'How could I have made such foolish commitments?' she reproached herself. 'Everyone engages in *lashon hora*. How can I be expected to contain my anger when so many things upset me? It is unrealistic for me to devote my energy to others when I do not have enough time for myself. And if I had enough time, I would pray, but surely not with such concentration.'

"In a few brief seconds, the woman had released herself from every obligation. At that very moment, however, the storm began to rear its ugly head yet again and a mighty gust heaved her against the railing of the bridge. Quivering with fear and trembling with remorse, she turned her face heavenward and declared, 'My G-d, I was only joking! I take my pledges seriously. I will even increase my commitments! O L-rd, let me just return home safely!'

"We often find ourselves in situations like this," Chedva explained. "During childbirth, in hard times, on the *Yamim Noraim*, we too feel as though we are crossing a narrow, teetering bridge, and we will pledge anything in return for safe passage.

"Inevitably, however, once the difficult times are over, we swiftly forget every one of our commitments. Is this woman not you? I know in my heart of hearts that she is *me*."

"My friends, you all know me, my story is no secret." Chedva was addressing her former classmates several years after they had graduated from Bais Yaakov Seminary. Ostensibly, they had gathered to hear a *shiur* from their illustrious colleague, but in truth they longed to hear what Chedva wanted from them, to find out what they could do to help their dying friend.

"I grew up with you and we attended school together. I was a student like everyone else, and afterwards a dormitory counselor, just as some of you were. I got married — most of you were at my wedding — and I had three children and a good job, thank G-d: I was lacking nothing, nothing at all. Everything was fine.

"Then, three months after my third child was born, I started feeling ill and a terrible weakness overcame me. I didn't know what could possible be wrong. After all, many women with many more children manage without feeling so exhausted. My arms began to ache, but I concluded that since I spent most of the day carrying the baby, it was only natural. I was also coughing a lot, but it was winter so I didn't pay much attention to that, either. That is, until one Friday.

"I had completed all my *Shabbos* preparations in advance so that I could see a doctor Friday morning. With no intention of undergoing a checkup, I figured I would merely ask my physician to prescribe some vitamins. At most, I thought, she'll suspect anemia and recommend a blood test. But instead she became concerned over my constant coughing and ordered a chest X-ray.

"No sooner had I taken the X-ray than the technician ran to her supervisor as if *her* life were in danger. 'Are you crazy?' she sputtered uncontrollably. 'What are doing walking around? you belong in a hospital — now!"

"I went to America for radiation treatments," Chedva continued. "It was *Shabbos* Purim — for them, that is. For me it was torture; I could barely speak. After a brief examination, the doctor said that I needed a blood transfusion and had to be hospitalized immediately. I began to weep; I just couldn't control myself. 'I don't want to go to the hospital!' I sobbed.

"I didn't know what was happening to me, what they wanted from me. 'I have three babies in Israel.' I whimpered, crying like a baby myself, 'and I want to return to them.' The doctor urged me to regain my composure.

"Nothing could be done, he explained, without my being admitted to a hospital, and I should prepare myself for a painful and protracted treatment.

"Of course he couldn't help," Chedva editorialized. "Only the Healer of All Flesh could, and did. I underwent two chemotherapy treatments in America and I was to undergo another eight in Israel at Tel Hashomer Hospital.

"After the first three, however, I once again felt ill and my lungs filled with water. I ran to my doctor, only to discover that he was doing Reserve Duty, so I called my doctor in America, but he was on vacation.

"Depressed and frustrated beyond description, I felt myself bracing for support on that narrow bridge in the grip of the storm. 'Master of the universe,' I called out, 'You are the Doctor of all humanity and You are always here! It does not matter to You if we suffer from a slight ailment or a major disease, You can heal all!' And of course, G-d helped."

"The week before Rosh Hashana, I was racked with pain again and delirious with fever. I trembled at the thought of being confined to bed on *Yom Hadin*, but thank G-d, my condition improved.

"I managed to finish all the cooking and even to invite guests, just as I had every other year, but I felt terribly unprepared for the holiday season. I was aching to attend a *shiur*, a *shmuess* — anything that would put me in the proper mood.

"Fortunately, a talk was being given not far from my home. I hobbled in at the very end, just as the speaker was relating a personal story about his *tzoros*. Old, frail and very ill, he had gone to see the Steipler זצ״ל for a blessing. But instead of a blessing, or even a few words of compassion, the Steipler had bellowed, 'You need a *zechus!*' — meaning that nothing else would help.

"I was unable to sleep that night, for his wise words kept ringing in my ears. I, too, needed salvation but had no *zechus*. As never before, I realized the truth of the Talmudic dictum that one should be careful to pray before one becomes ill, for once one's health is failing one must provide a *zechus*. My plight conformed precisely to the one described in the *Gemora*. I was like the man who was sentenced to death and my only hope lay in finding advocates powerful enough to stay the execution."

Perhaps others would have failed to see the analogy, but not Chedva. She refused to ignore what she had heard and gratefully and graciously accepted the challenge Providence had placed in her path. "Just as a healthy person has his particular duty," Chedva often said, "an unhealthy person has his."

"From then on, I felt the narrow bridge pitch violently and the tempestuous waters below churn menacingly. I was certain that I had to immediately create a *zechus* before it was too late."

"Practical considerations, however, foiled my every idea. With no energy, I found that even the simplest chores were major hurdles for me. Significant *chessed* projects also seemed out of the question, for my first priority was my own family, who had been neglected ever since the onset of my illness.

"Without stamina and certainly without money, I was baffled and irritated, and time was running out. Not knowing where to turn I opened my *Tehillim*, and the answer practically jumped off the well-worn page:'Come, children, listen to me,' proclaims King David, and are we not G-d's children? 'I will teach you how to revere the L-rd. Who is the man that desires life, and loves a long life of happiness? Guard your tongue from evil, and your lips from speaking falsehood.'

"It was so obvious! Advice that required neither strength, nor time, nor money, and involved the most important of all attributes: fear of Heaven, A guarantee of life in this world and the next, all for just guarding your tongue!"

From that moment on, every ounce of Chedva's dwindling energy was devoted to promoting *shemiras halashon*. Not a single day passed without Chedva addressing at least one group of avid listeners regarding the perils of *lashon hora*.

When she returned home from America after exhibiting some initial signs of improvement, she found her house bedecked with flowers and stocked with cakes. The garden-bakery atmosphere, however, did not bring her cheer. As appreciative as she was, she would not be distracted from her mission. "I don't need flowers and cakes," she announced. "I need a *lashon hora*- free environment!" From the day she landed, her phone rang off the hook with friends, relatives, teachers, and assorted well-wishers asking what they could do to help. Her response to one and all: "Simply refrain from speaking *lashon hora*."

Unfortunately her homecoming was unexpectedly brief. Only days after she returned, her doctor informed her that her condition was very grave and she had to go back to New York to resume treatments immediately.

With renewed faith in her *"Abba,"* Chedva left once again for New York. Before, during, and after her treatments, she pursued her mission singlemindedly. She traveled across Jewish America and Canada and the length and breadth of Israel, going from school to school, auditorium to auditorium, *shul* to *shul*, and house to house. Chedva delivered 75 talks per month, with two or three every day.

Her schedule was staggering — taxing enough to thoroughly exhaust a healthy individual, but she claimed that it gave her strength. Night after night, Chedva would stand up before a group of women, look them in the eye and pronounce, "Refraining from *lashon hora* requires no financial outlay, and no expenditure of time or energy. On the contrary, my very presence here tonight attests to the fact that such a commitment adds strength and lengthens your lifetime. And I assure you, the rewards are not only in this world."

Her friends and relatives, seeing how wan and weak she had become, tried to curtail her busy lecture schedule but their efforts were in vain. "Believe me," Chedva told them, "I'm doing it for myself. If the merit of what I am accomplishing will help me, then it is surely better than rest, and if it won't help me now, then it is *tzeida laderech*...."

As improbable as it sounds, Chedva somehow managed to squeeze her chemotherapy in between talks. Radiation exposure is not exactly a good preparation for air travel, but regardless, Chedva would head directly form the hospital to the airport.

One day Chedva's chemotherapy was scheduled for 9:00 A.M. and two hours later she was to lecture in Brooklyn. Her attendants had long since learned not to challenge the wisdom of Chedva's running around without allowing herself time to recuperate; they also gave up on persuading her to postpone a talk when she was suffering excruciating pain. But this time, sheer practicality mandated that an 11:00 speaking engagement was simply out of the question. After all, one never knew how long the wait for treatment would be nor how long the session would last. And even if everything went smoothly, the trip from the hospital in Manhattan to the Boro Park section of Brooklyn was an hour's journey at best.

But Chedva was incorrigible. "When there's a good cause, G-d helps out," she assured them, and sure enough she arrived on time. Even more miraculously, fifty minutes after radiation she delivered a talk as powerful, as impressive and as searing as any of her others. That morning in Brooklyn, like every other time she spoke, she had little difficulty injecting the personal elements: "For my sake, for my health, please don't speak *lashon hora!* Make a commitment to abstain from *lashon hora* for one hour each day. Just one hour! Increase my number of celestial advocates!"

Who could refuse? Who could refuse a sick young woman fighting for her life and asking that you contribute only an hour a day of spiritual bliss that would ensure a better life both in this world and in the World-to-Come?

Chedva's devotees were given an opportunity to challenge their mentor's "good cause" theory on erev Shavuos, when she was given a brief leave of absence from the hospital. Naturally she was anxious to fly home to spend the holiday with her family in Bnei Brak.

As soon as word got out that Chedva would be leaving the States, London was on the line, asking if she could stop over to deliver a talk. But even with her unshakable sense of mission,

Chedva knew that her time was limited and every moment with her children was precious. She had to refuse.

Her Divine Travel Agent, however, was not content that her *zechus* be confined to North America and Israel. He therefore arranged a major *aliyah l'regel*, resulting in no available flight except via London.

At 7:00 P.M., even as her plane was to depart from Kennedy Airport, Chedva was still being examined by her physician. Needless to say, the flight was delayed and Chedva arrived in time to deliver four talks on *Shabbos* in London (at four different venues, all of which she walked to unaided).

Back in Israel, a quiet revolution was underway. Every Friday evening after candle lighting, as the holiness and blessing of *Shabbos* filled their homes, elementary school girls were attending *shemiras halashon* groups designed to protect this aura from being squandered on frivolous chatter. There may still be a few isolated girls who do not attend "Shomrot" every Friday night, but you can be sure those who do won't talk about them.

A woman who attended one of her talks had claimed that she was unable to survive even one hour without *lashon hora*. "Gossip is my life!" she pleaded in self-defense.

Just one day later, this woman called Chedva to relate that she had resolved to go the entire day without uttering *lashon hora*. Chedva was both ecstatic and incredulous. "What happened?" she asked.

"You contaminated the entire neighborhood; that's what happened!" the woman countered. "No one wants to speak to me. Whenever I phone someone, she invariably tells me that she has just begun her *lashon hora*-free hour and hangs up. And whenever someone calls me, she is as brief as possible and a second later the line goes dead!

"I simply have no one to talk to. Look what you've done!

"But I'll tell you the truth, there's a bright side to all this: I never had so much time before. My husband blesses you just for the housework that I have managed to accomplish in all my newfound free time...."

"Pray that you will never suffer, that you will be able to reach sublime levels of service to G-d in good health and without pain. Have the foresight to prepare the cure before the ailment, and fulfill the mission the A-mighty has entrusted to you," Chedva pleaded.

"Everyone of us was created to serve the L-rd whether in sickness or in health. My job is to serve in sickness. Pray that you will never be in my place."

If ever anyone clung to the privilege of living, it was Chedva Silberfarb. She fought for every moment, yet she was remarkably unafraid to die. She publicly thanked G-d for giving her the opportunity to prepare for her own demise. "As long as there is still breath left within me," she said, paraphrasing the liturgy, "I shall gratefully thank the L-rd and take advantage of every moment of life."

This is precisely what Chedva did throughout her twenty-seven short years. Most of what the public knows about Chedva is culled from her last two years, but for family and intimates, those twenty-four months were but the ineluctable culmination of an exceedingly full life. It was as if she had always had a prescient awareness that her time on this earth would be all too fleeting and she must not waste a single precious moment of it.

Chedva Silberfarb's name, just like the Chofetz Chaim's, has become synonymous with the concept of guarding one's tongue. Indeed, as her husband pointed out at the funeral, the sum of the Chofetz Chaim's long life span of 93 plus Chedva's short one of 27 together added up to the very symbol of longevity awarded to those who refrain from guile and slander: 120.

Just twenty-seven years old, the mother of three children and a worldwide movement, Chedva Silberfarb crossed the bridge and left the world a more beautiful place than she had entered it.

Betsy Kaplan

"Chevra Kadisha" – A Woman's View

I WISH THAT I HAD written this article some months ago, soon after my first experience as a member of *Chevra Kadisha*. At that time, my feelings were so lofty, so poignant, and so fresh in my mind. I may have waxed poetic at this writing. Now, many months and several *taharos* later, I shall endeavor to recall how I felt at that time.

First, a little background: *"Chevra Kadisha,"* or "Holy Society", is a loosely structured organization of Jewish men and women who see to it that the bodies of Jews are prepared for burial according to *halacha* and are protected from desecration, willful or not, until burial. From time immemorial, it has been the duty of every Jew to bury his dead properly, according to certain rules. Two of the main requirements are the showing of proper respect for a corpse, and the ritual cleansing of the body and subsequent dressing for burial.

Last summer, a friend asked me if I would like to become a member of *Chevra Kadisha*, then being formed in Atlanta. This work had been done for some time here by an older couple who were soon leaving to make their home in Israel, and the growing committed Jewish community in our city made the need even more urgent. I immediately answered in the affirmative, thinking that not many would respond to this call, and knowing that even my sparse medical background would eliminate the "squeamishness" that many would feel.

A meeting was called, and to everyone's surprise, there was a tremendous turnout. A young teacher at our day school, Rabbi David Epstein, was leading the group, and outlined what the requirements would be, pointing out that two different groups would be needed. One would be for *shmirah*, or watching the body (for protection against desecration); the other for *taharah*, the ritual cleansing and dressing of the body. Naturally, many more volunteered for *shmirah* than for *taharah*, but we had enough for both groups.

Soon after the meeting, we were called to perform this *mitzvah* for the first time. We were nine women that evening, far too many, for we were getting in each other's way, and all of us novices, but we were to be forever bound by a common experience not known by many, but deeply felt by the privileged few. I remember calling my Rabbi later that evening and thanking him for the opportunity to experience what I still feel is the ultimate in awareness of the link between the human and the Divine . . . the sending off of a human soul to its eternal home. The trepidation all of us felt upon entering for the first time the room where the body lay, and the complete physicality of the preparations for *taharah*, served as a remarkable contrast to the spirituality of the occasion and the emotions of everyone present. We were the final human link between this daughter of G-d and her transition between her earthly and Heavenly homes, and we were all struck with an awe not subject to articulation.

There have been since that time two other deaths, which required our services. It so happens that two of the three women had been friends of my mother, who herself died many years ago, and having known them both in life and in death only served to enhance the devotion I had to this "*avodah*," a word meaning both "work" and "service to G-d."

Ruth Finkelstein

The Search

THE OLD WOMAN'S soul hovered above the open grave. In it rested the fancy coffin — *"She was a grand old lady, she deserved it,"* the mortician had told the family — which contained her "remains": the body of a woman in her late nineties, ostentatiously groomed and dressed in fashionable clothes. In the distances, the last black-clad backs of her children were vanishing from sight. Her soul shook to the vibrations of suppressed laughter wafting back.

The last spadeful of damp earth was now being flung carelessly upon the fresh grave by the alcohol-weakened hand of a stranger. "Better there in the grave," she sighed, "than laid out in the chapel." Her body — the part which disintegrates — had been decked out and put on exhibition, but her soul was still shamefully naked.

But this was nothing new. For years it had been the pattern. Her physical needs had been well provided for by the children but her soul had been left to yearn and finally allowed to shrivel in its loveless and lonely world.

"How can I come before the throne of the Eternal without one *z'chus* for my poor children?"

She made her way to the nursing home where she and her human form had lived for some time before their final separation. Her old room seemed strange and she looked around as if she were seeing it for the first time.

Two cleaning ladies were working in the stark, cheerless room. The bed had been stripped down — her closet, dresser, and night table stood open mouthed and empty. The only thing in view, besides the furniture, was a large, well-worn *Korban Mincha siddur* looking forlorn on the bare night table.

"What'a we suppos'ta do with this?" one of the cleaning women asked, pointing to the *siddur*.

"Dunno. The daughter said to get rid of it, but seeing like it's a prayer book, I don't have the heart to throw it away," replied the other.

"Just leave it there for the next one," she ventured after a while. "Looks to me that nowadays Jewish people have to get old and sick before they go back to prayin'. And that's the kind — old and sick, I mean — we get here, so just leave it be."

"Yeh, the young ones don't seem to have no use for prayin', do they now? I always say that's one sure sign that they need it all the more, but they gotta be taught when they're young."

When she heard this, she winced and fled. New thoughts of self-incrimination came over her and she decided to visit the home of her oldest daughter where the whole family was likely to be gathered. Maybe there she would find the one *z'chus* for her children which she was so anxious to find. On the way, a long forgotten memory forced itself upon her. She recalled the time this very daughter, then about six or seven, approached her tearfully.

"Mama, why do we have to be kosher? Nobody else is. I'm the only one who don't eat lunch in school. I sit by myself and everybody looks at me."

She remembered how her child's anguish had penetrated her. After a few more crying sessions she yielded and permitted the child to eat the school's lunches. But she *had* made sure to impress upon the child that she was never to bring any *trefa* food into the house.

Yes, that's how it had started. She had weakened — permitted her children to do what everybody else was doing and they had followed through by "laying out" their mother's body the way everybody else did.

Arriving at her daughter's split-level ranch, she brightened hopefully. Here she would find something — or would she?

She entered the smoke-filled living room and looked around. The spacious room was crowded with people, most of them middle aged: her two sons and their wives; her two daughters and their husbands; their married children and spouses; their many friends and acquaintances; and four or five of Grandma's own friends and some neighbors. There was a lavish spread on the dining room table; her oldest daughter was "presiding," making sure that everyone was properly served. The bar was open — a white-jacketed bartender was serving drinks. People were sitting in clusters, eating and chatting in studied restraint. Now and then, a spurt of suppressed laughter hung unfinished in the air.

"Look, she had a full life. All right, so there were bad years too, as well as good ones, but that's to be expected when you live as long as she did" — her oldest son was speaking.

"Yes, I'm sure she's better off now, but she suffered so at the end," replied his wife.

'What I always admired in her, though, was the way she never interfered in her children's lives...and I mean *never*. Even when she thought they were wrong, she bit her lips and said nothing. Remember the time — I don't know how many years ago — we were at her house on a Saturday and you lit a cigarette? She looked at you, but she never said a word. She just walked into the other room and came back with an ashtray."

"You know, Mom," a young woman in her late twenties spoke up, "maybe it's not nice to say, but I think another word for 'non-interference' is 'non-guidance.' I know if I'd see my Stevie do something I'd taught him was wrong — and I don't think a parent loses that responsibility ever — I'd make sure to correct him. I'd even go a step further; if I'd only *suspect* he was doing something wrong, I'd try to find out if he needs straightening out. That's part of being a parent. And why shouldn't it apply to smoking on Saturday as well as stealing, for instance?"

"But how can you compare smoking on Saturday to stealing?" asked another young woman who had overheard the conversation from several feet away. SUDDENLY THE ROOM WENT QUIET. Everybody turned to Stevie's mother — she'd been born a Gentile and had converted to Judaism.

Stevie's mother remained undaunted.

"Smoking on Saturday isn't a violation against society... it's not punishable in a court of law, that's true. But it is a violation of G-d's law and an affront to our elders. I've been taught..."

A hubbub of voices cut off the speaker:

"Listen to her — since when did she become a *rebbetzin?*"

"Hey, Joe, when did you become a rabbi? After all, you have to be a rabbi before your wife can become a *rebbetzin.*"

Grandma couldn't stand it any more. She fled from the room to the adjoining den. Here she found her grand- and great-grandchildren sprawled over the furniture and the rug, their eyes fixed on the television set — quiet, and out of the way.

Searching the room, she noticed a document in a fancy frame displayed between two sconces on the wall above the television. Not having visited the house for many years, she read the citation for the first time:

> AWARDED TO IRVING M. SOFER
> IN RECOGNITION OF MANY YEARS
> OF OUTSTANDING AND SELFLESS DEVOTION
> TO THE ZIONIST CAUSE
> AND THE STATE OF ISRAEL.

One of the little girls suddenly pointed to the citation. She giggled, "My grandfather calls it *'his religion'*."

Feeling utterly desolate, she made ready to leave, but as an afterthought, she went into the kitchen. In the corner of the counter, surrounded by the clutter of food serving, she noticed an eight-day *yahrzeit* candle flickering mournfully. Snatches of conversation came drifting in from the dining room.

"...Three days. And about *kaddish*... if you insist on it that way, I'll give you the name of an Orthodox rabbi whose *shul* has services three times a day. For about a hundred dollars they'll take care of it. Or if you prefer to have me make the arrangements..."

"Thanks, Rabbi, I'll send you a check for the hundred."

Not even time for the *kaddish*. But then her sons had never been used to disrupting their schedules on her account, and who knows if the remember how to read Hebrew. Saddened and contrite, she turned to leave... but she heard a voice — the voice of a child:

,,מכתם לדוד שמרני ק-ל כי חסיתי בך. אמרת לה' אד' אתה טובתי בל עליך"

A psalm dear to King David: Guard me, oh Lord, because I am dependent on You. [King David said to his soul:] You have said to Hashem, "You are Hashem; the goodness you have bestowed upon me, You did not have to bestow, because I am not worthy of it."

Swiftly and lightly, she reached the second-floor bedroom from which the voice of a child was coming. Stevie's mother stood in the doorway.

"Oh, there you are, Stevie. I missed you downstairs and I couldn't imagine where you were. Why didn't you tell me you were going upstairs?" Without waiting for an answer — "But what in the world are you doing?"

"I—I'm—I'm praying for Great-grandma's soul, Mom," answered the little boy, "my teacher in yeshiva showed me what to say."

Turning back to his *Tehillim*, the child continued:

„לקדושים אשר בארץ המה ואדירי כל חפצי בם."
For the sake of the holy ones who died and were interred in the earth and had been pious, in their z'chus do You help me; and they are the strong ones through whose z'chus all my desires are satisfied . . .

And on the wings of those precious words the soul was borne heavenward.

Sarah Shapiro

Shadows in the Kitchen

*A Housewife Views
the Holocaust*

SOME WEEKS AGO I happened to read the first few paragraphs of an article about a *baal-teshuvah* movie producer in America. The interviewer had asked him if he was interested in doing any films about the Holocaust. "No," said the producer. "Why not?" asked the journalist. "Because it's much easier for people to identify with the six million," he replied, "than it is for them to identify with Judaism. They get a sense of their Jewishness much easier that way, yet they're escaping their true responsibility."

I turned the page, furrowing my way through all the advertisements for *sheitels* and completely re-styled kitchens, on to the end of the magazine. The magazine has gotten lost now somewhere among the piles of crayoned pictures and bathing caps and all the odds and ends that summer vacation produces, but that comment has been on my mind ever since, presenting itself to me first from one angle and then from another, now in this light, now in that one. There's something so true about this man's statement. Every few years I go through one of my Holocaust periods: for a month or two I read nothing but histories, first-hand accounts, analytical studies. Is my interest in the Holocaust an obsession that I should curb? Is it a substitute for a higher level of Jewish awareness? Though I would certainly come under the movie producer's list of Jews who identify themselves properly with Judaism (after all, look at the scarf on my head, and the *Badatz hechshers* on my kitchen shelf), it could be that the time I devote to reading about the Holocaust is time that could be better spent brushing up on the *halachos* of *Shabbos*, attending *shiurim*, or getting the laundry done by Thursday.

What am I looking for? What drives me on from one Holocaust volume to the next? When I ask myself what it is that captivates me, I find I'm seeking something that can illuminate my own daily affairs — the truth that lies beneath the surface of life. How are we, really, underneath it all? What is revealed when all the props are torn away? What would remain of our *emuna* were virtually no sign of G-d's kindness in evidence, since even amidst the relative ease in which our generation is presently living, maintaining our *emuna* isn't easy? It's obvious that we're all being tested, day in and day out, from one minute to the next. Each person I know has his or her own personal share of suffering and there is no shortage of tragedy. Yet while we may find ourselves inwardly complaining that our difficulties seem undeserved, the suffering is usually meted out on such a scale that we are still capable of discerning the reasonable and kind Hand that's administering it. We can look for its meaning. We can conceive of the possibility that our pains are as precisely calculated to heal what ails us as are the pains we get in the dentist chair.

Here I am, thank G-d, in my daily life, where the worst thing that has befallen me this week was to be insulted by a friend on the same day that one of my children had an ear infection and another one wouldn't go to bed at eight. My telephone has just gotten turned off because I didn't pay the bill on time; now there's a legitimate problem for you. Yesterday was Tisha B'Av. I managed somehow to get all the kids out of the house, sank into the couch with *Slingshot of Hell*, by Rav Yehezkel Harfanes, Martin Gilbert's historical volume, *The Holocaust*, and *Responsa From the Holocaust*, by Rabbi Ephraim Oshrey. First I found the place where I'd left off in *Slingshot of Hell* a few days earlier. Like millions of other Jews of that era, Rav Harfanes lost almost his entire family to Germany's perpetration of the Final Solution. In the now familiar scenario, his wife and children were sent to the left, while he and one of his sons were sent to the right.

"We threw kisses in the air and promised one another that we would be reunited before long." After the war, he writes, "when I returned to my home, I felt the walls of my house to be the silent witnesses of the tragedy I had experienced. They were stripped of all plaster, thanks to the scavenging of treasure-seekers. They were windowless and doorless, a veritable shambles. This devastating sight reminded me of the destruction of my dear family. I regarded myself as a severed entity, an amputated limb. I was so depressed that for a long time I slept on the floor, not even sensing the lack of a proper bed. My spirit was altogether crushed. I felt as if my deceased ones were deposited right before me."

"... Not Made Me a Slave"

I arrived an hour or so later at the end of Harfanes' journal and rested. Lying there stunned by the nobility of his spirit, I found myself, after a little while, wishing we had an air conditioner, then uneasily picked up *Responsa From the Holocaust* and opened it at random:

"One morning during prayer, Rav Avrohom Yosef, who was leading the congregation in the morning service, reached the blessing, 'Who has not made me a slave,' and shouted bitterly to the Master of all masters, 'How can I recite a blessing of a free man? How can a hungry slave, constantly abused and demeaned, praise his Creator by uttering, "Who has not made me a slave?"' Every morning as he led the prayers, he let out the same cry! And many of those who joined him in prayer felt the same way. I was then asked for the Torah ruling on this matter. Response: One of the earliest commentators on the prayers points out that this blessing was not formulated in order to praise G-d for our physical liberty. I therefore ruled that we might not skip or alter this blessing under any circumstances. On the contrary, despite our physical captivity, we were more obligated than ever to recite the blessing to show our enemies that as a people we were spiritually free."

I skimmed along through the chapters, pausing at the case of a young man whose left arm had been amputated by a Nazi for the crime of stealing potatoes:

> "No words can describe this young man's anguish, not only because he has been turned into an armless cripple but because now he was prevented from fulfilling the commandment of the Torah to don *tefillin* on the left arm. Weeping bitterly, he came to me and asked whether he could fulfill the *mitzvah* of *tefillin* by donning them, with the help of others, on his right arm. Response: I ruled that even if someone else put the *tefillin* on his right arm, he would be fulfilling the *mitzvah*. He rejoiced at the ruling and, as he walked out in good spirits, remarked, 'The accursed Germans did not succeed in robbing me of the *mitzvah* of *tefillin*.'"

I flipped some pages.

> "After the Germans carried out the mass murder of Jewish children on 3 and 4 Nissan 5704, by butchering some 1,200 children and infants whom they tore from their mothers' bosoms and shot and burned, I was asked by the unfortunate parents whether they had the obligation to recite *Kaddish* for their children and if there was any distinction to be made between infants and older children. Response: I instructed the unfortunate parents to recite *Kaddish* for their beloved children, but only for those who were 30 days old or more."

☙ Yakov Grojanowski's Diary

My stomach was rumbling uncomfortably and my throat yearned for orange juice. I switched to Gilbert's history, opening to the fourteen-day diary of a young Jew named Yakov Grojanowski, who was assigned to a special work detail in a gravedigger squad:

"... The S.S. leader ordered the work detail to open the doors. A strong smell of gas prevailed. Five minutes later he shouted, 'Hey, Jews, go and lay *tefillin* (i.e. throw out the corpses)!' Meanwhile the gendarme ordered us to sing. At first we disobeyed. However when he threatened to shoot, Meir and Jehuda begged me to stand up and sing. I myself don't know from where I drew the strength to get up.

I addressed my comrades in a feeble voice: 'Friends and honorable people, get up and sing after me; first we will cover our heads.' They stood up. I began to sing: 'Hear! O Israel, the Lord is our G-d, the Lord is one.' Those assembled repeated each verse in depressed tones. Then I continued: 'Praised be the name and the splendor of his realm forever and ever,' which the others repeated after me three times.... [A few days later] after the morning prayer, we again talked about ourselves, politics and G-d. Our overwhelming worry was the fate of the Jewish people. All would gladly have forfeited their own lives if only the Jewish nation could survive. Monday, the twelfth of January, at 5 a.m. six people got up and recited the Psalms amid crying and wailing. Some of the others made fun of us because of our piety. This consolation struck them as youthful foolishness. We replied that our life was in the hands of G-d. If all this was His will, then we accepted it with love, all the more so as the days of the Messiah were approaching. After the morning prayer and *Kaddish*, we recited the prayer of penitence. At 7 a.m. they brought us coffee and bread. Some of the men from Izbica drank up all the coffee. The others got very annoyed and said we were already facing death and had to behave with dignity. It was decided to share out a little coffee to everyone in future."

Passing quickly through the 1940's, something caught my eye from June of '44:

> "One of those executed at Birkenau was the former Elder of the Theresienstadt ghetto, Jacob Edelstein. An eyewitness, Yossi Rosensaft, was present during Edelstein's last moments: 'It was about nine a.m. and he was saying his morning prayers, wrapped in his prayer shawl. Suddenly the door burst open and S.S. Lieutenant Hoessler struttled in. He called out Jacob's name. Jacob did not move. Hoessler screamed: "I am waiting for you, hurry up." Jacob turned round very slowly, faced Hoessler and said quietly: "Of the last moments on this earth, allotted to me by the Almighty, I am the master, not you." Whereupon he turned back to face the wall and finished his prayers. He then folded his prayer shawl unhurriedly, handed it to one of the inmates and said to Hoessler: "I am now ready." Hoessler stood there all the while without uttering a word, and marched out

when Edelstein was ready. Edelstein followed him. We have never seen Jacob Edelstein again.'"

Lying on the couch, riveted to each page, a queer self-doubt welled up within me. Was I entertaining myself, G-d forbid, with the drama of these Jews' ordeals? Was I getting a false sense of Jewish identity that could be better discovered by forcing myself, in spite of the fast, to go see what my children were up to? After all, the Jews of the camps and the ghettos had to continue functioning without nourishment for days and weeks and months on end... shouldn't I make a gesture of emulating at least this? Gilbert's volume in itself is, let's see, eight hundred and twenty-eight pages long, filled with seemingly endless, similar accounts. I'd spent four hours with this book alone and had only scratched the surface.

At last the fast ended and my husband and I gladly reentered the world, put the children to bed early and retired at nine. At 1 a.m. I bolted suddenly awake.

What was it I'd been dreaming? Of mothers being separated from their children? I think so.

Lying awake in the darkness, it struck me, as it has on other rare occasions in the past but as if for the first time: The Holocaust actually happened. It happened a few brief years before I was born. These things were experienced. It happened to them, my brethren, because they were Jews, like me. Why was I spared? Is my most profound response only to pray that I and my loved ones should somehow squeak through life without being similarly tested?

It was getting light before my conscience let me go back to sleep again.

So. Is this all I have to offer the Jews of the Holocaust: that meager, three-or-four-hour span of guilty sleeplessness? When I finish this book, I'll start another soon enough, perhaps on some other topic, and the keen knife of awareness that cut open my sleep last night will be misplaced along with the old magazines and children's drawings and bathing caps, and I'll think of other things. The movie producer was right, of course: My identity as a Jew cannot be found through the emotions to which stories of the Holocaust give me such easy access. But I can no more escape *from* stories of those awful times than I can escape *into* them.

At this moment, as I type, my four year old has just awakened from his afternoon nap. I chafe at the interruption and wish I could stay submerged in my own thoughts, but alas, he climbs up on my chair, taps me on the shoulder, smiles for my attention. As I go now to give my baby boy his lunch, shall I file the subject away in my mind somehow, under Q, perhaps, for question, or U for unanswerable? It seems the only thing to do is let the Holocaust's vast shadow — the small fragment of it, that is, which I perceive — follow me into my kitchen; its darkness can accentuate all the light in my life that now surrounds me. How lucky I am to sweep my own kitchen floor! How grateful I have to be to recite the morning blessings without Lieutenant Hoessler looking over my shoulder! How happy I should be to be able to let other Jews partake of whatever's most precious to me— "To share out a little coffee to everyone in future." The shadow can remind me that much of what I suffer from need hardly bring me grief at all, and can teach me to bear the legitimate sorrows nobly.

The greatest sign of respect I can accord those who underwent unimaginable tortures is not necessarily to lose sleep reading about the Holocaust and be too tired to wake up on time for my children the next morning. It would be to appreciate as fully as possible my opportunity to serve *HaKadosh Baruch Hu* with joy. To recognize, as did Yakov Grojanowski, that we are already facing death and must behave with dignity.

To rejoice in the gift of life, for as a people in possession of Torah we are spiritually free.

Yaffa Ganz

Standing Alone

ಆ Stop — And Take Stock

PAIN IS AN INTEGRAL part of the human condition. There's no getting through life without bumping into it — or having it bump into you. Or bowl you over.

I'm not talking about the minor aches and pains we all know, the ones that are scattered through our days like little stumbling stones. There are ways to mitigate and protect ourselves from these pint-size pains. I mean the major league events. The kind of pain that engulfs and overwhelms you, pushing everything else out and away.

The ear or tooth or stomach or knee which suddenly spreads and takes over, becoming You. You can hear the sounds of traffic or children playing or a telephone ringing, but it's coming from some other pain-free planet, far away; these things have nothing to do with you. Your world has condensed and blackened into a sort of womb-like knot which includes only you — and your pain.

What is the purpose of such deep, all-encompassing pain? Pain surely has its importance and place in our lives. It serves, firstly, as a warning that not all is well in our bodies. If a broken leg or an infected ear didn't hurt, irrevocable damage might ensue by the time we discovered anything was amiss.

Pain is also undoubtedly one of the many ways in which G-d signals to us that it's time to stop our mad race and take stock. That something is amiss in our psyche, as well as our body. Pain tells us it's time to think and evaluate, and perhaps to initiate a bit of remedial action somewhere along the line.

Yet none of these reasons necessitates the need for the huge wave of acute, crystallized pain we all experience at one time or another. What good is pain that leaves you alone, gasping for breath, unable to think or to function? Pain that completely demobilizes, demoralizes and debilitates? Pain that no one else can alleviate, or share, no matter how much they empathize? For real pain is exquisitely private. Since nothing happens haphazardly, and since everything serves some purpose, this pain, too, must be "good" for something. But what?

The Isolationist Quality

Perhaps the very isolationist quality of the pain provides a key. When all is said and done, we are, each and every one of us, an individual — a separate soul standing alone before G-d. But how often do we stand "alone"? Even the most unsociable of human beings is surrounded day and night by the world he lives in — the people, the material accoutrement, and the social and moral dictates that provide the framework for every society. How many of our thoughts and feeling are truly our "own"? How often do we strip ourselves of all extraneous "clothing" we have acquired, and stand, so to speak, naked and shivering, facing the Creator Who made us? How often do we remember the inside Me who inhabits the Outside Person we usually are? Rarely.

But when one is in the throes of gripping pain, everyone and everything else recedes. The kind and loving people who surround us, anxious to help, cannot reach us. As we are sucked into that awful wave of obliterating pain, helpless and completely alone, we would gladly give away our most precious of possessions if only our suffering would come to an end.

Yet, Not Completely Alone

We are not completely alone, of course, not even in our pain. In that black void there is Another, and in our free-falling terror, we find ourselves face to face with Him. For only when we are able to shed our superfluous, outer self — the self which deludes us into thinking we are stronger and richer and smarter, more competent and important than we really are — only then, as we realize the extent of our impotency, are we able to face G-d with true humility. Only then are our prayers sufficiently pure (*Please Hashem*, please, *make it stop!*), and therefore, powerful.

Perhaps the fact that we cannot tolerate more than a trifle of excruciating pain without losing control or consciousness is related to the fact that we cannot sustain "direct contact" with the Divine for any extended period of time. It's an interesting thought.

From the grievous sufferings of King David, glorious songs were born. From the desolation of *Iyov*, new faith was established. From an anguished slavery, redemption ensued. Evidently, when nothing is left, when we have been stripped of all illusions, when no hope, no help is forthcoming, only unremitting pain — then we remember the Rock, which has not only the power to crush, but also to heal.

It is undoubtedly preferable to find G-d through blessings and joy, but frail creatures that we are, we often tend to search more actively for Him in times of stress. Fortunately for us, He is to be found then too. Even when we think we are alone, in the throes of acute, overwhelming pain.

---

* This article is copyrighted by author.

≈§ Her Housekeeping vs. Her Soulkeeping

Time for Personal Growth
Housekeeping vs. Soulkeeping
Woman's Place in Torah Study
Jewish Women in a Torah Society
Letters in Response
In the Wake of the Thomas Hearings
Woman at the Crossroads
When Feminists Demand,
   Can Judaism Deliver?
Sanctity and Self-Expression
"Where There's a Rabbinic Will,
   There's a Halachic Way"
Music — By and for a Jewish Woman
Wonder Woman

Shira Silvers Frank

Time for Personal Growth

*Every woman requires some
time for herself to help her discover
the spiritual core in the midst
of material pursuits.*

∽ "From the Diary of Mrs. M...."

(The Seventeenth of Iyar)
   "I'm trying to find the time to hear myself think. Instead, a constant stream of actions seems to play itself out in front of me.... Looking back, the characters seem almost stage-like. I grasped this moment to stop and think why I perform these steps in a robot-like ballet.... When will the constant present be fused with the eternal goals we set for ourselves? Will I ever see a connection between the two almost-completely diverse worlds?"

∽ Values in Collision

THERE IS A CONNECTION between the spiritual and physical realms, not to be fully understood until *Moshiach's* time. Yet everyone strives to see how the two are interrelated, to recognize the ever-present redeeming spirituality in the material. This is a particularly difficult challenge for a woman. She's more deeply involved in the material-physical world. Her goal, of course, is to elevate her sphere of activity in the material world, yet many women do not actualize their potential to do so. The values of the contemporary secular world, which emphasize that a woman's place is definitely *not* in the home, may well be a major complicating factor in this dilemma. But regardless of where the cause may lie, this dilemma does exist and many women do attempt to cope with this problem.

Dealing with two sets of value systems — the secular and non-secular, which are often diametrically opposed to each other — can indeed cause tension, especially when a woman feels torn by the desire to cater to both worlds. There is no shortage of such conflicts: the desire to be strikingly fashion-wise or "sensible"... the denigration of a woman working in and with her home as opposed to outside activity.... Even the "super-*baal habosta*" syndrome, though it has its roots in a positive Jewish value, can also cause tension, for "nothing is ever clean enough." The crucial concern of the sanctity of family life becomes overshadowed by anxiety over the mess that children make. The disorder brings anguish to the mother, who often directs her resentments against her children.... When any single value is unduly stressed, desirable Jewish goals become deemphasized as a result. Even the pre-occupation with the technicalities of child-rearing and housekeeping can eclipse a woman's creativity.

✡ Time for Reflection

One way to deal with these conflicts and the tensions they produce is to follow a long-standing practice. Just as a man, by requirement, sets aside regular times for Torah study and contemplation every day, so should a woman create an island of time for herself, even on a busy day. This tranquil period in the midst of daily turbulence is a "*Shabbos*" of sorts, which can elevate the rest of the day, as *Shabbos* elevates the six weekdays of material involvement. It offers a woman a chance to reflect on her life more objectively, and help improve her sense of a deeper self. When the great *Mussar* teachers and Chassidic mentors call for *hisbonenus, hisbodedus,* or *cheshbon hanefesh* — various forms of introspection — their words speak to all humankind, women as well as men.

To carve out time for such purposes on a daily basis calls for great discipline. But, then again, no masterpiece was ever created without discipline and diligence — how much more so when the masterpiece is one's own *neshama*. Moreover, the emotional calm gained from truly hearing oneself and attaining some objectivity is a desired end unto itself.

A woman's exemption from performing time-bound *mitzvos* gives her the opportunity to use her time in a more unlimited, flexible sense. She should nonetheless structure this time and set up her daily schedule to comfortably fit in a period for herself and her spiritual concerns. Without disciplining one's hours, the days and years become an endless merry-go-round. Once a year, with the arrival of *Yomim Noraim* and the New Year, one looks at the completed year in retrospect, and one month seems to melt into the other, only distinguished by *Yomim Tovim* and children's illnesses.

☙ Enhancing Everyday Activities: Personal Spirituality...

This "time for myself" can be used in various ways, not the least of them *tefilla* (prayer) and Torah study. The significance of woman's *davening* and learning is not to be underestimated. At the outset, these activities may be difficult and unrewarding, but if one views involvement in spiritual endeavors as being compared to exercising a muscle, one's attitude can change. Once it becomes a regular experience, daily immersion in thought and prayer will become much easier. And when one eventually finds sufficient time to *daven* with depth, the experience will be realized much more easily, especially after having made recitation of the *Shemoneh Esrei* a daily practice.

Studying the Torah also has very strong ramification in one's daily life. As Ben Bag-Bag said: "Learn it and learn it (the Torah), for everything is in it; look deeply into it... for there is nothing more edifying for you than it" (*Avos* 5,25). Women are required to fulfill the *mitzvos* of loving G-d and fearing Him and studying those aspects of Torah that promote feelings of love and awe are surely in order. The Chofetz Chaim said that a woman is permitted to study those areas of Torah that inspire her to greater love of G-d, and she is to be commended for such learning.

Women's groups all convene the weeks before Pesach to review the festival's countless laws. But there are other *mitzvos*. How much more meaningful are the *mitzvos* of *Shabbos* and *kashrus* with a more in-depth knowledge of their laws. Studying the *halachos* not only guides a woman in faithful performance of halachic obligations, it also highlights the importance of significant details that might otherwise seem trivial. Only through study can one appreciate how meaningful every factor in *mitzvah* observance truly is. This involvement in Torah cannot help but bring benefit to the entire family, since Torah is the essence of goodness.

∽§ Creating Goals

One may complain that this idea sounds desirable in theory, but is difficult to carry out practically. This need not be so, since the scheduling and selection of a mode of study is really up to every individual. Besides the obvious *shiur* at night, one mother at home can team up with another mother in a similar circumstance to study together on the telephone or in person when the children are in school, when the baby usually naps, or when the respective fathers are able to take over at night... Or a woman can make time when she knows that she cannot do housework, and would otherwise read the paper or a novel for a short break. The frequency of such sessions would of course depend on each person's particular schedule.

Learning that is geared toward a goal usually brings the most satisfaction. Starting a *sefer* with hopes of finishing it, is usually a formula for frustration. It is much more realistic to concentrate on selected chapters of a *sefer* that you both find of interest, on certain commentaries on the *Chumash*, or the appropriate *Megillah* with *Rashi* before a *Yom Tov*, making sure to allow ample time to finish in a certain time period. Limited goals usually bring the best results because they are achievable, and with each completion comes an exhilarating sense of satisfaction and a better sense of self, adding positive reinforcement to future learning efforts.

∽§ Working With Creativity

So many women possess gifts of creative expression — be they musical, artistic, literary, or in other realms. But once they marry and involve themselves completely with their families, they seem to neglect developing these talents. A woman need not exclude this vital aspect of herself, but should rather channel it in a disciplined manner along the lines described previously in regard to other positive endeavors. Besides providing a sense of catharsis and offering a format for venting the frustrations of the day, being able to create is a special feature of a woman's makeup, and she can derive spiritual strength from creative activity. These talents can be used to bring joy to the entire family and invigorate an otherwise mundane day for children as well. Even though creativity tends to follow some internal stimulus, time structure and specific reachable goals can make the activity more meaningful.

"Chessed" — Even Without Organizations

Life's more conventional areas should also be explored for enhancement. When one mentions *chessed*, for instance, one usually thinks of intricate organizations with time-consuming activities, often involving work outside of the home. So one often abstains from them, no matter how worthy or important they may be. Whether or not this reaction is justified, there are some immediate forms of *chessed* that we all engage in that are so close that we tend to ignore them completely. One need not live in a Third World country to find opportunities to help others. Every individual has areas that need *chizuk* — encouragement, help, or comfort. Servicing them begins with looking at the other person and thinking:"What can I do to help him/her?" Thought soon finds oral expression, and when one's speech reflects such concerns, replacing mere small talk spoken to fill empty gaps of time, that is truly an achievement... How many hours a day do we find ourselves speaking "eloquent soliloquies" whose basic purpose is meaningless?

How does one begin? Won't the intrusion be resented? A person with sensitivity does not have to wait to be asked. Not only is this emotional reach-out a vehicle for *kiruv rechokim* — extending oneself to help fellow Jews alienated from *Yiddishkeit* — it can be a vital help to those closest to us. As a matter of halachic precedent, the needy of your family take top priority, while the poor of your city take precedence over those of other communities. This giving of ourselves to others is important enough for every one of us to spare some time and talent to pursue. In addition, on a personal level of growth, cultivation of this intimate type of *chessed* elevates daily physical endeavors, and gives more purpose to our temporal lives. (This is the כח הנתינה, power of giving, that Rabbi Dessler so often stressed.)

The Real Agenda

Growth, self-actualization, fulfillment of potential, development of innate talents — these are within the reach of every woman. These pursuits can enhance a woman in her role as *akeres habayis*

— the mainstay of the home, in a truly Jewish sense. When a woman — nay person, for that matter — feels better about herself emotionally and spiritually, her attitude toward life becomes completely transformed. The employment world offers workers a coffee break. We too need the respite during our daily chores to be more productive in the work schedule that follows. How many women, after a day of being super *baal-haboste* or fashion plate, and after having thought and spoken for hours of things that were truly of no consequence (sometimes *lashon hora* besides), feel a deep emptiness within them? They then look at their children as being a mere appendage to the house; or they lie down to read a novel or watch television, because their minds had been too empty all day to really sense their ultimate purpose or worth, and feel no need to crown the day with some elevating activity. Why does the beauty of her role with her family escape her? Are perhaps the fleeting moments of this true satisfaction so evasive because of her unending ride on a merry-go-round of *hevel* (hollow pursuits)? If someone feels that she did all the "right things" but still finds that something is lacking, that lack is a sense of purpose. The material needs were fed, but, not the *neshama*. Even children are not appreciated and enjoyed, for being in the way of "what we have to do."

☙ The Keys

The keys to a meaningful existence, then are goal-setting and structure. On the most practical level, being organized helps give purpose to daily activity. By being a "program planner," you can derive a great sense of satisfaction when schedules are met: Moments of your life are not merely passing unimportant time slots, but are parts of an organized whole, when you take charge. The special moments reserved for "positive outlets" inspire an awareness of fleeting moments of time. With this, a woman can re-awaken herself to periodically examine her individual life and see where improvements can be made. This not only promotes an advance in a spiritual sense, but constitutes a leap forward for the emotional self. Each person needs to search herself and see where she can best utilize a "positive outlet." This search will result in an elevation of each of us in our individual lives.

H. D. Wolpin

Housekeeping vs. Soulkeeping

CONTROVERSY, Thy Name Is Woman! Nearly every household magazine of recent vintage offers conflicting views on "the plight of modern woman." A rash of articles so widespread indicates that the symptoms of a dilemma must indeed be present. One school of thought pumps for the emancipation of the housewife. "Loosen Those Shackles — Get A Job And Find The True You!" shouts the printed page. The tired wife who, feeling rather pleased with herself as she surveys her tidy kitchen, has picked up a magazine to relax for an evening, learns to her bewilderment that she is considered utterly bovine, if not beneath contempt, to tolerate the indignities of housework. The other faction in the fray advocates finding oneself, or rather losing oneself, in the earthy joys of creative homemaking. What greater aesthetic bliss than dicing an onion! Surely, life's supreme goal is attained in the triumph of holding in one's palm an honest, hand-kneaded loaf!

The myriad details that twang at the core of modern woman have given rise to the existence of such a problem, unknown in a less complex age. Today's housewife is often a slave to the rigidly high standards of contemporary homemaking, her time-saving appliances notwithstanding. In addition to managing a household, with all this entails, she is expected to keep herself everlastingly chic and youthful.

The dizzying cycle of repetitious tasks leaves varying subconscious effects on different personalities. Simply living with head high can be a heroic womanly effort at times, for it involves constant coping. Illness, disappointment, and the bleak awareness of the frailties of others must all be coped with, smoothed, and filed into neat order. To live the soul-trying, *giving* existence of womankind with no goal hovering over head, or at best the dubious one of "social prestige," is a tremendous waste of human quality.

The position of women beneath the shadow of crumbling mores, with no clear values to maintain, is understandably pathetic. By contrast, the Orthodox Jewish woman, grasping the strong, silken cords of tradition, should logically be free of any troubles more vexing than getting her work done early enough to meet the Friday evening deadline. The charted paths she follows are infinitely more satisfying psychologically than those her secularized sisters walk. Most Jewish women accept their roles joyfully and fulfill them admirably, instinctively rising to every occasion. In the case of some, however, all is not calm beneath the placid surface.

Paradoxically, the wife who pursues society's nebulous goal of "contentment" is likely to be curiously restive. She views her typical day as one of undeserved drudgery. Furthermore, she feels that her education has been largely wasted. But her pride allows her no alternative; home and children must be cared for, regardless of how empty and meaningless she considers the daily routines. No wonder she feels trapped, and desperately seeks an outlet outside the home.

The importance of the Jewish woman's attitude should not be underestimated, for she is entrusted with much of the responsibility of translating a Torah-true life from the written word into practice. If she is dissatisfied, and views her duties in life as onerous burdens, her bitterness has a corrosive effect on an entire Torah unit, her family. How insidious an element is bitterness if allowed to seep into the veins of a people enjoined, *Ivdu es Hashem b'simchoh!* (Serve G-d in joy!)

What is there in the nature of modern life to have spawned such a problem? One evokes the hallowed mental picture of our grandmothers poring over tear-stained pages of *Tehillim*, the homogenous lines of the *Tzenah U'r'ena*. Why should it seem somewhat ludicrous to try to superimpose that image over the picture of the Jewish woman of today?

Our grandmothers' warm self-reliance stemmed from an intimate communion with the Divine coupled with a sheltered existence. Faith, in the form of various references and supplications to the *Ribono Shel Olam*, was summoned up in every other breath. Unadulterated faith in G-d and in the Jewish way was the vital force that infused toil with glory. Today, just as girls are no longer sheltered, this traditional picture has faded from the kaleidoscope of progress. Girls are educated much the same as boys, only to realize that most of the knowledge painstakingly acquired over years of study can never blossom into useful channels. What outlets, then, have they for the wellspring of zeal bequeathed them by their grandmothers?

The diligent observance of *Shabbos, Yomim Tovim, Taharas Hamishpacha*, and *Kashrus* has certainly been strictly preserved. Yet the very nature of modern times robs the woman of certain spiritual satisfactions which once used to be her province. For example, she is afraid to take a total stranger into her home for a meal, so instead gives him a monetary contribution which she never misses. Whereas on one hand she finds herself being further and further removed from personal involvement in *Yiddishkeit*, on the other hand she often stands as a buffer between her husband and the secular world as it is today. While her husband has access to the thirst-quenching waters of Torah, and strives to continue his Torah study, very little of this filters down to her. She is pitted against all the mass media: radio, television, movies, advertising, theater and novels — with woefully insufficient spiritual defenses. When her mind is already being subordinated by the multitudinous pressures of daily living, how can her observances help from being perfunctory?

As her husband chants the *Eyshes Chayil* on Friday night, she sits smilingly serene, but in her mind thoughts overlap with the speed of race cars piling up.... *I must speak to Benjy about his table manners again... I really should have shortened Ruth's skirt before letting her wear it... I hope David doesn't comment about the 'kugel' being slightly burnt...* and so on, *ad infinitum*. Proof enough — a complex and delicate problem exists. No pat solutions can be given, of course, but if we were afforded insight into the minds of sensitive women *not* similarly troubled, what vital difference of attitude might we find?

Nearly all share the common problems of fighting dust and civilizing children. But the enlightened Jewish wife measures all her activities against the yardstick of *Kol ma'asecho yihiyu l'shem shomayim*. (All your deeds should be for the sake of Heaven.) She knows the religious significance of her household tasks. Though she may not think about it (and even grimace while tackling the job), she knows that the act of cooking a meal, and even of scouring the pans afterwards, is the highest act she can perform in the hour or so she allots to this task. By cooking this meal, she is strengthening her husband and children for learning Torah and performing *mitzvos*. By cleaning and decorating her home attractively, she is giving her family the serenity of mind they need to flourish mentally and physically in the light of the Torah. All the capacities of her educated brain and heart are channeled constructively. Since she emphatically *doesn't* think that working in a research laboratory with experimental animals or keeping the books in an office are superior activities, it is apparent that her thinking is colored not by vacuous contemporary values, but by Torah philosophy. She doesn't suffer from malnutrition of the ego because she never loses sight of her goal of bringing herself and her family closer to G-dliness. If she can't afford a new breakfront, she cheerfully does without it; if she can, she may buy it for the added contribution it can make, or she may decide instead to spend the money on tutoring for a particular child, or the like. She weighs the purchase of a fur coat or a necklace the same way, willingly rejecting it if something else would better further her goal. It takes much intelligence and objectivity to try to make all decisions *L'shem Shomayim*; to realize that attempting to "keep up with the Kohns" would preclude spiritual growth. Where there is no such growth, there is, of course, stagnation.

"Holier-Than-Thou" Saintliness? Not Necessarily. Her attitude is encased in the recesses of the mind; outwardly she is as normal as apple strudel.

The average young woman, who has been weaned from the Torah outlook through continuous exposure to an alien culture, might shudder when confronted with such raw "piety," even though she, too, is formally observant. Standards of *social frumkeit* are evolving, and she wants to blend with the current mode. In some religious circles, wives instinctively know that fund raising and ticket selling are "in" mitzvos; *davening* and *bentshing* seem, by comparison, "square." And one who abstains from a little intimate, sophisticated *loshon hora* on purely religious grounds is hopelessly gauche!

Certain guiding realizations must be brought out into the open. The woman must become aware of the unique needs of the feminine *neshomah*. She was created as a "giving" being, and only in giving of herself will she find fulfillment. All Jews are dragged a little lower if she allows herself to be satisfied with a life of acquisition of trappings. No matter how frosted over with modern accoutrements, the essential earthiness of such an existence is refined very little. Nothing is wrong with gracious living, so long as this in itself is not the sole object. In one generation, the housewife might salve her yearning heartstrings with the possession of a well-dusted radio cabinet, a figured carpet in the parlor, and "a son a doctor, a son a lawyer." In a subsequent generation, the pot-of-gold at the end of the rainbow might be a well-tended half-acre in suburbia, a Paris-approved wardrobe, two cars in the garage and "a son a *yeshiva bochur*, a son a scientist." In either case, religious rituals are observed as part of household routine, and as such are secondary to the earthbound goals. The woman remains a fine, respectable Jewish wife and mother, but seldom utilizes the potential of her creative, resilient female nature to contribute to the universal Jewish goal of *Kiddush Hashem*.

If the same amount of surging energy she lavishes on trivia was directed, through the media of home and family, to serving *Hashem* primarily, with all other considerations secondary, some of the darkness shrouding the world today would be lifted. If she were joined by enough of her contemporaries, the ensuing brightness would be meaningfully felt.

Fraida Blau

Woman's Place in Torah Study

HOUSEWIFE ... MOTHER ... Secretary ... Administrator ... Storekeeper ... Saleslady ... Think for a moment. When was the last time you opened a *sefer?* Was it yesterday? Last week? Or was it perhaps years ago — when you last studied for your final exams?

Unfortunately, many girls view their Bais Yaakov diplomas as a formal farewell to serious Torah study. After all, they assume, women have no obligation to learn Torah, and therefore are exempt from this, our greatest *mitzva*.

Torah is the life force of Judaism that forms us into a unique and holy people, and is meant to be studied by women, too. Every word, every letter is filled with *kedusha* and has a profound influence on the *neshama* of anyone who engages in its study. Women are not without this need.

A Share in the Merit

In fact, the *Gemara* in *Brachos* asks, "What merit do women possess [to be revived at *techiyas hameisim* — when the dead will be resurrected]?" The *Gemara* replies: "They permit their husbands to study Torah and await their homecoming, and they accompany their children to *cheder*."

Asks the *Tashbatz*, "Why not credit them with the merit for the many *mitzvos* that are unique to them?" — and then explains: "While it is true that women do perform many *mitzvos*, the Torah is so vital for eternal life that we must find a *mitzva*-activity directly connected to Torah-study as a prime source of merit for them."

In the time of the *Gemara*, women apparently gained sufficient knowledge and inspiration from their environment and non-structured activity to lead a Torah life without resorting to formal study, but they still required Torah study as a vital source of merit and for this they relied on their indirect involvement. Today, such a level of involvement may not be sufficient.

This is not as radical as it may sound, for in truth, women have been actively involved in some form of Torah study for millennia. They were included in the *mitzva* of *Hakheil*, when every seven years, men, women, and children gathered in Jeruslam to hear the king read *Mishna Torah (Sefer Devarim)*. The men came to learn, we are told, while the women were expected to listen — a term that implies comprehension, not just hearing. The impact of the knowledge and inspiration of that gathering was strong enough to last seven years.

The *Sefer Chassidim* points out that some women made Torah study a more frequent experience. When the Shunamite woman told her husband that she was going to see the Prophet Elisha, he questioned her: "Is today then *Rosh Chodesh* or *Shabbos* that you are going to hear a Torah lecture?" Apparently, it was her practice to attend Torah lectures regularly.

There are other indications throughout Jewish literature of women's involvement in study, such as the reference to the canisters that served as "traffic dividers," to prevent the mingling of men and women — during Torah lectures, according to some commentaries. Obviously, the women of Talmudic times attended Torah classes in sufficient number and frequently enough to warrant such safeguards. (*Kiddushin* 81)

There is plenty of evidence in historical sources that Jewish women were always literate, for they were tutored by their mothers, aunts, or grandmothers. Only formal classroom education did not exist in earlier millennia.

Today, too, Torah study should be part of a woman's routine. Every morning, both men and women are required to recite the *bracha "la'asok B'divrei Torah* — to be occupied with the words of Torah." Not focused on merely listening to Torah, the *bracha* emphasizes being actively engaged in Torah study. True, the *Siddur* provides everyone, man and woman, with minimum Torah passages to follow the *bracha*, but there is certainly more for every person to study as is required for most men, and as is recommended for most women.

This may seem to be in direct contradiction to the classic *drash* on the *pasuk*, "*You should teach your sons (Devarim 6:7)* — but not your daughters." This limitation, however, refers to the Oral Law, which women are not obligated to study in the same manner as men are. But women are obligated to study those matters that pertain to them, says the *Bais Yosef*. In fact, *Sefer Chassidim* maintains that a father is *required* to teach his daughter *halacha*, and rather than limit himself to those areas that pertain exclusively to women, he should guide her to mastery of all *halachos* that apply to her. As verification, the author cites the description of the high level of Torah scholarship during the time of *Chizkiyahu*: Everybody, including women and children, knew the laws of *Taharos* (ritual cleanliness) and of *Korbanos* (Temple sacrifices), which are of universal application. This level is often cited as the ideal every Jewish society should strive to achieve.

The categories of what women should study have not changed over the years, but as the Chofetz Chaim explained,[1] the amounts have. This should not be taken to mean that the *halacha* has changed. Rather, women always have been obligated to acquire both sufficient knowledge and enough inspiration to dedicate themselves to live in accordance with the Torah. Many years ago, they could rely on our strong, viable tradition for their needs, and there was no necessity to teach women Torah in today's broader and more formal format. They never studied the Oral Law, and only approached the Written Law when it was deemed essential for them. (See *Rambam* in *Hilchos Yesodei HaTorah*.)

In his day, the the Chofetz Chaim recognized that women had need to increase their Torah study — in *halacha* for practical

---

1. "It would seem to me that this (limitation on women's study of Torah) only pertains to those times when everyone lived in the same place that his ancestors lived, and the ancestral tradition was very strong for each individual. This motivated him/her to conduct his/her life in the ways of his forefathers. Nowadays, however, when the tradition of forefathers has weakened and many people do not live close to their parents, and especially in view of the many who have had a secular education, it is necessary to teach them the entire Bible, *Mussar*, *Avos*, *Menoras Hamaor* (ethical writings of our sages), and so on, so they will be strong in the principles of our holy faith. Otherwise, G-d forbid, they may totally abandon the path of G-d, and violate all the *mitzvos*" (Chofetz Chaim, *Likutei Halachos*, *Sotah* 20a).

guidance and in Scripture and Mussar for inspiration. Today, when we are constantly being bombarded by influences that do violence to Torah values, women certainly should make a greater effort to study Torah than ever before, but in the same prescribed areas. The goals, and the areas to be studied to reach these goals, do not vary. Only what and how much should be covered does.

The Chofetz Chaim was not alone in his contention that the strongest weapon to combat alien influences is *limud HaTorah*. Six hundred years earlier, the *Rambam* stated: "Lewd and illicit thoughts only enter a heart that is void of Torah." There are no vacuums in life. Space will be filled, and if it is not filled with Torah, it will be taken by thoughts that are contrary to Torah. This is a concern that should touch everyone.

Just one word of warning: In the last paragraph of *Shemoneh Esrei*, we pray to Hashem: "My soul should be as dust to all, open my heart to Your Torah." According to one interpretation of this passage, only if we see ourselves as dust, as nothing, can we become proper utensils for Torah. Humility is a basic prerequisite for the successful acquisition of Torah. Unfortunately, some women who have learned "some" Torah become arrogant, and their Torah knowledge serves to corrupt their character. Such women are definitely misusing their knowledge, for the purpose of Torah learning is to improve character, to make a person more humble and sincere.

The approaches may undergo change from generation to generation, but they still lead to the same goals. A Torah-study frame of reference can bring fresh meaning to a woman's seemingly endless mundane chores, and certainly can give her the spiritual uplift she so desperately needs for her most sacred task — the *chinuch* of her children. Indeed, the fruits of Torah study may well provide her with the necessary element to help transform her home atmosphere into one of *kedusha* and *Yiras Shomayim* — sanctity and fear of G-d.

So it is time for all good women to grab a rag, wipe off that thick layer of dust from their old *seforim* and renew their Torah study. Not only will they be enriched personally from this great experience, they will also enrich the lives of all those dearest to them.

Nisson Wolpin

Jewish Women in a Torah Society

*For Frustration?
Or Fulfillment?*

I.

The Role of Women

✥ Differences in a Plastic Society

MEN AND WOMEN share a common humanity — an overwhelming bond, to be sure. But differences in their emotional makeup, their inherent personalities, and their basis for fulfillment are far more than some people are willing to concede. It would seem that biological differences testify to differences in basic function, and these should affect personality in ways profound and far reaching. It would seem that to deny these differences would be to shut one's eyes to the obvious. After all, in virtually every society, each sex traditionally has been assigned distinct life roles. And most significant of all, these differences are reflected in the variations in *mitzvah*-responsibilities mandated by the Torah.

Regardless of these differences, the claim is common today that preassigned sex roles have made women victims of discrimination, and that they are not allowed options equal to men in almost every phase of life — jobs available, compensation for work, opportunities for self-fulfillment. The role assignments that were once universal, social critics point out, may have had their place in a different time. Today things are different: The food conveniences and population controls available in contemporary society have rendered the kitchen-nursery axis obsolete to modern woman, and the hunter-protecter-provider is equally meaningless as the exclusive activity area for sophisticated man. The structuring of roles by sexes, they claim, is outdated and without any meaning.

The quest for *equality* to the point of *sameness* has even brought the dictionary to the chopping block. Directives have been issued to copy editors in the McGraw-Hill publishing house to purge their lexicon of sexist expressions. Hence, fires are doused by "firepeople" — not firemen; a "chairperson" wields a gavel — not a chairman, nor a chairlady. Further, book illustrations are to show television sets being repaired by women, while men cuddle the baby on the sidelines. "Equal" must mean "indistinguishable."

This urge to homogenize mankind has spurred some women to see every traditional separating and categorizing of human role and function by sex as a Bastille to be stormed and razed to the ground, leaving nothing sacred — including Torah and Judaism. Examining the complaints and criticisms they voice, some are obviously contrived: but others may seem to be of substance. As a rule, when one's attitudes and values are based fully on the Torah, such accusations can be dismissed as so much ignorant antagonism, so much gratuitous fault-finding. But these stirrings in the social order also mean that Orthodox women will be dealing with newfound freedoms and opportunities. To chart a sensible and productive response for ourselves, then, means taking into account the attraction of the new, and the inevitable unconscious absorption of foreign values. It summons deeper understanding of our own beliefs, a firmer anchorage in our own convictions, and it calls for a better assessment of the challenges to Judaism posed by forces of "liberation."

ৼ The "Faults"

The challengers seem to focus on the secondary status of women in Jewish society, and on her general stereotype by sex which limits her areas of activity, productivity, creativity. These, in turn, are viewed as stemming from a range of sources: Torah law and rabbinic ordinance (a woman does not wear *tefillin* and is not expected to *daven* with a *minyan;* she is passive in the marriage ceremony, and cannot initiate divorce proceedings; she is not obligated to engage in Torah study) as well as custom and specific education (women are only associated with nursery and kitchen and are generally excluded from aggressive "masculine" roles in life). Those with a non-Orthodox orientation ask, "How binding are the Torah laws, and to what extent do they take into account a woman's personal needs for expression, fulfillment?" Others join in questioning customs, wondering, "To what extent is confinement of women to home and hearth a reflection of the eternal. Torah attitude, and to what extent is this an outgrowth of external conditions, changeable cultural factors, that may be discarded without regrets?"

◆§ As the Torah Differentiates

To be sure, the Jew looks to the Torah to take human nature into account. But more: Human nature actually reflects the Torah's truths — truths that pre-date man to the extent of serving as the blueprint for all creation, including mankind. As the *Zohar HaKadosh* says: "*Istakal B'Oraysa...* He looked into the Torah and created the world accordingly." Many of our Torah luminaries have explained this axiom more fully: "The Torah did not examine the family structure and then issue the command to honor one's parents. On the contrary: Because the Torah's ideal society involves child-parent responsibilities, G-d found it necessary to create the family." The flesh-and-blood relationship between parents and children, then, is an expression of the spiritual relationship between Man and his source. For that matter, the entire Torah-dictated structure of society reflects a higher spiritual reality, and these realities are the starting point for biological and psychological aspects of creation. One simply does not deal with one without the other.

Woman, her personal role, her status in home and society, all reflect characteristics very much her own. These *halachic* particulars correspond to biological and emotional specifics — her child-bearing and nurturing capacity, her superior intuitive capacity. And all of these are part of the *"Vayiven* — He fashioned her..." according to a specific design (see *Bereishis* 22:3). And the details, the many facets of her design, are outlined in the Torah.

The woman's role is not the object of discrimination — just one of definition. There are many such assigned roles in Jewry that seem to spell advantage — or disadvantage — to the select: but, in truth, they are assignments of responsibility. The *Kohain* enters exclusive Temple areas to perform Divine service. Daily he blesses his fellow Jews, prefacing his words with the *bracha:* "Blessed art Thou ... Who sanctified me with the sanctity of Aharon..." — privileges denied all other Jews. Yet, he in turn, has no ancestral lands, and relies on "priestly portions" and gifts for his livelihood.

There are other roles of privilege and limitation that are assumed by choice rather than by birthright. "Whoever takes the burden of Torah upon himself is absolved of obligations to the government" (*Avos* III:6), referring to exemption from taxes and military service. Rabbi Shimon bar Yochai's exemptions went beyond this. He was so immersed in Torah study that for thirteen years he was absolved from *tefilla*. The rule "involvement in one *mitzva* frees one from other obligations" does not normally apply to Torah study vis-a-vis prayer. The Torah scholar is not exempt from *davening*. But Rabbi Shimon's involvement was so all-encompassing that it became the exception.... This supreme Torah-role was of Rabbi Shimon's election and, indeed, he succeeded in realizing his goal.

Women as a genre are also assigned to a pursuit all their own — as is the *Kohain*. And women are expected to become so totally immersed in the role of serving as the home base of all Jewish activity ("His wife, she is his house") to the exclusion of all distracting obligatory activities — as was Rabbi Shimon bar Yochai. Their child-bearing capacity should not merely be viewed as the source of this responsibility capacity. It is an expression of it.

Thus, a woman is not obligated in most *mitzvos* that are time-bound. Nor is she involved in those that require community, such as *tefilla betzibbur*, or bearing witness in monetary cases, and bearing arms is viewed as "masculine" and outside her purview. This is not meant to forcibly confine woman to her home. Yet, it is in the home where she finds her fulfillment.

When a woman does focus her interests, activities and designs for fulfillment outside her home, this can become a factor in the destruction of the family as a viable unit in society. Statistics need not be cited. Books, magazines articles, and the shocking crumbling of families within everyone's circle of acquaintances tells the reader that the family is not as healthy an institution as it once was. Freeing women from the responsibility of homemaking is a major factor: The woman who seeks and finds satisfaction outside of the home will view housekeeping as menial and a drudgery, and she gives it less of her attention and interest. Without the single control figure devoting her efforts toward its optimum function, the home deteriorates. In addition, freer mixing among the sexes, no matter how legitimate the premise, is bound to result in greater familiarity among men and women, offering more opportunities for violations of marital fidelity, wreaking further damage to the stability of the home.

⋽ But Where Is Fulfillment?

True, a women's sphere of activities in the Torah society are defined by an appreciation of her capacities, her strengths, and her predestined role. But women in many other societies persist in seeing themselves as members of an exploited class that is denied full function and equal rights with man. Part of this dissatisfaction is based on a lack of comprehension of the overwhelming importance that should be attached to "home-making."

Part is based on a realistic appraisal of ancient woman's status as chattel — to be purchased, used, and abused. While this treatment in primitive societies (and its modern-day implications) may seem similar to the Jewish woman's perpetuation of "Sarah...behold she is in the tent," it has no counterpart in Jewish tradition, where a man is enjoined to love his wife as much as himself and to honor her more than himself.

Part of this rejection of the traditional roles is based on a willful ignoring of the nature of man's volatile sexuality: for necessity in contemporary society often dictates excessive mixing of men and women in circumstances that might promote compromise. This vestigial note of caution is bound to be scoffed at by those whose ambitions exceed their moral sensitivities, or by those whose sensibilities simply offer no resistance to society's steady swing toward immorality. The Jew will still cherish *"Kol kevuda bas melech penima* — all that is glorious in the king's daughter is within" as an ideal, not as a closeting of half of humanity. The non-Jew may not have the benefit of such a tradition. Thus, the prudent Jew may be accused of not trusting human nature, when he really acts cautiously out of *knowledge* of human nature.

Yet, a Jewish woman may still complain. She still appears to be limited in her orbit of activity. Torah study, which occupies the most exalted position in Jewish life, is outside of her purview. All she can do is send her sons off to yeshiva, and patiently await her husband's return from the House of Study — making her little more than a grandstand-warmer on the fringe of the action, a mere appendage to the activists.

This complaint may come from the heart, but it ignores the soul of the matter: Judaism recognizes the blending of efforts and accomplishments that marks a true partnership. In the prototype of joint efforts — Yissochar in his tents of study and Zevulun in his mercantile ventures — both share equally in financial gain and ultimate recognition for spiritual growth. By the same token, man and wife not only find spiritual and emotional completion in merging with the other in marriage, but they also share in each other's growth; she in his Torah study and amelioration, he in her involvement in the perpetuation of *Klal Yisroel* through the primary unit of the family....And, as *Chazal* say, engagement in communal activity (such as the woman's family endeavors) is tantamount to Torah study; resulting in the wife providing Torah-merit for her husband, by virtue of *his* identification with *her* activity.

By contrast, when a woman seeks actualization of her "self" to the exclusion of involvement with her family, she not only denies her femininity, she also ignores her existing creative involvement in her husband's activities.

Worse yet, the woman who seeks the acceptance in a man's world on her own terms — on the basis of her intellect, her creativity, her sense of organization — often does so for the wrong reasons. She may well be entitled to have her efforts evaluated objectively and to be compensated accordingly. But this search can become tragic if she de-feminizes her self image to the extent of conceptualizing success as "making it as a man in a man's world." It is difficult to conceive of a greater triumph for male chauvinism than to put such a high price tag — surrender of femininity — on woman's liberation from exploitation.

৺ The Inherent Comfort

In addition, there is an inherent comfort that men and women experience in their respective assignments. This was so obvious to the Biblical Pharaoh that, when devising tortuous work for the Jews in his bondage (*avodas perach*), he reversed the accepted roles of men and women to induce a physical and emotional trauma upon his slaves. This was not merely a social trauma, for the switched roles were common to *all* Jews in his captivity, not just to exceptions. Today as well, uncharted paths in an open society can lead to a lack of definition in sex roles, and trigger a violation of equilibrium unequaled in modern times: for in spite of all claims to the contrary, men and woman find greatest comfort when working in traditional roles.

To be sure, exceptional women have succeeded in proving themselves in roles associated with men, and as a prime example many point to the Prophetess, Devorah the Judge. But even Devorah never disclaimed her gender. She refused to accompany Barak in leading the Jews in battle. And in her triumphant victory song, she referred to herself as "A mother in Israel." Even the woman who succeeds in a man's world must not cease to be a woman, or she loses far more than she gains.

Thus, abandonment of exclusivity of roles for men and women is not at all a liberation, as touted. It is the forcing of people into roles for which they are not suited, really limiting their opportunities for fulfillment. In addition, it signals the ushering in of the destruction of the family as a shelter of values and security for its members, eliminating the most vital unit in an orderly society.

II.

Education for Identity

✢§ The Schooling of a Tradition

Woman's struggle for liberation is certainly bringing new challenges to the Torah society. But it is hardly the first time that women are experiencing a threat to their Jewish equilibrium. One of the features of living in *Golus* is the apparent impossibility of escaping detrimental influences of the market-place. And during the past hundred years, this has definitely been the case.

Sure enough, when the intellectual enlightenment began to have its fullest impact in Eastern Europe, and the daughters of even simple Polish families were affected by universal education, Jewish girls were no exception. Ultimately, these girls began to feel superior to their "backward" parents by virtue of a few snatches of Polish poetry they had committed to memory. By token of this "superiority," they rejected their homes as a conveyor of values, and the values were abandoned along with their source.

This called for a radical solution, and indeed one was in the offing. Sara Schenirer succeeded in salvaging the post-World War I generation of Jewish girls, as well as subsequent generations in Europe and America, when she founded the Beth Jacob movement of formal schools of study for girls — truly a visionary solution to a most severe problem. But this marvelous innovation was not without its own complicating features. For it is another phenomenon of *Golus* that every contrived solution to an old problem brings new problems in its wake. This must inevitable be true in regard to the working solutions to any social problems that beset Jewish life, and the education of Jewish women to preserve traditional values proved no exception.

When the task of imbuing Jewish values became institutionalized, some flaws were bound to enter the process. The home is the natural setting for transmitting values, and the synthesis of a natural function is bound to be cumbersome, artificial, and imperfect. (A dialysis unit designed to replace the function of a person's kidney, which is smaller than a human fist, fills an average-sized room — and it is not fool-proof.) A school — regardless of how faithfully it spells out the philosophical outlook of the home, no matter how representative the faculty is of these ideals — is basically an institution of formal study. In addition to the school's success in teaching, imbuing, and exemplifying values, it also idealizes the method: intellectualization and formal study. This can be a decided advantage when dealing with the education of men, for Torah study is a goal unto itself for men, quite aside from its role as a means for gaining necessary knowledge. (One drawback to a yeshiva-ized society is that the yeshiva student who fails in his Torah-study pursuits can come to feel that he has failed in his Yiddishkeit.)

When imbuing women with values through schooling, however, two hardships are built in: The less bookish are educated for failure, and those of more scholastic bent are educated for education. A woman is indeed required to master all laws pertinent to her *halachic* role, but the study that brings her to the knowledge is basically functional. The girl of greater intellectual gifts may well pursue her interests in those areas that concern her, but this would be the exception rather than the norm. And as stated, schooling does educate for education.

Years later, when the graduate devotes her time and talents to making a home, rearing children, and creating a family, she'll comb her daily routine in search of some justification, some evidence of fulfillment along the lines of her education — and intellectually she may find herself wanting. Then the day comes when children are in school, and rather than recognizing the value of her most individual, highly specialized role of environment-creator and personality-molder, she sees all of her remaining activity so totally supportive as to have no intrinsic value, easily replaced by the latest convenience or the old-fashioned maidservant.

The inner vacuum she must then contend with is a very real one, created by the cessation of intensive study she was involved in during her school days.

Schooling Devaluating Homemaking

This is not meant to find fault with education, Beth Jacob-style, for without it there would be scant hope for the religious survival of modern Jewish women. Besides, the dilemma of "the means of schooling becoming the ends" results at least as much from general societal trends as it does from our own schools. Yet, it is the Orthodox Jew, more than anyone else, who feels the pinch of the problem of the-school-replacing-the-home to the point of devaluating home-making in comparison to all outside activity.

This dilemma and some of its ramifications are most poignantly captured in a conversation between the founder of the Beth Jacob movement in America and this writer. She remarked:

> "When I used to leave my family of little children every morning, in the early years in Williamsburg, I would feel terribly torn. I had entrusted them with a competent sitter, but how much more would I have preferred to be feeding them myself — I telling them stories, I imbuing them with values — instead of some stranger. There is so much one can implant in a child through mealtime distractions and bedtime stories — wrapping them in kedusha *instead of nonsense, telling them concept-building stories instead of 'The Three Bears.' I felt defeated every time I left for work, closing the door of my house behind me.*

I would wish for Eliyahu Hanovi to come and relieve me of my agony.

"Then I graduated my first class. My first *talmidah*, an American-born girl, married, and she put on a sheitel. This was in the early 40's — it was an unbelievable breakthrough, and I knew then that I had been correct in the way I was conducting my life.... I no longer needed Eliyahu to tell me so."

Not every woman is founding a movement. Yet when she is a product of the Beth Jacob movement, she embodies its highest ideals along with its imperfections and imbalances. At its best, the young wife may even take on a share of economic responsibilities of the family while her husband devotes himself as fully as possible to Torah study....And the result has been a revolutionary upgrading of the level of Torah life in America, while the home becomes permeated with the atmosphere of every member of the household responding to a higher calling. At the other extreme, "keeping house" is associated with menial tasks, and is considered a denigration of a woman's capabilities ("I guess it's all right if that's all you *care* to do, or if that's all you *can* do—").

Such is the *Golus* phenomenon. Perhaps we must wait for Eliyahu Hanovi to restore to us all our sense of balance. But even in our current social context, there must surely be ways to compensate for the massive shifts in emphasis that abound. There must be some ways to bring Jewish women home.

ೞ Repaving Traditional Paths

As stated, Jewish women seek greater participation in broader society because, in part, this is a logical extension of being successful in school. But we are not ready to tamper with our Beth Jacob schools, which have proven to be so eminently successful. Another source of this urge to find fulfillment in broader society stems from a general progression "from home to corporation." In this respect, at least, Jewish women can benefit from some of the widespread reassessment of this trend that is now taking place. While they may begin by "learning," they may well end up "teaching."

One aspect of the heavy air of disenchantment clouding today's society centers around the impersonalization of modern life.

Creativity, production, and consumption are all isolated from one another. Dwelling for a moment on any of the three, one sorely misses the other two: Most of a person's efforts to earn a living — especially in more complex establishments — seem far removed from the creative aspect of production (see Studs Terkel's book, *Working*); and the average worker can realize only a symbolic relationship between his job and "breadwinning" — even the paper bank-check he takes home at the end of the week must in turn be translated into food, clothing, shelter, and entertainment. Creativity and emotional fulfillment usually come from hobbies and other secondary preoccupations, not from one's employment. So people view with fond nostalgia The Good Old Days, when man grew his own grain, ground his own flour, baked his own bread. They search for pride and meaning in their daylong activity; not finding them, they often leave the beaten path of the highly industrialized society — grasping at every homegrown symbol available, from organically grown foods to worn-out denims.

The irony of it is that one could easily cite as the last vestiges of personal involvement the following fields of activities: molding and guiding personalities; working in plastic arts; preparing one's own food needs; and delving in the spiritual, so as to imbue the mundane with sanctity. These rewarding pursuits are found in greatest abundance in three activities that the Jewish tradition has entrusted to women: ushering in the Sabbath by kindling the lights on Friday evening; separating the *"challa"* when baking bread; and keeping the conjugal laws of family purity.

These, indeed, do touch on areas of most intense personal involvement:

☐ Bringing children into the world, guiding them, training them, imbuing them with love of G-d and respect for fellow man. When Eve conceived and gave birth to the first child ever born of woman, in exultation she named him *Kayin* — "*Konisi* — I have produced a man in partnership with G-d." What can match this achievement?

There is a well-known anecdote involving a young couple, cradling an infant, who approached a Rebbe for guidance on raising the child to be a *tzaddik*. "How old is he?" the sage asked.

"Two months," was the reply.

"Then you are eleven months too late in asking for advice."

Optimum preparation for greatness begins before conception, and surely does not end with birth. Raising and guiding children to their fullest potential is a full-time occupation, and a singularly rewarding one. One need not look beyond the confines of the home for this experience.

☐ Baking bread as a means of providing for the physical sustenance of the family: mixing, adding the yeast, kneading, twisting and shaping the breads; separating the priestly portion, allowing the loaves to grow, slipping the pans into the oven, serving and enriching the staff of life with love.

The dining table is likened to a *mizbei'ach* — an altar. Mealtimes are meant to be more than moments of nutritional replenishment. They provide those valued occasions when the family is in union; and they also could be sacred occasions. The care invested in preparation and serving meals adds immeasurably to their standing as salient moments in the day.

☐ Kindling the shabbos lights, bringing the glow of fulfillment, spirituality and tranquility to a hectic household. Uniting the *Shabbos* — an island of spirituality and calm in the week-long raging sea of mundane pursuits, with the home — an anchorage of permanence and dedication in a fickle sea of changing moods.

One might be quick to dismiss the discussion of these areas as an exegesis forced beyond its original intent. But that would be shortsighted. First, the *Chazal* underscore these three as the Jewish woman's special responsibilities. Second, so many of today's alienated are searching for the experiences represented by just these three activities.

All the more pity, then, if in search of greater fulfillment, the Jewish woman flees her home-centered orbit of activities to join her non-Jewish sisters in seeking liberation from tradition — in effect, abandoning her position as the last hold-out against assembly-line living, totally capitulating to the tyrannies born of the industrial revolution.

III.

A Postscript

The home should be the setting for the Jewish woman's most valuable, productive, and fulfilling efforts. But society has her conditioned to think otherwise; and her schooling has educated her to experience otherwise. Can there be some kind of corrective measure, realigning her goals and satisfactions with her traditional, ideal role?

Other women rise above the tidal pull away from home. They find challenge and satisfaction at home without apology, but do require an occasional change of environment, or need additional sources of income. Not everyone can or should become a teacher. Here, too, some innovative thinking should be encouraged.

On the first count, schools and organizations have both attempted to effect a subtle shift away from total stress on the intellectual. They have been incorporating hospital duty and visits to shut-ins into their regular curriculum schedules. This constitutes a small but meaningful step in the right direction.

Some creative women have come up with money-making enterprises they operate from their own homes — bringing themselves income, while performing invaluable services for others. These include:

☐ Operating nurseries and day-care centers for children of working (or shopping) mothers. Some gain government funding; other run their nurseries as part of a charity program, eschewing personal profit.

☐ Writing, editing, and translating stories, poems, plays, and news bulletins for schools, charitable institutions, and the general public. All of those erstwhile yearbook editors provide a formidable literary corps. And our children's library shelves are embarrassingly bare of worthwhile books, as are our schools and camps of worthwhile dramatic material. The supply should expand to meet the demand.

☐ Creating, designing, and hand-painting dolls, toys, favors for children, or for home decoration, or for original *tashmishei kedusha* (religious artifacts) such as *challa* covers, *Shabbos* aprons, tablecloths....Why must the full range of modern Jewish art be limited to Orchard Street chintz and Israeli antiqued brass?

☐ Jewish communal life once had a full range of activities — visiting and nursing the sick, the aged; supplying food and clothing for the impoverished; burial societies — run for women by women. There are some communities (such as Chicago and Baltimore) that still take pride in initiating younger women into their *Chevrai Kadisha* when necessary. Getting away from home for a spell need not be purely self-indulgent. It can be a purposeful and generous act, too.

The list should go on. At the moment it is limited by lack of experience and a limited imagination. Neither of these should shortchange women in their creative application of personal resources to new needs — without doing violence to their most treasured Jewish femininity. There must be feminine answers to Jewish women's continuing search for enrichment and fulfillment.

Letters and Responses to: Jewish Women in a Torah Society

⇢§Simplistic Treatment of Women

To the Editor:

Most men consider themselves experts on women. In the case of religious men, this knowledge is generally based on their observations of one woman, namely their respective wives. Thus, one man will state that "women" cry a lot, others that "women" are amazingly stoic. . . .. The article "Jewish Women in a Torah Society" does not take into account individual differences in women, but is as simplistic as would be a comparable letter written by a woman whose husband learns all day, chiding all men for not doing the same.

It suffices that men look upon a life spent within the *Bais Medrash* as an ideal, and women view a life spent within the home as an ideal, with both realistically aware that this ideal state may not be feasible for everybody. Just as men are not made to feel guilty for closing their *Gemaros* to make a living, women should not be made to feel guilty for working outside their homes for similar reasons of necessity.

Incidentally, there is no such thing as a "man's world," anymore; this is a people's world, and has been for some time.
A woman cannot lose her femininity by working outside the home, because it is an innate part of her. Woman is feminine, whether she is rolling dough, typing her thesis or working at a machine. Yes, Virginia, there are as many individual differences among women as there are among men. (I fear you are a male chauvinist lamb.) Possession of a master's degree does not mean that a woman cannot found a viable Jewish home, just as shuffling between stove and

sink all day does not automatically guarantee that she will be a good mother. It all depends upon her *hashkofos*, capabilities and determination. I do believe, however, that it is generally wiser for her to postpone outside commitments until her children are all in school, if possible.

Traditionally, women have been competing in the marketplace for some time, and have thus enabled generations of men to reach great heights in Torah. I believe the key to success in synthesizing homemaking with outside pursuits is the motivation involved. If she is working to evade domestic responsibilities or to attain luxuries, she may find her dual role difficult. If, however, she is pressed by economic necessity, because of absence or incapacity of a breadwinner, or if her husband is engaged in Torah study and she does not want to passively bow to the ensuing poverty, then I believe she will be helped from Above to achieve her goals.

There is an air of condescension throughout the article, particularly evident when the author suggests women make tacky aprons at home, probably netting for themselves a munificent three dollars for a day of toil. There is also a veiled implication that it is somehow tawdry for a Jewish woman to work outside the home. Rabbi Wolpin, don't for one moment underestimate the flexibility or *gadlus* of the Jewish woman. Though she works outside the home, she carries the *hinai Sarah b'ohel* concept around with her as a portable tent, surrounding herself with an aura of *tzenius* wherever she goes. The Torah-committed woman inspires the respect of all she meets and makes a true *Kiddush Hashem* in the world.

Bas Yisroel

ಈ Intellectual Stimulation — Unfortunate?

To the Editor:

Although I began reading Rabbi Wolpin's article "Jewish Women in a Torah Society, for Frustration or for Fulfillment " (Teves 5735) very eagerly, hoping to find, finally, an intelligent, reasoned discussion of the difficulties a Jewish woman may have in finding fulfillment within a Torah life, I completed the article feeling a great deal more frustration than would have met with Rabbi Wolpin's approval. After all, the article made me react intellectually, made me assess his arguments in the light of logic, as well as in the light of personal experience and the experiences of other Jewish women. This is not to deny Rabbi Wolpin's thesis that a woman's primary responsibility is to her home, to her family, and to the activities traditionally associated with the feminine role in Jewish life. This is not to put forth an argument for women's lib or equal rights. It *is* a challenge to all the Rabbi Wolpins who help to form the Torah society as we know it.

Rabbbi Wolpin argues that one of the unfortunate by-products of the Bais Yaakov movement is that it stimulated intellectual activity on the part of its students. Unfortunate byproduct? Isn't it rather a sad comment on the Torah society that the intellectual awakening of its women is a threat to that society? Isn't it rather the responsibility of that society to put all its resources — and, yes, even the female mind does occasionally have its strengths — to good use rather than to suppress those resources for lack of imagination on how to take advantage of them?

Rabbi Wolpin does offer some suggestions to the frustrated female: personal involvement in the three *Mitzvos* that evolve upon the woman. Again, I can't fault the author in his premise — only in his romanticizing of the actual practice of those *Mitzvos*. "...allowing the loaves to grow, slipping the pans into the oven, serving and enriching the staff of life with love..." —indeed! And this spiritual uplift is to take place during a day filled with doing laundry and scrubbing floors, or while the children are calling for a referee in their latest quarrel and the husband comes in growling for his supper because he has to go to a *shiur* in ten minutes and so what if the wife hasn't had ten minutes of his attention all week, on top of which little Berel's *Rebbe* called that the child misbehaved in *Yeshivah* again. And when a woman does fulfill life and still finds herself seeking something more, something different, something to occupy her mind rather than her hands, what then? Then, Rabbi Wolpin says, she should become involved in public works and good deed projects. His practical suggestions tend in one direction and, although beyond reproach, they are rather weak for the woman whose mind is — must I say unfortunately? — active, curious, alive, frankly not interested in *chessed* work. Is she to be condemned because she does not fit the stereotype?

Furthermore, Rabbi Wolpin takes no account of those women who have completed their tasks as mothers, whose children have grown to independence. Where should these women turn for fulfillment — to those same cliched, tired, old outlets? And still further, Rabbi Wolpin takes no account of those women who have no families from which to derive their satisfactions and fulfillment. Is there no place for such females in the Torah society? Isn't it difficult enough for them to be already deprived without their being made to feel that the Torah society cannot accommodate them because, once again, they do not fit the stereotype?

Surely Rabbi Wolpin would do well to come to grips with the realities of some of these issues. I found the ideas presented in his essay, although elegantly phrased, far too shallow to be a definitive statement on how a woman should find sufficient satisfaction in a Torah society. Once more, perhaps the finger should be pointed at the Torah society for failing its responsibility to its women, rather than at the women for seeking that elusive fulfillment wherever it might be found.

Eve Roth
Lakewood, New Jersey

৺§ Men and Women Shared Humanity: Intellect, Also

To the Editor:

You are so right! Man is meant to be man and woman is meant to be woman. The common denominator of humanity that you mention, however, refers to mind and *neshama*, and these are both shared by men and women.

The main problem regarding Jewish woman's role is not whether she belongs in the kitchen or in the intellectual world, but rather how much emphasis is to be put on her performance in the kitchen, and how much her intellectual needs and self-realization are de-emphasized. A woman's greatest and most fascinating blessing is her children, and the upkeep of a spiritually enriched home. But as the Rebbe Reb Bunim said: " 'These are the children of Noach, Noach ...' Noach's development was his greatest achievement. In man's involvement with his children, he must not forget to educate the child in himself." And that can take a lifetime. It would really be shortsighted to assume that the *hashkafa* (Torah philosophy) taught in high school or even in Seminary could last forever. As a woman matures and her inner and outer life experiences deepen, presenting new problems, it would certainly require new learnings and fresher application of the old.

Sure, it was natural for Avraham to ask Sarah to bake cakes for the *malochim* since she did make the kitchen her domain as much as Avraham supervised the farming and commerce connected with their possessions. But I am positive that Sarah's distinction was not totally based on her cooking skills any more than Avraham was just simply another wealthy land-owner. Her ability to reach out to women was, beyond doubt, built on her spiritual attainments. I would think that women are expected to emulate every aspect of Sarah's character.

Doing *chesed* should not simply be a vehicle for "getting away from the home," which was implied in your article. For this situation there is a classic joke: "Pity on her, she has no one to pity." A woman's lack of interest doesn't free her from the obligation to grow in *hashkafa* any more than it would free a disinterested man. By virtue of the humanity they share, they share this obligation to grow.

From a mother in love with her five children בלע"ה who enjoys cooking and baking for them:

Name Withheld by Request

Rabbi Wolpin Replies:

The three above correspondents are more in agreement with the premise of the article on Jewish women than one might infer from the tone of their letters.

The first letter (from Miss B.Y.) faults the article for projecting an ideal rather than facing reality. Indeed, the article was written on the assumption that women are fashioned biologically, emotionally, and spiritually to realize a specific ideal, and the article was aimed at encouraging pursuit of this ideal. Rather than inspire guilt, the intention was to spell out certain long-accepted goals which, for many of us, are in danger of getting lost in a scramble for liberation — a liberation that misconstrues our ideal to be a form of bondage. In addition, evasion of the ideal role can only result in frustration.

Of course, individual women do differ from one another, but there is an over-riding femininity common to all. Recognizing it should not make one a chauvinist or feminist, but a realist. As stated in the article, this femininity offers the basis for projecting the ideal, which revolves around the home.

For any number of reasons, work outside the home can be necessary at times, but certain considerations should be kept in mind. First (as Miss B.Y. points out), outside activity should not be sought as an escape from home responsibilities. That would be fruitless, and in the long run, self-destructive. In addition (as Miss B.Y. implies), outside employment and other involvements should not compete with home obligations for time or attention... This is something would-be women physicians, editors and lawyers should take into account.

Finally, the circumstances of the work should not conflict with basic tenets of *tzenius* and modesty. Miss B.Y. appears to prefer to overlook this consideration; yet, the moral looseness of modern society is so obvious that it would seem to take wishful thinking or deliberate blindness to make one unaware of it.

To be sure, the "*Hinei Sarah Ba'ohel*" concept is more than a designation of place; it is also a frame of mind. But place *is* a factor, and should not be forgotten in the rush of our mobile society. A good deal of *siyata dish'maya* — a generous assist from heaven — is needed for any of us to maintain the same levels of *tzenius* in an amoral society as in one's own home.

If this were truly a "person's world," conditions would be somewhat more compatible to Miss B.Y.'s portable *tzenius* concept. It takes more than a simple statement, however, to convert our universe into other than "a man's world." And it takes more than saying so to preserve a woman's femininity at a machine — or at a machine gun. *Chazal* expressed this long ago by frowning at any woman's tendency to leave home and hearth (even labeling the Matriarch Leah and her daughter Dina as *yotzanios* for "excessive" going-forth). Because of belief in pre-assigned sex roles, women are *halachically* excluded from specific occupations, such as any type of warfare, for being masculine. When working in a man's world, a woman should not lose sight of this.

The air of condescension detected was not intended. The various alternatives described in the article's Postscript were presented in only the broadest of terms. As for sewing and designing, Coco Chanel's successor may be creating tomorrow's fashions in a Boro Park walk-in or a *kollel* apartment in suburbia; a typewriter may be pounding out the Great American Novel or feature articles for *JO* at the same address — both activities being performed with consummate creativity and fidelity to time-honored standards of *tzenius*. I did not put the $3 price tag on Jewish women's productivity.

Miss Roth (writer of the second letter) accepts the article's thesis regarding a woman's primary responsibility, but seems to misinterpret the critique of intellectuality. She is certainly correct in viewing stimulated intellectual activity as a valuable resource. To be considered unfortunate, however, is the resulting expectation that a woman's entire productivity and creativity be measured by a yardstick fashioned in the academe. Her touching vignette of "The Harried Housewife" really proves the point, for it portrays a challenge that can be met by a woman employing her full arsenal of patience, compassion — and, yes, intelligence. But, intellectuality as such simply does not come into play. The intellectual pursuits of her student days ideally would yield a fuller appreciation for the spiritual values inherent in the nitty-gritty of homemaking. If, instead, it bred a contempt for the menial aspects of her job, something is amiss. (It brings to mind a famous Kotzker parable of the provincial bumpkin who visited the *Bais Hamikdash* and failed to see more than "a big slaughterhouse.")

Intellectual capacity is a gift, and like all gifts, should be nurtured and developed. Yet it should not, by any means, overshadow other obligations and other areas of activity. As a parallel, the woman who possesses unusual musical talents should by all means develop them in as much as they will afford her a means of expression and bring beauty and joy to the world. Beyond doubt, her musicality would find fullest expression as a concert performer or composer, but when these become a primary involvement, eclipsing her homebound activities, she should reconsider. While pursuing her career may result in a consummate gift to the music world, it would also constitute a denial to the full flowering of her feminine self. Feminists would surely say that full expression of the artistic self still comes first; that it can be shared with homemaking — so much could be delegated, or altogether avoided. But this would truly be denying the person's feminine aspects, with the one gift assuming a prominence out of proportion to the rest.

This does not mean that the intellectual gift inborn in some, nurtured in others, should be neglected. A Torah society does owe its women structured opportunities for intellectual growth after seminary graduation without forcing them to seek stimulation in the universities. If Miss Roth (and others) would consult local Beth Jacob Seminary alumnae associations, some synagogue and organizational groups, she would find that some significant strides have been made in this direction.

More important, women, especially in our society, should seek time and means to study on their own. In her vignette, Miss Roth weighed the elements too heavily against the heroine (or victim). Torah Society does not define the husband's role as a suppergrowler with only ten dyspeptic minutes to spend with his family. Rabbi Moshe Schreiber (the Chasam Sofer), leader of European Jewry in the early 19th century, devoted valuable time to joining his wife in study of *"Orach Chayim"* — the section of *Shulchan Aruch* that deals with daily *halachic* procedures. Rabbi Schreiber is known for his anti-innovation dictum: "The new crop is prohibited by the Torah." His sessions with his wife were surely a reputable practice that reflected no new trends in women's liberation.... His father-in-law, the famed Rabbi Akiva Eiger, was an intellectual and spiritual giant of his time (1760-1837). He wrote a letter turning down suggestions that he remarry after the untimely passing of his wife (in 1797), saying:

> *"...How can I forget my wife and all she has done for me? She has raised my children and instilled in them the fear of the Almighty. Whatever Torah I have learned, I have to thank her for. She cared for me in my feeble health, and, as I have recently discovered, she hid from me financial embarrassments and worries so that I would not be disturbed in my studies. Many times I have had discussions with her on interesting religious problems, until the late hours of the evening."*
>
> (translation by Rabbi Harold Leiman, from Dr. Leo Jung's *Jewish Leaders*)

Torah-study and analyzing "interesting religious problems" is indeed a prominent feature of marriage in a Torah Society.

As for the "public work and good projects" that Miss Roth finds "cliched, tired, and old" — I would remind her that cliches are not born; they develop through repeated use, and these particular ones do not wear out as long as there is a need for *chesed*. On the contrary, an educated woman has an obligation to join in reaching out to her sisters who are alienated from our heritage, applying her insights and understandings to stimulating fields where they are surely needed, without leaving the Tents of Sarah — much as Rabbi Field pointed out in his letter (which follows).

It is true that the article did not deal with the situation of many single women; even though all women are single at some time in their lives, almost all of them expect to change their status and visualize the basis of their fulfillment as someday sharing in the leadership of a household. This state of singleness is not the so-called norm situation, but surely does warrant a fuller discussion.

Nisson Wolpin

৶ More Opportunities for Women

To the Editor:

Your treatment of the role that Jewish women play (or should play) in a Torah society was excellent. I am sure it will meet with ridicule in many circles, which sometimes is an indicator of how close to home you are.

Today's feminist movement, although perhaps conceived in and motivated by high ideals, has spewn forth a host of related problems in its wake. We find ourselves in the midst of a very real "identity crisis."

Witness the fashions for both men and women today, the hairstyles, even the mannerisms and speech habits: Men and women both are confused about who and what they are. Who is to say that the recent concentration on subjects relating to homosexuality is not also a direct result of this confusion? Even amongst the "Orthodox" many scoff at the Biblical injunction of *"Lo yihiye kli gever al isha..."* against wearing the clothing of the opposite sex.

(See *Dvorim* 22:5 and commentary of Rashi there, also commentary of *Taz and Shach* in *Yoreh Deah* 122:2.) I would like to follow your lead in making some suggestions as to where the need is great for women to be active — without contradicting their Torah-ordained role.

Today a most essential area to Jewish survival is clearly *kiruv rechokim* — especially of young people lost in schools and universities across the country.

*One cannot over-emphasize the impact of a *Shabbos* dinner experience — including *candle lighting*, dinner and table preparations, and the special methods of cleaning up. — Who but women can help in this particular area?

*Today there seems to be (at least in this community) a widespread return to *kashrus*. Aside from giving practical suggestions regarding how to set up and maintain a kosher kitchen (leaving technical *halachic* questions to the rabbi), there is a need for direction on how and where to shop, what to look for, and so on. — Again, who but our Jewish homemaker?

*And is not the future of Klal Yisroel dependent so much on *taharas hamishpacha?* Who is to speak to the scores of interested, but oft-times ignorant young women on this all-important subject? — Of course, our *neshai chayil!*

Let us not forget the comment of Rashi that should serve as a pace-setter for all of *Bnai Torah* today: "...that they brought them [e.g., heathens] under the wings of G-d — Avraham worked with the men and Sarah worked with the women" (*Bereishis* 12:5) and the Torah credits them (Avraham and Sarah) as if they actually made people.

Rabbi Binyamin Field
Phoenix, Arizona

⋅§ Give Me Your Tired, Worn-Out Cliches

To the Editor:

Miss Roth's attitude towards *chessed* (*Letters*, Jan. '75) really evoked my anger — and then pity. She sounds as if she really *believes* that *chessed* is only for those whose intellects do not qualify them for greater things. Guess it was the lack of a good university that lead Avrohom Avinu *and* Sarah Imeinu to indulge so much. Pity!

Avrohom Avinu came to recognize God with his own intellect, and when he was ill and in pain, Hashem made the sun shine with special intensity to keep travelers off the road, so that Avrohom, who was 99 years old, could recuperate from his *bris-milah*. But Avrohom couldn't bear the spiritual pain — the vacuum created by this lack of *orchim* (guests) — so G-d sent the *malachim*. Could not Avrohom, an intellectual giant, have found something better to occupy himself with than being a waiter to a bunch of dirty wayfarers? Could he not have spent his time in study, or have welcomed the rare chance to meditate or reflect upon the universe and its many wonders?

And then again —

The scope of *chessed* is infinite! So much so that it is a challenge to anyone "who is active, curious, alive." It can mean a pause in one's rush-rush pace to simply cross an old lady to the other side of the street, or it can mean listening — really listening — to another person's problems so that he knows he has someone to share them with, and then applying one's perception and sound judgment to help him solve the problem. *This is redeeming the intellectual stimulation.* The possibilities are endless.

Which brings to mind an old axiom: As an *end in itself* the person who is writing his thesis for his Ph.D. is accomplishing nothing more than someone sitting in front of his TV, watching a ball game, with a can of beer in his hand. That is, he cannot be קונה חלקו בעולם הבא (gain his share in the World to Come) with his *or* her thesis, nor with his TV; he cannot — with listening to a great symphony, nor with Rock and Roll music. Likewise — not by reading a great novel, nor a cheap comic strip.

One may *enjoy* these various activities, his source of pleasure will vary with his intellectual capacity, and he may *develop* this capacity by doing these things — but find *fulfillment?* If he does, there is something sorely lacking in his or her *hashkafah* as a *shomer Torah umitzvos*, something very unclear in his mind about why he was put on this world in the first place.

We actually *verbalize* this every single day — a *Mishnah* from the Oral Torah which our sages thought wise to incorporate into our daily prayers in the hope that we would *listen* as we speak them: "These are the activities for which a person eats fruit. . . ." Six out of ten are forms of *chessed*, and within each there are a million possibilities.

Cliched, tired, worn out—? Never! Guaranteed to give fulfillment? Beyond question!

Mrs. S. Freedman
Brooklyn, New York

⇃§ The Role of Jewish Women: More Complex

To the Editor:

I would like to respond to your article "Jewish Women in Torah Society, for Frustration or Fulfillment?" In your preface you raised the question "To what extent is confinement of women at home and hearth a reflection of the eternal Torah attitude?"

A woman's duty is to bear and raise her children, and to imbue them with *Yiras Shamayim*. This is her basic responsibility but her duty to herself, her family, and *Klal Yisroel* does not end there. We can not be content with building our family alone, for we possess the talent to make contributions to *Klal Yisroel* as a whole. Yes, we start with our own viable home structure and from there help build a better world.

Having a part-time career or being intellectually stimulated does not necessarily mean one's responsibility as the *Aishes Chayil* will suffer. Education and career are not negative values for the *Bas Yisroel*. There are many years when the children are all in yeshivos. Should housework then be woman's all-consuming activity? I would rather have my children see me working for the community, organizing a school system, helping the elderly, or bringing better nursing skills to the community. Housework is necessary to the family unit, but it is not the goal. *Homemaking*, on the other hand, means promoting the value and scope of each member of the family. Being a good homemaker then means being the best human being one can be, and using all intellectual faculties to do so.

Today's society often demands that both partners contribute to the family's income. This is paralleled in the Torah family — we women work when we are young so our husbands can learn Torah.

During our child-raising years we work part-time so our husbands can pursue a career in *Chinuch*. Mothers of older children work to send them to the best yeshivos — no matter what the transportation, dormitory and living expenses are. Other women work so that their sons and sons-in-laws are able to learn in *Kollel*. Throughout her life the *Aishes Chayil* may be called upon to supplement the family income and she should be prepared with marketable skills or a career.

In regard to the education of girls, you stated that *"Schooling educates for education."* To want to use one's mind is a blessing, not a hardship. I have met many women well versed in Torah learning. They are to be praised for they are able to understand and appreciate the depth and beauty in Torah learning. They also have an enhanced ability to encourage their children in their Torah learning. — What better example is there for children than seeing their mother going over the *Parashas HaShavua* with Commentaries or studying a *Mussar sefer!* It is not enough for the father to be a *Talmud Chochom*.

You refer to "intellectual inner vacuum" felt by the Bais Yaakov girl who raises a family. There is no reason for this. The more profound the *Bas Yisroel's* education during her school days, the deeper her commitment to Torah life will be. It is better to be introduced to intellectual pursuit, even if it has to be put second place during the busy mothering years, than never to have felt its satisfaction at all.

No, being a *Bas Yisroel* does not mean that a woman's role is narrow or confining or non-intellectual.

Deena Holland
Los Angeles, California

Rabbi Nisson Wolpin

In the Wake of the Thomas Hearings

CLARENCE THOMAS'S nomination to the US Supreme Court hit a snag — or, one should say, a minefield — with the allegations of a former aide, currently a tenured professor of civil law at the University of Oklahoma, that the Judge was guilty of conduct that should disqualify him from serving on the Court. Quite apart from the shock waves that the accusations unleashed on the personal lives and careers of those involved, and the effects they had on the course of national politics, the entire incident should give us pause.

About a decade ago, a number of rabbis and *roshei yeshiva* went on the record to decry the growing trend of young ladies fresh out of high school seeking work in "downtown offices," where they are exposed to the spiritually corrosive atmosphere that often prevails. One or two even went so far as to caution young women who would seek gainful employment to enable themselves to support their husbands in their Torah growth during their Kollel years, asking them to consider very carefully the type of workplace that they might seek. The estimable growth that their husbands realize may be achieved at a loss in their own spirituality and innocence — a loss for which there can be neither compensation nor justification. (See "Raising a Torah Family," JO, March 1981, based on an address by Rabbi Elya Svei at a National Convention of Agudath Israel of America.) *"Die atzilus fun a bas Yisroel* — the inherent dignity of a Jewish woman" is far too precious to risk for any reason.

These cautionary notes were greeted by some with cynicism and a touch of disbelief: After all, this was 1980, and our daughters are prepared to meet the world on its own terms. In addition, people contended, the circulars and the public addresses were responding with exaggeration and alarm to a basically benign situation.

The 1990's have arrived, and in the wake of the Thomas hearings, a lot of dirt had that been swept under the carpet is suddenly being exposed. Responding to a *New York Times/* CBS News poll, over 38% of the women surveyed responded "yes" to a query if they had "ever been the object of indecent advances...or unwanted discussions from men who supervise you or can affect your position at work." That's more than a third of the women who were surveyed. *Not* asked was if they were ever witness to others being harassed in such a manner, or if they had every been exposed to unsavory discussions not directed at any women in particular, but ventilated in their presence. Undoubtedly, such questions would have resulted in more than double the positive responses recorded in the actual poll.

Our people — especially our mothers, wives and daughters — have always been distinguished by their modesty and sense of shame. Indeed, their exceptional sensitivities have been instrumental in keeping our people *"rachmonim, byshonim, vegomlei chassodim* — merciful, modest and generous." Concerns expressed in the 80's regarding preserving this source of national and personal pride are obviously no less relevant today.

Nechama Bakst

Woman at the Crossroads

I ease the car out of the driveway, and involuntarily steal a last hasty glance over my shoulder. Immediately, I am sorry, but the damage is done. The faces I have seen outlined in the window will remain with me. Forlorn, familiar faces — sad eyes following me. Impatiently, I wrench myself away, hating this maudlin melodrama.

What nonsense, to carry on every morning as though I am some sort of criminal abandoning my children, when in reality I am only one of millions of working mothers who spend some part of each day away from home. I speak to myself firmly: "In a few short hours I will be home. I will feed the baby, fold the laundry, cook supper and otherwise juggle my time as wisely or unwisely as other mothers do. I will be home in plenty of time to listen to Chanie's eager chatter, give Moishie his juice in his favorite cup, and read them each their special bedtime stories. Then why do I feel this jarring pang of guilt? Why can't I let well enough alone and incorporate two schedules into one as expertly as other working mothers do?

I suppose it's because I'm not at all sure in my own mind that this is the right thing I'm doing — for myself, for my husband, for my chidren. I've mulled over the pros and cons so often I can recite them with my eyes closed. The light at the corner turns red, and I find myself rehashing it once again.

✺ The Orthodox Scenario

THIS SCENARIO OUR Orthodox society has created seems so inconsistent to me — so paradoxical — it has us women scrambling back and forth like tiny figures on the chessboard, inexorably marching towards checkmate.

On the one hand, we are raised in the mold of our grandmothers. In age-old tradition, we are geared to accept the knowledge that a woman's place is in the home, at the helm of her household; that a mother's primary duty is to teach, to guide, to inspire her children. We are brought to realize that a mother is the instrumental factor in her children's future, no less important in her role than her husband is in his. We come to believe that these concepts are real and true and laudable.

In puzzling contrast, the Bais Yaakov schools, which we conscientiously support, transmit a contradictory message. From an early age, girls are systematically exposed to a curriculum that indoctrinates them with the concept that there is no woman more commendable than one who goes to work so that her husband may be free to learn Torah. In fact, many hundreds of students emerge from Bais Yaakov each year, eager to embrace this concept of *Kollel*, American style. Though a direct offshoot of *Kollelim* in Europe, it is a unique creation of our generation. For in Europe, where a select few were chosen to be supported by others, there were only a handful of prize young men who were allowed such status. In America, it has become a way of life for thousands in the Yeshivah community.

That may be a very worthy situation. In fact, the Torah builders of our generation saw widespread *Kollel* participation as an imperative for establishing a solid Torah society in the years ahead.

Nevertheless, if a woman is forced to leave her home in order to support her family, isn't she neglecting her primary obligation of serving as mother — teacher — guide? Should that function be relegated to part-time, as in part-time worker/part-time mother, making her only half-way effective? Or might one counter that in this instance her earning power is so valuable to the family as to justify this choice, without a sense of compromise? All these arguments I ponder and weigh, trying to evaluate each objectively.

✑ The Superiority Factor

The situation is even further complicated by another aspect of our changing society, the superiority of the Bais Yaakov education. With the rapid growth of Orthodox girls' schools all over the country, Bais Yaakovs have to be competitive to survive. Where curricula in the past dealt mainly with the basics of Torah knowledge and *hashkafah*, today we find a wide range of diversified subjects. Now, a girl who enters Bais Yaakov in the elementary grades can be expected to emerge a highly knowledgeable young woman. Again, this seems a very welcome change. The ramifications, though, may be far more serious than we realize. For having set a pattern of progressively intensive education in the earlier years, we cannot expect this education to end at grade twelve.

In truth, it could not possibly be otherwise, especially in view of the rush of intellectual stimuli women are exposed to today, and the great number of opportunities generally open to them. Jewish women are fully aware of this intellectual ferment and their religious education cannot afford to offer any less. So, here we have it: Where, previously, it was a rarity for a girl educated in Bais Yaakov to go on for further training, today it is the rare Bais Yaakov graduate who does otherwise.

To be sure, the Bais Yaakov-directed goal is to emerge as a teacher — or at least as a highly motivated, knowledgeable young woman dedicated to the loftiest standards of Torah life — and that, often as not, means being a struggling *Kollel* wife.

And then there are those who seek other kinds of professional advancement, whether for the purpose of being a better *Kollel* wife, or simply for self-fulfillment. So off they go to college or vocational school, and emerge as a computer programmer, dental assistant, or one of countless other forms of professions. No matter how you spin the dial, the step after Bais Yaakov is virtually the first on a progression that leads to a career.

But, then comes the question that teases, and then haunts us: if we (as the Torah society) honestly intend that these young women adhere to their traditional roles as mothers dedicating their lives to raising families, is it fair to gear them for careers they are not expected to follow? Thus, we pave the way for frustration and discontent in the contemporary, young Jewish woman.

ৼ The Unavoidable Environmental Pollution

Furthermore, it is an unfortunate truism that there are many places of business where women seek employment which do not meet the standards of our Orthodox society. In the face of the woman's contribution to the family welfare, making it possible for her husband to reach for the highest levels of Torah scholarship, are we to overlook this argument as well as the ones previously mentioned? Or, are there other alternatives for one who is seriously committed to helping in the support of her family? For example, there are surely scores of offices, in yeshivos and otherwise, where the environments do meet the standards of acceptability. Certainly, if a woman chooses to go out into the marketplace, she should do so only with strict limitations; she must be select, learn to discriminate among the myriad positions that have recently become accessible to the contemporary woman.

Of course, it is undeniable that there is a certain amount of contact with unwholesome aspects of the outside world present in any position, as reputable as it may be. Were we living in another era, that would surely be a basis for contention. We must reluctantly concede, though, that today there are no ivory towers where one can seclude himself from the rough edges of the outside world. One has only to enter a doctor's waiting room, for instance, or climb onto a public bus, to be immediately assailed with the sharp taste of reality. In fact, whether we go to work or stay at home, we cannot hope to deny the turbulent world which must inevitably touch our daily lives.

❦ A Mother's Contrary Emotions

This rationale seems so perfect — so logical — so — so *rational* — and yet — and yet — who can account for the contrary emotions of a mother. Instead of satisfaction, I feel only doubt and resentment; instead of fulfillment, I am racked with guilt.

And so I find myself at the wheel of my car, lost in thought, agonizing over my dilemma. The light turns green, but I, locked into a no-win situation, am too preoccupied to notice until it turns red again. Soon, I will have to come to some sort of conclusion — but what conclusion is there? For every argument, I cast in favor of going to work, I seem to find an equally reasonable argument to refute it. I am afraid I will have to go on in this unstable manner, careening between pro and con. Today for, and tomorrow against; today seemingly content, tomorrow torn with guilt.

Hazily I grope for direction, switching in mid-thought to a different angle. What if it were possible for a woman to go to work and be at the same time, not only as good a mother, but a better mother for it? What if the fact that she has an outside stimulus allows her to grow, to mature, thus giving her the impetus to meet her children's demands with patience and humor, rather than with pent-up anger and resentment?

The Individual Variation

Perhaps there is no ready-made solution, after all, nor a need for one. If there are no positives and no negatives, then there is no need for guilt. Perhaps the concept of what's right or wrong is irrelevant here. What should be relevant is the way each individual mother feels about her need to leave and her need to return. Who says that spending twenty-four hours a day exclusively with one's children is the only way to achieve perfect motherhood?

I know of mothers who work mornings and wouldn't dream of enrolling their three-year-old toddlers in afternoon school because they feel that a child that age needs to be with his mother at least part of the day. And I know mothers who don't work but send two-year-old children who can barely utter an intelligible syllable to school from 9 to 4 because of their own inability to cope.

I know of working women who have vacation during the summer months and spend hours each day taking their children on outings, while their non-working counterparts ship their youngsters off to camp for the entire summer to give themselves a breather. I would venture to say that if the hours could be counted either way, one might come up with some surprising figures.

It's true that when I come home from work, I am often physically worn-out. But what mother who has to care for small children isn't? And coming back from a few hours away from home leaves my mind fresh with ideas, keyed up with life, recharged for a new and better existence. No small measure of my satisfaction is due to the knowledge that with my support, my husband is attaining the highest pinnacles of Torah scholarship, and our children derive the full benefits of our combined efforts — So, perhaps when I leave each day and a little bit of me dies, at the same time something new is born. If I come home rejuvenated and refreshed with a renewed sense of well-being and value, doesn't that make me a better mother for it?

The light at the corner turns green; cars sound their horns impatiently, arousing me finally from my reverie, telling me there is work to be done.

Rabbi Yisroel Miller

When Feminists Demand, Can Judaism Deliver?

*Fulfillment for Women
Within a Torah Framework*

NON-OBSERVANT JEWS interested in the topic of Judaism and Feminism generally accept feminism as an article of faith, against which they measure the relevance or fairness of Judaism. While this is not the case with those who are *shomrei Torah u'mitzvos*, words of explanations aimed at the non-observant could be instructive to those with a strong commitment as well, to help them answer the questions of their alienated neighbors...or some gnawing doubts within themselves.

⊷§ Women, The Synagogue and the Rest of Judaism

Addressing a non-observant group should begin by exposing a damaging misconception:

The feminist movement took note that Judaism limited the woman's role in the synagogue. She is not a rabbi or a *chazzan*, she gets no *aliya* and she is not counted in a *minyan*. Many women demanded ritual equality, and the Conservative and Reform clergy gave it to them. To make such changes, however, one must overcome an objection: The Torah is transmitted from generation to generation by means of our *Mesora*, and the rabbis are entrusted with safeguarding that *Mesora*. Ultimately, the only way to cut Judaism down to egalitarian size is to reject the binding nature of our *Mesora*, and re-do Judaism unbound to Sinai. And once you've done that, why bother with Judaism at all? Why not Unitarianism, ח״ו?

So it appears that a sincere feminist must choose: either Judaism or feminism — a terrible choice to have to make. May I suggest an alternative approach to the whole subject: Women have been hoodwinked into believing that the synagogue is central to Judaism.

It is well known that our tradition contains 613 Biblical commandments, but synagogue attendance is not one of them; it is basically a rabbinic enactment. There are pious old Rebbetzins who never go to *shul*, on principle, even on Yom Kippur. When I say this, people sometimes look at me in bewilderment: Are we talking about the same religion?

And the truth is, we are not. Americanized Judaism, even some Orthodox Judaism, is a far cry from the Torah given on Mount Sinai. To be sure, the synagogue is a sacred institution. It is the setting of *tefilla betzibbur*, which is a fundamental obligation for men. But in the totality of Torah, the synagogue ritual is only one ingredient, a worthy rabbinic addition to the Biblical *mitzvos*. To mistake that component for the whole is like mistaking the leaf of a rose stem for the flower. and then looking at the leaf and wondering: Where is the beauty of roses of which the poets wrote so much? To truly understand the place of men and women in Torah, we must examine the list of the 613 *mitzvos* in the *Chumash*. This is the first task in our approach.

ೊ A Search for a Source of Fulfillment

There are some women who complain about the "restrictions" of the Torah because to them, the *dvar Hashem* is not of definitive authority. But there are other women who complain, or at least question, not from disloyalty, but to the contrary, because they do care; they want to feel the *dvar Hashem* in their lives, and they don't.

We teach women that their source of *kedusha* is to be found in the home, in raising a family with a Torah outlook — and rightly so. But what if a woman has a home and a family, and attends *shiurim*, and still feels unfulfilled? She's not asking for an *aliya* or a *Gemara*; all she wants is a feeling of spiritual achievement that she does not yet possess. What do we tell her?

Some may argue that in the Torah world there are no such women. Then what of the woman who has no family: single, divorced, or married and childless? What of the *baalas teshuva* who comes from a different world, and has a different set of self-expectations? Is there some direction we can offer, to make things more understandable — not an alternative to the *Mesora*, but a perspective on it?

A true *ben* Torah, however he earns his living, can wake up each morning and thank Hashem for the day that lies ahead, because each day he looks forward to accomplishing something. Like everybody else, he will spend hours at his job to provide for his family; as a Torah Jew, he will try to conduct himself with honesty and integrity, and be *mekadesh es Hashem*. But more important, all of this is framed in a structure that begins and ends with *tefilla* in the synagogue, and regular sessions of Torah study. And immersed in these activities, he can expect to experience growth: making progress on completing *Shas*; and perhaps also improving his *kavana* in *davening*, adding to his comprehension, line by line.

The feeling of accomplishment — that he is engaged in activities that are intrinsically important, which are also respected by his peers, and that he is making progress — this all provides a man with a sense of self-esteem and an inspiration to continue to strive to come closer to G-d. But for the woman who does not feel this sense of accomplishment, for whatever reason: What can we tell her to think about when she wakes up in the morning, to make her want to grab hold of the day?

∞ The Chofetz Chaim's Whole Life Catalogue

In his last years, the Chofetz Chaim זצ״ל wrote a *sefer* which he advised us to learn and review time and again. It is a *sefer* that most of us have never read, called *Sefer Hamitzvos Hakotzer*, a list of all the *mitzvos* that apply nowadays. The *sefer* is not that popular, perhaps because we tend to think in terms of the final *halacha*. What difference does it make whether a *halachah* is from *Chumash* or *d'Rabbanan*? One reason why the Chofetz Chaim may have felt that the *sefer* was important enough to write is that human beings are by nature goal-oriented. We need a structure within which to work and specific targets to aim at. With the Chofetz Chaim's list, one says *Modeh Ani* and then one thinks:

Such and such are the *mitzvos* that I hope to accomplish today.

Within this context, it is possible to address the women who are not yet *frum*, to give them a picture of what Torah is; at the same time, this presentation can help an observant woman perceive a picture within which she can see herself: The key to self-understanding for both men and women is to view *Yiddishkeit* as a structure of 613 *mitzvos*, and to see how one functions within this structure.

613 *mitzvos* may seem like a vast number, but many of them are a single commandment counted as two because it is stated several times in different ways, like the positive *mitzva* to honor parents and the negative *mitzva* not to hurt them; or the prohibition against idol-worship, which involves at least eighteen separate *mitzvos*, referring to its various aspects. In sum, there are considerably fewer that 613 *types* of obligations.

Of the remainder, many apply only at special times, like those associated with *Shabbos* and specific *Yomim Tovim*. So when one considers, how many different Torah obligations are there for us to fulfill on an ordinary Sunday?—how many different kinds of religious experience does the Torah want me to pursue on a weekday? — one finds that there are approximately forty different types of daily *mitzvos*...about forty things for Jews to think of when waking up in the morning besides *mitzvos d'Rabbanan* and *minhagim*. Let us sketch an outline of *Yiddishkeit*, by seeing what these forty types of *mitzvos* are.

One category is what some people call rituals: *mezuza, tallis* and *tefillin, kashrus*, the prohibition against *shatnez* and the *halachos* of *taharas hamishpacha*. Three *mitzvos* are included in our prayer: Affirmation of loyalty, with *Krias Shema* twice a day; expressing thanks to G-d with *Birkas Hamazon*; and to *daven* sincerely, to ask Hashem for help, at least once a day, plus whenever in trouble. Those are the minimum *D'Oraisa* expectations of *tefilla*.

Most of the remaining *mitzvos* are a sanctification of human relations: A *chiyuv* to try to love and help every Jew as ourselves, and an extra *chiyuv* to love the true *ger* even more; an obligation not to hurt people's feelings, and not to embarrass them and not to speak ill of them even if it's true.

A commandment to think before giving advice, to be sure that it is not harmful or self-serving; and not to help or encourage

When Feminists Demand, Can Judaism Deliver? / 129

someone to do an *aveira*. A *mitzva* not to take revenge or bear a grudge, or curse, and a *mitzva* to be always scrupulously honest: not to take from others improperly and not to fool them, and not to delay payment of wages; a *mitzva* not to overlook the obligation due to one's spouse; a *mitzva* to help others carry packages, and a *mitzva* to remove a hazard from your home — sweeping up a banana peel is an act of holiness.

We have a *mitzva* to honor the elderly, *talmidei chachamim*, and our parents. A *mitzva* to develop a relationship with *chachmei haTorah*. And an obligation to judge people favorably and assume that their motives are sincere, while at the same time offering constructive criticism when warranted.

We could spend a lifetime trying to perfect ourselves in any one of those areas, but there are also other *mitzvos* demanding personal sanctity in general: The *mitzva* of *Kiddush Hashem*, to always act in a manner that demonstrates to the world that goodness and *kedusha* are the only things that count, and to avoid even the appearance of unethical behavior; and *"Lo sikrevu legalos erva"* — the far-reaching *mitzva* to avoid any situation that might possibly lead to violating Torah laws against immoral conduct. The *chiyuv* is to be holy by avoiding compromising situations, even if nothing improper occurs.

Yet another obligation is to fulfill vows, and by extension, to keep commitments, and not to say one thing and end up doing another. The laws of these four personal *mitzvos* is *"Lo sasuru —* Do not stray after your eyes," which according to the Chofetz Chaim amounts to a warning against sinking into hedonism, even kosher hedonism; for us, it is a cautionary command against overspending on luxuries and status symbols, and frequenting even glatt kosher nightclubs.

৺§ Mitzvos of Mind and Emotions

The final category of *chiyuvim* are *mitzvos* of the mind and emotions: The *mitzva* of *emuna*, to think about *Hakadosh Baruch Hu* and make His presence come alive in the room; the *mitzva* of *Yichud Hashem*, to know that He is one, and not two or three, and also that He is the *only* One, that He is in complete control of my life — naturally, this implies that there is a *mitzvah* to develop emotional tranquility and peace of mind.

There is a *mitzva* to learn to fear Hashem, to love Him, and to continually contemplate His kindness to us. There is a *mitzva* to avoid non-Jewish religious services, even as a spectator, and not to busy our thoughts with alien ideologies.

There is a *mitzva* not to covet, not to spend time thinking of how we would like to have another person's sports car or spouse. And there is a *mitzva* of *teshuva*, to repent from *aveiros* regularly.

If you still need more to fill your day with spirituality and purpose, there are two other obligations: One is to learn Torah. Apart from the man's *mitzva* to learn Torah for its own sake, both men and women are obligated to learn those parts of Torah that are necessary to know how to fulfill all their *mitzvos*, which means enough learning to keep us all busy forever. And one last *mitzva*: "*Veholachta bidrachav* — walk in the ways of Hashem," which Rabbi Moshe Chaim Luzzatto explains to mean that we must each work to develop every noble trait of character: kindness, humility, honesty, industry, self-control, compassion, serenity, dignity and joy.

◆§ The Total Picture

That is our picture: forty different areas of *kedusha*, to think about, to work at, and to experience every day — forty goals to wake up to. None of these is considered extra *frumkeit*; it is all basic curriculum for every Jew. And they all apply to both men and women, except for *tallis* and *tefillin*.

Of course, there are also the *mitzvos* for special occasions, and the *mitzvos d'Rabbanan*. But this basic list, which most Jews have never thought about, are the building blocks of Torah living, the structure with which to begin. For the Jew who is not yet *frum*, this will not answer all the questions, but it offers an entirely new perspective, and it deflects his or her initial negativism, to enable him or her to ask questions and want to hear the answers.

As for the *frum* woman looking for more substance, she will discover that spiritual growth is not in the pageantry of carrying a *sefer Torah*, but in the *kol demama dakka* — the still, small voice of connecting with one's own *neshama* as the *neshama* connects with *Hashem*. None of this conflicts with the traditional role of wife and mother; it makes the woman the kind of wife and mother the Torah wants her to be.

For this approach to succeed, I suggest, it needs to be publicized; and it also needs status. *Daf yomi*, for example, has become an "in thing." To some extent, so has learning the *halachos* of *lashon hora* (slander). If we could embark on a campaign, in *yeshivos* and schools and publications, to extend this prestige to *chavos halevavos* (duties of the heart) and to these other *chiyuvim* — from honesty in business to wearing a smile on our faces — these could also become valued goals, sources of self-esteem, and sources of fulfillment and *simcha* for us all.

Some years ago, a middle-aged couple came to a certain *yeshiva* and requested that prayers be said for a sick relative. They explained that they belonged to the local Conservative Temple; and when the *talmidim* asked the couple. "Why did you come to the *yeshiva?*" they replied: "Well, we know that G-d is Orthodox." There are hundreds and thousands of Jews who, in their hearts, also know. If we can set the example, to structure our lives around the presence of *Hashem*, others will notice and try to do the same.

Yaacov Amitai

Sanctity and Self-Expression

Do women really need a minyan of their own?

❧ Once Upon a Time...

ONCE UPON A TIME, in the days of the Temple, there lived in the land of Israel a man by the name of Peloni ben Almoni. He was a pious and upright Jew, but also an unhappy and frustrated one. For on the occasion of the Three Festivals, when all Jews ascended to Jerusalem to rejoice before the Lord, and to bask in the majesty of His Temple, Peloni's joy would turn to bitterness as he cried out within himself: "Woe is to me! My limbs are truly burning with the sublime desire to take part in the Holy Service, but this is denied me because I am not a *Kohein* (priest)! My soul is fairly bursting with the urge to raise its voice in glorious song before Hashem, but, again, this is not given to me for I am not a Levite!"

And when Peloni's obsession reached the point where it could no longer be contained, he went and built himself an *almost* perfect replica of the Holy Temple, made himself vestments *almost* identical to those of the *Kohein Gadol* (High Priest), and instituted his own "holy service." Now, Peloni was a pious and upright Jew, so he made certain that all of his actions were strictly within the bounds of *halachah*. The lambs that he "sacrificed" twice daily were *not* consecrated beforehand,[1] the incense that he burned on his "inner altar" was *not* blended in the same proportions as the *ketores* was[2] and so on. So Peloni felt fulfilled, both for his "service" and in his knowledge that he had broken no law of the Torah....

Until a wise man of his town came to remonstrate with him: "Fool that you are! What have you done to yourself? You have thrown away the precious gift of coming face to face with the *Shechinat Hashem* (Divine Presence), which dwells solely in the place of *His* choosing! And for what? For a pretense, for a charade, for a chance to *play Kohein?!* Look, look with clear, unbiased eyes into your heart of hearts: Is it really *avodas Hashem* that you so ardently desire, or is it self-aggrandizement? Is it *Him* that you worship or is it your *folie des grandeurs?*"

New and Improved — or New and Prohibited?

In the *Long Island Jewish World* of July 13, 1984, we find the front-page headline: "Women's Prayer Group Gets a Torah." The extensive report, accompanied by two photos, tells of "a Flatbush Orthodox women's davening group"; of the opposition they have met among some rabbis; and of their having recently celebrated the dedication of their own *Sefer Torah*. There is also a companion article based on the remarks of a woman a prominent local political figure who donated the *Sefer Torah* to the group.

Whenever some new practice appears in Jewish life, it behooves us to ask, with the utmost concern, whether it belongs in the category of *"Chadashim gam yeshanim"* new and old (are equally precious to *Hashem*) a quote from *Shir HaShirim* (7:14); or rather with the Chasam Sofer's famous warning: *"Hechadash assur min HaTorah..."* the new is prohibited by the Torah.[3] In the present case, this writer feels, the question ought to be addressed in several stages. First, there is the technical halachic one: Does the new practice "break any rules"?

---

1. They were not in the category of bona fide sacrifices, which are prohibited off Temple grounds.
2. There is a prohibition against duplicating the Temple incense for outside use.
3. A halachic statement that the Chasam Sofer often borrowed from its original context to express his opposition to change inspired by the Reform doctrine of innovation in religious practice.

The article first quotes one of the organizers of the group:[1] "Just last week, I received a call from a local rabbi who assured me halachically we're all right." But then Rabbis Samuel Fink and Dovid Cohen, among others, are cited in the article as having the opposite view. Likewise, Rabbi Moshe Meiselman in *Jewish Woman In Jewish Law* (Ktav, Yeshiva University Press '78; p. 145, and note 64 to Chap. 20 in the name of Rabbi J.B. Soloveichik). Having said that much, there is really no need for further comment. *The Jewish Observer* is not the proper forum for a full discussion of a halachic issue.

܀§ Setting the Pace for the Future

Once this has been established, there is another concern. Is this incident a forerunner of possible future deviations from *halachah?* Again, the spokesperson quoted before: "But they're afraid... we're feminists and that soon we'll want to come into the *shul* and want *aliyas* there and women rabbis...If we wanted that, we could go to Conservative *shuls.* We're doing this precisely because we want to remain within *halachah."*

Reassuring words, to be sure. But did the donor of the *Sefer Torah,* for one, hear them or understand them? I'm afraid not: Let us listen to her own words, as she offers us her interpretation of a "Biblical precedent," and how it helps her understand her current spate of activity: "There was, however, an important and landmark occasion in Jewish history when a group of women challenged the established order (as we are doing today) and prevailed. Our forebearers might be legitimately considered the forerunners of the first Jewish women's liberation movement. They were known collectively as Bnos Zelophchad ... As simple as this request seems in the telling, it was an extraordinary act of courage, deeply motivated, no doubt, by a strong sense of justice denied.... What happened was that a group of courageous and intelligent women, who rightfully demanded justice, caused the laws of inheritance to be changed forever."

In all fairness to them and to history let us set the record straight. The daughters of Zelophchad have become favorite role-models for feminists, but they did *not* challenge the established order, they were *not* motivated by "a strong sense of justice the

---

1. All quotations are from the *Long Island Jewish World.*

Sanctity and Self-Expression / 135

simple reason that they approached Moses with their request *before* the law of inheritance was ever promulgated — as even a cursory reading of the relevant passages would reveal (*Numbers* 27: 1-11). Moreover, we find them specifying in their claim"... for he has no son," upon which *Rashi* comments:"... if he had had a son, they would not be demanding anything..." — hardly the stuff of liberationism! But be that as it may, the Torah donor has managed, in the process, to tell us in no uncertain terms that "a group of courageous and intelligent women" can cause laws of the Torah "to be changed forever," courtesy of the daughters of Zelophchad! I do hope that someone in her audience set her straight on this point.

For the sake of accuracy, I would like to also address some of her further remarks: "Since women could not own...property, according to existing laws...". Here she is totally mistaken. There is no difference whatsoever between a man and an unmarried woman as far as ownership of property is concerned. And a married woman also retains her ownership, with the profits going to her husband while control is shared (*nichsei melog*) but even this arrangement is of later Rabbinical origin; in Moses's time husband had no claim or control on his wife's property.

"Before their entrance into the Land of Israel, when Moses was dividing the parcels among the tribes..." Moses did no such thing; Joshua did, as is recorded in Scripture.

"Moses might well have looked aghast at this situation: About the unauthorized entrance of these women as they broke in upon him and the elders, he might have said, colloquially put, 'Stand behind the *mechitzah* (divider)... send a male representative. I do not speak with women.'"

An altogether preposterous statement: Biblical, Talmudic and later Rabbinical literature is all replete with examples of women having entry into the highest Torah councils as a matter of course. In our day, too, a woman can turn to any rabbi worthy of the name and find an open door and an open ear to her *she'eilos* (halachic queries) or claims of injustice. Only someone who has never asked a *she'eilah* can honestly believe otherwise.

"Unfortunately we have been met by fear, ignorance and arrogance." In light of all the above, a slight emendation is in order here: The fear, Ms. Torah Donor, very much ought to be ours; the ignorance and the arrogance are all yours.

✺§ Not a Fable, Peloni

There is yet another dimension to consider, and this is quite beyond *halachah*. For this, let us return to the story of Peloni. A fable, you say? Not necessarily. The *Mishnah* (*Menachos* 109a) states: "The priests who served in the House of Chonio may not serve in the Temple in Jerusalem." The *Gemara* explains as follows: When the High Priest Shimon Hatzadik died, he was survived by two sons, Shime'i and Chonio. Now, although Chonio had deferred to his elder brother for their father's exalted position, he could not free himself of envy a consuming envy which ultimately caused him to flee to Alexandria, where he built an altar and brought sacrifices *to Hashem. Tosafot*, however, maintains that it was all done in strict adherence to *halachah*. This raises an obvious question: If so, if indeed everything in that House of Chonio was glatt kosher, why then were its poets stripped of their G-d-given right to serve in the Holy Temple? The answer rings out, loud and clear: An altar conceived in egotistical jealousy is the very antithesis of *avodas Hashem* a "house of worship" born of a turning away from Jerusalem is nothing but rejection and spurning of the *Shechinah* itself!

So we call out to our sisters of the women's group: Why have you fled our *mikdash me'at*, the one place in *galut* where the *Shechinah* dwells, cast aside the *zechus* of saying the "*yehei Shemai Rabba*" and all the other *devarim shebikdushah*, which set the very angels and worlds atremble? And, yes, renounced *keriat haTorah betzibbur*, which is a spark from *ma'amad har Sinai*, and which, according to *Magen Avrohom* (282:6), women are obligated to hear? For what? For the chance to *play ba'al korei?* Is this bit of childish self-assertion your ideal of *avodas Hashem?* Or is it the furthest thing from it?

Let us be rid of our toys and trinkets, let us quit pandering to our petty psychological chimeras. Let us all unite, men and women, old and young, *Kohanim*, Levites and Israelites, to fulfill *His* will, for *His* greater glory!

Sanctity and Self-Expression

Rabbi Yissocher Frand

"Where There's a Rabbinic Will, There's a Halachic Way"

Fact or Fiction?

THERE IS A BRIEF and comprehensive answer to the title question: Fiction! But one-word answers do not clarify issues, and the topic does call for elaboration.

The title statement is heavy with implications: When the *Rabbanim* or *poskim* (rabbis and decisors) truly want to achieve something, an accepted halachic principle that indicates otherwise should not be an obstacle. Somehow, they can manage to sidestep the *halachah*. Whether by means of a *lomdus* or a *snif* (a clever piece of reasoning or a tangential argument), *Rabbanim* are ingenious enough to find a way around any difficulty. Therefore, where the *Rabbanim* do not find a way out of a specific halachic problem, it is only because there is no will to do so. Thus, one may assume, any number of problems could be resolved legitimately, if the rabbis only cared enough. This lack of resolve is to be read as a serious indictment of the rabbis: They just don't care enough.

Before exposing this accusation for the calumny that it is, let us first examine the specific problems to which the purveyors of this slogan apply it.

⋑ Turmoil Regarding Women's Issues

One area that has become a focus of the search for halachic innovations is a cluster of "women's issues." Women cannot be treated differently from men, we are told; they cannot accept old standards and, therefore, we must adapt religious practices to their new ways of understanding things. Thus questions arise: Why can't women have greater expression and participation in religious activities? What is wrong, for instance, with prayer groups for women? They feel alienated sitting behind the *mechitzah*, spectators instead of participants. Shouldn't there be a way out of this quandary?

In addition, the call for a Rabbinic will to find a halachic way has become almost synonymous with discussion of the tragic *agunah* problem. It is well known that some husbands who are estranged from their wives refuse to give them a *get*. A woman may be in halachic/social/economic limbo for years, or her fate can be tied to a "ransom" of thousands of dollars before the husband grants her a *get*. Can't we do something about this situation? Can't we come up with a *lomdus* to get around this problem?

And if the will-and-way formula is true, can't we do something about the *"Mihu Yehudi"* problem, which has splintered Diaspora Jewry? There are groups within Orthodoxy that have come up with a proposal for a joint commission of Reform, Conservative and Orthodox representatives that would recommend candidates for conversion, to be processed only by Orthodox Rabbis. This would spare us all the headaches we've gone through by rejecting Conservative and Reform converts and the resulting schisms within Jewry .... Can't we do this? *Shouldn't* we do this?

Under the Same Umbrella

The above questions are presented as though they are interrelated, all to be solved by some hypothetical "will-way" formula. Those who argue for such innovative approaches in halachic decision-making go back to earlier times for precedents in employing such tactics. Foremost among such cases is the creation of the *pruzbul* by Hillel *Hazakein* (the Elder). This, in effect, was a rabbinic ordinance designed to permit the collection of debts incurred before the *Shmittah* year debts that the Torah would otherwise annul at the end of *Shmittah*. This step was deemed crucial for promoting the lending of money for commerce, which had become curtailed with the approach of each *Shmittah*.

Pruzbul has been cited by Conservatives for generations as the model case of halachic innovation. (See, for instance, *Judaism*

1979, in which Robert Gordis argues in regard to *pruzbul*: "They [the Rabbis] did not hesitate to set aside what they understood to be the law in the Torah.")

In truth, however, even after a cursory reading of the *Gemara* (*Gittin* 36a), it is obvious that this is simply not the case. The *Gemara itself* asks: "Is it possible that Torah Law absolves the debt, and Hillel would rule that it is *not* absolved?"

The *Gemara* responds along two lines of reasoning: "First: Nowadays [when the *Yoveil*/Jubilee year is not in effect], *Shmittah* is only Rabbinic in nature, and as a result the *halachah* allows broader latitude.

"A second consideration: *Hefker beis din hefker*." That is, in *monetary matters*, the Rabbis have a power akin to eminent domain, which permits them, in effect, to take funds from one individual and transfer it to another. Obviously, this does not in any manner represent a precedent to "setting aside laws of the Torah."[1]

As for our particular problems in the contemporary scene, there is not one answer that fits all the above enumerated cases. One statement, however, can be made unequivocally: *halachah*, the bedrock of Normative Judaism, does not change. What was *assur* (forbidden) yesterday remains *assur* today, and what is *mutar* (permitted) today was always *mutar*. *Halachah* is absolute, *halachah* cannot be abolished, *halachah* cannot be fabricated. *Halachah* is not an amorphous area wherein changing social needs

---

1. Another citation, used by Conservative scholars and some of the left-leaning Orthodox, is the expression, "*Eis la'asos laShem, heifeiru Torasecha*," which implies that in a time of need, the laws of the Torah are indeed set aside.

But once again let us look to the halachic sources. The *Rambam* says quite succinctly: "A *beis din* has the power to uproot matters *lefi sha'ah* on a temporary basis ... When the *beis din* seeks to strengthen Torah observance and to create a protective ordinance so the people will not transgress the words of the Torah" — *Hilchos Mamrim* 2:4. Note three key elements.

One: That any such *takanah* (ordinance) be *lefi sha'ah* — only temporary in nature.

Two: That the motivation be for the overall strengthening of Torah observance and not, G-d forbid, the opposite.

Three: This power is exclusive to a *beis din* of *musmachim*, which we lack today. Thus, the *Shulchan Aruch* and all other decisors do not even mention this rule in defining rules of *halachah*.

For an in-depth discussion of the *Rambam's shitah*, specifically demonstrating how all other examples were indeed temporary in nature, see *Maratz Chayus, Toras Haneviim*, chap. 3-6. See also a responsum by Rabbi E.M. Bloch which argues that this rule was only applied in cases involving Rabbinic law.

can be legislated; it is the eternal truth of Torah applied to temporal activities reflective of Divine judgment; it corresponds to the "blueprint" role of Torah in the *olam hama'aseh*, the world of action. The so-called inflexibility of Torah law is a measure of its eternal truth an impregnable strength rather than a weakness to be contended with. It is this fortress of *halachah* that has guaranteed our survival throughout the millennia of *Galus*. When we see what appear to be changes in *halachah*, things are not as they appear. As situations change, so may the *application* of *halacha*, but not its basic core of principles. That remains constant.[1]

Let us examine some of the topical changes that *can* take place, as well as other changes that cannot take place, such as those regarding *agunos* or *battei dinim* for *geirus* (special accommodations for non-Orthodox converts).

৵ When Changes do Take Place

There is no question that amongst all the social changes of the last decades, beginning with the tumultuous Sixties, the feminist movement has had the greatest impact. Orthodox Jewry rejected the promiscuity of the Sixties as obviously *"treif"* but the feminist movement has threatened Judaism in subtle and insidious ways. The formation of prayer groups for women, for example, raises some troubling questions. Quite apart from those women who have a political agenda or women with a non-halachic orientation, we often deal with a core of serious, sincere Orthodox women. They come with halachic precedent in hand. They assert:

"It was *assur* to teach Torah to girls. Our *Bobbes* never went to Torah schools. But Sara Scheneirer recognized that if there would be schools to teach Torah to girls, there would be no future generation of Jews."

That is not an overstatement. The Belzer *Rebbe*, the Gerrer *Rebbe*, and other *Gedolei Hador* recognized this, and after

---

1. For instance, cattle farmers, faced with how to deal with first-born calves or lambs which must be set aside to be given to a *Kohein*, resort to selling a share of the flock to a non-Jew before birthing, thus circumventing the problem. This is akin to the standard selling of *chometz* to a non-Jew in advance of Pesach, to avoid the prohibition against possession of *chometz* on Pesach. These rabbinically mandated procedures are based on existing halachic structures, which exempt non-Jewish commodities from those specific prohibitions, but these exemption procedures were not institutionalized until the rabbis saw the need to do so.

consulting them, Sarah Scheneirer launched the Bais Yaakov movement. "Of course, some spoke out against Sara Scheneirer — she was a revolutionary in her day," argue the feminists. "Yet the Rabbinical leadership got around the prohibition against teaching girls (*Sotah* 21a). By the same token, why can't women have a prayer group? Some people will object, but they probably would have reacted negatively to Sara Scheneirer, as well."

If one explores the *sugya* (topic) in *Mesechta Sotah*, however, one finds distinctions between *Torah she'bichsav* (the Written Law), which is permitted and therefore could be taught, and *Torah she'ba'al peh* (the Oral Law), which is forbidden. Ethical teachings, *hashkafah* (philosophy of faith) and *mussar* (character development) are also among the areas that are permitted and, therefore, could be taught.[1]

That which had been *acceptable* was then put into practice when the need arose. We have indeed found ways to work innovatively within the parameters of *halachah*, but we never change the *halachah*.

✽ Minyan Impossible

On the other hand, a woman's *minyan* is a halachic impossibility. The *Gemara* derives hermeneutically (from a *gezeirah shavah*) that a *minyan* consists of ten males. One cannot change that, and it is futile to attempt to do so. It is sad, then, that women who want to *daven*, and strive to come closer to *Hashem*, are being so misled. As a result, they are missing out not only on the Torah reading and *Kaddish*, which women may not conduct or

---

1. In his *Likutei Halachos* to *Sotah* (*perek* 3), the Chofetz Chaim says in regard to the rabbinic statement that when a father teaches Torah to his daughter it is comparable to teaching her *tiflus* (foolishness): "This refers only to the Oral Law. As for the Written Law, one should not teach it to her *lechat'chilah* (as a first choice), but it is not comparable to teaching her *tiflus*."

The Chofetz Chaim then adds in a footnote: "It would appear to us that this was only so in earlier times, when everyone lived where his parents had lived, and the legacy from earlier generations was well entrenched, and everyone conducted his life in line with his parents' traditions. Then it was possible to say that daughters should not study Torah, and we could rely on the practices of our upright ancestors. Because of our lapses, however, our hold on our fathers' traditions has become extremely weakened. Moreover, it is common not to live where our parents had lived (further weakening our link with our tradition) especially in view of how widespread the practice is for them to become literate in foreign languages. It is thus a great *mitzvah* to teach [our daughters] *Chumash* as well as Prophets and Scripture, and ethical writings of the Rabbis, such as *Pirkei Avos*."

recite, but also on *tefillah betzibbur* (prayer with a *minyan*) and its special advantages, for it is always *nishma'as* — G-d *always* hearkens to it. The women that persist in *davening* in their ersatz *minyanim* are losing this incomparable advantage. One must wonder: For whom are they *davening*? *Tefillah* is called *avodah*, which means service. It is unheard of for an *eved*, a servant, to overrule his master in determining how to serve Him. Yet these women, ostensibly desiring to perform *avodas Hashem*, are determining for themselves how the *avodah* should be done!

This, in fact, is an old *yeitzer hara*. People have always tended to search for innovative ways to serve G-d, but for Jews, there is only the way delineated by *halachah*.

The *Netziv* (Rabbi Naftoli Tzvi Yehuda Berlin, צז"ל, 1820-1893) comments on the following *Midrash* in a way that illustrates this phenomenon:

> When the Jews prepared to consecrate the *Mishkan* (the traveling sanctuary), *Moshe Rabbeinu* told them, "This is the thing that G-d has commanded you to do: then the glory of G-d will appear to you" (*Vayikra* 9:6). The Midrash comments, *Zeh hadavar ta'aseh* — this is the thing that .... you (should) do: Be rid of that *yeitzer hara* from your hearts, and you will all be of one awe and one form of service before Me."
>
> Said the *Netziv*, "As the Jews were about to erect the *Mishkan*, they formed sub-groups, each wanting passionately to serve G-d in its own, innovative way. In response to this, Moshe exhorted them. 'Forget this *yeitzer hara*, and form one united approach to serve G-d, the way prescribed by G-d through *Torah* and *halachah*."

Unfortunately, this old *yeitzer hara* refuses to go away. Are these age-old desires perhaps ultimately rooted in a desire to serve one's ego, rather than one's G-d?

Example: A letter written to *Moment* magazine, from a female rabbi, asks for assistance in the following enterprise:

"As co-editors, we would like to see the following included in our book: rituals for adoption ... career or life change ... empty nest syndrome, commitment ceremonies, undertaking political action, baby naming, abortion, death and remembrance. The existence of such a book will include and encourage the definition of Jewish family and Jewish marriage and will include the contribution of Jewish feminists."

This type of travesty occurs when one fails to follow *Torah achas* one unifying Torah. I do not mean to mock this "rabbi"; she is in the category of a *tinok shenishba* — a captive child, brought up without benefit of exposure to Torah teachings and Torah values. Rather, it is incumbent upon those of us who believe in *Torah she'ba'al peh* to eschew the stumbling and groping of the uninformed, and to exemplify for them unadulterated, purely motivated service to G-d, in the ways precisely outlined by Torah directives.

The Travails of the Agunah

The *agunah* problem is one of the most tragic of modern halachic quandaries. This is not the classical *agunah* discussed in the *Gemara* and *poskim* where the *Rabbanim* cannot establish for certain whether a woman's husband is alive or dead. We are referring to the *agunah* who is married to a man who is very much alive, but refuses to grant his wife a *get* and leaves her in halachic limbo for years, or attempts to extort from her thousands of dollars.

I personally recall a case in which the husband abandoned his wife, took their baby and refused to give her a *get*. After a time, I was informed that the woman was finally receiving her *get*. I was so elated that I exclaimed, *Mazel Tov!* Then the irony of the situation struck me: According to the *Gemara*, the *mizbei'ach* sheds tears at the dissolution of a marriage, and here I am shouting *Mazel Tov*. Yet we live in a time when on occasion we do say *Mazel Tov* on the giving of a *get*.

Such being the case, there is an anguished, legitimate cry: "*Rabbanim*, can't you do something?"

To illustrate how far from reasonableness this particular argument has strayed, permit me to quote from an article[1] by an Orthodox woman who should know better:

> "In an attempt to close the gap between men's power and women's powerlessness in the divorce issue, the rabbis tried hard, but not hard enough. *It would have taken a little more collective maturity to close the gap altogether.* (Italics mine — Y.F.) This leads one to conclude that, in their heart

---

1. Published in *Lilith* Magazine, Summer 1977.

of hearts, many would like the gap to exist, apologies not withstanding."

In other words, "There is no Rabbinic will."

If these women — and their advocates — would but be aware of the *teshuvos* written on behalf of *agunos* they could never write such drivel.[1] I heard from my *Rosh Hayeshivah*, Rabbi Ruderman ז״ל, that the very last act that Rabbi Yitzchok Elchonon Spektor, the Kovna *Rav*, performed from his death-bed, was to write a *teshuvah* to permit an *agunah* to remarry... It is told that Rabbi Moshe Feinstein ז״ל suffered from a stomach ailment. Every time he had to deal with an *agunah* question, it is used to flare up because Reb Moshe took the woman's plight personally. He felt that he had to find a *hetter*, but he could not fabricate a *halachah*. Yet these militant feminists claim that the rabbis don't care!

To claim that the rabbis do not have compassion is comparable to saying that an oncologist who cannot cure a cancer is indifferent to the plight of the patient. The problem is that the *halachos* of *gittin* and *agunos* are complex. They deal with the termination of one marriage, and the feasibility of entering another one — no light matter. The classical *agunah* case involves reconstructing an event on the basis of incontrovertible evidence, without the benefit of conventional witnesses. An area fraught with severe prohibitions, it is no field for well-meaning amateurs or politically-motivated agitators. It calls for vast knowledge, years of *shimush* (apprenticeship of *poskim* in the field), and *breite pleitzes* (a sense of responsibility broadened by years of study, experience and resolve). The greatest scholars in every era devoted their vast talents and energies to resolving such problems. For example, the late *Dayan* Yitzchok Weiss of the *Eidah Hachareides* distinguished himself with his exceptional accomplishments in freeing large numbers of *agunos* following World War II from their paralyzing status through his tireless efforts, investigation and expertise in *halachah*.

---

1. Another example: "It is precisely this Rabbinic will that merits more attention... who are the rabbis whose will we are to consider? And is it not possible that the will of even the best of them derives from sources not altogether impeccable mistakes of fact, mistakes in judgment and even personal feelings not necessarily saintly?" from Rabbi Emanuel Rackman's nationally syndicated column, including New York's *Jewish Week*, January 12, 1990.

By the same token, attempting to force the hand of a husband who is withholding a *get* flirts with the same highly sensitive areas of *halachah*, as will be discussed in the next section.

⋅§ Prenuptial Agreement

For years now, some have proposed the idea of drafting a prenuptial agreement to be incorporated into the *tena'im* (premarital contract). Briefly, it would state that in the event of the breakdown of the marriage, the wife would receive a large sum of money should the husband refuse to grant her a *get*.

This approach would seem to assure that a husband would not leave his estranged wife stranded without a *get*. Why, indeed, can't this be done? Unfortunately, this approach has serious problems. For this agreement to have teeth, it would have to be enforceable in secular courts, and according to legal experts in the U.S., this type of agreement is probably not enforceable in most jurisdictions. In legal terms, it would not stand up in the courts. Moreover, the halachic ruling of *asmachta lo kanya* applies here; meaning that if a person obligates himself, but thinks that he will never have to pay the obligation, it is not considered binding. (This is the same reasoning that underlies prohibitions against gambling, quite apart from the ethical-*mussar* factor.)

Moreover, if a person swears to give a *get*, or otherwise places himself under circumstances of coercion, this may become a *get me'usah* — a *get* not issued willingly, and thus invalid. The problem is complex and intricate. A workable solution has not yet been found. This does not necessarily mean that the situation is without solution. But one thing is certain: Proposed solutions must meet with the approval and sanction of *Gedolei Hador, Gedolei Haposkim*, the leading Torah authorities of our time.

Rabbi Elya Svei, שליט״א, the Philadelphia *Rosh Hayeshiva*, once commented: The *Gemara*, in *Derech Eretz Zuta*, relates that Rabbi Akiva said, "At the time when I first started learning, I found a *meis mitzvah* (an unattended corpse), and I carried the body four miles to bury it." When he proudly told this to his *Rebbeim*, they responded, "With each step you took, you committed an *aveirah*, because the *halachah* says that a *meis mitzvah* must be buried right where it is found." As a result, Rabbi Akiva said, "*Lo zazti mishimush chachamim* — I never ceased being an apprentice to the Sages." Without the guidance of *Gedolei haTorah*, what one thinks is a *takanah* — a positive ordinance — might instead be a *kilkul* — destructive.

The sub-theme of this discussion is "a Jew thinks differently," and we may add to that, "A *Gadol* thinks differently." What we may deem to be a good and kosher proposal could in fact be disastrous. Our solution could inadvertently cause more harm than good.

In the time of Reb Meir Simcha Hakohein (the Ohr Somayach), a secular Jew was charged with making communal policy in his region. At the outbreak of World War I, he came up with a creative idea: The Germans were moving East, taking over town after town; they were laying waste to the communities, confiscating the Sifrei Torah and burning them. This fellow proposed leaving every community with one Sefer Torah and collecting the rest to be sent to St. Petersburg for safekeeping. A brilliant plan!

He approached Reb Meir Simcha in Dvinsk for his cooperation, but he refused categorically. Reb Meir Simcha quoted the Chazal: Tzeddakah assah Hakadosh Baruch Hu leYisroel, shepizram bein ha'umos — G-d acted charitably with the Jews by scattering them among the nations. He then added, "We are more secure when we are spread out, and I won't permit putting all our assets in one depository."

The war was lost by the Germans, but when the Communists took over Russia, all those Sifrei Torah that had been stored in St. Petersburg were lost.

The communal leader seemed to have had the right solution at the time, but a *Gadol* can *feel* what is right with his heightened sensitivity before formulating policy or drafting *takanos*.

◆§ A Ray of Hope

Because of the severity of the problem, we dare not relax our efforts and tell ourselves that since no definitive halachic solution is as yet available, nothing can be done. Even if the halachic avenue is complex and for the moment unclear, certain social means are at our disposal for exerting pressure on recalcitrant husbands. *We cannot do everything, but that is no excuse not to do anything.* Specifically, when it has been determined by a duly constituted *beis din* that the husband must give a *get*, and that the husband either fails to appear before that *beis din* or refuses to obey the *p'sak* of that *beis din* (and as such, has the status of not being a *tzayis dinah*), that husband should face the most severe form of social ostracism that a community can muster. For instance, *no Rav* should permit that husband to receive an *aliyah* or *daven* before the *amud* or say *Kaddish* in his *shul*. This man should also face various forms of social humiliation until he agrees to grant the *get*. (As long as these means are not linked or tied to the mention of giving a *get*, it is not considered a *get me'usah*.)

Unfortunately, the above approach is not always feasible. Such a person can easily find another *shul* or another neighborhood and become a member there, no questions asked. (Generous contributions always help.)

Even more disgusting is the scenario of this scoundrel "buying himself a *beis din*" which rules in his favor, thereby saving himself from the title of a *lo tzayis dinah*, in effect making the above mentioned sanctions impossible.

When we lived in our land and had our own judicial system of *batei dinim* with ultimate authority, such travesties did not take place. But in *Golus*, things are not as they should be. Thus, when we are *mispallel* three times a day: "*Hashivah shofteinu kevarishona* — Return to us our judges as we once had," it is to rid ourselves of all the plagues of *Golus*, including the tragic plight of the *agunah*. When we mourn the *churban* of the *Beis Hamikdash*, we should also mourn the *churban* of our societal integrity. In the meantime, however, we must continue to seek social cures for what is essentially a social malaise.

◆§ Cooperative Conversions

We have stated that *halachah* does not change. In its immutable form, it has kept us together, and preserved us as a nation. Now we are faced with a proposal to establish a joint Orthodox-Conservative-Reform commission to deal with non-Jews who would like to convert to Reform or Conservative Judaism. These potential converts would be referred to an Orthodox *beis din* for *geirus* (similar to the discredited Denver Conversion Plan; see JO, Jan. '84). Why should this long-abandoned plan be revived? "As a *takanah*, for the sake of *achdus*, unity of the Jewish People," its proponents cry. A worthy goal, but the plan is a sham.

The *halachah* requires that to convert, one must have true

kaballas hamitzvos, complete acceptance of all the *mitzvos*. The *halachah* is clear: If one is *mekabel* all the *mitzvos* except for even one *deRabannan* (a *mitzvah* of Rabbinical origin), the *kabbalas mitzvos* is invalid. The leading Rabbinic figure of pre-World War II Europe, Reb Chaim Ozer Grodzenski זצ״ל, *paskened* that a candidate for *geirus* who is *misgayer* even through bona fide *Rabbanim*, but does not have true intentions to keep *kashrus*, is not a true *ger*. Do the authors of the above-mentioned proposal really believe that when a Reform Rabbi has informed a non-Jewish candidate of his obligations as a Jew, and has not included belief in *Torah min haShamayim* (the Divine origin of Torah), that his acceptance of Judaism is valid? Should we be partners in this illusion, and help perpetrate this fiction for *Shalom*, peace? The suggestion is so absurd as not even to be worthy of discussion.

Ha'emes vehashalom e'ehavu — Truth and Peace must be paired together. *Emes* without *Shalom* is worthless. "*Lo matza Hakodosh Baruch Hu kli machzik brachah elah haShalom.*" *Shalom* is the ultimate receptacle for blessings. But we must also examine what else it contains. If its contents are fraudulent, of what value is the container?

The Kotzker *Rebbe* commented on the following Midrash: The *Ribbono Shel Olam* wanted to create the world, and asked *Chessed*, "Should I create the world?" *Chessed* answered, "Yes, *sheha'olam kulo Chessed*, the world is full of loving-kindness."

He went to *Emes*, and *Emes* said: "Don't create the world, because the world is full of *shekker* — falsehood."

He consulted *Tzeddakah*, and *Tzeddakah* responded, "Yes, *sheha'olam kulo Tzeddakah*, the world subsists on charity."

When he went to *Shalom*, *Shalom* said: "Don't create the world. It will be full of *machlokes*."

It was two against two. The *Midrash* says that G-d threw *Emes* down and created the world.

Said the Kotzker *Rebbe*, "But what did G-d do with the opposition of *Shalom*?" The pungent response: "*Onn Emes is Shalom shoin gring* — without *Emes*, *Shalom* is easy to achieve."

We want *Shalom* as much as anyone else. But we want *Shalom shel Emes*, a peace based on Torah truth — that which has kept us together and preserved us since time immemorial.

Nama Frenkel

Music –
By and For a Jewish Woman

*Asking Questions
When I Know the Answers*

RECENTLY, IN A *Shabbos*-table discussion with Rabbi Mordecai Twerski of Denver, I remarked somewhat self-righteously that when I hear stories, albeit beautiful ones, about Chassidim visiting their Rebbe for *Yom Tov*, I can't help thinking about their wives who stayed home. "And what kind of *Yom Tov* did they have?" I demanded.

He reminded me of a fact that I already knew. I ask this question often, always receiving the same answer: "Nama, don't judge their time by imposing our social limitations. Their mothers and aunts and grandmothers lived upstairs, next door and downstairs. A *Yom Tov* in a *shtetl* offered dimensions and a variety of experience we can barely imagine. They might find our life unbearable—living as we do isolated in our little families, far from everyone, worried about privacy."

Of course, he was right. So why do I keep asking this question? I'd say that I find myself worrying about the isolation of other women because I feel isolated in what I do as a woman. In spite of the hours spent on the telephone, the meetings, the *tzedaka* work, taking the kids places together, and even the unique intimacy generated in a bungalow colony, I still cannot feel that I share in the lives of other women. I'm not really talking about loneliness. I have friends, thank G-d. What I miss, ironically, is the sense of family-community my *shtetl* sister had when her husband went away for *Yom Tov*. I feel as though my *avodah* — service to G-d — as a Jew depends on finding it.

My Rebbe, Rabbi B.C. Shloime Twerski זצ"ל, often said, "Geniuses are created before the age of six." He usually went on to explain that the important qualities a person possesses — curiosity, determination, trust and *Yiras Shomayim* (fear of G-d) — are learned at home. He refused to be defensive about the so-called "woman's role" in creating a home, saying that maybe we've never really tried to figure out what the Torah thinks, but simply imposed our private agendas. One thing he was sure of, though, was that most women possesses a special capacity for creating and changing the "emotional environment" that they exist in. It was this "feel" for the subliminal that gives them an edge in creating a home where it "feels" Jewish. It was the talent for bringing the ideas of Torah into every nuance of everyday life, and into the inner workings of the personality that was referred to in the fundamental phrase, "*Kol kavoda bas melech pnima* — The princess's glory is within."

Practically speaking, a greater use of our human potential ought to be possible when we learn with the joy and curiosity fostered in a balanced emotional environment. Our academic learning of Torah could be backed up with an ability to concentrate our total selves. Our resistance to subliminal influences from billboards and stores — even people — ought to be higher. We ought to be able to encounter both success and failure with a greater sense that we're not alone. All because we have a "Jewish Home."

☙ "Feeling Inadequate and a Little Frightened..."

I'm supposed to be responsible for all that! Frankly I feel inadequate and a little frightened because, from the day I left seminary where we talked about these things, I've had very little chance to "brush up" on just how that environment is created. I may have innate ability as a woman, but I need colleagues to go beyond *seforim*, as valuable as they are, and into the laboratory of human example, where I can learn with all my senses for a job that requires all my senses.

I'm looking for a way to draw on the experiences of others. Many of the questions I would ask other women, if we could really talk, are matters I could learn better subliminally. *How do other mothers discipline their children, how do they teach them? More importantly, how do they settle arguments with their husbands, how do they face tragedies, what do they daven for and when do they find the time?* Some of us are lucky enough to have mothers who are in themselves the answers to those questions. I hope they can be the same for their daughters.

I didn't learn those answers from my mother, I don't know whether she knew them, but I would like to teach them to my daughters. My real question, it seems, ought to be: *What can we do to build Jewish womanhood, so we can produce more geniuses, more excited, creative children filled with the wonder of the Ribbono-shel-olam's world?*

Rebbetzin Sara Freifeld, ע"ה, like many great teachers of women, knew that learning for women had to include practical advice about how to develop that "inner guidance system." In the content of her curriculum, she emphasized *Tehillim* and *tefilla* — psalms and prayer — an education we could put to use every day. In her teaching style, she constantly emphasized the real-life component, pausing often with observation about child raising, husband raising, etc. She expected us to participate in our community; doing a *chessed* was unquestionably part of our assignment as her students. In her presence, I felt a sense of sisterhood with all Jewish women, a current of connection that extended to *Har Sinai* and before. With her inspiration, it all seemed possible. But she's not here now and I often wonder about ways to really communicate that feeling. After all, it's not words alone that say it.

"I Sat Down and Cried..."

I had a hint when I heard a record called "Ashira, Songs By and For Jewish Woman." Jewish records have a very special place in creating our environment. For many women looking for a concrete way that our toddlers can imbibe Torah even before they make their first *berachos*, records like *The Mitzvah Tree, 613 Torah Avenue*, or the albums from groups playing what I call for lack of a better term *"chassana* music," offer a real tool. If you cannot quite manage to entertain your children as much as you would want, you feel a little better knowing they are clapping and dancing, or just humming as they bang the pots or build with blocks. I approach every new Jewish album with excitement. It's a new companion — a little energizer — when I have to wash a huge stack of *Shabbos* dishes or clean the floor. It reminds not just my kids, but me, that all this means something; keeping a Jewish home clean has a purpose far beyond "keeping up with the Rosens."

I have to admit I sat down and cried when I heard *Ashira*. I've been told my reaction was not uncommon. It was relief I felt. Someone is speaking about my life, my questions, my joys. Things only a woman would think of. And always tied to Torah. I listened to it day and night and bought copies for all my friends, who felt exactly as I did.

The songs deal with things only women would wonder about! Like how did the Jews manage to get packed to leave Egypt on such short notice, and how did Miriam manage to remember her tambourine?

> *How did she know that on this journey*
> *There would be cause to sing?*
> *Take the baby, Sara*
> *and wrap him up real tight*
> *Leah, get the baskets*
> *we're leaving here tonight*
> *Avi, bring my tambourine*
> *And take your father's hand*
> *We are going from this land*
> *far across the desert sand.*
> English lyrics and music: 1983, © Ashira

I personally have two favorites, "Two People," a song about marriage, and "Letters and Spaces," which talks about the fact that G-d's presence is hidden within His Torah. Both rely heavily on very haunting lyrics and marvelous music to communicate what I, with my description, cannot. Many of her pieces will have a surprisingly universal appeal among Jewish women of all backgrounds. Others that are directed to the searching woman from Western society are in a contemporary idiom, and might prove jarring to some ears. I find them all of a refreshing immediacy.

⌘ A Tenuous Breakthrough

The record represents a breakthrough for Jewish women because it is by and for the principles that rule our lives. It is recorded under a pen name, so that if a man would hear it, he would not know who he was hearing and thus further reduce the *kol isha* factor. "*Kol isha*" — the prohibition for a man to listen to a women singing — does not apply to a recorded voice, according to many authorities. While Ashira is acting under halachic guidance, some may find this recording an imprudent breakthrough in making a woman's singing available on a mass-marketed basis. I suppose that just as some irreligious Jews will ignore the caveat "Do not play on the Sabbath and Festivals" that appears on many records of "religious music," others will ignore Ashira's intention of making this record exclusively "By and For Jewish Women." My comments are on my personal reaction to discovering this record.

The concerts that Ashira gives are even more exciting. First, consider what doesn't happen. No men are allowed. Not the janitor, not even the Prime Minister. "Don't you know what you're giving up? Do you know how many groups would be *honored* to be asked to play at the President's reception?" she has been asked.

Ashira is a Jewish woman first, a performer second.

⌘ Where All Women Are Sisters, Mothers, Aunts...

She's not the only one. Women have gotten together to play and sing in huge women-only concerts several times in New York and in Jerusalem, in the past few years.

To me her concerts are special. I hear that ladies with *sheitels* sit next to girls in blue jeans, in Moshe's Cafe in Jerusalem, on Monday night, women's night. Moshe doesn't come.

The girl in blue jeans may have never been in any group that's exclusively women. She's never met a lady with a *sheitel*. She's on vacation in Jerusalem, from Kansas or California, maybe even Brooklyn. Some vague inkling brought her.

The lady with the *sheitel*, on the other hand, very seldom gets a chance to go somewhere for entertainment that she really feels is Kosher. She hates to take her husband away from learning, but what can she do that's relaxing that isn't for couples? When she talks to the girl in blue jeans during the break, she's surprised to find she has wisdom to share; and that for once this college girl who intended to have no children at all is willing to listen.

At a women's concert, all Jewish women are sisters and aunts and nieces, grandmothers and granddaughters to one another, brought together in a setting that really opens the way for talking about the things we somehow never get a chance to discuss.

I am not suggesting Ashira or any singer or musician will replace asking advice from a Rebbetzin, G-d forbid, or saying *Tehillim* or learning. Ashira herself seeks out all these things, as should every Jewish woman. She also manages to put the feeling and struggle of doing those and other *mitzvos* into a form that reaches us beyond the limits of our intellect. She touches us on the level we have to operate on as women, if we want to give our full power to the words of Torah we have learned. She calls us to take our goals seriously and gives us tools to do so.

If we think about the fact that G-d reveals Himself through history, we can find some significance here. After the destruction of European Jewry, it is not enough to rebuild yeshivos, schools, and *mikvaos* — as vital as those things are. We need to build the sense of community, the sense of family. This is up to women. If a spirit or a movement sweeps the world that says "women should take responsibility for their lives," let us consider the revelation that is in it, not the many distortions. Within our community, we can show the world that Jewish women understand what it means to take *real* responsibility for the world and its future. Maybe by creating our own music, and getting together to share our lives as sisters while we listen to it, we'll be able to hear and use the message our mothers have passed down since Sara, and our husbands will be able to fulfill "*Shma b'kolah* — hearken to her voice" (See *Bereishis* 21:12).

Bracha Druss Goetz

Wonder Woman

I worked hard just to make them all so proud
Pre-med grind — way back to spelling tests.
I worked hard just to make them all so proud.
Then they'd know — it would *show* — I was best.
So why'd it always happen I could not convince myself?
Awards just made a hollow sound when placed upon the shelf.
And why'd it always happen that the praises stopped so fast?
Isn't there a goal to reach where my glory will last?

Then one day I got tired of this game
Wonder girl, though you've won, what's it worth?
Then one day I got tired of this game.
Craving more, is it found here on earth?
Well it has not been easy putting old wishes aside.
While washing piles of dishes, my hands burn with swallowed pride.
No, it has not been easy putting old wishes aside.
Though I'm called a mother now, the old dreams never died.

This afternoon it was raining very hard.
My little ones were getting bored — nowhere to go.
This afternoon it was raining very hard
I decided to put on a puppet show.
Lining up their kiddie chairs, they sat there in a row.
I peeked out at them a moment and their faces were aglow.
Lining up their kiddie chairs, they sat there in a row.
Their eyes were full of wonder as they watched my puppet show.
My whole life I've been waiting for applause.
Well it came — and it's true — it was great.
My whole life I've waited for *this* applause.
Their little hands — clapping for joy — were worth the wait
If I could only realize that here within these walls
I did something much greater than in all the lecture halls.
If I could only realize that this glory does not leave —
Why are elusive tapestries the hardest to unweave?

❧ She Longs for the Whole Family

High in the Hills of Yerushalyim
A Daughter Recalls a Great Father
Rebbetzin Henkin and Me
Avraham's Household
Letter in Response
This Side of the Fence
Letters to the Editor
Love and Marriage
A Private Waterloo
The Battle for the Jewish Family
Sidney (Also Known as Steven)
Invisible Ledgers
Life-styles of the Childless Poor
Jewish Kids up for Grabs
My Children's Brother
Reflections of a Parent
Dear Mom
An Open Letter to My Questioning Friend
Kids on the Fringe
Letter in Response
The Seed of Hope

Malky Brailofsky

High in the Hills of Yerushalayim

High in the hills of Yerushalayim
Where the sky is ever a cloudless blue
And children dance in the sparkling sun
My Zaidy and Bubby chose to dwell
For reasons only they can tell
Leaving their children so far away.
Will we see you again? Who can say?

High in the hills of Yerushalayim
Where echoes of Torah fill the streets
And *kedushah* feels completely at home
My Zaidy wears his *tefillin* home from *shul*
The *sefer* in his hands is a willing tool
He turns its pages, caressing each one
His eyes shining like the brilliant sun
But he's white-haired, frail, and he trembles with age.
What more can he offer us at this stage?

High in the hills of Yerushalayim
Where women go to the *shuk* to shop
And strollers fill the back of the bus
My Bubby sits at the window and stares out
Wishing to go and venture about
But her years forbid her to do so on her own.
Can old age be sweet when one feels so alone?

Deep in the darkness of Germany
Where Jewish life once grew and thrived
And our great *gedolim* learned and taught
My Zaidy was young! My Zaidy was strong!
His life was a harmony of Jewish song!
My Bubby was lively! My Bubby was gay!
She had too many tasks to do in one day!
The years of their life still lay ahead.
Will they shine with success as one life's path they tread?

Deep in the darkness of Germany
Where the Nazis destroyed all that was ours
And flames reduced Jewish homes to ashes
My Zaidy's family all breathed their last breath
Every one was led to his death
He alone lived to see Germany die
He had a goal, a dream to live by
He and his wife would continue to build
In spite of Hitler, who thought all'd been killed
They would plant a tall tree whose branches would spread.
Who could count the generations that lay ahead?

High in the hills of Yerushalayim
Where a summer spent is a golden gift
And just walking the streets is a joy
My Zaidy and Bubby were taken by surprise
You should have seen the delight in their eyes
As my husband and I walked through their door.
Is this not what they have lived for?

Sitting in the sun of Yerushalayim
I stared at my Zaidy and wondered
I looked at my Bubby and shook my head
Could it be the talk back home was true,
"You'll have to teach them your names anew
Their minds have dulled, comprehension is weak
They won't understand the words you will speak."
I smiled at my Bubby and she smiled at me.
Was this all I had come to see?

Sitting in the sun of Yerushalayim
My Zaidy suddenly glanced at his watch

Then he rose to his full height
He said to us, his face aglow with bliss,
"In New Jersey, right now, is Yitzchok's son's Bris.
I was one lone *neshomah* many years past
When I planted a tree and made it fast
We are now one hundred and fourteen souls."
"And Zaidy," I said, "the tree still grows."
I left that day with an opened eye.
Hadn't Zaidy taught that the Jewish nation does not die?

Adele Engel

A Daughter Recalls a Great Father

I SEE MY FATHER seated with his *gemara* in our book-lined study where he spent almost every waking moment he could spare from his other duties of the day. This was his sanctuary, and of a quiet evening — with the younger children asleep — my mother would join him with her sewing. Occasionally she would look up and smile and exchange a word with him.

This was the family harmony that permeated our home, as I remember it. Father was the dominating, quiet focus of our life, with our mother the ever-present smiling buffer between the lively activities and noise of nine children with their problems and varying activities. Our father's deep *Yiras Shomayim* and love of Torah were the guideposts of much of our development.

He was ever available to us. The three meals each day were family gatherings where we aired views and exchanged news, with our father listening, smiling and advising. Ours was a lively family — no limits were put on our conversation until a hint of *lashon hara* would reach his ears. With a word or a look he was able to put an end to any expressions which bordered on *lashon hara* or *rechilus*. And so we were early taught by example the trait of guarding one's speech.

Seated at the head of the table, we anticipated his needs, for in all his life, father never *requested* anything at his own table. Unless it was provided, he would go without food; he often said to us,

"Never ask for anything, unless it be given to you voluntarily."

Shabbos and *Yom Tov* were focal points of our lives. How I longingly recall the Friday evening when our father — in our beautiful large dining room — presided over the long table with gleaming silverware, the children ranged by age along the table. His high melodious voice rang out at *Shalom Aleichem* when we stood, with our mother at his side, each child grasping one finger of his hand, as a tree with the branches springing from its roots. Each blessing with his hand resting on our head was given with such warmth and feeling that his words permeated our whole being and created in us — even at a very young age — the *Shabbos* spirit which *we* in turn have tried to impart to our children. No *Shabbos* meal was complete in our home without two or three guests. They came from far and wide whether it was a *yeshivah bachur*, or a famous *rav* from the East. A procession of fascinating travelers, scholars, writers and rabbis graced the Rosenheim table every *Shabbos*.

I recall our excitement and interest when an outstanding *rebbe* would be our *Shabbos* guest. His *shtraimel* or *tallis* or coat would be in our keeping until after *Shabbos*, so once or twice we could not resist snipping off a small piece or thread of a garment as a memento of an unforgettable visit. From East or West — every guest in our home was a king in his own right — the *Shabbos* at the Rosenheims was an experience not easily forgotten.

In his earlier years and in my earlier recollection, Father often traveled away from home in connection with his work for *Klal Yisrael*. He would always return home in time for Shabbos. In our possession today is — as we called it — "fathers *sefarim* suitcase." It is a small object and battered, proof of frequent use. On one occasion, at least, this suitcase had to be left at home, much to our father's chagrin. Prior to a trip to Poland, he was informed of a border restriction which did not permit foreign language books into Poland. Our father recalled with a smile and relish how his essential two or three *sefarim*, without which he would not travel were smuggled into that country. A kind lady, sharing his train compartment spirited them across the border —at his request — *in her personal hatbox*.

Forever mindful of his family and the importance and impact of a *Yom Tov* celebration, our father introduced and continued a *minhag* for each of the *Shalosh Regalim*. Each family member —

the servants included — received a personally selected *sefer*, appropriate to his age and interest. All his children own many books of lasting value, each with his loving personal inscription, ranging from children's stories by M. Lehmann to newly published rare *sefarim*. His satisfaction and contentment at our expressions of joy is part of our warmest memory.

It is well known that the *Gedolei Yisrael* honored our father with the unusual title of *Moreinu*. It is, however, not known that no one in his home was every permitted to discuss or even mention this honor. Some time after this memorable *Knessia Gedolah* we found the folded parchment document hidden in the *far back* recesses of one of his bookcases.

My mother, always his companion and confidante, often was torn between her great pride in him and the humility he wanted everyone to show concerning any honors or tributes he was awarded. On the many occasions of an address, lecture or *shiur* to large audiences, we, his family, were always seated in the rear row of the hall or room. This was an unspoken rule in our family — never requested by father, but showing him our understanding of *his* and therefore, *our* concept of living, forever shunning pride or ostentatious behavior.

Our father was known as an outstanding orator. His speeches were masterworks of organized thought which held his audiences spellbound for as long as an hour or even two. And yet, after such an address, we would find a small while 2x2 card in his pocket with perhaps four or five points arranged by number, penciled in his beautiful Germanic script.

We left Germany in 1935 after two years of living under the Hitler regime. Nothing has every been told of the actual circumstances of our flight or of our father's difficulties prior to his departure.

Father was greatly respected by the city government and police authorities of our native city Frankfurt-am-Main. As publisher of a German-language weekly newspaper, he had frequent and cordial contacts with the authorities. At one point, early in the Hitler regime, he published an editorial expressing his dissatisfaction with an order to all Jews (as well as all citizens) to fly the German flag in celebration of some Nazi anniversary. This resulted in a peremptory summons on *Shabbos* morning to police headquarters — a walk of three-quarters of an hour. I accompanied

Father on this walk on an icy cold winter *Shabbos*. We had spared my mother any knowledge of this, and set out on what may well have been the road to a prison or concentration camp. I will never forget our conversation, warm and yet casual on my personal problems, on my school studies as well as the *Parshah of the Week*. He was calm as always, exuding faith as always. As we were about to enter the imposing Police building, he turned to me: "Wait for me here; if I have not returned within thirty minutes, you will know where I am. Return home and be of good cheer." The Almighty was with us and we returned home together after he was issued a "warning" to "temper" his editorials.

Our actual departure from Germany was caused by a set of circumstances, known to few people. We had returned on a Friday morning from a trip to Holland. We were told of the shocking morning edition of *the Voelkischer Beobachter*, the leading Nazi-newspaper, which had splashed across the front page our father's name and that of two other Agudah leaders (one already out of the country, another passed on). They were accused of being traitors to the Third Reich and of having plotted behind the scenes against the Nazi regime. It was almost *Shabbos*. Uncertain of the consequences, our father left his home again for a small town nearby to avoid possible arrest and yet not to desecrate the *Shabbos*. After *Shabbos* he continued his journey to Berlin where he learned the origin of the newspaper attack.

In early 1933 Father, with other Agudah leaders had an audience with the Pope in the Vatican to discuss a possible Nazi victory and to try to forestall utter disaster. One of the printed reports of this meeting issued to top Agudah leaders was lost in a hotel room in Berlin and found by a member of the Nazi party. Two years later the report was sold to the highest bidder — the infamous *Voelkischer Beobachter*.

Father returned home and quietly continued his work untouched by the fear of those around him, his deep faith unshaken as ever. He had friends amongst notorious Nazis and the local government. Guided by their old past friendship and their deep-seated respect, the "powers to be" issued their "last warning" and thus *Moreinu* Rosenheim was put on the infamous Nazi "blacklist". Two months later, we were on our way to England and thus new Agudah World Headquarters were established in London.

A Daughter Recalls a Great Father

Joanne Jackson Yelenik

Rebbetzin Henkin and Me
– A Story

THE DEPARTURE LOUNGE of El Al terminal is full. I try, without too much success, to divert my attention from the knot in my stomach and the tightness in my throat, by looking around and discovering who my son's traveling companions will be. Here, an old women is being embraced by two toddlers. Over there, in the corner, a middle-aged man gently touches the cheek of a younger man who resembles him strikingly. Small groups huddle together, talking enthusiastically and then, without warning, falling silent. Suddenly, it hits me. The departure lounge is a metaphor for *galus*. The history of our separations whether voluntary or involuntary, is dramatized and recreated in this airport setting. My eyes return once more to look upon the sweet, handsome face of my son.

He is leaving now, for the second time in five months, to go to yeshiva in Israel. His first departure, in August, was so overwhelming as to be indescribable. This visit of two weeks, to share in a family *simchah*, emphasized the reality of the good-byes, but also left my husband and me with wonderful memories and a clearer understanding of what our son's yeshivah life is like. We embrace, each of us trying to be braver than the other. " 'Til Pesach," my son says, and the Jewish calendar I have come to love takes on still deeper meaning. *"Gey gezunt und kum gezunt,"* I say, remembering from an unknown past, and the salutations of my father and aunt, the few words of Yiddish I mastered, and which remain in my sub-conscious mind for occasions like these when English is useless.

As I stand watching the now empty-space where my son stood on the security-check line, my glance takes in the many black-coated figures boarding the plane. At least, I think, he will have a *minyan*. The thought makes me smile for the first time in what seems like hours. I guess I am becoming a real *Yiddishe Mamma*.

Once again I scan the figures in the departure lounge, those with whom I have shared such a peak moment. I search out the women in *sheitels* and the men in *kipot* and hats. They look familiar to me, or maybe it is that I just long for companionship. My eyes rest on one man accompanied by a small child, his daughter. He smiles. As remarkable as it may be, it turns out that we do know one another. His wife, who has just boarded the plane, is a friend of mine. My husband and he exchange greetings. I being to tell him some of my feelings. "Let me tell you a story," he says. The vision of this family's Shabbos table appears before my eyes. I remember our discussions on *Yiddishkeit* lasting far into the night. Almost all of them begin with this man saying: "Let me tell you a story."

"There was this very famous and revered rabbi from the Lower East Side: Rabbi Yosef Eliyahu Henkin, by name. He was very wise. When this rabbi was about twelve years old, he was asking questions that proved very difficult to his teachers, and he realized that he had learned all he could in the tiny *shtetl* where he lived. He decided he had to go to a large yeshiva all the way on the other side of the country from where he lived. Times were hard, and he had no money, so he chose to walk there."

I think, *What could it have been like for him, walking in the freezing cold, across a land? What if his shoes fell apart? Perhaps he was able to make the hard decisions for the Yidden of his times because of this walk that he took at twelve years old.*

"You know," the man continues, "when you were talking now about your son, and when you happened to mention even the number of the seat he was assigned, I thought of this rabbi's mother and of how little she knew about what was happening to her son while he walked from one end of the country to another to reach yeshiva."

As we continued speaking, I felt more and more the presence of this woman: *What did she pack for her son to carry with him? What thoughts of him did she have as she went through her daily chores, as she thought of him when she prayed? What would this* woman think of us, the mothers of today's yeshiva boys? Would she smile at the voluminous packages of food substances and clothing articles sent from America to Israel? Would she think we were foolish? Would she marvel, as I do, at the blessing of the telephone bringing our sons' voices to us? Would she tenderly remind me, who is new to this way of life, of the tradition of sending one's son off to yeshiva? Would her voice join with those of my own grandmothers and great-grandmothers who would joyously clasp me to them, telling me how happy they were to know that in today's world of choice that my son and I had chosen the old patterns, which is tried and true?

One of the luxuries of being a *baalas teshuva* is that in the search for one's *frum* past, one can adopt along the way any number of pseudo-relations — that is, those from our common Jewish ancestry whose life histories touch you or provide you with something that you do not have from your own background. In such moments, like this one in the airport lounge, one welcomes someone new to the family tree, just as I now make Rebbetzin Henkin, with all due respect and affection, one of my own. My sense of her missing her son, of her longing for him, of her wondering how he was progressing in yeshiva is as much a part of me as is my sense of my own grandmother's efforts to make *cheder* a pleasant experience for my father, which unfortunately it was not, and of my grandfather's devotion to a Law which he could study in only the most elementary fashion.

Yes, Rebbetzin Henkin is a wonderful addition to my store of figures who, by the example of their lives, teach me how to set priorities and formulate goals. Yes, it is good to have Rebbetzin Henkin as a resource, good to be able to call up her memory and the strength of her character on cold, winter nights, and before lighting candles on *Shabbos*. Oh, and yes, it will be good to have her with me, in my heart and soul, at other times, in the departure lounge of the El Al terminal.

Fayge Osnat Levy

Avraham's Household

*Relating to Jews
of Different Backgrounds*

✑ Love the Hungry

"THERE WILL COME a day when I shall send a hunger into the land; [it shall be] neither a hunger for bread, nor a thirst of water, but for the words of G-d" (*Amos* 8:11). This is surely an apt description of the *teshuvah* phenomenon emerging in so many parts of the world today.

A less-known side to the *teshuvah* movement is the significant number of non-Jews who are also seeking something more satisfying than bread or water, and are finding it in Orthodox Judaism.

Gerei tzeddek (converts) are not new to Jewish history. The number of great people who were converts, as well as their influence on the Jewish nation, is phenomenal. From Yisro, Moshe Rabbeinu's father-in-law, to Ovadiah the Prophet, through Shmaya and Avtalyon, teachers of Hillel and Shammai...from Tzipporah and Rachav (wives of Moshe and Joshua) through Ruth the Moabite, great-grandmother of David — converts have been prominent amongst Jewry's leaders. This was all merely history to me until the day I befriended a very special woman in Jerusalem and learned that she was a *gioret tzeddek* (female convert).

Since then, my awareness of the unique qualities and singular problems of *geirim* has increased considerably. What do today's righteous converts have in common with their distinguished "ancestors"? They have a high level of sensitivity, which means that they are attracted to truth and repulsed by corruption, immodesty, coarseness and lack of *chessed*. They are courageous people who leave the security of their families and friends (and, often, their countries as well) to break away to live where truth and *chessed* are found in larger quantities.

From Isolation to Psychic Suspension

There are 33 references to converts in the *Tanach* alone, most of them saying something like: "Love the *ger*," and "Do not cause pain to the *ger*" (*Bava Metzia* 59b). No word is superfluous in the *Tanach*. Why should there be so many references to this one *mitzvah?* We can find a clue to the answer in the fact that converts are frequently grouped with widows and orphans in *halachah*.

All three have no family; they are alone in every sense of the word. A convert leaves his family in order to live as a kosher Jew, and the family members will often consider him or her their black sheep. Communication is often broken off for good, effectively ending emotional security and support as far as the family is concerned. Everything from the past is suddenly pulled out from under their feet. *Rashi* speaks of their situation as follows: (*Bamidbar* 5:8 referring to *Sanhedrin* 68b).

"Our rabbis asked: 'But can you find anyone in Israel who has no kinsman whatsoever — neither son nor brother nor other relative...going back as far as Yaakov?' The person referred to is a proselyte."

The *dinim* that deal with the treatment of widows, orphans and converts are saying, in effect, that people who feel isolated need every bit of support and encouragement; and, conversely, every negative word — even those said inadvertently — hurt their recipients much more than they do people who enjoy more secure circumstances.[1] The Torah recognizes this extra sensitivity and deems it so important that it is mentioned thirty-three times.

---

1. About half the converts I have met during my five years in Israel did not have any of the experiences mentioned in this article; the other half did. Again, some of these experiences are familiar to *baalei teshuvah* and a few also to new *olim*.

The sudden loss of support is only the beginning. Next, the *ger* struggles on all levels — she[1] must discard old attitudes and concepts and take on new ones; *midos* must be changed; at least one completely foreign language must be learned (Hebrew), and sometimes a second (men learn Aramaic when they study *Gemara*), and some converts even take on a third, such as Yiddish or Ladino. If Israel was chosen as "home," then there are still more changes. And all this happens at the same time.

This is still not the end. When a convert leaves the *mikveh* with her conversation certificate in her purse, she is officially Jewish and intellectually she knows she is Jewish. But it can take a while for her feelings to catch up with the new status; she has built up an identity for the past 18, or 25, or 35 years, and changing it is not as easy as taking off one jacket and slipping on another. For several years a convert may feel as if she is suspended in mid-air, not belonging not being here or there. This is the identity problem.

৺ Opening up to a Newcomer

What can a well-meaning born-Jew do to give the *ger* a hand? One key word is "understanding"; it cannot be stressed enough. The convert is making a strenuous effort to find a niche in Jewish society. Realize that a perceptive, sensitive person has chosen your group or community because she admires something about it. Maybe it is the *chessed* that attracted her — perhaps it was your group's reputation for learning. Maybe the convert saw the way you live up to your ideals, and wants to be like you. Born-Jews should make the effort, from their side, to understand where the convert is holding with regard to the community.

The second key word is "acceptance". This is a broad, general term with several subcategories, all of equal importance. Welcome is a good starting point. This means the friendly word in the street, the "hello" on the stairs, the small talk in the supermarket checkout line. One of the most important elements here is a smile. It means a lot to a newcomer; it says "I'm glad to see you" (as any new *oleh* can testify).

---

1. I have written in the feminine gender because my contact with converts has been limited to woman.

Conversely, "I'm busy, goodbye," thrown over a shoulder while passing on the sidewalk can hurt. Hurry away, if necessary — but say "hello" and smile. It leaves a warm little memory.

Welcome, too, in your home, if you can. *Shabbos* is an especially good time to invite a single person. Such a visit says "I care," for one thing. It is also an educational opportunity, for it is the only way a convert can see a Jewish home in operation. The non-Jewish home is not the same, and knowledge of how a Jewish home functions cannot be gotten out of books.

If a married convert moves into your neighborhood, talk to her. Invite her for coffee; introduce her to others in the neighborhood. If your neighborhood has a *chessed* organization, include the *ger* in its activities; she may decide to become a participating member.

Invite her to *bar mitzvas*, *brissim*, etc. Let her help you with them, too, if they are small, homey affairs. Introduce her to others at family festivities. If you are too busy as hostess, then introduce her to one of the guests who will make her feel part of the group.

Fortunate is the convert who lives in a *chessed*-oriented neighborhood — and blessed are her neighbors.

☐ **Differences:** Acceptance also means accepting differences, ones that are an inseparable part of a person — part of her package, as it were. Don't come down heavily on things that concern identity, either the old or the (hopefully) budding new one.

The convert wears dresses that are longer than you are used to seeing? Let her — It's not against *halachah*. She might have worn jeans all her life and is now experimenting with styles to see which one is really hers.

She doesn't like some traditional Jewish food? Nothing in the *Shulchan Aruch* says she must. If you went to live in Japan — how would you feel about *sukiyaki* the first (or even the tenth) time it was set in front of you? If she observes *kashrus*, that's quite enough.

She refers her questions to a different *Rav* or *Rebbe* than you do? More power to her, if she has found an approach she feels close to. It is her anchor. Remember, she has given up her family and all the emotional support of a familiar environment. Her Jewish group is her family now and any aspersion on it is painful. (All insistence that your *shitah*, *Rebbe*, or group is *the* one, whether stated subtly or loudly-and-clearly, can be interpreted as aspersion.) If you don't approve of the group, *Rebbe*, *Rav*, *Siddur*, or customs she is in the process of adopting, it is best to say nothing.

Then there are the nuances of social behavior: the customs, the little gestures, reactions, facial and verbal expressions that are so natural and automatic that we are not even conscious of them—until we meet someone who has different ones. The problem here is the unconscious factor; there is something about the new person that is felt as different, and the gut-level reaction can be uneasiness, or even fear. (If you feel this uneasiness or fear because of insignificant differences, imagine how much more uneasy and fearful a convert could feel facing so many monumental differences all the time!)

The antidote, perhaps is *awareness* — awareness of our own reactions and feelings, so as to bring them up out of their hidden depths and examine them in the upper chamber in the light of Torah and reason. At the same time, concentrate on the virtues of the convert, such as courage, and the deep spiritual sense that has drawn him (or her) toward Judaism. Try to find other connecting factors as well, and focus on them.

☐ **Visiting the Sick:** Imagine yourself alone in a little room in Tokyo or Taiwan — with a 103° temperature. Wouldn't you be frightened? So might the convert (or any new *oleh*, for that matter), alone and sick in a little room anywhere in Israel. The average person, secure and comfortable in his own country, may find it difficult to realize that the convert (especially the one who lives in Israel) feels like she is in China. Nothing, but, nothing beats a *bikur cholim* in these circumstances. The convert will bless you for the rest of her life. If you really can't go, pick up the phone and get someone else to go. And while on the phone, why not call and wish her well? Better yet, get several friends to drop in, one each day, to see how the sick person is doing. This is Torah Judaism in action. The convert's reaction is: "They really practice what they preach: I did the right thing by becoming Jewish. I want to be like that, too."

☐ **Help!** The following situation is similar in some ways to the *bikur cholim* one above. A *ger* might come to you, saying that she is in need of urgent help. In Israel, this might mean that she needs to know where there is a room to rent, or a job opening. Or, she might be sick and not know where to turn. She might come to you because, in this particular period of her life, she is sometimes desperately lonely. (A person who has never made a major life change may even be afraid of the feeling of loneliness per se, which is also unfamiliar.)

Why is the convert coming to you? You might be the only address she has. Blessings upon you if you can tell her where to go to get the help she needs — or, better yet, if you can help her yourself.[1]

If you feel overwhelmed by such requests — or if this is your first contact with a convert — the best solution might be to say, "Why not have a cup of tea while I call so-and-so? She might be able to help you."

"I'm busy" or "I don't have time" can deeply wound the convert. Like everyone else, she has dignity and she has had to swallow a considerable portion of it to personally ask a stranger for help. This alone should indicate to you that the situation must be urgent in her eyes. A curt "I'm busy" adds to the humiliation and can compound the identity problem too — for she can feel rejected both as a Jew and as a person (depending on the strength of her new Jewish identity at the time), even though the refusal was not meant that way. She willnot respond this way, however, if you can give a warm smile, a kind word, and a cup of tea. On the contrary, she will go on her way with a blessing for you in her heart and on her lips.

Admittedly, it is not easy to deal with a request for help from someone with whom you feel you have nothing in common. But the Torah (*Mishpatim* 23:5) mandates a course of action that points to a rather extreme example of such a choice: It requires a man to help load a donkey, even when the donkey belongs to an enemy. How much more so must one respond to a request for help from a person you have no rapport with!

Moreover, the *Gemara* puts a preference on helping an enemy load up his donkey over unloading an over-burdened donkey belonging to a friend, because the former would promote control over one's emotions. Our situation, then, offers a twofold opportunity — helping a righteous convert and strengthening one's own *midos* at the same time.

---

1. I had so many questions of my own of this kind, as a new *olah* in Israel, that I started a loose-leaf notebook with helpful addresses, which I now use to help others.

☐ **Hospitality:** Some converts (admittedly, not all) are deeply hurt when a born-Jew comes to their home and refuses to eat or drink. From the convert's point of view, this is another encounter with the identity problem. Illogical, perhaps, but feelings tend toward the illogical.

The convert feels that she is making a supreme effort to keep a super-kosher kitchen, with all the proper *hechsher* labels, and so on, and yet her hospitality is refused. She wonders if she is *treife* or *tamei*, and if her best efforts to become part of Jewish society are to no avail, and if her touch will forever necessitate throwing out the wine.

If you know of such a convert and enjoy her company, ask your *Rav* or *Rebbe* if there is a way you can accept something to eat or drink in her home. If not, it is strongly advised not to visit the home of a convert who might be offended. It would be better to make a date to meet outside, perhaps to plan a shopping trip and end it with a Dutch-treat coffee in a shop of your choice.

☐ **Speech:** Verbal support is important to a person who might feel as isolated as if standing alone in the middle of a desert on legs made of jello. *You long for a wall beside you somewhere, just so you can reach out and touch it once in a while*, I have been told, *for reassurance's sake*.

"Say, that's a nice dress," goes a long way, when the newcomer turns up in a new dress with high collar and low hem.

"I heard you are doing a great job on the *chessed* committee. What exactly do you do?" — is very encouraging.

If I were a man, I would probably be especially glad to hear a sincerely interested "How are the studies coming along?" once in a while.

Encouraging remarks or queries regarding any accomplishment that the convert has managed to rack up in her new life are sure to be appreciated — cooking, sewing, learning, children, *chessed* activities — whatever she happens to be involved in. A convert told me that one of the nicest things anyone ever said to her was that someone admired her courage.

☐ **Lashon Hara:** *Lashon hara* is bad anytime, but it can be especially harmful to anyone with a social disadvantage. When you hear *lashon hara* about a convert, it is a *mitzvah* to speak up in her defense. Remember, she has no one to defend her; blessed is the born-Jew who does.

Lashon hatov is a powerful helping tool. Wherever possible, throw in an extra good word about the convert (and about converts in general).

Sefer Hachinuch (*Mitzvah* 63) comments about the vulnerability of the convert:

"...and he, having entered our Faith, is now an Israelite. *Scripture* added this caption about him for us, and the warning is even repeated, as on another occasion it is written: 'You shall not oppress him [the *ger*]' (*Vayikra* 19:33). For the matter of oppression is close to him (i.e. more likely to happen to him) than to the Israelite, since the Israelite has redeemers (defenders) who would demand satisfaction for his disgrace."

☐ **Face to Face:** When a convert acquaintance of mine became engaged, a woman stopped her and said loudly, in the middle of a crowded area of a neighborhood shopping center, "Oh, I hear you're engaged! Is your *chattan* Jewish?"

This might sound quite extreme, but it can serve as a magnified reflection of the kind of inconsiderate comments that can devastate a convert. What this woman probably meant was, "Is your *chattan* a born-Jew or a convert like yourself?"

So the woman was off-base on two counts: one, the public humiliation; and, two, reminding the girl that she is a convert. The *Midrash* (*Sifra, Vayikra* 19:33) says: "You should not say to him, 'Yesterday you were worshiping idols and now you have entered under the wings of the *Shechinah*.' "

In this instance, the kindest thing would have been to contain curiosity and simply say, "*Mazal tov!* I'm so happy for you!"

Many converts do not want to be reminded, nor have it spread around, that they are converts. Some, however, do not mind. I have met both kinds. How can the born-Jew know which is which? You can't — unless the convert brings it up. Until that moment, however, the best policy is "better safe than sorry."

If a convert is quite open and comfortable about her status, there are "good" questions, which can be thought-provoking for both the convert and the born-Jew. I once heard a joint lecture by two converts on some of these topics, which included: "Why did you do it?" and "What do you find in Judaism?"

Discussing the convert's choice of approach to Judaism, her Rebbe's or *Rav's shitah* and customs are welcome — if asked with sincere, kindly interest. This can be a source of joy and enthusiasm for the newcomer, who may be happy to talk about her newfound "family," her first tenuous emotional link with the Jewish people. And it can be instructive, inspiring, and fascinating for the listener. "What are you reading now?" and "What are you studying?" are also good lead questions.

To sum up with a standing-on-one foot rule, it is best to be as careful not to say negative things about — or to — a convert as you would be regarding what you say about or to your *Rav* and his wife.

☐ **Shidduchim:** Making a *shidduch* is one of the greatest *mitzvos* and even the effort to do so is greatly appreciated by the principals, *if* the effort is made with the utmost tact and thoughtfulness.

Imagine someone telling you about a nice-sounding possibility and you go to the first meeting with high hopes and a light heart. You sit down to talk and all goes well for the first half hour; then the other party leans forward in a confidential manner and says, with a meaningful smile:

"You know, I am the Moshiach" or "I must be extremely cautious. My room is bugged, THEY'RE after me."

A little superficial investigation turns up the obvious: He has just been released from the local mental institution. Worse, yet, is when the discovery is made after the *chupah*.

The might sound like a ludicrous story — but again, it has happened more than once, and to *ba'alei teshuvah*, as well.

If you really want to help a convert with a *shidduch*, *tizku lemitzvos!* But do check out the dates before suggesting them. If you don't know any normal ones, wish the convert well and let her know that you are praying that she will find the right match. *Tefillah* is one of the finest signs of caring.

There is a second type of *shidduch* interaction that falls into the "speech" category. A young friend of mine went to see a highly recommended person about a *shidduch*. This woman concluded the conversation with: "Don't be discouraged; I know of a girl with cerebral palsy who just got married — if she can, so can you!"

Apparently, she thought she was encouraging the convert; instead, the comment turned out to be the last incident in a series that pushed this girl a significant distance from Judaism. What should have been said is something like: "I am sure you will have the Jewish home you want, probably very soon. I will keep looking for you."

☐ **Listening:** A convert is likened to a newborn baby (*Yevamos* 22a). Little children are fascinated by all the new things they discover every day; and so is the convert in her new world. Children like to ask questions and share their exciting discoveries with someone; the same can be said for the convert.

The new Jew's discoveries may include points in Jewish history, *mussar, haskafah, halachah, customs* — or just the happy feeling that life's great under the Wing of the *Shechinah*. A willing ear is a *mitzvah* at these moments.

The convert has questions, too. Her religious questions will most assuredly not be anything like the ones the born-Jew asks his rabbi. You may be shocked by some of them — those that touch on subjects you started learning at age three — or some you never heard of. These queries do not come from *apikorsus* or anything equally threatening, they are just a sign that a new soul is groping for Truth. She is asking you because she doesn't know where else to turn. The best thing to do is to refer her to a Rav who is experienced in dealing with *ba'alei teshuvah*. (Of course, without giving the impression that you are shocked by the question!)

The *Rambam* received numerous questions from converts; two of his letters to them still exist. One, addressed to an anonymous inquirer, concerns a question the convert had asked another rabbi. The *Rambam's* reply follows:

"...When your teacher called you a fool for denying that Moslems are idolaters he sinned previously, and it is fitting that he ask your pardon, though he may be your master. Then let him fast and weep and pray; perhaps he will find forgiveness. Was he intoxicated that he forget the thirty-three passages in which the Law admonishes concerning treatment of 'strangers'? For even if he had been in the right and you in error, it was his duty to be gentle; how much more, when the truth is with you and he was in error?

"And when he was discussing whether a Moslem is an idolater, he should have been cautious not to lose his temper with a righteous convert and put him to shame, for our sages have said, 'He who gives way to his anger is comparable to an idolater.'

"How great is the duty the Law imposes on us with regard to proselytes. Our parents we are commanded to honor and fear; to the prophets, we are commanded to hearken. A man may honor and fear and obey without loving. But in the case of 'strangers,' we are bidden to love with the whole force of our heart's affection. And he called you a fool! Astounding! A man who left father and mother, forsook his birthplace, his country and its power, and attached himself to this lowly, despised, and enslaved race; who recognized the truth and righteousness of this people's law, and cast the things of this world from his heart — shall such a one be called 'fool'? G-d forbid!

"Not witless, but wise has G-d called your name, you disciple of our Father Avraham, who also left his father and his kindred and inclined toward G-d. He Who blessed Avraham will bless you and will make you worthy to behold all the consolations destined for Israel; all the good that G-d shall do unto us He will do good unto you, for the L-rd hath promised good unto Israel."

And, in another letter to a convert named Ovadiah, the *Rambam* writes:

"...Ever since [Avraham Avinu], whoever adopts Judaism and acknowledges the unity of the Divine Name, as it is prescribed in the Torah, is counted among the disciples of Avraham, our Father, ע"ה. These men are Avraham's household...While we are the descendants of Avraham, Yitzchak, and Yaakov, you stem from Him through Whose word the world was created. As is said by Isaiah: "One shall say, I am the L-rd's, and another shall call himself by the name of Yaakov."

Take good care of the converts in your community; they are precious to G-d. Who knows: You may even be nurturing another *Onkelos* or Ruth!

Letter in Response: Children of Avraham's Household

To the Editor:

I would like to add a footnote to Fayge Levy's excellent article on *geirim* ("Avraham's Household," JO, Mar. '86). It is not uncommon for someone who is trying to make a *shidduch* for a convert to suggest another convert. Such a match has at least two points in its favor; namely, that a *ger* usually understands another *ger's* background and feelings better than a born-Jew does, and that in such a match, neither party has to bear the potential hostility of in-laws who resent the fact that a *ger* married into the family. However, there are several reasons why this practice is a bad idea, and should be discouraged. Here are four of them:

    1. The marriage of two *geirim* creates a halachic situation in which the daughter of such a union cannot — *lechatchila* — marry a *kohein* (*Even HaEzer* 7:21). If their daughter becomes aware of this fact, she will, most likely, feel stigmatized and inferior because of it. If she remains unaware of it, the stage is set for all sorts of human tragedy.

    2. The marriage of two *geirim* puts the couple's children in the same awkward existential position as a first-generation *ger* is in, of being spiritually and culturally part of the Jewish people, but not having the link of a family tree that extends back towards the generation of *mattan Torah*.

    3. Rightly or wrongly, if a *ger* finds himself constantly being set up with *gioros* (or vice versa), he cannot help but begin to doubt the warmth of his welcome.

4. When two *geirim* marry, the potential for *chillul Hashem* with regard to their non-Jewish parents is great. While the parents may be relieved that, against all odds, their child wound up marrying" one of his own kind" (!), they must also be darkly suspicious that the reason their child is marrying another convert is because no "ethnic Jew" would have him. Their suspicions may be totally unfounded, but it is unlikely that any assurances from the young couple will succeed in dispelling them.

My own mother assured me, a few years back, that born-Jews "will never allow you to become a rabbi or to marry their daughters." *Baruch Hashem*, I have been able to prove her wrong on the first point. And, while I have never refused a *shidduch* with a *giores* as such, it would be nice, for the honor of the Jewish people, to be able to prove her wrong on the second.

David Hoffman
Kew Gardens, N.Y.

Miss Anon

This Side of the Fence

As a single woman in her late twenties, I would like to share with you my feelings about the pressures of being single in the frum *community, and how some of these pressures can be eased. Although I am writing from a feminine perspective, I'm sure many aspects will apply to men, as well.*

◈§ Exploding the Myths

SO OFTEN WE HEAR someone say, "Such a lovely girl — why isn't she married yet?" Comments like this aggravate our frustration with our single state. Being married is a central concept in *Yiddishkeit*. It is considered not only a major *mitzvah*, but a condition of life that the *Ribbono Shel Olam* prescribes as necessary for optimal function as Torah Jews and as human beings. Since marriage is considered to be the normal state of existence, being unmarried is viewed as "abnormal." So people relate to singles, at least subconsciously, as they would to a person missing an arm or leg; they feel sorry for them and don't quite know what to say. Often people with the best intentions say hurtful things, and this only widens the "Great Divide" that exists between married people and single people.

To begin with, I would like to explode two widespread myths about single people: 1) There is something wrong with them. 2) It's their fault that they're not married.

Upon meeting older single people, we want to know what their "problem" is. With the exclusion of individual situations, the contrary is usually the case. Not only is there nothing "wrong" with older singles, but they are often high-caliber people. My single friends are conscientiously committed to *Yiddishkeit* and would make wonderful wives and mothers, and I consider myself fortunate to be in their company. Yes, there are a lot of wonderful single people around, and our first step as a Torah community is to give them the benefit of the doubt.

On to Myth No. 2: When people ask, "Why isn't he/she married?" there is the intimation that it is the single person's fault. Actually, this question is no different from any other question in life for which there are no ready answers: "Why did so-and-so make a fortune in business?"

We are trained to believe in *Hashgachah Prattis* — that G-d has a plan for everything. Somehow *shidduchim* are perceived differently, as though the single person is to blame for his own sorry state. Yet it is often no more a person's fault than other life situations beyond their control.

We often feel these vibrations from the most well-meaning people who try to help us, and we immediately put up our defenses. It is saddening, indeed, that in an area where people need to work together the most, the schism seems to be widest. When a person requires other kinds of help, we don't question the need for a warm hand and sympathetic smile. Why should we be any less understanding of singles?

Singlehood is lonely. Despite having loving parents and good friends, a single person is still very much alone emotionally, and in solitude must face the major decisions of her life as well as her emerging identity as a person. In our community this is complicated by the fact that we must be concerned with what people think about us — about the way we dress, talk and act — for fear that an unfavorable remark may get around and "spoil our chances." It is never a completely natural existence.

৵ Eliminating Negatives

There are many positive steps to be taken to break down the communication barrier and ease tensions, and they begin by eliminating the negative. When dealing with single people, especially concerning *shidduchim*, there are some key phrases to avoid:

☐ **"You are too picky."**

This line is the all-time hands down winner of the Most Hated Remark Award. If you are sincerely interested in bringing two people together and you care about others' feelings, don't ever say this to anyone. It causes alienation.

If you were about to invest millions of dollars, which could either make you or break you, would you do it lightly? No one questions the urgency of caution when entering financial risk for gain; and yet how much greater is the investment we make in a marriage — an investment that is priceless and one that has the potential for greater spiritual returns than we can ever imagine!

"Pickiness" is a relative term. I'm not referring to hair color, style of glasses, or width of hat brim, but to such matters as compatible values and perceptions in life. Is this being picky? Then a single person has every right to be picky. She will spend the rest of her life with the person and the framework she has chosen.

The area of personality is also crucial. No matter how well one knows the principals, one can never make a decision about what is "right" for someone else.

☐ **"You have to compromise."**

This is a restatement of the "too picky" indictment, implying that older people are unrealistic and that they do not need to be as happy or fulfilled in marriage as those who married at a younger age. There may be a positive message somewhere, but it sounds and feels like a put down.

☐ **"She doesn't really want to get married anyway. She's too happy/too busy with her career."**

This statement, besides being painful, is also false. *Everyone* wants to get married. Being alone is unnatural and oppressive, and even physically harmful. I don't know anyone who is happy being single, no matter how cheerful she may seem to be.

And then, we are warned not to "get too happy," the

implication being that if we enjoy our work or get too "comfortable," we'll become satisfied with our singlehood.

Many people mistake a person's active single life for a confusion in priorities. In most cases, it is a brave attempt to lead a productive life and to achieve personal growth in the interim before marriage. Most married people are unaware of the tremendous strength it takes to maintain good spirits and to be involved in worthwhile projects without the support and friendship that only a spouse can provide. As singles, we walk a very fine line between wanting to reach out for comfort and guidance, and the need to project a strong image and a sense of control.

As far as our jobs go — if lucky enough to have good ones, we are very thankful, and they are in no way contradictory to our priorities. Marriage and family are first for us, and in the meantime, we are very grateful for all the benefits provided by our jobs (many of which will come in handy in our married lives). These include the opportunity to mature socially, the sharpening of ethical awareness, the refinement of *middos*, the improvement of skills, and last, but not least, the self-esteem and independence that come from earning a living. We count our blessings while we wait.

Also, please remember that you never see a total picture. No one sees all the private and often painful *hishtadlus* that goes on behind closed doors in a single person's life; the heartfelt talks with friends and mentors, the self-searching, the *tefillos*, and the many, many tears. All of this is hidden from view.

The Torah does bid us to be happy at all times, no matter what the circumstances, and we try to take that directive seriously. Happiness doesn't necessarily mean that we are content with our status.

☐ **"Enjoy yourself."**

This pre-date advice, though well-meaning, is illogical. Going out is *not* fun oriented — although time pleasantly spent can be a fringe benefit. For non-Jews, dating is a social activity, but for us it is a means toward *tachlis* — a serious goal.

As a rule, dating is a necessary evil, and it can be severely stressful. After being brought up on a lifetime of strict separation of the sexes, we are suddenly told to go out and find a husband/wife, and not only that, but we should "relax and enjoy ourselves"!

The dating situation itself is an emotional Catch-22. Both people get all dressed up and are on their best behavior. Every word is weighed and stored, so that ordinary comments, which would be bypassed in daily conversation, become disproportionately important and/or misconstrued. There is also a lot of inspection going on, no matter how much anyone wants to deny this. So after an average of three hours of being thoroughly investigated, during which our performances may rival those of anyone on or Off Broadway, we then say good night and close the door on someone we may never even see again!

There is so little opportunity to see the other person in a normal context. (I sometimes even find myself praying for a flat tire just to depart from the script.) We probably know our co-workers better than we know our prospective husbands/wives before we marry them.

We're aware that when people tell us to enjoy ourselves before a date, they are only looking for a way to wish us luck. Perhaps "Hatzlachah" would be more appropriate.

☐ **"What do you have to lose? It's only one evening."**

No date is "only one evening." Each one involves much preparation, as well as pressures of some sort. A single person's careful consideration of a prospective *shidduch*, and her decision about whether to continue a relationship — or to begin one at all — should be respected.

☐ **"So what's new with you?"**

We know that people are interested in our welfare and do sincerely want to see us married. But there are other aspects to our lives. When someone asks us "what's new," they usually have only one topic in mind, and it gives us the irritating feeling that our only worth as a human being is in marriage, and that nothing else we do could possible be important.

I have been extremely grateful for the few *Shabbosos* I spent with families where the topic of dating did not come up once. These people were just as concerned about me as anyone else, and would be the first to call me if a suitable name came up. But in the meantime we talked about my ideas, my job, my outside activities and friendships, my efforts to be a good person. They made me feel worthwhile, and because of that I am most comfortable talking with them, in particular, about *shidduchim*.

"How's you social life?" is a related question, but one that is obviously more direct — and intrusive, unless asked by someone who is really a close friend (in which case it would certainly be worded in a gentler way), especially when no concrete help is being offered. I would never go up to a married person and ask, "So how come you don't have any children?" By the same token I would like my privacy to be respected. Dating is a sensitive, personal issue and should be treated as such.

☐ **"Listen to me—"**

Not always spoken, this message is often conveyed by body-language or inflection: The single person is not really capable of making good judgments and should take others' advice.

Of course we need advice, just like anyone else, and we often seek it. And we are willing to listen — especially when we feel we have been listened to. But many times advice is forced on us without regard for our own feelings. In certain situations I sometimes wonder why my own adult judgment is not considered as sound as that of a married person who may be five years my junior.

A case in point might be the person who is seeking to marry someone who wants to live in Israel, and is constantly admonished "not to limit herself." She is not necessarily unrealistic. Nor will she definitely wind up in Israel. What it does mean is that living in Israel is central to her value system, and not just an item on the notorious "checklist." Dismissing this hope as unrealistic, or even petty, is a dismissal of much of what the person stands for, and is counterproductive.

Many of us find ourselves at the mercy of too much good advice. We are pushed and pulled in so many directions, frightened into thinking that we may have "missed" our *basherte*, or that we did not make the right decision — in general, discouraged from developing confidence in our own sense of judgment.

✺ Of Gratitude and Positives

Let my complaints not eclipse my gratitude to the very many who try to help us. Perhaps some positive suggestions can further help these sincere friends in their efforts.

• Please realize that there are many single people around you, and they need your help. This may be a neighbor's son or daughter, or an out-of-towner in the apartment next door, with no family nearby and few contacts. We singles are painfully aware that we are almost totally dependent on the help of others to get married — not a pleasant situation for anyone to be in, and one that you can alleviate with just a bit of thoughtfulness. *Shadchanus* is not just the province of professionals; it's everybody's private *mitzvah*, and it should be done responsibly. This means following through on suggestions, collecting the necessary information, returning phone calls, and listening objectively to feedback.

• Next: Listen. Sometimes an open ear can be the most valuable gift you can give anyone.

• And then — perhaps most important of all — treat your single friend just as you would anyone else.

• One final thought: Singlehood should not be considered a wasted time period. It can be very positive. And it can serve as significant preparation for marriage — if viewed that way. Single people develop strengths and awarenesses in life that would otherwise remain dormant, often becoming more sensitive to the needs of others. I am certain that I will be a better hostess for having so often been a guest, and that I have already become a better listener.

Being single can even be seen as a *chessed*. We always learn that *Hashem* gives *nisyonos* to those who can pass them; it is a testimony to my friends' character that they have been given the opportunity to demonstrate their faith, and that they have done so admirably.

May we be granted the opportunity in the near future to implement our own suggestions — from the other side of the fence.

Letters to the Editor

◆§ Problems On Both Sides of the Fence

To the Editor:

"This Side of the Fence" (*The Jewish Observer*, May 1990)... seems to say that being single includes a set of problems that disappear upon getting married.

As for Miss Anon's being asked to explain "Why" and, in effect, to demonstrate that she's doing "her part," *at least she can*. She can say she went out on a recommended date, or consulted another *shadchan*.

People who don't as yet have children aren't about to say what they're doing — operations, medical "procedures," test, consultants, etc. (and, of course, doing things *b'zchus*, hoping to be asked to be *Kvatter* at a *bris*, etc.).

From my "side of the fence," your problem is more readily solved than mine, but I don't envy you. Just don't envy others — even those with children may have their own *peckel* of *tzuros*.

Remember, Hashem gives us only what we can handle, *if* we use what we have and meet the challenge.

Mr. Fence
Brooklyn, New York

◆§ Not All Singles Are Equal — Or Blameless

To the Editor:

I feel sympathy for Miss Anon when callous comments — whether intentional or casual — are insensitively passed her way.

There are, however, some occasions when the attitudes of some singles give well-meaning *shadchanim* pause. May I mention some?

Frum singles are not immune, unfortunately, to the non-Torah values with which we are bombarded on a daily basis. External factors — extraneous to the intrinsic worth of a person, and to a lasting relationship, such as age, looks, and money — have become more and more important to even the cream of our crop!

When did a Bais Yaakov girl begin judging *bachurim* on the criterion of "what he does," rather than "who he is"? When did a learning Yeshiva *bachur* begin asking for wealthy girls who portray the "Barbie image" over the "Yiddishe mamma" image?

I will not dwell on the 47-year-old male who stubbornly insists on someone no older than 30, nor the 42-year-old grandmother-divorcee who requested no one who earns a salary of less than $75,000 year!

And then there are those singles who show the simple unwillingness or inability to make the most of their appearance (sporting sloppy or soiled clothing, dirty fingernails).

These are but a few of the cases of some singles' own undoing that I have encountered as a *shadchan*.

May I suggest that all singles evaluate — and constantly re-evaluate with shifting age and circumstances — their expectations in finding their *bashert?* In doing so, they should realize from whence their often great "over-expectations" come — from a world which stresses values that are not ours! And may I further suggest that the yeshivos and Bais Yaakovs implement classes which will have a *hashpa'ah* on our *b'nei* and *b'nos* Torah in their decision of what is important to look for in a potential spouse, and the makings of a good marriage. Then the singles in our *frum* communities will more fully reflect our Torah-true values, enabling us to tear down the fence!

(Mrs.) Margie Pensak
Baltimore, Md.

◆§ The Value of Friendship to Singles

To the Editor:

Thank you for your interesting and timely series of articles on singles in the Iyar/May Issue. My married friends show a great deal of concern and interest in helping single people, and tell me (as I see from experience) that when they meet an unmarried person, they always try to think of a possible *shidduch* for him or her... They are generally hospitable, frequently inviting singles for Shabbos. Those people who are not as involved are usually extremely busy with small children, or may live in cramped quarters, lacking space for Shabbos guests.

We must face it: It is very difficult to make *shidduchim* for people past their twenties, when the parties are experienced enough to be discerning, yet the choice is just not there. As a result, there must be a certain amount of burn-out among friends who have been trying on our behalf.

These are, of course, married people who make insensitive remarks, and the article brought this to their attention. However, I take such comments as a sign of caring and a well-meaning (albeit clumsy) attempt to help the unmarried person.

Among the married people who try to make *shidduchim*, there is unfortunately not much follow-through, so well-meant first steps often lead nowhere. But I appreciate just someone's thinking of me, even if it doesn't lead to *tachlis*. I enjoy the company of my married friends, aside from their role as sources for *shidduchim*.

Finally, being single is not the only problem in life. If there is a way to perhaps ameliorate one's own private sorrow, short of marriage, it is by recognizing and caring about the pain of others. I see married people with insoluble life-and-death problems. How I wish I could help them! But their problems are not amenable to solution by making *shidduch* phone calls or by extending an invitation for Shabbos. I am truly less fortunate than my married friends, not because I am single, but because I can never give them what they have given me.

Eileen Pollock
Lakewood, New Jersey

➳ Picky No More at Forty

Dear Editor:

You did a public service by focusing on the loneliness of the singles, and by letting others know their needs and sensitivities. At the same time, however, I'm afraid that you did them a disservice. Now men and women in their late 20's, 30's and upward will be reinforced in their sense of entitlement to pickiness and refusal to compromise. I know whereof I speak, because I was there.

I had a very clear picture of Mr. Right, and all those young men that came calling — this one couldn't speak English straight, that one was too much of a dandy, and the other one couldn't learn half as well as my brothers — they all fell short. When I passed 35, I realized that even those not-quite-good-enough fellows stopped coming, but I refused to panic. Finally as my fourth decade of life was coming to an end I gave up on Mr. Right, and settled for Mr. O.K. — a divorced man that I wouldn't have even looked at twenty years earlier. I compromised. I stopped being picky. But at least I'm not alone. I don't care what the feminists (and their champions) say. The *Gemara* is right. The Aramaic expression, ridiculed by the women's rightists, is as true as ever: "*Tav lemetav tandu milemetav armelu* — Two is better than one. Period."

It's probably too late for us to have children, but at least we have each other. I can't sign my name out of respect for my husband — but I'm sure tempted to, just so his first wife should recognize what a fool she was to dump her imperfect husband for a life alone.

To all well-meaning, would-be-*shadchanim* out there: Be gentle with your single friends, and don't use negative words like "compromise" and "pickiness." But — for Heaven's sake — don't encourage them to indulge in their fantasies! Loneliness gets worse as the years advance, and compromises become less and less attractive, and less and less available, for countless reasons.

Name Withheld by Request
Ocean County, New Jersey

David Gottlieb

Love and Marriage

ONE OUT OF EVERY two marriages in North America ends in divorce. Of those that survive, some *should not*: The relationships have deteriorated to the point that dissolution is the only way to relieve the misery. *Thus, the majority of North American marriages are failures.* The explanation for this enormous human suffering is not easy to see, especially since the statistics for the best educated, most sophisticated and least inhibited segment of the population are just as bad.

For *frum* communities, the figures are much lower. In addition, the symptoms of failed marriages that have not divorced (child abuse, wife/husband abuse, alcoholism, disappearance) are also much lower. Some take pride in our relative success at marriage; others emphasize that we still fall far short of our marital responsibilities and should regard our rate of failure as an "epidemic" or "crisis" which requires emergency measures. Without taking sides in this debate, we can all agree that we are doing *something* significantly better than the rest of North America. Perhaps, if we understand that something, we will be able to use it even more effectively in the attempt to improve our own marriages.

◆§ Biblical Marriages

When the patriarch Yitzchak met his future wife Rivkah he "... took her into the tent of his mother Sarah, married her, and loved her, and was comforted from (the loss of) his mother" (*Bereishis*

24:67). From a Western perspective, the sequence of events is puzzling: Shouldn't love come before marriage? And why is the development of their relationship bracketed by Yitzchak's concern for his mother? *Chazal* tell us (*Bereishis Rabbah*) that during Sarah's lifetime, her tent — which was Yitzchak's home — experienced open manifestations of *Hashem's* presence. With her death, these signs disappeared. Yitzchak's criterion for a spouse was the ability to recreate the Divine environment he experienced in his mother's home. It was her proof of this ability that determined Yitzchak's decision to marry Rivkah. Love for her was the *outcome* of the marriage commitment based on that foundation. Note that the love which grew between them is not unimportant: The fact that the Torah mentions it shows that love is one of the goals of marriage.[1] However, far from being the *prerequisite* for marriage, *love is a consequence of marriage based upon a common vision and goal of life, and the perception that the partners are suited to achieving that goal together.* Only when Yitzchak found a partner for such a marriage and experienced the resulting love — only when the divine environment was recreated — could Yitzchak be comforted for the loss of his mother. (Of course, *some* emotional bond must be created during the testing period before a commitment is made to marry. This is included in the "perception that the partners are suited to one another." How to characterize the required bond exactly requires investigation.)

The following generation gives what appears at first glance to be a contrasting paradigm for love and marriage. Yaakov meets Rachel at the well and immediately kisses her. Within thirty days he loves her so completely that he is prepared to work seven years for the right to marry her. Here Yaakov's love explicitly *precedes* marriage, and in fact develops so rapidly that it appears to be almost "love at first sight" — the very antithesis of his parents' example. But this appearance is immediately dispelled by a closer look at the *pesukim* and the supplementary comments of *Chazal*. (a) When he meets Rachel at the well, Yaakov *first* waters the sheep, then kisses her, and then *weeps*. This behavior is not typical of infatuation! (b) The offer to work for her for such a long period, and the choice of

---

1. This gives the lie to the *Fiddler on the Roof* slander of Jewish marriage as a love-less relationship.

seven years in particular, needs to be explained. (c) The Torah's description of the passage of the seven years "... as but a few days in his eyes due to his love of her" like a beautifully romantic sentiment — until we reflect that while waiting for a longed-for event, time passes *slowly*, not quickly.[1] His love for her should have made the seven years feel like a hundred! (d) When the time is finally up, Yaakov requests the promised marriage with the words: "Give me my wife that I may go in unto her." Such a statement seems gross in the extreme.[2] How can we imagine Yaakov making it?

A Common Goal of Peoplehood

The key to the whole story lies in the answer to the last question. *Chazal* explain that Yaakov saw his marriage to Rachel as the instrument for bringing the Jewish people into existence. Since the Jewish people is the goal and the justification of the whole of creation, and the Creator made marital relations the only means of procreation, *those* marital relations achieve the pinnacle of holiness. As Adam and Chavah before him, Yaakov saw no embarrassment in that process *when dedicated to such a goal*.[3] His statement "... that I may go in unto her ..." expressed the height of sanctity which he achieved.

Understanding that the creation of the Jewish people was Yaakov's goal in marrying Rachel, we can answer questions (a)-(c) as well. He used the seven years as a *period of preparation* for such an awesome task.[4] The choice of the time period is not arbitrary: seven units of time connote a complete time-cycle, and a period of purification.[5] When one is preparing for a challenge which will test all one's abilities, whose outcome is of enormous importance, and

---

1. See, for example, the discussion of *Sefiras HaOmer* while waiting for *Mattan Torah* in *Sefer HaChinuch*.
2. Cf. *Yalkut Shimoni*.
3.. Cf. *Iggeres HaKodesh* of the *Ramban*.
4. This task is what distinguishes Yaakov from Avraham and Yitzchak, and makes him "*bechir she'b'avos*": They each had non-Jewish children and thus were only *ancestors* of the Jewish people. Yaakov and his family *were* the Jewish people in microcosm.
5. The week, *shemittah, yovel, Pesach, Shavuos* and *sefiras ha'omer* illustrate time periods composed of seven units of time. *Tumas mes, yoledes, zav* and *zavah* illustrate seven units of time as a purification process. The *Zohar HaKadosh* says explicitly that Yaakov used the seven years to prepare himself for the union with Rachel.

which requires the meticulous strengthening and training of all one's talents and abilities, how does the time pass during thepreparation period? Quickly![1] *His* love for *her* was predicated on such a challenge, *therefore*, the seven years "... were as but a few days in his eyes." Finally, we must remember that when Yaakov first saw Rachel he was already a prophet. A prophet by definition sees what the rest of us do not: Yaakov saw in Rachel *the mother of the Jewish people*. His love for her and all his subsequent actions were consequences of this vision. Thus we see that Yaakov and Rachel, instead of contrasting with Yitzchak and Rivkah, in fact exemplify the same principle: *Love and marriage are consequences of a common vision and a goal of life and the perception that the partners are suited to achieving that goal together.* This principle is one of the two pillars upon which Jewish marriage rests.

✎₰ The Integration of Two Into One

The second pillar of Jewish marriages is found in the Talmudic dictum that Adam was (or was originally destined to be) *androgynous*, i.e., a being combining male and female characteristics in all human dimensions — physical, emotional, intellectual and spiritual.[2] What are we to learn from this piece of historical information? (*Mai d'hava hava?!*) We are to learn that *marriage is the context in which a man and a woman attempt to recreate or approximate the perfect male-female union represented by Adam.* Let us examine this lesson in detail.

Human relationships differ in the quality of integration they achieve. On the lowest level is the pure business relationship: each partner enters the relationship solely for the personal gain he can achieve thereby.[3] Personal integration with the partner is nil. We may label this relationship "I plus": Each partner is to himself a completely self-interested "I," but he recognizes that the cooperation with another "I" can profit him more than can his individual efforts.

On a higher level is the "We" relationship, in which individuals identify with the needs and goals of a group, and

---

1. Think of preparing for an exam, a performance, etc.
2. *Eruvin* 11a.
3. Of course, many business relationships become more than purely business.

experience events in terms of their significance for the group. "We" replaces "I" in the thinking of the members of such a group, at least during group activities. Anyone who has played on a well-knit sports team, performed with a music ensemble, or engaged in a similar activity has been part of a "We" relationship. A score by the opposing team is *our* loss; my successful play is *our success;* the notes I produce is a contribution to *our* sound; *that is how the activity is experienced.* In this context a new entity is formed; namely, the *group.* Individuals relating with one another in the "We" mode become members of this new entity and are integrated (partially) into it. Their individuality becomes subordinate to the group's needs and goals.

Although it is a significant improvement on the "I plus I" relationship, the "We" relationship does not embody complete integration. The group is an *association* of *individuals* each of whom retains his own identity. He merely *plays the role* of group member at certain times, and at these times accepts the group's goals as his own. This relationship does not affect his *essence.* Such a total integration, which transforms the essence of the individual to the extent that *he is no longer truly an individual*, is the highest form of human relationship. The new entity formed by this relationship is not a *group*, but rather an *organic whole*, of which the erstwhile individuals become *parts* (rather than members, as in a group). This relationship may be labeled "I," for two reasons. The singular pronoun indicates that the new entity does not have the multiplicity of a group, but rather is a *single* entity; and the use of "I" indicates that the new entity is a *totally integrated individual*, which supplants the individuality of those who stand in the relationship.

The husband and wife who achieve the "I" relationship do not form a two-membered group, but rather a new organically integrated whole. Compare, for example, the human body. It can be divided into head, trunk, arms and legs. Nevertheless, we do not say that each person is a group of six! The reason is that the head, trunk, etc. are *parts* of one whole, rather than individuals merely associating with one another. What makes the difference? *Integrating functioning*: Each of the parts is totally dependent upon its connection to the rest of the body for its life and ability to function. Similarly, the "I" relationship produces integrated functioning for the individuals who stand in that relationship.

❧ Unique, and Therefore Integrated

It must be emphasized that this integration does not compromise the *uniqueness* of those who achieve it. That x and y function together as a unit does not imply that x=y. On the contrary, integrated functioning usually presupposes crucial differences which are so related that the whole may vastly transcend its parts. Some examples: a violin and a piano playing together; forwards and guards in basketball; a surgeon and an anesthesiologist in the operating theatre; Sanhedrin, King and prophet for the leadership of the Jewish nation. The uniqueness of the individuals forming the "I" is the very foundation of the integration: It is because they are unique in precisely these ways that they can coordinate their functioning so as to form this integrated whole.

How is the "I" relationship expressed in the context of marriage? It is as if when Yitzchak says "I" and Rivkah says "I," instead of each referring to his/her own self, they *both* refer to the *same new amalgam* of which each is a part. If you write "I" on one occasion and speak "I" on another, we do not understand the written "I" as referring to your arm and the spoken "I" as referring to your lungs, larynx, mouth, etc. Although produced by different *parts* of your body, each refers to the *whole*. This is because "I" refers to the smallest *whole* encompassing the part which produces it. In the case of Yitzchak and Rivkah, neither of them individually is a whole any longer; thus the "I" produced by either refers to the whole of which each is a part.

The "I"-relationship marriage is experienced differently from other human relationships. Imagine that Leah is a social worker having difficulty convincing a client to get psychiatric help. Her husband Reuven encourages her and gives her advice, and the following day she succeeds. If Leah and Reuven are related as the "I plus I," the success is *hers*; he is at best an enabler, expecting her help in his projects as *quid pro quo* for his support of her. If they share a "We" relationship, the success is *theirs*, but it accrues to the pair (the two-membered group) through *her* action which she performs *as an individual*. If they form an "I," the very action itself is related to Reuven as well: The success was accomplished by a *part of the very same whole of which he is a part.*[1]

---

1. When my hand imprints my name on a check, it is *I, the whole person*, who signs the check; the action accrues the *whole* even though only a part is in motion.

A second example: A husband and wife are together when one receives a gross insult from a third party. The spouse protests: "Your words affect me as well — I take that insult *personally*." He responds: "Don't talk nonsense: I didn't insult *your person*, I insulted *your spouse's person*." Is the protest nonsense? Not in the context of the "I" relationship. Just as any insult to my face is an insult to me as a whole, so an insult to my spouse is an insult to the whole of which I am a part.

This, then, is the lesson of androgynous Adam: Man and woman are created as incomplete parts of a larger organic whole which comprises both of them. Their complementary gifts and needs enable them to integrate with each other on the pattern of that original whole. It is this which gives them the capacity to transcend the "I plus I" and "We" levels of human relationship, and at least approximate the integration of the single "I" of which Adam is the paradigm. The goal and challenge of marriage is to recreate Adam's wholeness to the extent possible for physically separate beings.

Love — a deep and abiding attachment to and identification with one's spouse, coupled with the joy of that attachment — is the result of forming the "I" relationship. Without this, there may be a temporary thrill, an infatuation, a mutually beneficial satisfaction of one another's needs (characteristic of even "I plus I" relationships), but not love. The "I" relationship, at once the challenge and the fulfillment of highest human integration, is the second pillar on which Jewish marriage rests.

Practical Applications

The two pillars of Jewish marriage — suitability for achieving the common goal, and the "I" relationship — have many implications for practice. The *shidduch* system is designed to produce the first pillar. This subject has been discussed by others (cf. "Shadchanim — Matchmakers" by Chaim Shapiro, JO, Summer 1985) and I will not pursue it here. The second deserves very extended treatment, of which what follows is only *a few* of the *roshei perakim* (salient points).

The "I" relationship will not create itself. It must be actively pursued with intelligence and dedication. No matter how well suited husband and wife are to one another when they marry, life's experiences work to drive them apart. No man has even a vague inkling of what it is to carry, birth and suckle a child. The loss of a parent cannot be fully experienced by the mourner's spouse. Unless there is a commitment to *rebuild* lines of communication and modes of sharing, husband and wife will inevitably drift into private worlds, becoming less and less relevant to one another. Love cannot be strengthened, or even sustained under such conditions. This means that time, effort and resources must be dedicated to constantly renewing the relationship. In my opinion, the failure to take responsibility for creating the "I" in marriage is the single most common factor in divorce. Western culture has evolved a passive attitude towards love and marriage: "Let's see if it works. If it does, fine; if not, why spend life chained to unhappiness?" "If *it* works" — not "If *I* will work" — and certainly not "It *will* work: I will *make* it work!" How does one relate to other difficult and important life tasks — a school exam, a musical performance, and athletic competition, a medical problem? One undertakes to practice, study, train, prepare and strive to achieve (with *HaKadosh Baruch Hu's* help) the desired result. This is the attitude one should have in marriage. A successful marriage is the personal achievement of the husband and wife who worked to create it. A failed marriage is often their personal failure.

Adopting this attitude of responsibility towards building the "I" with one's spouse provides a new understanding of typical marital occurrences. For example, it often happens that the wife (or husband) starts to tell the husband (or wife) an experience or feeling of hers which is immensely boring to him. What should he do? There are two common schools of thought. (1) Marriage is based on *chessed*: He should listen anyway as a favor to the wife. (2) Marriage is based on *honesty*: He should tell her frankly that the subject is boring to him and expect her to respect his feelings. From the vantage point of building the "I," both approaches miss the crucial point: *He should not be listening to the story, but to her.* The story is boring; if he saw it in a newspaper or heard it from an acquaintance he might immediately put down the paper or change the subject. But this communication from his wife indicates her present state of mind, her present feelings. He wants to know where she is so that he and she can continue to build their whole together.

A second example, consider the adage: It is easier to give than to receive. Why is this so? Because receiving often implies weakness, insufficiency, dependency and failure on the recipient's part, while giving implies strength, surplus, independence, success, and also magnanimity. The ego-impact of giving is positive, of receiving, negative. If so, *one of the greatest gifts is to provide another with the opportunity to give.*[1] Often one spouse will not share problems with the other "in order not to burden her/him with my problems." The effect is to deny the other a chance to help and thereby confirm her, his own self-worth. (And the cause is often an attempt to save one's own self-image.) After a disagreement we are willing to forgive, but are we willing to ask for forgiveness? Forgiving, as a form of giving, is *easy*: It implies that we were right and the other party was guilty! Asking for forgiveness allows the *other* to be charitable in excusing *our* fault.

It is hoped that these brief examples will indicate how the goal of creating the "I" provides a new perspective on marital experiences. Consistent application of this perspective yields a new *integrative* approach which helps cement the marital bond even as life's vicissitudes assail that bond.

Klal Yisrael needs to strengthen itself against the tide of marital misery which surrounds us and threatens to undermine our marriages as well. *Shiurim, sefarim,* counseling (before and after marriage) and group discussions are needed to help us construct our marriages in the image of the Talmudic vision of Adam, and thus fulfill the destiny for which we were created.[2] [3]

---

1. See *Michtav MeEliyahu*, v. 1, *Kuntres HaChessed*, chap. 12 where Rabbi Dessler distinguishes between *notail* and *mekabel*, the taker and the giver. Much of the description of the "I" is derived from *Kuntres HaChessed*.

2. Some will worry that expenditure of time and effort will deplete our resources for other necessary goals. For example, men learning full time will regret lost hours of *talmud Torah*. This view is shortsighted: *Much more time* will be lost (not to mention qualitative deterioration) from learning *in the long run* due to the consequences of lost integration and communication than is needed to prevent that loss. Compare *Rashi's* explanation of Rabbi Yishmael's *"minhag derech eretz"* (*Berachos* 35b): "for if you become dependent upon charity, in the end you will be prevented from (learning) Torah." *Rashi* sees a regular job as the most efficient way to maximize hours of *talmud Torah*; the same applies to investment in marriage.

3. I am deeply indebted to my wife, who introduced me to many of the ideas expressed in this article.

Libby Lazewnik

A Private Waterloo

I.

Oh, I could bite my tongue!
That treacherous double-edged sword
Has, in a single unmeditated sweep,
Altered the course of my history.
I should have detoured 'round the battlefield.
(Whoever really desires life
Ought to know that!) Instead
I sought the glory of confrontation:
Unwittingly stalwart in the service of
Life's enemy.
The skirmish was short but savage.
Among the casualties:
    Your sensibilities wounded
    My happiness killed
    Our friendship, reeling from a mortal blow.
My swordsmanship was dazzling.
Yes, in this particular battle I may count
Myself (though sprawled among the slain)
A victor of sorts.
Flinging wide the heedless gates, I struck
Sword a-glint in the simmering sun of your wrath.
You cowered; I pressed my advantage, drew
First blood. My sword proved the swifter.
A triumph.
And now I bury my burning face in
The Victor's wreath:
A malodorous bouquet of Regrets.

II.

What wouldn't I give to have
Those five miserable words
Back again!
If only for the space of a minute
I had them in my grasp,
Here's what I'd do:
Ruthlessly stamp them down,
Syllable on ugly syllable, till
The whole dismal sentence resembled
One tiny, twisted comma;
And I'd lodge that deformed thing
In a casket all of lead
With a dozen shiny seals,
Three on every side;
And I'd ride with that casket
Far out to sea,
Fling it into the deepest,
Blackest pit there —
A watery grave.
Then I'd plant my feet on the shore, and
Drain away the sea
(With that evil leaden mass at its heart)
Into a huge plastic bag
Sealed tight, tight;
And I'd hurl that bag
Up to the voiceless
Vacuum of space:
Silvery fairy bubble,
To toss in their own midnight ocean.
That's what I'd do, if only I had them back:
Those nasty, over-hasty
Words
That made you go.

III.

(sigh)
Instead, they live on,
Echoing in your memory
And my conscience.

Only forgiveness will bury them, one day.
There's no doubt how the history books
Will record this one.
The sword's snug in the scabbard.
Vigilant, I guard the gates
And gird my loins for the next battle.

Rabbi Mattisyahu Solomon

The Battle for the Jewish Family

✺ Reb Moshe's Last Message

THE JEWISH FAMILY is under assault. This needs no documentation, but it does need greater awareness on our part. It is a battle that requires leadership. The Jewish community is still suffering from the trauma of the loss of two of our greatest leaders, Rabbi Yaakov Kamenetsky and Rabbi Moshe Feinstein, זכרונם לברכה. They are gone, but their light will never be extinguished: "From their illumination we will continue to see light." I would thus like to draw from a message I had heard expressed by Reb Moshe in one of his last public addresses.

The *Gemara* tells us: When Pharaoh decreed that all male babies born be thrown into the Nile, Amram, the *Gadol Hador*, said, "We are toiling in vain; it is futile to bring children into the world," and he divorced his wife.

His daughter, Miriam, admonished him, saying through the power of prophecy, "Father, your decree is even harsher than that of Pharaoh, for Pharaoh only decreed against male children, but by divorcing your wife, you are also preventing the birth of girls. Pharaoh's decree was only against life in this world, and you have made a decree on *neshamos* that they have neither *Olam Hazeh* (This World) nor *Olam Haba* (The World to Come)." *Rashi* explains that even if a *neshamah* passes but briefly through this world, it will merit *Olam Haba*.

Upon hearing this, Amram took back his wife. And *Klal Yisrael*, which had emulated Amram's example in divorcing his wife, also followed suit, and returned to their wives.

The purpose of having children (said Reb Moshe) — in fact, the whole family structure — is to ensure that *neshamos* come to *Olam Haba*, and it was for this purpose that Amram took Yocheved back. *Klal Yisrael* learned from this that even if a child would be with them but a few short months, it is worth all the effort and all the later disappointment, to prepare a *neshamah* for *Olam Haba*.

The same idea is expressed in *Igros Moshe* (*Even HaEzer*, chap. 62), where certain methods of contraception are forbidden even if it is determined that the child that would be born would not live more than a few years — the purpose of bringing children into this world is that they eventually achieve *Olam Haba*. This fundamental concept was one of Reb Moshe's last messages to us.

This is even implicit in *Rashi's* commentary on the passage, "You should keep the *mitzvos* and you should live with them" (*Vayikra* 18:5). *Rashi* explains "living with them" as referring to *Olam Haba*. In other words, one should keep the *mitzvos* so as to merit life in the next world. Asks Reb Moshe: The Talmud infers from this *pasuk* that when a person is confronted with the choice of transgressing a *mitzvah* or losing his life, he should choose to transgress rather than be killed (aside from the three cardinal sins). So it would seem that as "You should live with them" is referring to life in this world, to live with the *mitzvos* and not be killed for their sake! Why does *Rashi* explain "living with them" as referring to life in the next world?

Reb Moshe explains that the *halachah* of "*ya'avor v'al yehoreig* — transgress rather than be killed" does not mean that one's life in this world *per se* is worth more than the fulfillment of *mitzvos*. Rather, the value of life is measured by how much potential for *Olam Haba* it possesses. A person is expected to transgress the one *mitzvah* so as to gain a longer life, thereby being able to perform more *mitzvos* and increase his share in *Olam Haba*. The focus of a Jew's life, its end goal, then, is *Olam Haba*, and this goal must always be served.

৺§ Brothers in Combat

The Torah relates that at Yaakov and Eisav's first encounter since Yaakov's escape after having received the blessings from

Yitzchok, Eisav saw Yaakov's wives and many children, and asked him, "Who are these to you?" To which Yaakov answered, "The children with whom G-d has favored your servant."

What is the nature of Eisav's question, and how did Yaakov's response answer the question?

Pirkei D'Rebbi Eliezer informs us that an entire dialogue took place between the brothers at this meeting. When Yaakov had purchased the *bechorah* (primogeniture) from Eisav, the two agreed to divide their areas of activity and concentrate each on his own domain. Eisav would rule over *Olam Hazeh* and Yaakov would be a man of *Olam Haba*. For Eisav was interested in the pleasures of this world, and he was content to concede to his brother *avodas Hashem* and all that went with it. Upon seeing Yaakov's large family, he asked, "Who are these to you? — this family is *Olam Hazeh*! What does it have to do with your domain?"

Yaakov *Avinu* replied, "You are mistaken. These children are my *Olam Haba*! G-d gave them to me to develop my share in the next world."

This is the issue in a nutshell. Eisav's philosophy — and that of contemporary society — viewing this world as an end unto itself, for its pleasures, for the sake of enjoyment — is in confrontation with the Jewish family, which has *Olam Haba* as its only goal. This is our adversarial relationship — the war of Yaakov against Eisav — *Olam Hazeh* versus *Olam Haba*.

◈ Strategy for Victory

How do we engage in this war and protect the Jewish family? How do we assure ourselves that the family and we ourselves not lose sight of *Olam Haba*? There are no shortcuts. But no matter how difficult or prolonged the battle, it can be expedited by establishing a clear understanding of how best to wage the war.

First, once one views the problem as a battle between *Olam Hazeh* and *Olam Haba*, and recognizes the home as the chief battleground, half of the battle is won. For then we have a better insight into what is at stake. True, we are already aware that we are surrounded by a society of alien values, hostile to our more spiritual life-style. But when we permit these alien, *Olam Hazeh*-oriented values to penetrate our defenses and infiltrate our outlook, through the various informational and recreational media

The Battle for the Jewish Family / 207

that have free entry into our homes, these do damage to the *Olam Haba* content of our lives and diminish the goals we pursue.

It is important that we recognize the extent to which we compromise the *kedushah* content of our homes by ignoring the command "And your camps shall be holy." A home of *kedushah* is but one side of a coin, the reverse side of which reads: "but if an *ervas davar* — a nakedness — appears in your midst, then [G-d's presence] turns away from you." What a costly loss!

We can gain a deeper insight into the implications of this loss if we but consider the riches that G-d's presence can endow a home with. Every day we ask G-d to bless us with *"Ohr Panecha* — the light of Your Countenance," and we follow with just such a list: "because of this light ... You have given us a Torah of life, love of kindness, *tzedakah, brachah, rachamim, chaim,* and *shalom!"* Can one wish for anything more in one's home than life, goodness, compassion, and peace? Yet through a silly indulgence or an unfortunate indiscretion, through an indiscriminate display of nakedness, G-d turns His face away from a person, and he forfeits all of these blessings!

Our times are plagued with so many broken families, members of our communities are beset with so many personal problems. If only the *Ohr Panecha* and its attendant blessings were not banished from our homes!

On the positive side, there is an old-fashioned means of expressing oneself that has gone out of vogue. I refer to employing terms that reflect *emunah* and *bitachon* in our everyday speech. As Rabbi Simcha Zissel Ziv, the Alter of Kelm, said in regard to the passage from *Mishlei,* "Faith is lost, it is excised from our mouths," we have discontinued the practice of our grandmothers, that of pointing to the miracles that surround us in our daily lives, expressing our faith in G-d's help and our gratitude for His deliverance. The *"Baruch Hashem's"* that punctuated the speech of our predecessors should once again become incorporated into our daily speech, eventually strengthening our convictions. In this way, faith will be restored.

Sforno interprets the description of "You are a holy nation" as being "*Mezuman* (in readiness for) *Olam Haba.*" Making sanctity an integral part of our lives means raising the level of our aspirations and of our very lives to *Olam Haba*. It is not enough just to appreciate the fact that our goal in family life must be *Olam Haba,* we must be conscious of this goal all the time. We should measure this goal against everything we do: What does this activity, this practice, this mode of dress and behavior do for my *Olam Haba*?

A Blessing of Numbers

I would like to conclude with a *brachah*. In the preface to Moshe's *brachah* to *Klal Yisrael* he noted their numbers: "Hashem has multiplied you like the stars in the sky." Then, he offered his *brachah*, "He should multiply you a thousandfold, and bless you as He has spoken to you." What do these words, "Hashem ... should bless you as He has spoken," add to Moshe's *brachah*? *Rashi* explains: When Moshe blessed *Klal Yisrael* that Hashem should multiply them a thousandfold, they were shocked — "You are limiting our *brachah*! Only 1,000 times the number of stars, our present number?" He answered, "This is only my personal *brachah*. But Hashem will then bless you with an unlimited *brachah*."

The *Chasam Sofer* asks, "Why didn't Moshe simply give them Hashem's unlimited *brachah*?" Moshe knew that people do not always appreciate the *brachah* of a large family. Perhaps their involvement in *Olam Hazeh* will distort their values, and the troubles involved in raising children will detract from appreciation of how giving enriches one's life. So he tested them — he knew Hashem's *brachah* would not be bestowed upon people who would not appreciate it. He started with a limited *brachah* and when they showed a true Jewish reaction, "You are limiting our *Olam Haba*? We are not Eisav's children!" he said, "That is from me — if you appreciate my *brachah*, then Hashem will give you a further *brachah* without bounds."

So in our *tefillah* to Hashem, we must pray for unlimited *brachah*, understanding that our life in *Olam Hazeh* has worth only if it is used as a means towards a spiritual existence. If used properly, we will merit fulfillment of the *Harachaman* we say in *Bircas Hamazon* (Grace After Meals): "May we be *zocheh* to the Advent of *Mashiach* and to a life of *Olam Haba* — in the way we lead our lives here and now."

Yaakov Jacobs

"Sidney (Also Known as Steven)"

ANY COURTROOM BATTLE for the custody of a child has unhappy — often tragic—undertones. It bespeaks an unsuccessful marriage, a broken home, and broken hearts. Whichever way it is finally resolved, the pain lingers on.

But a recent case which came to our attention, which revolved around a nine-year old boy — as the court described him "Sidney (also known as Steven)" — bespeaks the story of a broken people. The case was described in the decision of Justice Ostrow which appeared in *The New York Law Journal* on June 14 last. In the cold legalisms of "habeas corpus," "custody" and "visitation rights," a tale unfolds which has all the elements of the tragedy of a people divided between those who have left Torah and those who stubbornly cling to it.

We saw "Sidney (also known as Steven)" in a Shabbos visit to Camp Dora Golding, popularly known as Camp Deal, a camp for underprivileged *yeshivah* students in Deal, New Jersey. "See that boy" — a camp official pointed to a youngster with a clean white *arba-kanfos* draped over his shirt, jet-black *peyos* neatly tucked behind his ears, *siddur* in hand, and swaying as though he had been *davening* for a thousand years — "last year he was going to church on Sundays."

Sidney was born into tragedy — his mother is chronically ill and hospitalized, and since the first day of his life he had been in the care of his grandmother. When he reached school age, he was sent to a public school where he was considered to be a "slow" student and was transferred to a New York City "600"-school where he spent three years in the first grade.

It became increasingly difficult for Sidney's grandmother to care for him and give him a proper home; she was in her seventies and her husband in his nineties. When friends on the block invited Sidney to Mass on Sunday, his grandmother dressed him appropriately and sent him off to church.

In September of 1966, Sidney's grandmother entered the hospital for surgery. She placed the child in the care of Mr. and Mrs. Bernard Ostreicher, a *chassidic* family living in Boro Park, and distant relatives of the boy.

Sidney was enrolled in a *yeshivah*, and enjoyed the love of his temporary parents and the companionship of their six children. He made remarkable progress in his religious and secular studies, and it became clear that his failure in public school was not due to lack of intelligence.

"Sidney was unusually thin, and emaciated, quiet and withdrawn," so testified his principal — but "he demonstrated remarkable improvement within two months. He gained weight, took on a happy mien, became well adjusted and there was no indication that he was retarded. He showed an aptitude in his studies and earned good marks."

When the grandmother came home from the hospital and asked that Sidney be returned, the Ostreichers refused to give him up. The grandmother then instituted a habeas corpus procedure and petitioned the court to order the boy's return.

Mid-way in the proceedings it became clear to the court that the grandparents, because of their advanced age, could not cope with the needs of a boy nine, and it was agreed by both parties that an uncle of the boy be permitted to become a co-petitioner with Sidney's grandmother, to obtain custody of the boy.

Sidney's uncle told the court that — in the words of the court — "the Orthodoxy of the respondents is of such extreme nature that it would be detrimental to the welfare of the child," but the court noted that "the well-being of Sidney, his progress at the *yeshivah*, belie any adverse effect resulting from his studies."

In questioning the boy's uncle, who was seeking custody, it was revealed that he (the uncle) had been divorced from his first wife, had made no request for visitation rights to his child; had not seen her for the past eighteen years; and had not contributed to her support. But he was asking the court to take Sidney away from his foster parents because of their 'extreme' Orthodoxy.

"Sidney (Also Known as Steven)"

Justice Ostrow rejected the petition to remove Sidney from the Ostreichers, and awarded custody to them because, "in the opinion of the court ... the respondents [the Ostreichers] have demonstrated clearly and convincingly their ability and desire to give Sidney a good home and proper care."

"Sidney (also known as Steven)" is now living in Boro Park with his "new" parents and brothers and sisters where he is now known as "Shmuel."

Libby Lazewnik

Invisible Ledgers

They went shopping for shoes today
Three children and a mother
Riding home in the bus
She observes the day's acquisitions:
Six shiny shoes neatly laced in a row
Three bobbing balloons at the ends of sticks
Definite gains.

Then she pats her depleted wallet, remembering
There are losses, too.
In her mind's eye she sees
The balloons next week
Sagging, airless skins, sticks broken in half
While the children cry for new toys.
The shoes that gleam so bravely today
Will be scuffed later, and frayed
Bursting at the seams, ready for the trash-heap
Demanding further outlays
Of cold, hard cash.

She is tired, so tired
Of adding up
    shaping up
    keeping up.
Riding through the dusk
The years hang heavy on her

And the losses.
She ushers the children home
Still and sad in a twilight hush
Watching them admire the new shoes,
Caper with balloons
And sitting there, she begins
To notice things.

Her daughter, the older one
Makes a thoughtful remark
She could not have made a month ago.

The middle one endures the wait till supper
With a little more patience
Than before

The youngest boy says his *brachah*
Clear and proud
And does not dispute his mother's "no."

The sighs shrivel and die
Pain turns to wonder
A mother stops counting the minutes.
In an invisible ledger she tallies instead
Each nugget of hard-won wisdom
Each treasured shred of *nachas*
And her soul, radiant balloon
Greatly expands
With her knowledge, her joy:

Thieves may pick her pockets
And the years steal her strength
But they cannot take even the tiniest part
Of what she has
This moment
In this room
She smiles.
Though her wallet be thin
Her coffers are full.

Anonymous

Life-styles of the Childless Poor

YOU KNOW US. We're the couple from your *shul/kollel/ chevrah* who have no children. We've been married quite a few years, and we know you realize something's wrong. Your curiosity is understandable and excused, and we're sure many of you even keep us in mind when you *daven*. For this we are grateful.

In the *yeshivah* world, infertility is an excruciatingly difficult condition to deal with. Non-Jews and irreligious Jews are not questioned when they remain childless for a number of years. It is assumed that they are planning careers and waiting until "the time is right" and their fortunes are adequate. Most of them do plan things this way.

But what about us? You know that is not our case. We've watched all our peers *Baruch Hashem* give birth in a year or so, sometimes even less. Many of you got married long after we did and already have two or more children. We are part of the growing community of "the infertile."

Often you have offered us the "*kvatership*" at your son's *brisim*. What an honor! Such gratitude we felt, such hopes we had that maybe this time the *zechus* of this *bris*, with the visit of *Eliyahu HaNavi*, would bring us good tidings. But it was not to be.

So why am I writing this? No, not just to thank you for your concern and *tefillos*. I am pleading on the behalf of the "childless poor," to those of you who are less sensitive to our pain.

I think you know what I'm talking about.

How often have we women gathered at a meeting or *tzedekah* function and all the conversations would be about your babies' accomplishments? How many agonizing minutes did I have to spend holding back tears until one sensitive mother noticed my silence and tactfully changed the subject?

Not that I prefer the sudden and abrupt "Let's drop the subject" silence when mothers see me approaching. It's rather obvious and hurts almost as much.

What about you, "Mrs. Pregnancy"? That's the nickname I gave you years ago, for though you'd only been through two pregnancies, I've never heard conversation in which you did not mention them. No matter who is present, no matter how many, you are still forever telling us how your "nausea the first time through was much worse than the second one ... but *my* second one was harder because..." Or worse yet, you call me up to complain about how ungainly you look in maternity clothes.

Countless times I have listened to pregnancy and motherhood complaints, with fury building up inside me. I must hold myself back from screaming, "*Baruch Hashem* you are tired and nauseous! *Baruch Hashem* your baby kept you up all night. Don't you realize what a *brachah* you have?

But those are minor incidents compared to other experiences. At times, the brutal insensitivity of some women seems to overshadow all the stories I have heard about *nashim tzidkaniyos*. Like the mother who said to my childless friend after Pesach, "You just won't know what Pesach is until you have a child — *shepping nachas* as he asks the Four Questions..." My poor friend cried for hours after this. What was the mother trying to do, rub it in?

I personally will never forget the mother who got married long after me and gave birth within a year. The tactless things she would say to me and my friend *Akarah* II, the only two childless wives in our *shul/kollel/chevrah*, were unbelievable.

We're already used to ordinary boasting, but she'd bring the baby to *shul* and show him to us, with: "Have you seen my baby yet? Isn't he adorable? Come hold him." Yet even that was nothing compared to the last straw, the incident that compelled me to do something.

Akarah II and I were at a *Bar Mitzvah*, sitting together as we always do, so we can compare infertility treatments, while everyone compares baby stories. This proud mother, who had been seated at another table, was on her way out of the room. But she went out of her way to stop at our table, just to tell us (the only two women she knew at the table), "I've got to call my baby sitter to see how my little Dovid is."

The stinging pain I felt at the moment was enough to make me write this. The circumstances surrounding this were just too overpowering to ignore. What happened to the characteristics of *Am Yisrael* — *baishanus, rachmanus* and *chessed*, modesty, compassion and generosity? It brought back memories of my single days when my *kallah* friends would talk about nothing else but their *chassanim*, and make the rest of us feel miserable. And how I vowed, and kept my promise, not to bring such pain to my single friends upon my engagement. It was difficult, minimizing the excitement and joy for the sake of their feelings. But it just took a little sensitivity. And I know that *Baruch Hashem* I succeeded because my single friends specifically told me so and thanked me. I am not trying to sing my praises, but rather to make you realize that it is possible. If I could do it, anyone can. We know you women are thrilled to be expecting and to be mothers, and we are happy for you. But a bit of sensitivity would be appreciated.

Luckily, the men have it easier because men don't talk about their children as much as women do, and have no "pregnancy experiences" to compare. Yet on Simchas Torah I still cried for my husband, feeling his anguish as fathers danced with their children on their shoulders. He too feels envy in *shul* as fathers hold their sons, read the *parashah* with them, and hold out their tiny fingers to kiss the Torah. So let us not forget the pain of childless men. They, too, yearn for fatherhood.

I beg of you please to think before you speak. I do not write this to instill guilt feelings but rather to open your eyes and ears to the hurt of infertile couples. May you be rewarded for your compassion with many healthy children to give you much *nachas*. And may your prayers and ours be answered, so that stories like this need not be written again.

Vicki Krausz

Jewish Kids up for Grabs

◆§ It Began With Nelli K.

UNDER A QUESTIONING headline, "Who Best to Care for a Child, Body and Soul," *The New York Times* ran an article in July about a Jewish girl, Nelli K., who was almost adopted by a Roman Catholic couple. Almost adopted — but not adopted, *Baruch Hashem*, because the Jewish Children's Adoption Network (JCAN) was aware of this Jewish child's existence and was informed that she was going to be placed in a non-Jewish home.

Re-assigning Nelli to a Jewish home was not simply a matter of just being aware she existed. Nelli was a ward of The New York Foundling Hospital, a foundation run directly by the Archdiocese. She was listed in the Blue Book, the state's register of children available for adoption, without any mention of her religion. The non-Jewish couple saw Nelli's picture and chose her with no idea of her Jewishness. They called the hospital and were told they would be able to adopt Nelli.

It was at that point that the JCAN was informed about Nelli and her proposed placement. Not only did we (at JCAN) feel it was morally wrong for Nelli to go to a non-Jewish home, we knew it was illegal. New York State adoption law states that, where practicable, a child should be placed in a home of the same faith.

At first, our urging that Nelli be placed in a Jewish home fell on deaf ears. We already had the choice of several perfect Jewish homes lined up for Nelli. All we needed was the hospital's cooperation. We, therefore, contacted Agudath Israel of America, whose general counsel, Mr. Chaim Dovid Zwiebel, fired off a letter to the hospital, threatening legal action. Rather than facing such a risk, New York Foundling approved Nelli's placement with a Jewish couple.

Nelli K. has a major *zechus* in being a "media" child, the child who brought the focus on a major problem across the country. Every day there are Jewish children being placed in non-Jewish homes. But that did not become general public knowledge until major newspapers did an article on the Nelli K. story, until she was featured on Gabe Pressman's show, and until the non-Jewish couple filed suit over their not getting custody of her.

⋑ A Commitment Born of Tragedy

Looking back today at the road we traveled, to bring us to forming JCAN and being contacted about children such as Nelli, it becomes more apparent than ever how our lives are guided by *Hashem* in mysterious ways. As our lives move on from tragedy, from loss, a new task sometimes evolves, an added *mitzvah*. A seemingly negative experience can become a catalyst for a positive outcome. From death sometimes life blooms forth. When I was expecting my third child, I suffered a miscarriage. All parents know the joy and anticipation for each awaited child. They can perhaps fathom, then, how my husband, Steve, and I were totally devastated by our loss.

G-d had seen fit not to give us an additional biological child, but He did have another child in mind for us. Because of our loss, we resolved to adopt a child. Our commitment to adopt was so strong, we were willing to take any child, healthy or otherwise. Such a couple should be a boon for adoption agencies, we naively reckoned. However, agency after agency found some reason not to give us a child: We were too old, too distraught, too young, too rich, too poor. The excuses never ended.

Most Jewish couples who attempt to adopt will probably run head-on into the same walls we did. They too will start believing the myth that there are no Jewish children up for adoption. The various agencies and social service departments almost had us convinced. Finally, G-d sent us a present, and a lesson — a little Jewish girl.

Elisheva was a four-month-old ward of a local county social service department. Elisheva was placed in our care, but ours was not the first home she had been in. Before being placed with us, Elisheva had been bounced around between five families — the most recent one, a Mormon family.

To us, Elisheva seemed part and parcel of our family as soon as she entered our door. According to state law she still was a ward of the social service department, to "dispose" of as it saw fit. The department soon saw fit to try placing her with a Christian couple.

Elisheva is a Jewish child. We are Jewish. Logic would dictate she stay with us. Social service departments do not operate on conventional logic. And to the social service department, Judaism was not an issue. To them, Elisheva's Jewishness was a minor detail, like the color of her hair.

To us, Elisheva was *our* daughter, and we would not let her be taken away. She was born Jewish, and no one had a right to deny her her heritage. Like a mother lion defending her cubs, I knew I would fight for this child. The matter went to court, and after a nineteen-month battle, Elisheva was legally recognized as our daughter.

Learning Through Necessity

Going through those long and hard months, I came to know the intricacies of adoption practices. I came to recognize the blatant anti-Semitism often apparent in placements. And I came to realize there was no agency fighting for these Jewish children as Jews.

When a problem is so pressing, there is no time to sit and discuss whether or not it will be easy to solve. You just get hurtled into action. The problems we had encountered threw us unprepared into a fight for Jewish children across the country, giving birth to the Jewish Children's Adoption Network (JCAN).

We got started with nothing more than a phone, some pens, a stack of paper, and a large measure of experience from our own case. We knew there was a need, but had no idea how much of a need. Our phones were swamped by people willing to adopt, by social workers who were about to place Jewish children, and (tragically) by parents who wanted to give their children up for adoption. The overwhelming majority of these children were special-needs children.

A special-needs child can mean anything, from hyperactive to mentally retarded, from an abused child to an older child. Each child comes to us with his own problems, each with his own story of tragedy. As I heard each case, my heart cried for a world going out of control. We had to place a few drug-addicted babies and a number of abused children—innocent children wounded and scarred by an irrational society!

There are other cases that make me shudder at how the value of each Jewish child is simply not appreciated. We had a father who wanted to give up his six-year-old son because he didn't speak. One couple did not want to take their baby home from the hospital because he did not have muscle power in the lower half of his face... We have children being put up for placement because they are hyperactive or learning disabled. We all understand and sympathize with parents who give up severely disabled children because of their inability to cope with them. In some cases, it is easy to understand why children are being placed for adoption. In other cases, however, it is very difficult to relate to relinquishing a child because of minor problems. Where does this phenomenon of disregard of every child's value come from? The question echoes around and around in our hearts, without an answer. (When first contacted about children, we try to have the biological parents rethink the issue. We urge them to go for counseling, to get help from various support groups, and to try and work with the child.)

܀ۣ The Way the Social Services Operate

Across the country, there are few laws to protect Jewish children. In several states, such as New York and Massachusetts, there are limited laws on the books that say, when "practicable," children should be placed in a home of the same faith as them. In New York and Massachusetts these laws often go ignored.

Social service departments operate under a "confidentiality" clause. They do not have to tell anyone anything about the children they place. This makes it close to impossible to monitor where Jewish children are being placed and how many Jewish children are in the adoption/foster care system. A religious social worker in a large Western state had access to the files, and just to get an idea of the number of Jewish children who are wards of the state, he went through all the files. Since he had no way of knowing who was Jewish or not (as one social worker told me, "You can't even be Jewish on our forms"), he picked out children with obviously Jewish last names. His count was 1,500! And that social service department will tell you that they have *no* Jewish children up for adoption.

In Massachusetts, where the law is on our side, we were informed that three Jewish children had been placed in non-Jewish homes. An *askan* (community activist) in Massachusetts contacted the local social services and requested the children be placed in Jewish homes. To quote their response:

"Please be advised that the Department considers your office's involvement in this matter to be inappropriate. State laws preclude the Department's even acknowledging, not to mention discussing, specific cases that are opened in this office. Therefore, your inquiries of Department staff, and the inquiries of others who, we are told, have been encouraged by you to call the Department of Social Services, will not be responded to."

We called the executive office and complained. In response we received a letter stating that Jewish children should be placed in Jewish homes. However, the letter then went on to say,

"Because of the various statutes and privacy interests that are involved, I am not at liberty to discuss any particular child or any particular foster care placement."

Fortunately, in this case, we were able to contact the biological mother, the children's lawyer and the judge in the case. The matter went to court and the judge ruled that a Jewish home must be found for the children. Most often we are not so lucky. After a stone-wall response based on "confidentiality," we have no way of helping the children. We have no way to prove they "exist" and have no rights.

◆§ A "Lone Voice in The Woods" No More

Some days I clench my fists in frustration. I'm a mother of four small children who deserve my attention. But I can't just turn my back on all the other children — can't walk away from the thousands of *neshamos* who are being denied what is rightfully theirs.

JCAN had been a lone voice in the woods. Working with no equipment and no support does limit our effectiveness. *Baruch Hashem*, more organizations and people are acknowledging the problem and pitching in to help. At a recent meeting of the *Nesius* (the Rabbinical Presidium) of Agudath Israel, the *Rabbanim* discussed the entire problem and explored the implications, and the possible steps to be taken; the Orthodox Union's Institute for Public Affairs has taken up the issue and is putting together a task force on it; and the Jewish Community Relations Council has set up meetings with various agencies in New York to try and impress on them the importance of Jewish children being placed in Jewish homes.

For the meantime, each case we take on is an individual fight for that particular child only. We must launch a collective battle for *all* the children. There is a federal law that protects Native American children from being placed in a non-Indian home. We should push for a law on behalf of Jewish children, even if it is not as comprehensive as the one that protects Native Americans.

Slated for August '92 is the National Association on Adoptable Children's seminar, considered to be *the* major adoption seminar by adoption activists and government workers. In the past, there were only three Jewish voices being heard at such seminars: my husband's, mine and that of Hillel Rosenfeld, a government employee who devotes his spare time to providing post-placement help for Jewish people. This year there should be one voice, a collective voice of the entire Jewish community demanding, "Let us have our children!" How strange to be forced to such extremes in our free society! But it is one of the blessings of living in this free society that we can mobilize our forces and make a difference in the lives of these unfortunate children, if we only care.

Malka Schaps

My Children's Brother

Once again, when trouble falls,
My foster children's mother calls.
All I can give is sympathy,
But worry cuts through my empathy.
"Where is Meir? Where will he go?"
"I don't know," she cries, "I don't know."
My children's mother is on the phone.
Will we take him or leave him alone?

G-d sent me down a different path.
My husband learns — I do math.
How dear to me those hours at work,
The last of tasks I want to shirk!
"They called to say they've started out,
They'll be here in an hour-about."
The social worker is on the phone.
Will we keep him or leave him alone?

His brother and sister beam with joy
And change him to a different boy.
Long pants, long sleeves, four *tzitzis* show.
The clippers shear, leave *peyos* below.
We cannot put him in *cheder* yet.
First we teach him the *Aleph-Bet*.
Their father's mother is on the phone.
Will we keep him or leave him alone?

Fusses, tantrums, winning smiles,
New clothes, parks, we must walk miles!
Dentists, doctors, loom ahead.
When he's asleep I fall in bed.
Fierce bursts of sibling rivalry
"Is there another family?"
Yad L'Achim called today.
Will we keep him or send him away?

Our own children and his siblings too —
Now they don't want him and now they do.
After a hundred and twenty years,
Which are the hours that pay the arrears?
Those beloved hours of abstract thought,
Or the painful ones when I do as I ought?
My husband's doubts are like my own:
"Will we keep him or leave him alone?"

Ambitions ask, "What could I do
if instead of one hand I could use two?"
Our Rav relieves the dreariness:
"You can't belittle a woman's weariness."
Am I tired or just short-sighted?
You want us to keep him, I know you do.
Would you feel the same if they asked *you*?

Ephraim Milch

Reflections of a Parent

Euphoria and Joy—Interrupted

THE WEEK OF *Parashas Vayetzei*, 1987, my wife gave birth to Sheryl, a little sister to our 15-month-old son. Excitement, euphoria, happiness and joy — the miracle of birth. Yet, those feelings were suddenly interrupted (I use the word purposely) with the doctor's statement that our precious daughter had Down's Syndrome and possibly a severe congenital heart defect.

Indeed, as a parent of a child with Down's Syndrome, the struggles and challenges, fears and frustrations, center around the physical infirmities that our child must overcome or learn to live with before she can even attempt to reach the classroom or playground. Perseverance, commitment and a unique temperament are critical to parent and child, in order to cope with the higher incidence of ear infections, eating disorders and often life-threatening heart defects. These concerns and difficulties deflect the parents' attention from other less apparent problems — the low muscle tone, late physical development and mental retardation. There is pain knowing our child will always struggle and still never attain what most people take for granted. But the pain is more intense when our child lies at the *akeidah* of an operating room or intensive care unit and we wait for G-d to say: "Do not stretch out your hand to the child," so to speak, to grant her survival.

~§ Groping for Understanding

Down's Syndrome (Trisomy 21) is a genetic accident; indeed, medical science cannot identify a cause or reason why any specific child is born with Down's Syndrome. Accordingly more than other disorders, it is one of those rare situations that point directly to *hashgachah*. G-d decided that this child should be born with this specific handicap and G-d decided that our family is where this child is destined to be. The child comes to this world with its own soul and its own mission for reasons we do not know. At the same time, G-d surely has complex plans, which often call for creating specific familial and community relationships, in order to test, purify and bless each of us.

We lack clarity of vision, a prophecy that can inform us what G-d has in mind and what path we are to follow to best serve Him. Instead, G-d sends us the directions by way of life's "turn of events" which, with the help of the interpretation and guidance of our Torah leaders, can lead us to our eventual goal — a goal we do not fully recognize until the trip is over. Our family portrait obviously required a child with Down's Syndrome. If that child is removed from the picture, then the entire picture and all those in it cannot accurately reflect what G-d has intended. I am a different person as is each person who had been touched by a child with Down's Syndrome. That is what G-d intended. There could be no other way. As the Chazon Ish wrote in *Emunah U'Bitachon*, *emunah* is the trust and realization that everything that happens is determined by *hashgachah* — decided by a loving Father. There is no fate or chance. *Bitachon* is living with this realization.

A couple in their early twenties does not give much thought to an event like this happening to them; accordingly, one cannot be prepared with any answers. Yet, G-d provides the strength. He does not guarantee that we *will* be successful in raising such a child. He does guarantee that we *could* be successful, by providing us with the potential to properly manage the situation.

~§ Negotiating the Rough Spots

In attaining the achievements, we pass through a series of rough spots:

Can I love this child or grandchild as I do the others? The question itself presents fear and pain. The answer lies in seeing and holding the child. Love of a parent to child and child to parents quickly replaces the feelings of doubt and aspects of rejection. Human love transcends the experience and allows us to develop an all-encompassing bond with this child, as with any child, a bond that cannot be severed, despite moments of difficulty. To hold and to care for; positive emotions surface and continue to assert control.

We stand outside the operating room of Children's Hospital, our daughter undergoing open heart surgery, and we realize through the heart-throbbing tears and desperate prayers that the love is forever present and that the parent-child attachment cannot be severed nor described. Through a most trying experience, G-d has reassured us of the love and commitment that He knew we had and we, as human beings, needed to recognize.

This cannot be happening to me, or my child, or my grandchild. Parents and grandparents awake together to face G-d's complex world as never before experienced. Perhaps we previously deluded ourselves that life presents such situations only to others. Perhaps we refuse to accept imperfections or human limitations.

To a great extent, family members take their lead from the parents of the handicapped child. When the grandparent sees strength and stability in the parents, he too, develops the courage and guidance necessary in such a situation.

There are also moments, particularly early on, when the pain is so great that we lose self-control and dare ask, "Why me?" G-d is surely aware of our belief and trust despite the confrontation.

We face challenges and, of course, our reactions are human. G-d does not demand a uniform response. We are tested because we are human. Because we are human, we react individually. Some people grapple alone with the pain, questions and fears, and find meaning and strength on their own. Others find comfort, encouragement and answers by opening themselves and sharing with others. Some will cry longer. Others will question harder.

☙ Better than Reuvain? Or Worse?

"Why me?" Am I worse than Reuvain, that G-d has decided to punish me in this world? Am I better than Reuvain that G-d is sending me direct punishment in this world, and treating me to something better in the world to come? If a child with Down's Syndrome is G-d's way of pointing out the failure of the "me" generation to properly give as parents, have I been a parent long enough to have failed in that area that G-d must punish me? If G-d is *not* punishing, but looking for "special" parents, have I been a parent long enough and acquired the maturity, extra sensitivity and special caring, to deserve and properly deal with such a child? If we are being challenged, to question is normal. To feel the pain is normal. It is our task to come up with the responsive action.

☙ Seeing the Beauty in the Test

Our struggle to deal with our child is our private *akeidah*, and we continue to refer to the original incident to better understand what is expected of us:

Avraham awoke early in the morning. G-d had called, and he was ready to respond. Yet, obviously he harbored doubts, or it would not have been a test. Who accompanied Avraham and Yitzchak to the *Akeidah*? *Chazal* tells us: Eliezer, Avraham's chosen servant, who later was trusted to select a wife for Yitzchak, studied with Avraham and, indeed, walked up to his neck in water in order to travel to the *Akeidah*. Yishmael, as well — the son of Avraham, who underwent circumcision at thirteen, and now traveled the same course to the *Akeidah* as Eliezer. At that point, say *Chazal*, Avraham compares them to a donkey. The greatness of Avraham and Yitzchak that distinguished them from Eliezer and Yishmael was their ability to see the cloud of Glory hovering over the mountain, while the others saw only a hill. Eliezer and Yishmael recognized that this mission was a calling from G-d. They trusted and believed. But they failed to see the potential in the event ahead.

The key to transcending mortal shortcomings is not to dwell on the questions of "Why?" and "How come?" but instead to pray to G-d for the strength to ask "What can we do?"; to see the mountain and the enormous potential that this child has to serve G-d — as does any child, in its way. Once again, *emunah* and *bitachon* slowly reassure us and human love helps provide the needed strength. The questions, although perhaps not completely answered, no longer seem so pressing.

◆§ Advancing Toward the Future

A person with Down's Syndrome is a complete Jew and is obligated as all people to serve G-d to his or her full potential. We have the responsibility to educate her in Torah and *mitzvos*, and because she is no different than you or I, she will enter the community of Israel at the age of twelve and will assume all the obligations of an adult. Having a handicap does not diminish a person's human status. To the contrary, each *neshamah* is placed on this earth to perfect itself; a *neshamah* placed in a *guf* with limited faculties obviously has fewer weaknesses requiring perfection. The Chazon Ish would stand before those children with limited mental capacity and note that they are particularly holy and pure.

Through it all, one continues to live with dichotomies. Tears emanate from the pain and frustration; tears emanate from joy and happiness. Tears flow from beings overwhelmed by the moment; tears flow from the love and concern of others. Helping hands of family and friends at a difficult time are so important — their just being there—suffering in our difficult moments and rejoicing in our happiness, dreams and hopes—friends who not only presented a shoulder to cry on but who cried themselves— And some tears are shed in intense moments of prayer — alone, man and G-d.

We seek answers, to explain the past; G-d continues to provide solutions for the future. A world of sophisticated medicine and special education continually affirms the Hand of G-d and His greatness on earth, and we benefit from the selfless dedication showered on individuals — indeed, our daughter — who but a few years ago society ignored.

Sheryl provides us with a continuous lesson in true parenting. It is difficult, as a parent, to live vicariously through a child with Down's Syndrome, to dream that she will live out your unfulfilled dreams and carry on your hopes after you have passed on. The joy is in the achievement, the communication — at whichever level — of each child as himself or herself. The greatest proof of our humanity is in the non-comparing love we can show for our children and for each other. At the same time, she provides abundant love in all directions. She showers us with more satisfaction, more love and more personal growth than we could even hope to instill in her. As Dovid *HaMelech* wrote in *Tehillim*, "The stone which the builder rejected has become the chief cornerstone."

Bracha Druss Goetz

Dear Mom

Dear Mom, *Shalom!* How are you? I hope you're feeling well.
Thank G-d everyone is fine. And I have some news to tell.

    It's hard for me to write you,
       these words which should cause joy.
    Soon we will have, G-d willing, a brand-new girl or boy.

Already I can picture your look that's on your face.
Daughter dear, must you produce the whole human race?

    I'm thinking of your health, you'd say with genuine concern.
    You want to save the Jewish People —
       but give someone else a turn.

Your body needs a rest, my dear, why can't you take a break?
If you will not listen to me — do it for the children's sake.

    Until you gave me my first grandchild, I could hardly wait.
    But every year you're giving birth —
       and now it's number eight!

Of course I love each little face. I treasure every one.
But don't forget you're still my child —
   and I'm worried about you, hon.

    Physically, emotionally and financially too,
    Children are very draining. What will be left of you?

And then come your closing words —
   Mom, they always pierce through me.

Just remember: What's important is quality, not quantity.
    The other arguments never swayed me —
        but this one would sting.
    Quality — not quantity — that does have a good ring.

Your words never leave me, Mom, they won't go away.
But this time as I write to you, I now know what to say.

    Better quality than quantity, which one must I lose?
    Who says that you can't have both?
        Who says I have to choose?

I don't see why I should settle and sell myself so short.
I'm trying to make good human beings —
    this isn't merchandise I've bought.

    This job would be too much for me
        if it all fell on my shoulders.
    Their father and I do our parts —
        yet it is G-d who grows them older.

You're worried if we'll have enough —
    but can't you see my wealth?
I am glowing from my diamonds
    and these children give me health.

    Do you think more pleasure will drain me?
    Then let me say one thing —
    All that I can give to them does not compare
        with what they bring.

Why don't you understand me? Really you're the one to blame.
You filled my life with so much love, Mom, I want to do the same.

    I'll keep wishing you will share my joy —
        I hope someday you'll see
    All my children are an expression
        of all the love you put in me.

An Open Letter to My Questioning Friend From That Mother of the Boy on Crutches

Dear *Reb Yid* (or *Rebbetzin Yiddine*),

You don't know me, and I don't know you. We will probably never meet again, so I am writing you this open letter in the hope that you will see it and know how I feel. It just might give you some food for thought in the future.

This morning on your way home from *shul*, you passed my house just as two of my children were boarding their school bus. You stopped and spoke to me. My parents taught me to have *derech eretz*, and seeing a respectable-looking person, old enough to be my father, I felt compelled to stay and answer you.

You had noticed that one of my children boarding the bus has only one leg, and you wanted to know what had happened to him. Now, logic would dictate that there could be only three possible answers to this: (a) He was born like this, or (b) he lost it to an illness or (c)injury. Whatever the reason, it is done already and cannot be glued back on! So, why ask? Another thing my parents taught me was not to stare or point at people, and *never* ask personal questions of strangers, as this may cause them pain or embarrassment, *chas vashalom*. However, I am certainly not ashamed of my son, so I answered you very simply that he had lost it to an illness.

This should have been enough for you, but apparently you needed all the details — when it happened, the exact location, etc.

Again I answered your questions, even though I could see no purpose behind them other than idle curiosity. But, true to my upbringing, I could not act with disrespect. (To be perfectly honest, had you been an old lady with a funny-looking hat, I still would have felt compelled to treat you with *derech eretz.*) You then needed to know how many doctors we had consulted and if they all really felt that an amputation was necessary. I told you which *Rebbe* we had consulted and which prominent surgeon he sent us to. I even explained to you the unusual details of the case that made this course of action absolutely necessary.

Did this satisfy you? Of course not. You still had to know why I didn't seek yet ANOTHER opinion. (I wonder if you meant another *Rebbe* or another surgeon.)

By now, my friend, you had certainly gone beyond the bounds of common decency.

I'm certain that at this point even my parents would have given me permission to close the door on you and terminate the conversation. But you see, by this time, I felt that I had to justify myself. After all, what kind of mother WOULD allow her son's leg to be amputated unnecessarily? And what kind of stupid people would make such an important decision on one man's say-so? I had to make you understand that it was unquestionably *bashert* and that we have to believe that it was for the best.

✑ Attitudes and Such

I am sure that some people reading this will be saying, "Oh, she just has a poor attitude. She shouldn't take things so personally." But you can't get much more personal than to question a person's decision-making ability, especially where her children are concerned. As for "attitudes," permit me to tell you: Some time ago my son was in a grocery store and an old man asked him a question about his condition, which my son calmly answered. The man then asked my son if it was all right that he had asked him (a little too late, I would think). My little boy answered that people are always asking him such things and that he understands that they do this because they care about him and want him to get better. I am very proud of the way this 5-year-old handled the situation; I don't think we have any attitude problems here!

Perhaps you feel that I am overreacting to one person's curiosity. But you see, *Reb Yid*, although we don't know each other

— I MEET YOU MANY TIMES A DAY. Sometimes you are wearing a long *rekkel*, sometimes a sports jacket, sometimes a Windbreaker. Sometimes you have on a *Chassidishe* hat, sometimes a suede *yarmulke*. You may appear as a man or a woman; sometimes old, sometimes young. Your accent and vocabulary vary, but I recognize you just the same. Occasionally I get lucky and meet your brother. Even though he doesn't know me, he will stop and tell me that he once knew someone who went through the same thing and is now grown and married, with children. Then he will wish me *nachas* from my son and go on his way — without asking any personal questions or questioning my judgment or abilities. He always brightens my day and I am happy to meet him.

This is not to say that I don't want to answer any questions. On the contrary. I am always happy when friends and acquaintances call to ask how my son is doing. There is also a time and place for giving out information. My son has explained to all of his friends and classmates exactly what was wrong with him. He has showed them his prosthesis and explained how it works, adding, "This is just until *Mashiach* comes. Then I get the real one back."

What I really object to is being expected to give a complete *din vecheshbon* to every stranger who demands it. Would you ask a childless couple if they are really sure that they cannot have children? Would you ask an older single person if he is really trying to find a *shidduch*? Would you be insensitive enough to ask a *baal teshuvah* how it really feels to eat pork? (On second thought, considering some of the articles I have read recently, I'm very much afraid that you just might!)

৵ Guidelines for Greeting the Handicapped

The Torah obligates us to judge our fellow Jews in the best possible light. After speaking with you, I am sure that you are not cruel by nature. Nor would you willingly cause another person such pain. Perhaps you never had the benefit of parents who taught you to deal sensitively with other people, as I have. Maybe, like many people, you just don't know how to react to handicapped people when you encounter them. If that is the case here are some guidelines. If you follow them, you can't go far wrong:

1. Don't stare, but don't avert your eyes either. Being invisible is worse than being stared at. A pleasant and cheerful "Good

morning" is always nice. (Note: This works well with non-handicapped people also.)

2. Don't ask personal questions. Just don't! The exception here is if you need information for some practical reason. I am often approached by parents of children who have been diagnosed with illnesses similar to that of my son. I am more than happy to answer any questions they may have (no matter how personal) and to help in any way that I can. I also belong to a support group for parents of children with life-threatening illnesses. The purpose of this group is to meet other people in the same boat and give *chizuk* to each other. This is not the same thing as asking questions out of idle curiosity.

3. If you see a person in need of assistance (handicapped or not!), by all means offer to help. The person then has the option of accepting or refusing your help. If the person refuses, smile politely (see #1 above) and keep moving. Some people derive immense satisfaction from accomplishing a difficult task alone. If the person accepts your help, ask first how you can best be of assistance. Sometimes what YOU feel is needed may not be appropriate. Never assume that you know what needs to be done without asking first. I do not refer here to holding open a door for someone loaded down with packages. I refer here to something like lifting my son up steps — he can do it perfectly well himself, and you could startle him, causing him to lose his balance. Always ask first.

One final thought, *Reb Yid*. You mentioned that you were compelled to stop me because it hurt you to see a Jewish child like this (trust me — it hurts me more than it hurts you). You are not a bad person, *Reb Yid*. On the contrary. This compassion for another's suffering is what marks you as a child of *Avraham Avinu*. I would not have it any other way. The next time you see my child, or any other person in unfortunate circumstances, by all means feel for them. Experience their pain. But don't take it up with me. I am not the one responsible. Take it up with *Hakadosh Baruch Hu*. He is the one responsible for everything that happens in this world. Perhaps if enough people will talk to Him, He will rectify the situation by bringing *Mashiach* speedily in our days.

Name Withheld

The author of this article, a principal of a high school in a large metropolitan area, has requested anonymity to protect the identity of the people described.

Kids on the Fringe

OUR EDUCATIONAL institutions are embattled — beset by a variety of difficulties. In the previous issue of *The Jewish Observer*, Rabbi Yaakov Bender eloquently highlighted one critical problem: What about the large number of students who cannot find their place in our schools because of academic weakness, poor preparation and background, or limited ability? Great effort and large resources are required to meet their needs. Can the *yeshivos* carry the burden? If not, who will?

There is yet another problem that poses this question in an even more serious form but has not been given the attention that it most urgently demands: the issue of our problem students. I do not refer here to children who are severely emotionally disturbed. These are tragic cases that are clearly not within the purview of the regular schools. My concern is with the growing number of our children that cannot or will not adjust to our institutions and their standards.

Rabbi Bender touched on this problem in passing when he spoke of youngsters being told to leave their respective *yeshivos* "for even minor infractions" and refers to "the boy who has even slightly strayed off the well-defined *derech*, the boy with the so-called 'bummy appearance'... whom most high schools will not touch." He reminded us of the time-honored approach of our *gedolim* that a student should not be expelled unless he has a definite, clearly defined detrimental effect on others. This is such an obvious and logical guideline that it would seem very simple to apply.

But appearances often are deceiving.

Mother and daughter walk into the principal's office. The family just moved from another part of town. They are *shomrei mitzvos*, and want the daughter to attend the school. The mother does all the talking while the girl silently watches the proceedings through the curtain of hair cascading over most of her face. She seems to be reasonably well prepared for the academic work, and the transcript from the school she attended raises no questions. *Why not take her in?* muses the principal; *she will adjust*. However, before ushering them out of the office, the principal draws attention to the dress code and uniform of the school, and diplomatically points out that the teenager will have to do something about her hair; "After all, we want to be able to see you." The mother assures her that this is no problem at all.

Indeed it is not; on the first day of school, the new student appears with her hair neatly tied back — wearing a shiny leather jacket over her uniform. There is something of a stir in the classroom, but it passes as the class settles into its routine. A goodly number of her classmates stay out of her way, feeling ill at ease with the new arrival — especially when it is noted that on the way to and from school she uses a walkman to listen to her favorite popular music. Others, however, flock to this intriguing and different creature, and soon she has her circle of admirers.

✑§ The School's Dilemma

It was only a few days into the term when a mother called to protest about the school accepting this student. The principal explains: "After all, this girl grew up in a somewhat different environment. We are working with her, and she doesn't wear here leather jacket any more. If your daughter and her friends will be *mekarev* her, I have no doubt that she will soon adjust to our standards. Do you really think that the things you object to warrant sending away a child and maybe losing a precious *neshama?*"

Indeed, they do not — so we all agree. Were not our schools built to recapture our children from an alien environment? Should we now lock our doors to the children that need us most? But wait a minute: What about the girls who are attracted by exactly those things about her that we object to? With alarm, the teachers note that, not surprisingly, it is precisely those girls in the class who are the most vulnerable — with the weakest background, the least academic success, the most complex home situation — who flock to her and begin to imitate what we sought to discourage. Before long the battle is joined between those who decry our readiness to exclude children who are a little different, and those who see the need to protect the children entrusted to us. The school is squarely in the middle — condemned by both sides for failing in its educational task.

This scenario could just as easily be presented with a *Mesivta* applicant as its "hero" — and it is played out in innumerable variations throughout our educational institutions. Thus the question is raised: What can and should schools do? Perhaps, however — and this is the thesis of this article — this issue is a community problem that is deeply rooted in our society and must be tackled by the community at large, and should not be dumped into the lap of the school.

◆§ Saturday Night Live

Let us be clear about what we are discussing. At issue are not children from "modern" homes whose parents approve of, and indeed desire, a life-style incompatible with *yeshiva* and Beth Jacob teachings. These children will attend the type of day schools that accommodate such parents — and very often do the very best for these children within the confines of the parents' ideology. We are talking about parents who do want *us* to educate their children — and increasing numbers of these children turn out to be problems for us. Take a stroll on a *Motza'ei Shabbos* to the local delicatessen, pizza parlor or shopping mall — whether the locality be Brooklyn, Monsey, or the Catskills. By the standards of contemporary society, the scene is tame indeed; but it hurts deeply to find here boys and girls who have gone to our institutions, or still do, whose attire and behavior is in glaring contradiction to all the Torah standards that we have been trying to teach them — and it is not just their present situation that frightens us but, much more, the future toward which they appear to be heading.

✢ A Worsening Problem or an Optical Illusion?

Some hard questions must be asked. Is it only an optical illusion that this is a worsening problem, and the larger number of such cases is merely a result of the increase in *yeshiva* and Beth Jacob students in general? Or is it a sign of the increasing difficulties our schools face in countering the influences of an evermore radically demoralized society? Surely both are factors to be considered — and there are others. Most important for our considerations, however, is the role played by the deterioration of family life even in the *frum* community.

I cannot provide scientifically obtained statistics. However, in case after case that I have been involved in, the parents were divorced, there were serious problems of *Shalom Bayis*, or there were other major family problems — an extreme degree of parent-child friction, with one or the other parent far too rigidly authoritarian or else too permissive or ineffective, or stresses due to major sickness or bereavement.

Let me not be misunderstood: I do not suggest that only children from troubled homes become problems, or that all or even most of the children from such homes get into trouble; in fact, many children faced with such situations ultimately emerge stronger as they struggle to contend with their problems. But alas, too many do not — and thus, a majority of problem children come from such background. We have to realize that children differ in their reaction to strain and stress. Some show a remarkable resilience; through the mercy of Heaven, they are the fortunate ones. But there are also all those who withdraw into themselves, develop nervous systems and actual illness — or compensate for their problems by "acting out" or indeed becoming full fledged rebels against adult society.

Yet we should not automatically assign blame or guilt to any of the parties involved in these problem situations. In the first place, some of them cannot be controlled by human actions, such as severe sickness, G-d forbid, or inability to earn a living. But even when the problems appear to derive from human failure, marital or parenting, we must realize that, to a great degree, the adults involved are victims of a society in which there is confusion about one's personal rights and duties in marriage and child rearing, great emphasis on material possessions and self-gratification, vast variations in religious standards and understanding, and an unremitting pressure from the outside world. (It was Reb Boruch Ber, זצ״ל, the Kamenitzer *Rosh HaYeshiva*, who before the war corrected a man criticizing American rabbis: "It's not that the American *Rabbonim* are smaller. The problems they face are larger.") The fact remains: Problem situations are proliferating — and the children all too often are the victims.

This is easy to understand. Negative childhood experiences have serious consequences (and these tend to surface during adolescence, which can be a turbulent time in even conventional families.) In the first place, there is a deep-seated alienation from adults and their efforts to provide direction. Respect for their authority is lost — and, worse, so is the confidence in their wisdom and trustworthiness. In contrast, the hedonistic values and standards of the outside world appear most attractive.

Secondly, there is the harm done to the self-image of the child. He may feel guilty about what is going on; he is embarrassed and will desperately try to hide it from others; he lacks positive experiences and, in the face of glaring adult failure, becomes convinced that failure is unavoidable in life. He needs to feel that he is somebody — and he gains this feelings from association with others who are in the same boat. Moreover, he has to be reassured that somebody not only respects him but likes him and cares about him — and here the girlfriend (or boyfriend, in the case of a girl) plays a crucial role.

If a child is fortunate enough to be befriended by a trustworthy adult, a neighbor, teacher, or relative — in effect, a surrogate parent figure — this will go a long way to provide reassurance and to nurture the resilience that the child needs in order to cope with his problems. Given at an early stage, such help is likely to make a difference in the child's life. But time is of the essence here. Once he starts to develop a negative attitude toward adults, and links up with like-minded friends, it becomes very difficult indeed to reach him — and I pointed out previously that these children tend to find each other and flock together. That is why schools can usually handle a single student who poses problems, but will fail if he becomes a catalyst in the forming of what might be called a cell.

If this analysis is correct, it follows that we cannot expect our schools to solve problem situations that are so deeply rooted in the failures of our society. The community, whether it is a single congregation or a whole neighborhood, must realize that the weakening of families does not just spell heartache for individuals but is a real danger to the *Klal* and its future. The great rise in the number of divorces and of troubled youngsters found in our communities is surely a warning signal. In this connection we must face the fact that the problem is particularly serious in the most intensely *"frum"* localities. Firstly, children who "act out" do not stand out so glaringly in other communities; this does not diminish the heartache of the parents, but the youngster does not see himself (or herself) shunned and rejected so much, and can therefore be reached more easily. Secondly, there is the tendency, all too natural, to deny the existence of a problem until it is too late, and to reject outside help — instead, all too often severe punishment makes the situation worse, or children are shifted from school to school, with teachers and principals being blamed. Thus, there rests an enormous responsibility upon the community and its leaders.

In the first place, major efforts are called for to buttress our families. Effective intervention measures need to be put into effect by *Rabbonim, talmidei chachomim* and *askonim*. Torah guidance to newlyweds and help to families in trouble, *shiurim* and lectures on family life and education, all will help to shore up our families.

Social service agencies must not only be prepared to provide material help to the needy but to deal with families at risk, at their own request or that of *Rabbonim* and neighbors.

Secondly, much more has to be done in the area of providing guidance and counseling to children. This need not necessarily be done by professionals — quite often, individuals with intelligence and skill, warmth and the right *hashkafos* can help just by lending an understanding ear. Counseling centers should be made readily available in every community. For a variety of reasons, such counseling can probably be done most effectively within the confines of each school by a competent teacher or a guidance counselor. But the community must provide the means needed. How many of our schools have enough manpower for this purpose? How many could afford it? In truth, we cannot put a further burden on the schools; and even if they are enabled to provide adequate counseling, it must be clear that the problem cannot be vanquished until the community accepts its responsibility for the Jewish family and its children within twentieth-century society.

Letter From a Mother of "Kids on the Fringe"

To the Editor:

Thank you, thank you and *yasher ko'ach* to both *The Jewish Observer* and your anonymous author and educator for having the courage to finally address this most painful but pervasive problem in our community ("Kids on the Fringe," May '91). I write, unfortunately, from first-hand experience as a single mother and custodial parent of my children (all boys). Needless to say, my teenagers fell prey to exactly the life-style you describe, and possibly for many of the same reasons. And the pain of this situation is multiplied many times beyond the pain of the so-called good child rejected on the basis of his scholastic prowess. Here, there is the failed marriage, the children having to bungle through the separation, the anger at the parents who put them through this, the complication of remarriage on one or both sides with step-siblings and new grandparents, and possible additions from the new marriage, anger frequently left over from unresolved issues in the old marriage, and the shame of facing friends with this new status of divorced parents.

Picture a boy sometimes having to go to *shul* and sitting alone while his friends sit with their fathers. Then there's the mother trying to *"fere tisch"* until her boys hit Bar Mitzva age and they assume the position their father is supposed to be holding (which he does, on alternate *Shabbosos*). Imagine your children not bringing home *Shabbos* guests for one of two reasons: either he is ashamed, or other parents don't allow it because there is no intact family at the table. Your child, however, is frequently welcome at other tables because he *"nebach"* does not have a home. Message to child? I am different, and that is exacerbated by your intact family at your *Shabbos* table.

Feelings of sadness and anger frequently overwhelm the child, resulting in the acting-out behavior so accurately described by your author. Now the problem becomes more complicated. "Acting-out" child is given the feeling that he is tainted and spoiled goods. Even Rabbi Bender, who did the lost children an ultimate *chessed* of bringing problems to the forefront (JO May '91), still could not tackle this more pervasive problem beyond "the boy who has even slightly strayed off the well-defined *'derech,'* the boy with the so-called 'bummy appearance'... whom most high schools will not touch."

Imagine being the parent of the boy whom most high schools "won't touch." Think how you want to protect your children from "the wrong element" and then think again what it would be like for your child to *be* "the wrong element." Do you know what it's like to work a full day(because a single parent, no matter how generous the ex-spouse, can't support a family on "child support" alone), come home to a house full of children, with no one to shoulder any of the burden? Not the housework, not the shopping, doctor appointments, all aspects of child-rearing, bill-paying; and now complicate this by children acting out, while you yourself are trying to deal with being single. This child cutting school, that son running around with a pack of friends like himself (boys and girls), this principal calling you for another report of what this child's done now, and he's hanging on to his place in this *yeshiva* by a hair. One false move and it's *"ois yeshiva."* How much good parenting is left in this mother who has to juggle such a load?

And finally, to add insult to injury, there is the community, which sees your child in these "bummy" clothes, with his "bummy" friends. They notice that maybe you couldn't even get them off to *shul* Friday night because their rebellion extends this far. They have *rachmonus* but somehow sense that you have really failed. Or the ex-spouse has failed. Even the very compassionate author of this article very mildly points a finger at these parents, even while bending over backwards to temper that blame: "...But even when problems appear to derive from human failure, marital or parenting..." So imagine now you are that parent, and you feel, on top of all this, that you have overwhelmingly failed. How many children emerging from this situation feel anything more than "on the fringe"?

Letter from a Mother of "Kids on the Fringe"

☙Does Klal Have a Role?

The author is most correct in saying that the responsibility should be shared by the *Klal*. Perhaps the first thing a community inbued with *chessed* needs to do is not to treat these children as if they have some contagious disease. The children know full well how they are regarded in the community, and this alienates them further. It's true, all *yeshivos* cannot bear the burden of all children, but in a community where we are taught to do *chessed*, surely we should not throw these souls (*neshamos*) away because we fear for the *yeshiva's* good name, or our emotionally stable child's good name who by association with the troubled child might *shter* his/her own *shidduch*. Even public schools have programs for the most difficult of what *goyishe* society must deal with; surely some *yeshivos* can deal with these problems which usually don't even approach the public school type problems! Especially to insure that they don't become such problems. (This summer I learned of two *frum* boys who died of drug overdoses!)

There are wonderful people who have tried to help. I have dealt with many of them personally: Principals and *Rebbeim* who have spent long hours in conference with me on the phone and in person, hanging on to the child who ordinarily would have been thrown out long ago. Another principal, knowing the extent of one son's "history," accepting the child in his *yeshiva* anyway and working hard with him to give him that chance. An older *bachur* who has kept a strong *kesher* with the son and his harried mother to try to keep the boy straight. The *Rav* and *Rebbetzin* from my *shul*, who open their hearts and home whenever they can, if accomplishing nothing more that giving the *chizuk* this stressed-out single mother sometimes needs to go on another day.

Finally I'd like to mention people I've met along the way who have opened programs for these "throw-away" children. Rabbi Avi Davidowitz heads Torah Academy of Brooklyn. With minimal space and even less funding he tries hard to accept every boy who has failed in the mainstream. The boys are constantly guests in his home and the homes of his staff. He takes them on trips, he and his *Rebbetzin* have them for *Shabbos* and *Yom Tov*, he is on the phone with them day and night. He has reached the point where he has to often say no to *Rebbeim* who ask him to shoulder the burden they cannot carry in their *yeshivos*. The *Rebbeim* have been frustrated by the refusals he must sometimes give, and have asked *him* how *he* can turn down their souls. Yeshiva R'tzahd is another such institution, which accepted a problem child, sight unseen, just by virtue of my phone conversations with the principals.

Yes, there is *chessed* out there but the problem is great. It is time for us to open our eyes to the fact that we don't all live on 613 Torah Avenue, that even if we all follow the same timeworn recipes of all the Dov Dov books etc., our children will not necessarily be on the proper *derech*, and that if we are truly as *frum* as we say we are, that we should deal *b'chessed* in the same way with our lost souls as we ask *Hashem* to deal with us. If we can't do something personally, perhaps we could delegate our *tzeddaka* dollars to those institutions that are trying their best to pick up the broken pieces. Perhaps we can all have a *zechus* in rescuing a precious soul, and as we all know, "He who saves one soul is as if he has saved the entire world."

Name Withheld Upon Request

Shaindel Weinbach

The Seed of Hope

It lay still, looking up at me,
Hard and black and round.
I studied it dispassionately
And thrust it in the ground.
And then a wave of panic
Made me choke and gasp for breath,
Was I, perhaps, consigning
This little seed to death?

Buried in the suffocating earth
How could it possibly give birth?
Seen in the sunlight, an unlikely thing,
Could it, deep under, be a harbinger of spring?

Was not this earth the place of no return?
Where dead were buried — not where things were born?
Who would touch off the stirring of new life?
Help pierce the loamy blackness like a knife?

For spring to life it would
And stir and grow,
Upward, outward, sideways and below.
A root, a shoot, and lo!
A miracle occurring down below.

It breathes! It is alive!
It has a purpose, an unconscious drive.

The germ of continuity activated,
The thirst to live, to give, to grow as fated.
My gasp turns to a sigh,
Relieved, I cry:
So will the dead spring up in future time.
What is the wonder if it happens all the time?
Is not this little seed a balm, a suture,
Against the pain of death? And a promise for the future?

◆§The Mother Is The Teacher

"Chinuch" — Whose Responsibility Is It?
Shabbos — A Time for All Ages
Training Children Not to Speak Lashon Hara
How to Raise Children by Really Trying
The Critical Parent's Guidebook
Letters in Response
And He Who Knows Not How to Ask

Rabbi Yisroel Reisman

"Chinuch" — The Training of Children: Whose Responsibility Is It?

When a Child Comes

A MARRIAGE IS blessed with the arrival of a child. A husband and wife become parents and the couple becomes transformed into a family.

The new father's routine expands, but the entire focus of thought and activity of the mother is shifted to her new child. Yet the mother's total involvement in her child is hardly reflected in *halachah*. In fact the Talmud states, "A man is obligated to train his son in (the observance of) *mitzvos*, (but) a women is not obligated to train her son" (*Nazir* 29a). This is a view taken by most[1] but not all[2] *poskim* (halachic authorities) as law. How strange that the mother, whose talents and energies are described by *Chazal* as the mainstay of a home and who truly contributes more than anyone else to the child's physical and spiritual growth, does not bear the primary responsibility for *chinuch*!

Actually the *mitzvah* of *chinuch* itself is puzzling. It is undeniably a keystone in perpetuating Jewish life and values over the generations, yet the Talmud tells us that it is only rabbinic in origin (*Chagigah* 4a). None of the *Rishonim* (early commentators — 11-15 centuries) count *chinuch* as one of the 613 Biblical commandments. The teaching of Torah to one's children — in contrast to *mitzvah* observance — would seem to be a clear Biblical commandment: "And you shall teach them to your children" (*Devarim* 11-19; see also *Ramban* ibid.). The *Rishonim*[3] do not even count this as a *mitzvah* per se; instead, theyview this as part of the more general *mitzvah* of *Talmud Torah*.[4]

The unique ability of our people to persevere and grow throughout generations of exile certainly stems from our obsessive dedication to the *chinuch* of our children. How strange that at the Giving of the Torah at Sinai, G-d did not specifically command us to ensure the continuity of generations!

৵ "Chinuch": Two Understandings

In attempting to attain a deeper understanding of this *mitzvah*, we come across two distinct explanations of *chinuch*.

While we generally define *chinuch* as training, the Torah uses *chinuch* as a term of *has'chalah*—beginning.[5] These two definitions parallel two distinct explanations of the *mitzvah* of *chinuch*, as found in *Chazal*.

Some commentators[6] see *chinuch* as an early beginning of *mitzvah* fulfillment. Although a Jew is required to perform *mitzvos* beginning at age twelve (for girls) or thirteen (for boys), *chinuch* calls for these *mitzvos* to be performed at a younger age. According to this view, parental responsibility only extends to the mechanical performance of the deed.

Others[7] see *chinuch* as the parents' obligation to make *mitzvos* and Torah values a part of their child's life, so that he will be accustomed, from an early age, to perform Hashem's *mitzvos* regularly and eagerly. Although this view certainly acknowledges mechanical *mitzvah* observance as basic, the emphasis is placed on attitudes and feelings. Accordingly, a parent who cannot afford to buy his son a kosher *esrog* might be fulfilling his *chinuch* obligation by buying his son a flawed *esrog*[8] (providing, of course, that his son is unaware of the imperfection). Although this does not fulfill the technical requirement of the *mitzvah*, the father is still training his son in being accustomed to perform *mitzvos*, which is his basic obligation.

In short, we can refer to these two aspects of *chinuch* as the "*Mitzvah* observance" — or activity facet—and the "Torah value"

— or moral facet. Involving a child in the mechanics of *mitzvah* observance is not necessarily a Biblical obligation. This waits until maturity. It is the Torah-value aspect that would seem to be of utmost importance. So, while a child is technically incapable of moral intent in the performance of individual *mitzvos* (and, indeed, the Torah mandates no such morality[9]), a general education in moral values is not essential to his development as a Jews. This teaching of Torah-value morality to children may, indeed, be mandated by Torah law.

◆§ Pouring Foundations for Torah

G-d created man with many natural instincts. Among them — anger, haughtiness, lust — are some that we are taught to stringently avoid. Yet, nowhere in the Torah are we specifically commanded to distance ourselves from these *midos* (character attributes). This puzzling omission was explained by Rabbi Chaim Vital:*[10] "Proper *midos* provide the foundation for Torah. Without them, a Torah life would be unimaginable. Their acquisition, therefore, requires no specific commandment."[11] This observation can easily be applied to the Torah-value aspect of *chinuch* as well. At Sinai, G-d did indeed give *Klal Yisroel* the responsibility to pass down the Torah for all generations. But precisely because this is so self-evident, it was not specifically commanded.

The Sages of later generations simply added a second phase to the *chinuch* obligation; namely, the technical inclusion of minors in *mitzvah* observance. But the basic *chinuch* precept existed earlier.[12] We find that *Avraham Avinu* influenced vast multitudes to accept monotheism, converting these people into truly righteous men.[13] Why do we find no reference to their descendants anywhere in the *Mesorah* (tradition)? Rabbi Moshe Feinstein, זצ"ל, pointed out that notwithstanding their righteousness, these men had failed to grasp the significance of *chinuch*.[14] As a result, not one of their descendants perpetuated their convictions after the passing of Avraham and Sarah.[15] *Chinuch*, then, is the most basic lifeline of *Mesorah*, surely a Torah foundation of the type explained by Rav Chaim Vital.

---

* 16th-century Kabbalist, disciple of the *Ari Zal*.

~§ Allusion to the Heart

While a mother's role in *chinuch* is not specifically defined in the Talmud, it is alluded to: "Three partners form a human being — G-d, father and mother. The father contributes the white, from which are formed the bones, sinews, nails, brain and white of the eye. The mother contributes the red, from which are formed the skin, flesh, hair and pupil of the eye. G-d gives the soul etc."[16]

In Kabbalistic teachings, we find that white is symbolic of purity of thought;[17] red and the faculty of vision are symbolic of proper action.[18] Reb Tzaddok *Hakohein** explains this *Gemara* in a spiritual sense.[19] He describes the father's contribution toward the development of his child as the *he'lem*, i.e. implanting in the hidden depths of the mind of proper ideas and plans. Proper actions, however, does not necessarily result from this knowledge.

The mother's contribution includes the formation of the heart — the center of a person's drives, emotions, and desires, which motivate him to act. Her task, referred to by Reb Tzaddok as the *nigleh*, is to inspire the child to transform the *he'lem* into physical action. Or, in the words of *Maharal*: "The task of a righteous woman is to prepare her offspring to accept and then apply Torah ethics and thought."[20]

Sacred literature likens a woman to a garden (*Pirkei d'Rav Eliezer*, Ch. 21). Just as a seed is planted into the earth of a garden, where it is nurtured and fed until it blossoms into a majestic tree, so too, does man contribute the seed from which a child is formed; but it is a woman that G-d has blessed with the anatomy capable of nurturing that seed and forming it into a human being.

~§ A Spiritual Garden

This analogy is true in the spiritual sense as well. As Reb Tzaddok explained, the father's *he'lem* role is to plant seeds of *chinuch* by giving his child the basic knowledge necessary for *mitzvah* fulfillment. To accomplish this, it would be sufficient to acquaint a child with the mechanical observance of *mitzvos*. The mechanical *mitzvah* observance of childhood, however, will not automatically guarantee that a child will continue to perform *mitzvos* as an adult. This is only a beginning aspect of *chinuch*.

---

*Famed author of works on Kabbalistic themes, in 19th-century Lublin, Poland.

The mother's role in forming a child, spiritually as well as physically, is far more complex. Hers is the training aspect of that will influence the child to want to do *mitzvos*, to appreciate *mitzvos* and Torah values. Her task is to imbue him with the feelings that will inspire him to act upon his father's teachings. She is to provide him with the moral basis in which Torah and *mitzvos* will take root and flourish.

When *Chazal* say that women are exempted from the *mitzvah* of *chinuch*, they are referring to the *mitzvah* observance aspect of *chinuch*, the mechanical part. The Torah-value aspect of *chinuch*, however, falls under her jurisdiction. This is the *chinuch* role whose paramount importance can be presumed to be such an obvious Torah foundation that it is not specifically commanded.

Just as G-d endowed woman with the anatomy necessary for the forming of a child, so too did He provide her with specific talents and abilities necessary for *chinuch habanim*. When *Chazal* describe women as *"dabraniyos"*[21] — more talkative — their intention is not to belittle them. The same applies for their observations that women are more shy,[22] more merciful,[23] emotional,[24] and less physically active[25] than men. Although these factors may seem to handicap her, in truth they are invaluable tools necessary for her life role.

◆§ A Man's Faults, a Woman's Strengths

As *Ramban*[26] points out, a woman's tendency towards shyness is a positive attribute, not a fault. Her lack of aggressiveness and physical restlessness make her less likely to thrust herself into the competitive business world for personal fulfillment. Perhaps these very tendencies enable many a mother to ignore pressing tasks and deadlines to spend unhurried, unscheduled time with her children when they need it. *"Kol kevodah bas melech pnimah* — the princess's glory is within" refers to a woman's unique ability to find her main satisfaction within the four walls of her home. This happiness is absorbed by her child, who has a keen awareness of his mother's feelings. Because she is more emotional and expresses her feelings more openly and readily, her attitudes have a profound impact upon the development of her child.

Have you ever stopped to observe a mother putter around the house with a toddler at her heels? Listen and you will hear her non-stop commentary on the workings of a household and the mysteries of the grown-up world. Almost out of habit, she will describe each item she removes from the grocery bag, explaining its use as she puts it in its place. Now imagine a father unpacking the same bag of groceries. He will have the job done in half the time, but his child will be ignored during those few minutes. Our *nashim dabraniyos* have a natural quality that they use, almost subconsciously, to educate our children.

Indeed, the three basic qualities in which our nation prides itself — "*rachmanim, beishanim, v'gomlei chassadim*, being merciful, modest and charitable" — are all attributes in which a mother excels. Her *chinuch* activities cultivate these values in the hearts of our children.

◆§ Failing to Grasp Her Significance

Today's society is seeking to obliterate the social implications of male-female differences. "Liberation" demands that women seek to overcome what they perceive as feminine handicaps. As much as we may recognize this attitude as inimitable to a Torah perspective, the values of the society around us invariably invade our own. The common perception of a housewife-mother as a maid-babysitter is diametrically opposed to *Chazal's* understanding of her role. A mother who stays home with her children should view herself as a full-time *mechaneches* — an educator of the young, not a simple babysitter.

A mother's failure to grasp the significance of her role can have a detrimental effect on her children. Aware of this, a mother who elects to go to work should make certain that her replacement, too, is a capable *mechaneches*. Parents who would shudder at the thought of sending their children to public schools, nevertheless allow people with hard secular values — even non-Jews — to tend their school-age children for many hours a week. Would this mother truly appreciate her child's needs and the ways in which she is constantly contributing to his development, she would select a babysitter with much more care. This is not to say that a babysitter must be well educated — only that she have basic, simple, Torah-oriented values. And while it may not always be possible to obtain an observant babysitter, a *chinuch*-conscious mother should put every effort towards attaining this ideal.

⌘ Big Bird or "Imma"?

Because many women fail to see themselves as educators of their children, they often entrust this assignment to Sesame Street-type programs. Big Bird and Captain Kangaroo might indeed have training abilities in certain areas that are superior to those of many mothers, but those areas do not constitute *chinuch*. Children raised on the lap of their TVs often learn to count at an early age and become conversant in many relatively worldly matters. But, experience has shown that these children are often lacking in many *midos* notably *beishanus* (sense of shame) and *yiras shomayim* (fear of Heaven). While one may argue that educational programs can be beneficial as a supplement to *chinuch*, it is extremely difficult to limit such programs to a supplementary role. Children will absorb more from funny characters, bedecked in colorful costumes, than from low-keyed, one-to-one experiences in their homes. Unpacking a bag of groceries can hardly seem exciting to a youngster accustomed to seeing Cookie Monsters and cartoon characters performing impossible feats. Professional educators perceive television as an impediment to *chinuch habanim*. If mothers saw themselves as educators, perhaps they too would feel that way. Again, the child is hurt by his mother's failure to appreciate her own importance.

Hakadosh Baruch Hu has blessed every child with a thirst for knowledge and a strong desire to imitate the grown-ups around him. These are his tools for building a proper foundation for his life. A parent—*mechanech* must supervise the use of these tools. This constant viligance often causes inconveniences, but the rewards are great. As *David HaMelech* said, "Those who sow with tears shall reap with joy." Is there another harvest in life that is more important?

---

1. *Tosefos Yeshanim Yuma* 82a; *Terumas Hadeshen* 94; *Magen Avraham* 343:1; *Birkei Yoseif*, ibid.; *S.A. Harav*, ibid.; *Kaf Hachaim*, ibid.; *Matei Efraim* 616:6.
2. *Orech Mishor, Nazir* 29a; *Aruch Hashulchan* 343:1.
3. *Sefer Hachinuch* 419; *Rambam, Asei* 11; *Yereim* 254; *Rav Sadya Gaon* 14.
4. See Rabbi Yerucham Perlow's commentary to *Rav Sadya Gaon* Vol. 1, p. 234.
5. *Bereishis* 14:14; *Devarim* 20-25; *Rashi* in both places.
6. *Magen Avraham* 658:8; *Igros Moshe* Y.D. 137.
7. *Rashi, Sukkah* 2b; Rav Meno'ach, Comm. to *Rambam, Shvisas Asor* 2:10.

8. See *Mishnah Berurah* 658:28; *Biyur Halachah* 657.
9. *Turei Even* to *Chagigah* 6b.
10. Quoted in introduction to *Sefer Even Shlomo*.
11. Quoted from *Koveitz Mamarim* p. 34.
12. Rav Meno'ach, Comm. to *Rambam*, *Shvisas Asor* 2:10.
13. *Tifferes Tzion*, *Lech Lecha* 39:21.
14. M.T.J. *Melaveh Malkah* Address, 1976.
15. ArtScroll *Bereishis*, footnote to 12:5.
16. *Niddah* 310.
17. *Maharal*, *Gevuros Hashem* Ch. 28.
18. *Alshich* on *Shmuel I* Ch. 16, v.12; *Abarbanel*, ibid.
19. *Dover Tzedek* 22:1.
20. *Drashos Maharal* p. 28.
21. *Berachos* 48b.
22. *Kesubos* 67a; *Yevamos* 42a.
23. *Megillah* 14b.
24. *Lekach Tov* on *Esther*.
25. *Yerushalmi*, *Pesachim* 1:4.
26. *Ramban*, *Bereishis* 3:16.

Dr. Meir Wikler

Shabbos: A Time for All Ages

Crescendo at Dusk

JUST AS *SHABBOS* can be divided into stages and phases which may differ in degree, theme, mood or intensity, *Erev Shabbos* also has its own subdivisions. Perhaps the best-known and most respected (and feared) stage of *Erev Shabbos* is that final stage, ushered in with those familiar words, often uttered in shrill tones of urgency: "It's almost *Shabbos!*" From that signal until the onset of *Shabbos*, the pace of preparations picks up steadily and the sun seems to descend more rapidly, voices are sometimes raised and expectations for what can still be accomplished before *Shabbos* are sharply reduced.

During one such *Erev Shabbos* finale, not too long ago, my family and I began our usual race against the clock. Everyone over the age of four was automatically conscripted into compulsory *Shabbos* preparation and everyone's leisurely weekday gait was replaced by a more frantic pace. In the midst of this flurry of activity, three-year-old Yeshayale rushed up to me and demanded to know, "It's *Shabbos* now?"

"No. But it's almost *Shabbos!*" I had answered in motion and was down the hall by the time I completed the sentence. A short while later, Yeshayale repeated his question and received a similar reply, a few decibels higher.

What I had neither the time nor the patience to realize then was that my son was feeling totally swept up in the family's collective anticipation of *Shabbos*. Freed from the concerns of responsibility, he was able to experience this anticipation with unadulterated glee. His excitement was marred only by his undeveloped, three-year-old's awareness of time. He was frustrated by his inability to discern just how much longer it was until *Shabbos*.

So Yeshayale took what must have been an enormous risk, considering my volatile emotional state at the time, and he approached me again a few minutes later. "Tatty, Tatty," he pleaded desperately, "when it be *Shabbos?*"

"Soon, very soon!" came my wholly inadequate reply. A lengthy diatribe was prevented only by the lateness of the hour.

⋓ Lost in Outer Time

Later on that evening when the commotion of the *Erev Shabbos* finale had been replaced by the serenity of the *Shabbos* table,* I began to reflect on the implications of my hallway encounter with Yeshayale.

In adult terminology, the proper answer to his third question would have been, "Approximately thirty-seven minutes." But to a three-year-old, "thirty-seven minutes" means about the same as "thirty-seven months" or "thirty-seven miles." Three-year-olds are simply not able to conceptualize time or distance in quantifiable, adult terms.

Most of us cannot even imagine what life would be like without the awareness of time, which we take for granted. Of course, in a spiritual sense, there is no limit to the depth of time awareness an adult can achieve through prolonged and diligent Torah study and observance. But since the most elementary level of grasping the concepts of minutes, hours, and weeks usually comes in the fourth or fifth year of life, most adults cannot remember what life was like before these fundamental lessons were learned.

Just try to imagine a trip by car to a beloved relative whom you have not seen in many years. Your preparation for the trip is effortless, as you are buoyed along by your eager anticipation of that long-awaited reunion. Once you are finally on the road, you follow the travel directions with the precision of a watchmaker.

"Take Interstate 91, North to Route 86, East," you repeat to yourself as your car gobbles up the miles. After twenty or thirty miles you begin to wonder, "How many miles on 91 is it until we hit 86?" After a half hour, you wonder out loud.

"The directions don't say," comes the helper's reply. After an hour, everyone begins to wonder if Route 86 was passed, as accusations for not being more observant are now exchanged between the driver and passengers.

After two hours on Interstate 91, without the aide of maps or the reassurance of gas station attendant you would probably begin to experience the same frustration of uncertainty that three-year-old children live with every day.

Reassurances of, "You can have the candy in an hour," "Mommy is coming back at 2:30," or "Bubby and Zaidie will be here on Tuesday," are as useless to a three-year-old as a sextant would be to a lost motorist.

The Need for Predictability

Small children live with the frustration of uncertainty every day. They never really know what to expect or when to expect it. And don't be fooled by their apparent calm. They are constantly groping, struggling, and searching for any clue that can help them order, structure, and comprehend their somewhat chaotic worlds, devoid of time awareness.

Their thirst and yearning for structure, order, and predictability are familiar to anyone who has experienced the joy of playing with pre-school children. The games they enjoy most are always those that involve an inordinate amount of repetition. While this may bore an adult, it offers an oasis of security, stability, and reassurance for the very young child.

In short, small children look for any recognizable order in life which they can use to orient themselves in a world of time, until they develop their own awareness of the units of time.

"No, Mommy! I wanted the milk before the chocolate!" a three-year-old will complain.

"What's the difference?" Mother protests. But her child cannot possibly explain that the routine of milk first and chocolate second provides a tiny source of security to a three-year-old.

Robbing a child of that security would be tantamount to stripping a prisoner of his calendar and wrist watch. Just as that prisoner would pay greater attention to the setting of the sun or the changing of the guards, so too small children become preoccupied and seemingly obsessed with routine and repetition.

~§ Anchors in the Waves of Temporal Confusion

So how can parents assist young children in their struggle to bring order to their lives? The best way is to provide and impose structure, limits, and routine — all within reason, of course. One of the best ways to provide that for children is with rituals. Rituals are so important for children that in addition to religiously meaningful rituals taught to them by their parents, children often create their own rituals. Milk first and chocolate second, a drink of water before going to sleep, or avoiding cracks in the sidewalk are some typical examples of children's rituals.

The repetitive, daily *mitzvos*, therefore, such as *brachos*, *neigel vasser*, and *krias Shema*, provide children with invaluable signposts which help them navigate through the world of time without a mature awareness. Even before reaching the age of *chinuch* (according to any halachic opinion), observing and imitating their parents' performance of daily *mitzvos* can give small children many anchors to balance themselves in the waves of temporal confusion.

Perhaps the greatest temporal anchor, for all ages, is *Shabbos*. That island of tranquility and sanctity provides reassurance and hope to adults as well as children. As the humorous bumper sticker proclaims, "Hang in there: *Shabbos* is coming!"

One day passes like another to a small child who has not yet learned the meaning of "Monday" and "Tuesday." But *Shabbos* is so mistakenly unique that even pre-school children can recognize its presence.

When Yeshayale's older sister was three years old, she overheard a discussion of a plan to spend *Shabbos* with Bubbie and Zaidie. "When are we going?" she asked with unabashed excitement.

"Not for another two weeks," came the reply.

"But I mean, how long until we go?" she persisted, showing me how much off target my answer had been.

"Not this next *Shabbos*, but the *Shabbos* after that," I explained, trying a different tack.

"You mean in two *Shabboses?*" she asked, to confirm the date. "Yes," I explained, "we'll be going to Bubbie and Zaidie in two *Shabboses.*"

Sarah Dina walked off with a perturbed look, shaking her head as if to say, "Then why didn't you say so in the first place!?"

I had learned my lesson. I learned that well before children understand the meaning of days and weeks, they can grasp the difference between weekday and *Shabbos* which can help them, on their level, with their developmental needs.

So, returning to that *Erev Shabbos* finale described above, when Yeshayale looked up at me—as my wife *benched licht*—with confidence in his voice and a smile on his lips, "Now it's *Shabbos;* right, Tatty?" I learned my lesson all over again.

Rabbi Zelig Pliskin

Training Children Not to Speak Lashon Hara

EVERY JEWISH PARENT is concerned that his children develop as responsible, Torah-observant adults. Some aspects of this growth can be promoted by a supportive environment, while others are constantly challenged by widespread indifference to the specific goals they entail. Probably one of the most worthwhile and yet most difficult of goals parent entertain for their children is that they learn to refrain from speaking *lashon hara* — slander. Before discussing details regarding pursuit of this goal there is an incident described in the Talmud that can offer us some understandings that can serve as a foundation for a program for teaching *Shmiras Halashon* — Guarding One's Tongue:

Traveling to a specific city, Rabbi Avuhu asked Rabbi Shimon ben Lakish (Reish Lakish), "Why should we go to a place full of blasphemers?"

Upon hearing this, Rabbi Shimon ben Lakish alighted from his donkey, picked up some earth and put it into Rabbi Avuhu's mouth. Rabbi Avuhu asked for an explanation for this behavior, to which Rabbi Shimon ben Lakish replied, "The Almighty does not want us to speak evil about the Jewish People."

At first glance, Rabbi Shimon ben Lakish's extreme reaction to Rabbi Avuhu's comment is quite astonishing. Perhaps this can be understood in the context of how Rabbi Shimon ben Lakish became a Torah scholar (See *Bava Metzia* 84a). Reish Lakish, then the leader of a gang of bandits, spotted Rabbi Yochanan swimming in the Jordan River. He dived into the river and swam over to Rabbi Yochanan, who immediately told this robber, "The strength you demonstrated in swimming should be utilized for toiling in Torah study."

Reish Lakish retorted to Rabbi Yochanan, a strikingly handsome man, "Your beauty should have gone to a woman."

Rabbi Yochanan responded, "My sister is even more beautiful. If you accept upon yourself to study Torah, you can marry her."

Reish Lakish accepted the offer. At the outset, Rabbi Yochanan was his teacher, but eventually they became colleagues of equal stature: Their *halachic* disputes are cited throughout the Talmud.

The incident is truly remarkable, but also puzzling: How could Rabbi Yochanan offer his sister in marriage to the leader of a bandit group? The answer is — he really didn't! What he saw was not Shimon the robber, but the potential Rabbi Shimon ben Lakish, whom Rabbi Yochanan recognized as possessing outstanding abilities — abilities that would enable him to achieve greatness in Torah study. Rabbi Yochanan was so confident in his appraisal of Reish Lakish's potential that he did not consider his offer a risk, only an enviable opportunity.

We can now understand Rabbi Shimon ben Lakish's censure of Rabbi Avuhu. When Rabbi Avuhu was repulsed by the city of blasphemers, he saw its citizenry as they were at that moment: people to be avoided. By contrast, Rabbi Shimon ben Lakish drew from his own background. He knew that even people who are blasphemers can have the potential to be righteous. They only need someone with vision and ingenuity to motivate them to change.

Note also that Rabbi Yochanan did not try to influence Reish Lakish by lecturing him on the supreme value of Torah study. Rather, he entered the reality of Reish Lakish's world at that time, and influenced him in a language that he could understand.

Thus, Rabbi Shimon was taken aback when he heard Rabbi Avuhu's statement. He may well have been thinking: *These people are children of the Almighty, the grandchildren of Avraham, Yitzchak, and Yaakov! If they are far from Torah observance, they are not necessarily to blame. Perhaps we only have ourselves to blame for lacking the wisdom and creativity to motivate them. Rather than condemn them, perhaps we are responsible to help them improve.* People with an attitude like that of Reish Lakish are not likely to speak negatively of others. They will endeavor always to see the potential for greatness in people and will search for ways to help them realize this potential. This is most helpful when dealing with our brethren who have not yet come back to Torah observance, and crucial in refraining from speaking evil of others.

Yet another insight can be gained from this episode: Rabbi Shimon ben Lakish's putting sand in Rabbi Avuhu's mouth strikes one as a very cruel act. Reish Lakish obviously wanted to illustrate with the strongest technique possible how a person defiles *his own mouth* by slandering others. Having sand in one's mouth is a tactile experience — one actually feels the invasion of filth on one's tongue. *Lashon hara* is no less an invasion of filth.

The insights culled from these passages from the Talmud give us a basis for fashioning an approach to educating our children to *Shmiras Halashon.*

The first step parents should take when influencing their children to refrain from *lashon hara* is to clarify their goals. Basically, the goals are twofold — behavioral and attitudinal. The behavioral goal is obvious — to stop one's children from speaking negatively about others. The attitudinal goal is much more complex, both in substance and in the ways in which to achieve it. Most important, one cannot expect one's children to develop positive attitudes unless one has assumed them oneself. To begin with, one must ask oneself: "How do I feel about talking *lashon hara?* Do I find it more difficult to speak derogatorily of others, or more difficult to *refrain* from speaking against others?"

Unfortunately, many find it painfully limiting to avoid speaking *lashon hara.* The prohibition actually frightens them. But one should be embarrassed — yes, *embarrassed* — to speak *lashon hara.* Would anyone willingly make the following proclamation in front of others? "I am totally insensitive. I do not feel love towards others and do not mind if I cause them emotional pain and humiliation, or even if I cause others a financial loss and provoke strife." Yet when one speaks *lashon hara*, that is the message one is implicitly conveying to others. Were someone else to say this about him he would be highly indignant. Why should a person say it about himself?

Whatever a person's attitude is towards speaking *lashon hara*, this is what will be transmitted to his (or her) children. Bearing that in mind, when one feels an impulse to pass on a morsel of juicy gossip or a witty remark about someone, one can muster the self-discipline necessary to control that impulse. And then the self-discipline itself becomes a source of pleasure. If a person can also master the attitude of *simchah shel mitzvah* — feeling joy for having performed a *mitzvah* the great satisfaction and even joy that one can experience in *not* speaking against others can more than compensate for the forfeited pleasures of sharing information with others.

To be the consummate teacher of *Shmiras Halashon*, one should strive to reach a level of *ahavas Yisroel* that would not permit one *even to think* of slandering another person. One would never speak negatively about one's own child; one's attitude towards speaking against anyone else should be no different.

Another attitudinal goal is to be so sensitive to the pain of others that one would not speak against someone because it would be too painful *for the speaker*. People go to great lengths to avoid pain. Simply keeping in mind the suffering one causes others by speaking against them will eventually bring one to feel that pain, making it virtually impossible to speak against others. It would simply be too painful to do so.

Since helping children gain these awarenesses and sensitivities is a key to their development, how does one actually awaken these attitudes in children? Not with just one lecture, for sure! As we mentioned at the outset, if a person succeeds in integrating these concepts into his personality, then his children will gradually develop these attitudes as well. A person must bear in mind at all times that he is always serving as a model for his children. If a person *must* relate derogatory information to someone for a constructive purpose (in accordance with the laws of *lashon hara* as delineated by the Chofetz Chaim), one should make certain to do so out of the hearing range of the children. And if one is ever suddenly aware that he is speaking *lashon hara*, he should stop in the middle, as awkward as it may seem. And, furthermore, should others ever point out that what one was about to say might be *lashon hara*, one should endeavor to overcome the resentment and embarrassment of being "caught"; it would even be in place to thank them — just as if it were a warning that one was about to flick on a light switch on *Shabbos*. Objectively speaking, it should be no different. This, then, is crucial. First, parents should try to view the prohibition against speaking *lashon hara* with the same severity as they do other serious *halachic* matters; then there can be hope that their children will learn to follow suit.

Another important aspect of teaching children to avoid *lashon hara* is guiding them to judge others favorably. This is significant because, first of all, much derogatory information is simply not true: Wrong information is frequently passed with ease from person to person. And even if the information is true, there are frequently extenuating circumstances that would render the "wrong" action permissible and sometimes even obligatory. Moreover, one can never know on what perceptions or misinformation the "guilty" subject based his behavior. It could very well be that according to the way he perceived the situation, he acted properly, even if in fact he was mistaken. Even though the person has an obligation to correct his error, he does not deserve condemnation. Here, too, serving as role model for one's children is important; but in addition, it may prove necessary to verbalize as well, so children will understand their parents' thinking.

Most of the attitudes that one hopes to imbue children with are best taught by example, as stated. They then tend to filter down from the concept level to the nitty-gritty of daily life. The lessons of *Shmiras Halashon* that grow from consideration of others can be reinforced with a number of teaching techniques and tools:

☐ One should praise people who do not speak *lashon hara*. What we praise reveals what we truly respect. One can even comment jokingly on an infant who cannot yet speak, "What a *tzaddik!* He has never spoken a word of *lashon hara!*" When serving pickled tongue, one can say, "This is an exceptional tongue — never spoke a word of *lashon hara.*" While one normally makes such comments with tongue-in-cheek, the child hearing such comments will get the underlying message.

☐ By relating stories about the Chofetz Chaim to one's children, they will be inspired to identify with him and will try to emulate him. Telling children creative stories about the harm caused by derogatory speech and greatness of boys and girls who avoid speaking *lashon hara* can also help them. Bedtime stories can have lifelong positive effects.

☐ Stickers near telephones and other strategic places reminding people to refrain from *lashon hara* may strike some people as lacking sophistication but they are surprisingly effective. So are key chains with plastic chips proclaiming such messages as: "The key to keeping *shmiras halashon*: Give your friend the benefit of the doubt and the *lashon hara* you will wipe out." And then there are bumper stickers.

☐ One can help children structure their day to refrain from *lashon hara* for specific periods — for example, by setting up a two-hour period during which they mark off on a chart every ten minutes (5:00, 5:10, 5:20, etc.) that their speech was *lashon hara*-free. It is relatively easy to be careful for just ten minutes at a time, and the child will have a successful experience in *shmiras halashon* — to be capped off with a prize for a "clean" week.

☐ Knowledge of the laws of *lashon hara* is crucial, and even young children should be taught the basic rules. It is important to teach children to differentiate between information that is necessary to relate for constructive purposes and hence permissible, and information that is destructive and forbidden. The knowledgeable parent and conscientious teacher can give quizzes and award prizes for correct answers.

☐ It is also important to teach children how to stop their peers from telling them *lashon hara*. Of course, this will be dependent on the self-confidence and assertiveness of the child, as well as his relationship with his friends. Some children will find this much easier than others. As a rule, the more sensitive a child is to the suffering of others, the more sensitive he himself is likely to be, and many such children may find it quite difficult to muster up the courage to correct others. By the same token, a bolder child may have to be coached on how to point out others' shortcomings without being offensive. But even if a child is unable to correct someone who relates *lashon hara*, he should learn to declare that he does not want to hear *lashon hara*. (As an adult friend once commented self-deprecatingly, "I have enough faults of my own, I don't have to collect data on the faults of others." The subject was quickly changed.)

☐ A person who relates *lashon hara* will only keep on doing so if he is positively reinforced. If a *lashon hara* speaker finds that others react with displeasure, he will avoid repeating the experience. Adults can have their own approach to defusing a potential *lashon hara* situation. For example, heading off a defamatory comment at the pass with: "Someone must really be suffering from an inferiority complex to have to raise himself up by putting others down" — a sure squelcher. Children have their own level of communication, and can, perhaps, more easily put it directly to their friends, "It's wrong to speak against others." Children can also be taught to change the subject with grace if *lashon hara* threatens. As a youngster, I had a friend who had memorized a number of totally irrelevant but interesting entries from *Ripley's Believe It or Not*. Whenever the conversation seemed to be directed toward *lashon hara*, he would throw out an incredible but kosher fact; the topic would invariably switch to a discussion as to the veracity of his statement.

❧ The Key

As stated, the underlying key to training children in guarding their speech is probably the parents'/teachers' attitude towards refraining from *lashon hara*. It is this attitude that one will convey to one's children. I vividly remember my father ז״ל, a disciple of the Chofetz Chaim in Radin, quoting directly from his illustrious Rebbe ז״ל, "The *sefer Chofetz Chaim* is not a book about refraining from speech. Rather, it is a book that allows one to speak about everything else. If you are not familiar with the laws of *lashon hara*, how can you speak? You might be guilty of violating the prohibition against *lashon hara*. Once you know the laws, however, you can speak about everything else. The *sefer Chofetz Chaim* actually gives you permission to talk." This is a powerful, positive message, emphasizing that refraining from *lashon hara* forces a person to broaden his horizons and elevates the level of his conversations.

Refraining from speaking or listening to *lashon hara* is an expression of a beautiful concept of love and sensitivity. If we truly view it in that light, we will succeed in teaching it to our children in that way, as well.

Rabbi Chaim Dov Keller

How to Raise Children by Really Trying

THE PHENOMENAL resurgence of Torah Judaism in our day can, in great measure, be attributed to the great emphasis placed by Orthodox Jews on *chinuch habanim*. We have created an impressive network of educational institutions for boys and girls, from pre-nursery through Seminary and *Kollel*. We have been eminently successful in training a generation of *bnei Torah* and *bnos Yisroel kesheiros*. But have we been as successful in raising well-balanced children? Or have we, in our great preoccupation with the schooling of our children, in our zeal to impart Torah knowledge and inspire *mitzvah* observance, neglected what may be at least equally important — their development as well-adjusted human beings — as *"mentschen"*?

Obviously the subject of raising children is one of great importance to many people. In order not to mislead or disappoint anyone let us state at the outset that what follows is not a discussion of child psychology. It will offer no specific solutions to specific problems. It is, rather, a general discussion of some basic Torah principles which (to borrow a phrase from the *Mesillas Yesharim*) have been neglected precisely because they are so well known.

Although *Sefer Mishlei* is replete with advice on child-rearing, one *pasuk* (22:6) summarizes it best: חנך לנער על פי דרכו וגו' — "Train the child according to his way, then even when he grows old, he will not turn aside from it." This *pasuk* is the source of the *mitzvah d'Rabbanan* of *chinuch* — training children in *mitzvos* (to be distinguished from the *mitzvah d'Oraisa* of teaching one's son Torah, which we learn from "*Veshinantom levonecha...* and you shall teach your sons" [*Kiddushin*, 31a]). Let us examine this *pasuk* according to the profound yet remarkably simple insights of Rabbeinu Yonah[1] which encompass the basic rules of raising children. Then, as Hillel said, "The rest is commentary — go forth and learn."

The first word, "*chanoch*," is the source for the term *chinuch*, which is usually translated as "education." Actually it has the same root as such commonly used expressions as "*Chanukah*," "*Chanukas Habayis*," and "*Chanukas Hamizbe'ach*" — it denotes an initiation, a dedication of something by its initial use. For example, the dedication of the *k'lei shareis*, the utensils of the *Beis Hamikdash*, was through their initial use — *avodasam mechanchasam*. This initial use invested them with the *kedushah* for which they were intended. In its narrowly defined sense, the *mitzvah* of *chinuch habanim* refers to the introduction of a child to the observance of *mitzvos*. In a broader sense, says Rabbeinu Yonah, "You must train the child in the ways of *midos tovos* and in the ways of proper conduct," a much-further-reaching imperative. Unfortunately many of our most dedicated young parents in their zeal to initiate their children into the study of Torah and the service of *Hashem* come to look at them as mini Torah tape recorders or little *mitzvah* machines. They fail to realize the obvious — that children are developing human beings, and that someone has to assume responsibility for the course of that development.

The next word in the *pasuk*, "לנער — the child," is the object of our *chinuch* efforts. *Chinuch*, to be effective, explains Rabbeinu Yonah, must begin when the person is still young, and there is the possibility — and the necessity — to train him. In the early stages of his growth, his intellectual skills have not yet developed. He does, however, have an inborn nature all his own, and tends to behave in ways that are often socially unacceptable. Without the intelligence required for self-criticism and improvement, that nature, left alone, will take its course. Without benefit of *chinuch*, he will grow accustomed to certain patterns of conduct, and will later find it extremely difficult to change those patterns. The classic simile is

---

1. Rabbeinu Yonah Gerondi (of Gerona, Spain), 1180-1263.

that of the bent sapling that can easily be set straight while it is still young and pliable. Once it has grown crooked and hardened, little can be done to straighten it.

The *Mishnah* tells us that when one learns with a child, it is like writing with ink on a clean piece of paper (*Avos* 4:20). That clean slate is the *neshamah* of the child himself. What we too often fail to realize is that writing on that slate takes place not only when we formally teach the child. The myriad impressions he receives from those to whom he looks for guidance and from his peers are written almost indelibly on that slate. In the positive sense, *chinuch* is most meaningful and most effective when dealing with the *naar* — the young person.

Al pi darko — in accordance with his way." When training a child, being a role model for a child, directing a child, or correcting a child, one must bear in mind *his derech*, his way. Rabbeinu Yonah explains that the process of training a child must start with focusing on those areas of improvement that are closest to his nature, proceeding step by step, in accordance with the child's stage of development at any given time. This is implicit in the word *derech* — path — referring to the road the child is traveling.

Being on a *derech* — on the road, so to speak — implies movement. And, indeed, every human being by nature is not static; he is dynamic, in a constant state of change. Regarding the *pasuk* in *Mishlei* (15:24): ארח חיים למעלה למשכיל למען סור משאול מטה "For the wise man, the path of life leads upward, in order to avoid the grave below," the Vilna Gaon comments that a person is forever moving from one level to another. If he is wise, his way of life — the road he travels — leads constantly upward. If not, he will inevitably head downward. How much more so is this true of children. There is *nothing* constant about a child. Anyone who has ever observed a child knows that from the day he is born he is constantly changing.

In addition to telling us that everyone is on a path, the words "*al pi darko*" inform us that the path is individualized — the path is exclusively his own. Losing sight of this obvious fact can lead to disastrous consequences — some correctable, some unfortunately not. It is thus important to consider the various factors that define the child's own *derech*. Rabbeinu Yonah lists three considerations: (a) the child's current stage of emotional and intellectual development, (b) his potential rate of comprehension, and (c) the direction of his natural inclinations. For example, if you want to teach a child

Aleph-Bais, you have to know: Is this child emotionally and intellectually ready to learn *Aleph-Bais*? Then, how much can he absorb in each session? You may think, "My son is an *illuy*, a genius, so we'll start him on *Aleph-Bais* at two years. He should be able to get up to *Yud* by the first day. Another ten letters the next day, and by the end of the week he should be ready to start the *Siddur*. After another week or two, he'll be starting *Chumash*." For an exceptionally gifted child this is theoretically possible. But for most it is patently ridiculous. But don't we make similarly ridiculous mistakes all the time? In the case of the *Aleph-Bais*, we all realize that this program is beyond the normal two-year-old child. Even if we give him another year, and he's three, what is the length of his attention span? How long can you talk to a three-year-old on *any* subject? Not more than minutes at a time.

But do we keep these considerations in mind when it comes to inculcating a child with *midos tovos* — developing a sense of responsibility, a well-balanced personality, concern for others? Before trying to imbue a four or five-year-old with weighty concepts, do we take into account if he is even prepared to deal with these concepts? And if so, do we try to determine the rate at which he is able to absorb the concepts? What sort of timetable are we making for this child to become a *gaon*, a *tzaddik?* A parent must recognize that a child is not an adult; he is an adult in training — no different from an adult being trained in any new skill. One cannot expect anyone to become a master craftsman when he has just started the training course. It takes a while. In this case, the course is a long one. It takes a lifetime and then some for a person to become a "*mentsch.*" As Reb Yisroel Salanter comments on the latter half of the *pasuk* of "*chanoch. . .*": "And when he is old, he will not depart from the path" — that is, the path of self-improvement, of training one's self in the *midos tovos.* Setting someone on a lifetime course surely requires at least a bit more thought and effort than most people put into it.

Finally, and perhaps of greatest importance, do we ask ourselves: Does this program fit the child's individual nature?

Let us elaborate on each of these three points.

Actually, the *Gemara* deals with how to determine an individual's starting point for *chinuch* in various *mitzvos*, for there is a degree of maturity necessary for assuming each of the various responsibilities one has as a Jew. Among the examples cited by the

Gemara (*Succah* 44a): When a child knows how to talk, it is time to train him to say, "*Torah tzivah lanu Moshe.*" When a child is able to dress himself, he is ready to wear *tzitzis*. When he demonstrates a degree of independence of his mother, he is ready to dwell in the *succah*. To put *tzitzis* on a boy still in diapers or to force a child that cries repeatedly for his mother at night to sleep in a *succah* is not an act of *chinuch*, it is counter-*chinuch*. *Chinuch* is training a child to do a *mitzvah* properly; not to make a sham or *shpiel* of it, nor to teach him concepts that he's not prepared to accept. Similarly, at a later stage to force a child to sit and learn *Gemara* for long uninterrupted periods of time when he simply is not prepared to do so can turn him off from learning.

No less an authority than the *Rambam* gives us guidelines for motivating children. The *Rambam* tells us that Antignos Ish Socho was sharply criticized by the Sages for saying: "Do not be like those servants who serve their master to receive a reward, but be like those servants who serve their master not to receive a reward" (*Avos* 1:3 — See *Pirush of Rambam*).

Two great disciples of Antignos Ish Socho, namely Tzaddok and Baysus, misunderstood his words. When they heard this reference to serving G-d without any ulterior motives, they reasoned: "Is it possible that a person should work for a master and not get paid? Does this mean that we're going to serve the *Ribbono Shel Olam* our entire lifetimes and not receive anything in return?"

As a result, they rejected all rabbinic teachings, and founded the Tzedukim and Baysusim movements, which were the forerunners of all the deviant groups in Judaism, up to and including the present-day Reform and Conservative movements. All because Antignos Ish Socho preached a level of service that was beyond the reach of *Tannaim!*

This moved the *chachamim* to direct all future generations of teachers: "Wise men, be careful of your words" (*Avos* 1:11). Do not make lofty pronouncements, be they ever so true, unless you are sure of your audience. Don't give any high-sounding *mussar shmuessen* to kids who don't understand what you're talking about, or to common people who are not able to grasp the message, or even to *talmidei chachamim* who are liable to misunderstand your words.

∽§ The Rambam's Timetable

The *Rambam* (*Pirush Hamishnayos Sanhedrin*, Introduction to 10th *Perek*) applies the concept of tailoring the message to the listener in advising the parent how to train his child: When the child is taken to a *melamed*, he is not intrinsically interested in learning. Tell him, "I'll give you some sweets." The child responds to this. When he gets older, he'll learn for a new pair of shoes, or a new suit. Later he responds to financial rewards. After a while, he can be told: "You will be a great *talmid chacham*, and everybody will stand up for you. You may be a *dayan*. *Kavod HaTorah* will be yours." That level of motivation can last for quite a long time. It is also essential to know the proper timing for substituting the pair of shoes for the package of nuts, the money for the shoes, and so on. When a person gets older, you can tell him about the rewards of *Olam Haba*. But even that level of learning is still not one hundred percent *lishmah* — not purely for the sake of Heaven. Finally, he will attain the level of being able to pursue truth for its own sake. In summary, the *Rambam* says: Don't try to convince young people to learn Torah for its own sake. Of course they should learn Torah because *Hashem* wants them to, but make sure that there's something in it for them as well, until they are able to deal with the concept of Torah *lishmah* (*Pesachim* 4).

This is what the sages meant when they said that a person should always engage in the study of Torah and in *mitzvos shelo lishmah* — even if his activity is not for the highest motive — for he will eventually reach *lishmah*. Any person, and surely a child, cannot be treated as though he is only in the heavens. Like Yaakov's ladder, his feet must be on the ground. But ultimately, his head must reach heaven. He must have something higher to which he aspires.

Children must see in their parent that they too aspire to something loftier — not money, not a new house, or a grand vacation. They must see by their conduct that they too aspire to learn Torah *lishmah* — and to be better persons.

∽§ The Various Facets of "Darko"

Now let us discuss the third of Rabbeinu Yonah's aspects of *darko*: dealing with the child's individual nature. In explaining the word *darko*, the Vilna Gaon says that every human being is born under a certain *mazal*, with specific natural tendencies. The *Gemara* tells us that a person born under the *mazal* of *Maadim* has a tendency to spill blood. If he grows up to be a *tzaddik*, he will be a *mohel*; if he grows up to be a *rasha*, he will be a bandit; as a *beinoni* (of average righteousness), he will be a *shochet*. No matter what his level, shedding blood is in his very nature and cannot be repressed. To this, the Vilna Gaon comments that any attempt to mold this person into something other than one who sheds blood is doomed to failure. He will never be a concert pianist! All efforts to train the child must be *al pi darko*, consistent with his own tendencies. Then "even when he grows old, he will not turn aside from it." But if he is forced into a mold not in accord with his nature, when he grows older and is on his own, he will revert to his natural tendencies.

How many people are frustrated because they had wanted to be one type of person and their parents pushed them in a different direction. One cannot make a child into something that he's not. Every person can fit into Torah and *mitzvos*. Every *neshamah* can develop into a *tzaddik*. Yet G-d made each *neshamah* different. Just as no two people are identical in appearance, so are no two people endowed with identical characteristics (*Midrash Bamidbar Rabbah* 21:2). There is a fulfillment for each *neshamah* that conforms to its own natural pattern of behavior. The Gaon warns us not to force one *neshamah* into the mold of another.

ೞ The Ideal School: At Home

But we must raise a question that may disturb some people. Who is responsible for putting this *chinuch* into effect? Contrary to the literature disseminated by schools and *yeshivos*, the ideal *chinuch*, system is not to be found in educational institutions. It is not a product of modern facilities, state-of-the-art equipment and the pooled efforts of great principals and master teachers. The ideal system of education is, as the Torah says, *"v'shinantom levanecha"*: The parent teaches the child, one to one. This is the optimum situation because the parent ideally knows his own child and knows what the child is prepared to do, how quickly the child can advance and what the child's nature is.

Our contemporary system of public education, consisting of classes and schools, which was instituted by Rabban Yehoshua ben Gamla 2,000 years ago (*Bava Basra* 21a), was a necessary accommodation for those children that either had no parents or whose parents were incapable of teaching them. Our schools, with their tightly structured programs, represent a compromise involving necessary evils.

One of the basic shortcomings is the grouping of twenty or thirty children of different natures, different backgrounds, and different needs into one class. Furthermore, classes, for the most part, are put together not by tests of individual ability, but by an artificial standard — age, with all sorts of artificially determined "cutoff" dates. Are all adults of the same age as smart as one another? Then why assume that all children of the same age are of equal intelligence? And then, there are different aspects of intelligence — and emotional maturity — that develop independently of one another. Only an unusually gifted teacher can treat 20 or 30 children as individuals, use the program that was designed for an entire class, and tailor it to the needs and capacities of each individual child.

By necessity, the teacher in the classroom teaches at a median level, which will more or less satisfy the needs of the majority of the class. Then, depending on the skills of the *rebbi* or *morah*, he or she will devote special attention to exceptional children — both those that are especially gifted and those below class level, so that these children can also be gainfully occupied and benefit.

Our system is not optimum but merely the best we can come up with. Parents must therefore realize that if they intend to slough off the entire responsibility for the *chinuch* of their children onto the school, they are looking for trouble. Parents must be actively involved in what the school — almost by definition — cannot do, in the way of training the child according to his unique individual *derech*.

This individual consideration is especially crucial in molding the character of the child to be a *mentsch*. It is virtually impossible for a teacher with a number of children in a class to raise well-balanced children. That teacher can teach Torah, can pass on certain general rules in *midos tovos* to the children, and can serve as a role model to a certain extent. But the main work of character building, whether consciously or by default, is done by the parents. Unfortunately, many parents are very poorly equipped for the task. And not because they did not take Child Psychology 102, or read the almost inexhaustible current literature on the subject, but because of certain basic inadequacies in their understanding of what it means to be a parent.

◈§ No Magic Formula, but. . .

This is a challenge for which there are no magic formulas. Sometimes a solution may emerge from simply recognizing the problem and diagnosing its source. Once the attention of an intelligent person has been directed to a problem and he has been acquainted with certain general principles, he can often manage to work out the details or at least have the awareness to ask for advice. (1) Parents must realize that school is not the all-encompassing vehicle for their child's *chinuch*, but that they are also prime doers in his *chinuch*; that to simply provide for their child's needs, offer him tender loving care, and then just react to problems as they arise are not enough. They must assume an active role in directing his development. If a child is not directed, there is no doubt about it — he is going to have bad *midos*. It doesn't help if we just scold him or punish him when he's bad. We have to train him to be good.

(2) Whatever parents do in terms of directing their children, it is crucial that the child feel that his mother and father are on his side, that they are there to guide him and help him find his direction, not just to knock him down when he steps out of line. Most problems arise when parents and children become adversaries. As the *Tanna* says in describing the chaotic era immediately preceding *Mashiach's* coming: אויבי איש אנשי ביתו — "A man's enemies are the members of his household" (*Mishnah* at end of *Sotah*). This does not mean that the parent never punishes. On the contrary, *Shlomo Hamelech* tells us — "Whoever spares his rod hates his child but he that loves him chastises him early" (*Mishlei* 13:24). A good rule of thumb is: "Be firm, be fair, and be friendly."

Finally, (3) the parents — both mother and father — must realize the simple truth that not all children are alike. Everybody who has more than one child recognizes this immediately. You can serve them all the same supper, but you can't give them all the same *chinuch*. Parents, then, cannot relinquish the responsibility of raising their children. The mother and the father must take the time to figure out what makes each child tick, to determine his individual *derech*.

But one must walk a very fine line between treating the child as an individual and the equally important principle of the Sages:

"A person should never favor one child over the other children" (*Shabbos* 10b). The *chachamim* illustrate the potential for destruction that can come from favoritism with the fact that because of two coins worth of wool that Yaakov invested in a coat for Yoseif, over what he spent for his other sons, the brothers envied Yoseif, and this triggered the sequence of events that led to *galus Mitzrayim*. Treat each one as an individual, yet one must not receive more than the other: If you do something for one child at a certain stage of his/her development, you must do the same for the other children.

And of course, a mother or father should never say or even intimate that one child is the favorite. My grandmother had four sons and one daughter, who was the youngest. Friends would tell her, "We know who your favorite is." And she would lift up her five fingers and say, "Which one is my favorite? They're all my fingers."

⋅§ Whose Road Is He to Travel?

Al pi darko also means to consider the child's *derech* — his way, in contrast with the *derech* of others. The *chachamim* tell us that a person should not change from the profession of his father (*Eirechin* 16b). It should be easier for a person to be brought up in a family which has a certain tradition, and it is obviously easier for him to adopt the family profession. But this is not an absolute. Many parents make the error of trying to recreate the child as a carbon copy of themselves, even when the child is obviously not fit or inclined to follow the parents' *derech*, even when the profession is not an established family tradition, but just that of the father. When carried to the extreme, this can seriously disturb the character development of the child and even inflict him with severe emotional damage.

Another common phenomenon of misjudging the child's own *derech* is what can be called the *Bechor Syndrome*. In this manifestation of the problem, the parent, usually the father, has typically not realized his own full potential; his game is halfway played out. He's not going to change. His son, and it's usually the first-born son, carries the burden of his father's unfinished agenda. He is going to be his second chance. What makes the *bechor* particularly susceptible to this type of mismanagement is a combination of the parents' romantic enthrallment with having brought a new human being into the world, with an unlimited potential for accomplishment, coupled with their lack of experience and knowledge of what to expect from this little *neshamah* at any given time. The child's *derech*, if properly understood, will take him to his own destiny, not necessarily to that of his parents'. The parents must always bear this in mind, as painful or disappointing as this may be.

It is equally important to realize that the second child is not a clone of the first. The second child also represents a new experience for the parents. It is their first "other child." This can be especially burdensome to number two when the parents succeed with child number one. Hence the celebrated "middle child."

৺ The Road Well Traveled

The emphasis on *darko* — the child's own individual path — has yet another implication: not living for the neighbors. This statement may sound rather superfluous, but people have a tendency to neglect what is essential for their own well-being, and pattern their lives after their social milieu — even in spiritual matters. We must meet our own children's needs, not have them simply follow in lock step with the neighbors' children. Ben Zoma in the *Mishnah* tells us, "Who is the *gibor*, the man of strength? He who conquers *his* evil inclination." The stress is on *his own yeitzer hara* — not on someone else's. In our society, there is a trendiness in *mitzvos* and in areas of study. What may be fine for the population at large, may not necessarily be the thing that my child needs at this stage of his development. Others may require emphasis on avoiding *lashon hara*, while mine may still need to be taught to keep his hands to himself. Someone else's child may benefit from enrichment in *Mishnayos*, while my little boy may need the time to review his *Chumash*. While the "in-thing" in the *yeshivah* may be to say over a "Reb Chaim," my son may still need training in how to learn *pshat* in a *Tosafos*!

After all is said and done, after we have ingested all the words of the *Chachamim* and all the advice of the experts on raising children, after we have used all the accepted methods and applied our own innovation we must realize that, just as in every human endeavor, without *Siyata D'Shamaya* — the help of G-d — we can never succeed. It's not for nothing that *frumme Yiddishe mammas* pray to the Almighty before *licht bentschen* for the *zechus* to raise children and children's children who will be *Chachamim* and *Nevonim*, wise and understanding, who will be *Ohavei Hashem v'yirei Hashem*, who love and fear G-d, who will be men and women of truth who will enlighten the world with Torah and *ma'asim tovim*.

Every morning we pray to Hashem: אלוקי נשמה שנתת בי טהורה היא... — "My G-d, the soul that You have put in me is pure." To paraphrase that *Tefillah*: May we be given the understanding to realize that the soul that You have given *to me*, the soul of my child, which You have entrusted to me, is holy and pure, and that as long as I have that trust, I will do whatever I can to ensure that purity and raise him to do Your will.

Avi Shulman

The Critical Parent's Guidebook

Is criticizing children perpetual "nudging," or a lifelong aid to growth?

After what seemed like many years in a dentist's chair, I opened my eyes to signal the desperate need for a moment of relief. I noticed on the wall a caricature someone had playfully drawn of the dentist and whimsically entitled "Painless Dr. Smith." I pointed to the caricature and mumbled, "Painless?" He answered, "Doesn't hurt me a bit."

CRITICIZING CHILDREN has much in common with good dental care. Mostly unpleasant, vitally necessary, and greatly dependent on the attitude and sensitivities of both parties: dentist and patient/parent and child. Sensibly introduced, emotionally supported, and administered with sensitivity, good oral hygiene can give the person healthy, sparkling, trouble-free teeth for many years. Likewise, positive criticism, well-thought through and sensibly administered can help a child with attitudes that say "criticism helps me grow."

Criticism — or as we euphemistically qualify it, constructive criticism — is to many of us a never-ending battle in which we find ourselves an unwilling participant or combatant. Especially during the child's formative years when natural curiosity gives way to exploration, life styles questioned and parental views tested, many parents view their primary roles as critics. "Is it not my duty — or better stated, my sacred obligations to right wrongs, point out weaknesses and generally set them straight?" the parents emphatically say. And the response is, "Yes, you are 100% right."

The purpose, then, of this article is not to challenge the need for criticism — it's an inherent part of our expression of love and concern, in addition to being a *mitzvah* of *chinuch* — but rather to discuss ways to make criticism effective.

⋙ Like a Scalpel in a Surgeon's Hand

Why should we be concerned with *effective criticism?* Because criticism often touches the most sensitive chord of the human personality, the innermost psychic "spinal chord" which supports the entire fabric and make-up of the person. Criticism often touches on the child's self-image — the raw material of which feelings, emotions and self-confidence are shaped — and can have desirable or undesirable effects years or decades to come.

To indiscriminately or thoughtlessly "dish out" criticism can cause great harm and achieve the direct opposite effect the well meaning parent intended.

Just as the experienced surgeon — knowing how disastrous and far reaching the most minute slip of the scalpel can be — operates with utmost care, precision and determination—so too the parent — realizing how devastating, destructive and counterproductive criticism incorrectly given can be — will want to proceed with utmost caution and concern.

If we can imbue young children with an attitude that criticism is really a tool that can enhance personal growth and relationships, if we can convey the message that criticism is not a deprecation of their personal value but rather the sum total of society's experience that can ultimately make their life more effective, more pleasant, productive—then we will have equipped them with one of the most powerful aids to continual improvement and growth.

⋙ Two Views: The Long and Short of It

Whether this child, when grow up, will view criticism from superiors, spouses, co-workers as *"nudgerie,"* become defensive, withdrawn or hostile, or will interpret criticism as a necessary and healthy means of improvement is to a very large extent dependent on how we express it. Thus, we should always view criticism on two levels: (a) to achieve the immediate result (i.e. have the room clean, homework done, fighting stopped, etc.); and the second, perhaps much more important, level (b) to teach the child how to react to criticism. To achieve the first (and have the child clean his room) but have him respond negatively to criticism is a very high price to pay for a clean room.

One more point before we start. The purpose of the article is not to scare the parent. Few of us always do what is right and yet, ב"ה, most children survive. The purpose of the article is to develop a sensitivity and provoke one to think about the fact that there is perhaps a better way in this area, as there may be in every other field. Our objective is to stimulate your thinking about the subject.

☙ "Didn't I Tell You?"

> *Sarah, a playful three-year-old, is building a tower of blocks, which is growing higher and higher. Her mother sends out warning signals from the kitchen: "Sarah, be careful. Don't build the tower any higher. It is going to fall...Don't...Sarah..." "BOOM! "Didn't I tell you?"*

There are many situations where allowing for a small mistake can prove to be a much more effective way of teaching. While we don't want to risk physical harm, irreversible damage or the formation of undesirable habits, if the situation at hand is a relatively minor one, learning by one's own mistakes can be the more meaningful experience.

The parent may want to discuss the incident allowing the child to draw the correct conclusion...guide the conversation and squeeze out the lesson value, but the more "personal experience" the child can derive, the more forceful, unthreatening and long-lasting experience it will be.

Here is another point. Rather than yield to the natural tendency to blurt out the criticism, consider the alternative. Would a simple substitution or distraction of the young child's action accomplish the same result? Instead of scolding a young child who picks up a valuable object to play with, consider casually handing him a substitute toy.

Could someone else — spouse, sibling, teacher, counselor, or, under special situations, a close friend — make the same criticism and gain more receptivity? While it may be true that the parent is responsible to put into motion the corrective action, Father or Mother may not always be most effective.

◆§ The "Potch": Conveying Differences in Gravity

> *Chaim accompanies his father to shul and today is annoying and obnoxious. His father does not say anything to most of Chaim's antics but when he can't take it any longer, Father strikes out with several painful "potches."*

Because criticizing someone — especially a child — often comes easy, we not only point out the mistake—to make sure the message gets home—we are tempted to add emotion and usually some drama. The result is analogous to using the proverbial sledge hammer to kill a fly.

While a child who runs into the street may well deserve a strong reprimand including being yelled at and a sharp swat where it hurts, mistakenly breaking a plate does not deserve the same treatment. In fact, if you do respond to the broken plate in the same strong measure, you will have effectively blurred the lines of differentiation between minor and major infractions.

In his *sefer*, Rabbi Mayer Munk of Bnei Brak lists fifteen levels of punishment and points out that it is the wise teacher that portions out the punishment according to the *least* amount that would be effective. The same concept applies to parents. Obviously, there are many forms of criticism — ranging from a show of minor displeasure, from a casual observational comment, "perhaps this way would be better..." to the last straw, the yelling and the *potch*. Understatement — saying *less* than expected — oftimes speaks louder and is more effective than over-reacting.

The quick swat may release some of the parental frustrations and is definitely an approach to consider; but it may create more problems in the parent-child relationship than it solves.

◆§ The Time, the Place, and the Word

> *At the Shabbos table, Father casually asks 11-year old Noson how he's doing in school. Mother suddenly reminds herself that the teacher sent home a note admonishing Noson for failing a test and being the class clown. Father responds by a barrage of criticism.*

The time and place of the criticism can sometimes be as important or even more important than the criticism itself. The rebuke that could have been offered privately, but instead performed in front of family or friends, hurts much, much more.

The key word here is *feelings*. Children really do have feelings, and as adults and parents, we are not only obligated to be sensitive to these feelings, but our ability to win or *chas v'shalom* lose the child's respect is based on this sensitivity.

For the families undergoing stress or excitement, such as preparing for a *simchah* or a trip, criticism may be self-defeating by casting a cloud of negativism which envelops the whole family. Even a family meal may be the wrong time for criticism that can wait. The mood and temper of the entire family can be altered by harsh criticism of one child. If the intent is to correct instead of to embarrass, then privacy is not only desirable but imperative. Make certain that the privacy afforded your child is the same you would like for yourself. Use a room away from people. Close the door, and don't speak loudly enough to be heard outside. There are few more humiliating or degrading situations than being ranked out in front of siblings, peers, or friends — which is also extremely uncomfortable for the observers.

◆§ Effective Anger: Skin Deep

> *Spilling the groceries on the way home, reporting a half hour late for car pool, Mother has had an extremely frustrating day. 14-year-old Leah ignored Mother's instructions to prepare supper. Mother comes in and lets Leah "have it."*

Personal hurt and humiliation surely need venting, but to use this opportunity is all wrong. Anger clouds our minds so we cannot even think clearly. We scream, we rant, we pontificate in long, heated, excited statements that do or don't make sense. We may even hit but more often than not, aren't hitting our target (no pun intended). And we are not being effective.

Is there a place for anger? Yes, but only when it is totally controlled, or as *Baalei Mussar* put it, כעס הפנים ולא כעס הלב, anger of the face, not anger of the heart. Anger should be used to indicate how deeply you are concerned about the subject at hand, but *only* when you can position it, control it, portion it out, use it to underscore a point. This is only feasible when the anger is objective, a tool — not when you become subjected to it. If you can't control the anger but rather it controls you, there are few times when you can use it effectively for criticism. It is unnerving to hear *adults* tell of criticism and punishment that was meted out to them — justifiably or not — in anger decades ago, and for which they never forgave parent or teacher.

◆§ Shouting Softly

> *Michael brings home a disastrous report card. Father takes one look at it and goes into a frenzy. Every time Michael tries to say something, Father yells louder and louder.*

A story is told of a presidential candidate who, whenever he spoke outdoors, was disappointed with the public address system. Finally, in desperation, an engineer set up a huge amplifier directly underneath the speaker's platform. When the candidate heard his own voice being amplified many times, he was finally satisfied. We seem to think that the louder we raise our voice, the greater the impression we make. When speaking in public, raising one's voice can convey strength of conviction; in private discussion, the opposite is almost always the case. Here the lowered voice — almost a whisper, causing the other person to have to lean forward to hear — is most effective. Raising your voice tends to overwhelm and wash right over the listener; lowering your voice allows you to penetrate into the listener's thinking. Especially because the child *expects* to be yelled at—and sets up a mental block to tune out the admonition—the calm, lowered, whisper-like voice accomplishes much more. With some thought, you can learn how to communicate deep feelings in a whisper.[1]

◆§ Save Face for Him

> *Rabbi Avrohom Pam, שליט״א, told of an incident some thirty years ago that had a lasting impression on a student. During a written examination, the Rebbe spotted a student obviously cheating, and said to him, "If you need help with the questions, ask me."*

True, this method might not be applicable or even desirable in every situation, but whenever you can save face for someone

---

1. Perhaps this is the intent of the Gemara in *Shabbos:* "When we speak it should be בניחותא — calmly — כי היכי דלקבלינהו מיני — that it should be received well from him."

you are criticizing, do it and it will become a powerful, very appreciated tool.

Rubbing someone's face into the ground, even when you are perfectly right, rarely accomplishes what you want it to. "I told you so" is more than a stinging reprimand. Since the child usually knows very well that you "told him so," the child perceives the statement as nothing more than the perverted pleasure of making someone wallow in his mistake and lose his self-respect.

Listen Before You Leap

> *During a family crisis, when a member of the family was ill, 14-year old Yankie failed to express any emotion. At one particular point, Mother demands an explanation for his lack of feeling. When none is forthcoming, she screams, "You should understand. If I have to explain it to you, it is of no use."*

It has been said that "assumptions are the mother of all foul-ups" and that can be true in our situation.

Don't have an itchy "trigger finger," but rather ask first and listen intently to the answers. Don't assume the child always knows precisely what's expected of him or how he should feel or show his feelings. Even when you're "sure of the facts," ask — because it not only conveys a feeling of mutual respect but, equally important, you can learn much about the child. In fact, sometimes the reason for his behavior may be more important than you think. Hastily dispensed criticism can effectively lock off an important avenue of communication. Ask questions — honestly, probingly — and you may be surprised at what you learn.

On the other side of the coin, having to apologize to someone you mistakenly chastised is a humbling experience, one you could easily do without.

Don't Dump

Dumping is used here in its simplest meaning, such as in "dumping the garbage." Once we have the culprit at hand, few of us can resist the temptation to dump all the grievances and complaints we can think of. If one is good, two is better, and five is great! — Right? Wrong! The assaultee's defense mechanism blocks out too much. Just as a whisper is more effective than a scream, understating — the ability to hold back and say less rather than more — is *more* effective.

Moreover, piling together different sins committed at different times under different situations allows the person to deflect the criticism in a barrage of defenses. Unless all the situations are identical, we get into tangential arguments — into a "great debate" — instead of focusing on one single issue at hand. If our purpose in "dumping" is to strengthen our point, we may be dismayed to find it doing the opposite.

❧ Suggest Corrective Action

Listen to a standard criticism. The person criticized will seldom be provided with any direction as to how he should have performed the contested act, and more importantly, how it should be done correctly in the future. We assume (again that trap word!) that everyone else knows what we know, so we don't bother telling them. "You should have," "you could have," and "if you only would have" do not necessarily help the child know what to do the next time. The only really helpful suggestion is "next time try to do it this way." *We* haven't done *our* task fully if we do not discuss the right way of doing things.

❧ Request Cooperation

Instead of "telling, ordering, commanding, or instructing," try requesting cooperation in a friendly manner. Young children can be very understanding when spoken to in a language of cooperation. Being firm does not preclude an ability to be nice, to be understanding, or to be warm. Project a feeling that says: "I am here to help you."

❧ Reaffirm Continual Positive Assocation

Since we cannot read the mind of our child, we don't know what outlandish ideas this confrontation could trigger. The young child may interpret the stern reprimand as a rejection or as a permanent loss of parental love — all absolutely untrue. But it is not enough that you, your spouse, and everyone on the block knows that you love Chaim; what is important is that Chaim knows. So find a way to say, "Even though I scold you, I love you" or better, "Only because I love you do I care enough about you to reprimand you."

Especially after an unnerving encounter, a kiss, a hug, an embrace or other tangible expressions of love are important. Remember: What you know to be true is not nearly as important as what the child *perceives* to be true.

Develop Monitoring Formulas

O.K. We've corrected a wrong. The child knows what is right. He knows we love him. What now? Build in a system to make certain that the error will not be repeated or the mistake won't "happen" again. As adults we take for granted that once we have corrected an error, more is not necessary. But human nature being as it is, the child thinks: "If it's really important, they will monitor my performance."

Just as a teacher who issues homework assignments to children of younger grades and doesn't check the homework is really saying, "I am giving you the homework assignment because I was told to, but I couldn't care less if you do it or not" — so, too, the parent who doesn't follow up the new behavior is signaling to the child: "Don't take me too seriously." The contradictory signals are confusing. If it is important enough to be made into a big deal — to be criticized in the first place — it would be important enough to occasionally be checked on, which leads us to...

Create Opportunities to Commend Improvement

"Why is it you yell at me when I'm bad but never say anything when I'm good" is far more than a childish lament. It is a serious parental accusation. And the statement, "Because we *expect* you to be good," is not enough of an answer. Is that a justification for not noticing good behavior? Not acknowledging it? Not commenting on it? Since the child cannot read your mind, thinking cannot do what verbalizing can. Underscore good behavior by showing approval and pride rather than by cold indifference.

Why not go one step further, and complete the full circle? Recognizing the power of positive motivation, find opportunities to compliment the new behavior. If the child did not share with others but now does so, find an opportunity at the supper table to "officially" recognize it. Do it openly, unstintingly.

Of course there's a time for a no-nonsense, "it must be done this way, no questions asked" confrontation. Of course, the positive, sweet, suggestive method doesn't always work...and you need authoritive instructions with clearly responsive physical punishment for its violation. But the thrust of this article is that, unfortunately, most parents know that part of criticism. The multiple choices outlined in this article are available to the parent. These should also be taken into consideration.

◆§ Criticize Positively — an Art Worth Cultivating

Positive criticism — finding a base of strength on which to build — is by far the most effective method of criticism and an art well worth cultivating.

Positive criticism focuses on the child's strong points saying, "You do so well in organizing your Pirchei outing. You can surely do so much better in helping me organize the *succah* supplies." Contrast this to finding a weak spot and zooming in on it, emphasizing it, underscoring it and in a sense reinforcing it: "Why are you such a slob? Just look at the mess in my storage shed!"

אל תוכח לץ פן ישנאך הוכח לחכם ויאהבך — "Don't admonish the scoffer for he will hate you. Admonish a wise person and he will love you" (*Mishlei* 9:8). This passage is usually interpreted as referring to *two* separate people, the scoffer and the wise person. One commentary explains it to refer to *one* person: When admonishing a person, do not address the "scoffer" — the negative part of his personality — but rather appeal to the wise, virtuous side of the person.

There are usually two ways to view a child's misdeeds:

"You wild, undisciplined child," "You sloppy kid"; and "You are usually such a well-behaved child..." "You are usually so careful about keeping your things neat..."

There are obviously times when each approach is valid. For example, when repeated discussions, warnings and criticisms are ignored, then, of course, the stronger method might be necessary. But there are many, many times when the "Admonish the wise," the stressing of the positive, can work more effectively and at less emotional cost.

The "Admonish the wise" will be effective if you say only what you believe to be true, and you speak about the child's potential not exclusively when it is accompanied with an admonition, but at other times as well.

The child whose parents instill confidence on all levels, whose big and small accomplishments are fully acknowledged, and whose potentials are discussed in glowing terms, will benefit from the positive approach. He will be inspired to live up to the great expectations his parents hold out to him.

> A wise man once said to his children, "I pray that you will never speak evil of anyone. Not only because it is a grave transgression — but because you will have more important things to do with your time."

Rabbi Wolbe, שליט״א, one of today's leading *Mussar* exponents, recently spoke for several hours about the individuality of the child. When he concluded, a friend turned to me and said, "I think I know what he meant." When I responded with a puzzled look, he said, "I think Rabbi Wolbe was saying that a five-year-old child is not a 25% adult. He is a 100% five-year-old child."

One wrong criticism rarely if ever inflicts irreversible damage. It is *continual* deprecation, the constant putting down and embarrassment that can and does do the damage.

Enjoy you children, laugh with them, occasionally play with them, learn with them, set and retain guidelines, and appreciate them for what they are and אי״ה will be. With *tefillah* and *siyata diShimaya*, you will have much *nachas*.

Letter in Response to: The Critical Parent's Guidebook

Criticism, Toys, and Love

To the Editor:

"The Critical Parent's Guidebook" (*JO* Nov. 1983) was truly wonderful. Just as the *Ramban* instructed his son to read his letter to him once a week, so too would we parents all benefit if we would read this article regularly — perhaps marking paragraphs that are most pertinent to us.

Most parents *are* too critical. In our defense, our sharp words and impatience are often the result of undue daily strain. On the other hand, most of us overwork not out of necessity, but to obtain a newer car, a larger apartment, a better vacation spot. We women insist on producing fancy pastries, attending too many luncheons — when we could be excused with a mailed-in contribution. Parents often have an insatiable appetite for attending *simchos*, social events, and testimonials, staying until the last *l'chayim*, and then the next morning, letting it out on the children, not having the patience that is needed to "Train the youth in his way." We forget that, in its literal sense, *Shema* commands us to talk with our children about Torah — morning, noon and night. Instead, the baby sitter is often expected to take over our parental duties. No wonder if our children repay us with like measure in our old age and transport us to some nursing home.

We must realize that there is nothing that money can buy which can substitute for GIVING OF OURSELVES to our children.

My maternal *Zeida* and *Bubby* raised eleven children, working long hours for small wages here in America, but the evenings belonged to their children. Lacking a Bais Yaakov, he was his daughters' Rebbe. My mother would tell me how much his wonderful stories from the Torah and his instructions meant to her. He could have worked harder and bought toys for his children, or moved to a bigger place. I am sure that all his children approved of *his* choice of utilizing the evenings. My beloved *Bubby* worked endlessly by doing factory "homework" at night. There were times when she could not afford a baby carriage and she had to carry her youngest in her arms...

When my grandparents died, they were surrounded by eleven children, all Torah observant and all financially comfortable. They all gave their parents the highest respect, so much so that most parents would have envied them. All our bribery rarely yields the return that parents most covet: deep love and obedience. It is only the true value of life that we are obligated to pass on to our children, and that yields results.

Name Withheld by Request
A mother, grandmother,
and great-grandmother,
by Hashem's blessing.

Shani Perr

And He Who Knows Not How to Ask Open for Him

IT WAS A MAGICAL moment. We were alone in the kitchen, just the two of us — mother and child caught in a fragment of time.

Bright sunlight streamed in from the window, unusual for a brisk November day. Supper, half cooked on the stove — productive sounds from washer and dryer whispered the message that work was getting done, releasing me for the moment.

He was lying on the floor with the abandon only known to children, observing the world from a new perspective. Soon the others would arrive — big and small, each waiting to be seen, to be heard, to be listened to, to be loved, each one claiming his inalienable uniqueness. But not just yet.

"How come nothing comes out when you laugh?" he asked from nowhere.

I had been stunned before by the workings of his little mind, the scope of his imagination. "Prunes are raisins when they grow up," he once announced using all the reasoning and experience of his four years on this earth. "I love you till the end of counting," he once declared with all the poetry and intensity of his little being.

There is nothing second hand about children, I once read; no layers, no levels. In children, we see learning at its freshest. Hungry for knowledge, they taste and touch the things they see. They test everything grown ups take for granted. They want to know. They dare to ask.

His little world had categories, information filed in tiny discs, amassed from his tiny wealth of knowledge. He made associations, drew conclusions.

Chickens lay eggs, cows give milk, crying produces tears. And laughter?

"How come nothing comes out when you laugh?"

When was the last time I had asked a fundamental question?

Finding the universe as it is, we continue, accept the status quo, follow the daily routine. Our inability to ask results in our inability to dream.

"When Israel was a child, then I loved him," says the Prophet. "One should remain a child forever, always learning," says Reb Yisroel Salanter, "always asking in order to learn."*

I've heard it told that the *keruvim* that covered the Holy Ark with their wings had the faces of children, telling us to learn as only children do with body and mind, with heart and soul, straining their very beings to find out, to discover.

The Torah speaks of four sons, three who ask, and one who cannot.

It is the custom at the Seder that the youngest child asks four questions, for he gets down to the heart of the matter.

If there are no children, only a wife at the table, then she asks, for women retain their childlike quality longer than men.

If one is alone — with neither a child nor wife — he must summon up the child that lives within all of us but is deeply buried, and bid him to ask!

---

* *Tnuas HaMussar.*

... And Vice-Versa

The Teacher Is the Lesson

Were It Not for Her

An Overwhelming View

Dear Morah

Dear Mother

R= I

Teaching the Learning Disabled Student

In Search of Chavie

Miriam Zakon

The Teacher Is the Lesson

*Sarah Schenirer:
Her Lessons and Her Legacy,
Fifty Years After Her Passing*

~§ This Legend Lived

THE MEDIUM IS THE message. Marshall McLuhan's aphorism has become something of a byword for any discussion of effective communication. How something is said or presented — the medium — is inseparable from what is said — the message.

If this rule is true in the world of television, McLuhan's area of expertise and interest, it is perhaps even more important in the world of education. Education is possibly the purest form of communication, the communication of the mores, beliefs, ideals, and knowledge of one generation to the next, of the wiser to the less knowledgeable, of those closer to Sinaitic revelation to those one step further removed. If "the medium is the message," then "the teacher is the lesson." That *Rebbe* who stood next to the blackboard taught us as much by his gestures as by his lectures; we remember *Morah's* smile or frown more than we do her stencils. Truly, the lessons of our teachers' lives and behavior are unforgettable ones.

If you are reading this, and you are a Torah-observant American woman of a Torah-observant background, the chances are great that your most unforgettable teacher was a woman whom you have never met. If you are reading this, and you are a man who is a *ben Torah*, the chances are great that your wife supported you in *kollel*, urged you to attend a *shiur*, or encouraged you to find a *chavrusa* partly because of the influence of a woman whom you, and she, never met. And if you are of the growing numbers of *chozrim b'teshuvah*, the newly observant, chances are great that many of your teachers, many of your mentors, many of those who helped you find your way owe an enormous debt to a woman whom they, and you, never met.

The woman is Sarah Schenirer ע״ה. The debt owed her by women, by men, by children, by all of *Klal Yisrael*, is an enormous one. She was our teacher. And if "the teacher is the lesson," we would do well to study her life,* and the lessons that can be learned from this extraordinary woman.

The story, familiar to almost all graduates of Bais Yaakov schools, has an almost legendary quality about it. It begins, always, with the compelling image of the seamstress toiling with her needlework in her Polish city, watching with anxious eyes as the rift grows between Jewish mother and daughter, as girls untutored in the splendors of Jewish thought and learning seek escape in secular philosophy. The scene shifts to a small school that the visionary seamstress has begun. The idea takes hold, captures the imagination, and suddenly a dream becomes a movement, an idea turns into an ideology. Bais Yaakov has been born!

Like many legends, we begin to take it for granted, to accept what is told without examining its implications. The mythical quality of the story makes it difficult to grasp, to understand. But in the case of this particular legend there is one difference. You see, this legend is true, this legend lived. And therefore this legend — no, this living, breathing woman — has much to teach us. This teacher, truly, is the lesson.

∞§ Lessons in Change and Revolution

It has been said, by those who have little understanding and less love for Torah-Judaism, that we are an obstinate and unyielding lot, a group that makes no concession to reality, that

---

* The reader is referred to Joseph Friedenson's biography of Sarah Schenirer in *JO*, Feb. 1964 and Chaim Shapiro's "The Flame Called Sarah Schenirer," in *JO*, Dec. 1974.

remains conservative and inflexible in the face of new circumstances. The lesson of one woman's life proves this to be no more than a canard, a false accusation.

Frau Schenirer changed her world. She found a Poland that was offering an endless supply of tantalizing ideologies to girls ignorant of the riches of their own heritage. These "isms" — secularism, socialism, nationalism, communism — posed a potent threat to the very core of Jewish life, the home.

When Sarah Schenirer, pious and devout woman that she was, sensed the need for a change in the world of Torah education, she followed the path trodden by many Torah-true "revolutionaries" before her. She consulted *da'as Torah*, sages steeped in Jewish learning and wisdom. *Da'as Torah*, in this case, was the Belzer Rebbe, then staying in Marienbad. At her request, her brother, a Belzer *chassid* dubious of her plans of opening a school for girls, sent a note to the Rebbe outlining her dream. The Rebbe wished her success, and she was ready to begin her remarkable venture. Later, encouragement by the venerable Chofetz Chaim and other great men gave her additional confidence to enlarge the scope of her work.

Yes, when times demand change, Torah-true Jews are not afraid to answer the call. We do so not by abandoning our beliefs and our laws, but, conversely, by studying them even more deeply, searching within our Torah for the answers which we know are there, seeking out our "living *Sifrei Torah*" for their guidance and advice. Change there may be, but the goal — a life of Torah study, *mitzvah* observance, and doing G-d's will — is eternal.

With the fervor of a revolutionary and the piety of an *aishes chayil*, a woman of valor, Sarah Schenirer gave generations of girls and women the means to fight the false allure of endless "isms." At the same time she gave us a meaningful lesson in how an authentic Jew effects change.

৺ Lessons in Tznius and Simplicity

Pashtus — simplicity — is a quality that, more than any other, has been attributed to Sarah Schenirer. One of Sarah Schenirer's students in the seminary in Cracow, now a respected educator in her own right, remembers with fondness her first lesson with Frau Schenirer. At the time that this student first met her, Sarah Schenirer's reputation had reached far past the borders of her own native city, and the newly arrived girl expected a lesson full of deep insight and learning. What she got, instead, was a simple review of the laws of *neigel vasser*, washing the hands in the morning.

How disappointed all the girls were! — she remembers with a smile. Now, over fifty years later, she realizes the great depth of that simple lesson, and all the lessons which followed.

Simplicity was the motif of her lessons, of her life. Not the innocence of naivete, this, but the true simplicity of one who knows her goals, who trusts in her G-d. She was much like her namesake, Sarah, in this respect, as Rabbi Shamshon Raphael Hirsch (whose work had a great influence on Frau Schenirer) points out: "Sarah took the beauty of childhood with her into her womanhood, and the innocence of the twenty-year-old girl with her into the grave. How

Yaakov's Interior Strength

Rabbi Shimon Schwab

Chazal tell us that in times of old, when somebody did an extraordinary *mitzvah*, the *Navi* — the Prophet — was commanded to write it down and it was preserved for us in the *Tanach*. But later when there are no more *Neviim* to record history, Eliyahu *Hanavi* writes it down and *Hashem Yisbarach* Himself signs it. My heart tells me that Eliyahu *Hanavi* has written down the epic story of this *Ishah Gedolah* — this great woman — and that Eliyahu *Hanavi* will probably write down the names of thousands of Bais Yaakov students, Bais Yaakov-educated Jewish women, wives and mothers of *Bnei Torah*, who are the blossoms and fruits of the tree which Sarah Schenirer planted. All of the *Kollelim* today — in America, in England, in Europe, in *Eretz Yisrael* — are possible because of the Bais Yaakov education, because of the seed planted by her.

The word *bayis* means "house." And Bais Yaakov is the house of Yaakov, the Jewish house, which is a domain of a Jewish woman. "*Bayis* — house, this refers to the woman." But *bayis* also means "the inside" — as in "*mibayis umibachutz tetzapenah,* you shall coat it *inside* and out" . . . and Bais Yaakov means the inside of Yaakov. Think for a moment about a beautiful *Kiddush* cup, a *becher* made of sterling silver. The outside is shiny, glitters, is artistically embellished and far... does this point of view of our rabbis contrast with that of our days! (Our Rabbanim) look for beauty, not in the twenty-year-old, but in the child, and innocence not in the child, but in mature adolescence... only the girl matured to womanhood... can crown (her) head with the wreath of innocence." (Rabbi Hirsch, commentary on *Genesis* 23:1).

This trait of simplicity was certainly not indicative of ignorance or a lack of depth. No simple-minded pietist, she, the woman with the blazing eyes whose most beloved *sefer* was Hirsch's *Nineteen Letters* (read, naturally, in its original German). Hers was a total, complete singleness of purpose, her life absolutely dedicated *l'shem Shomayim*, for the sake of Heaven. If she lacked complexity, it was only the complexity of life that man creates for himself by doubts, by errors. The world — if one is totally and completely dedicated to

---

attractive to the eye — but this is only the outside. The inside holds the wine. Without the ability of the inside to hold the wine, the outside is a mere shell, without meaning: no wine, no *Kiddush*, no *brachah*. The outside of *Klal Yisrael* is the men; the inside, the *bayis*, is the Jewish women, *Bais Yaakov*. There is no inside without an outside; there is no outside without an inside. True, the eyes of the world rest on the outside, its most prominent feature. As far as the wine is concerned, however, the inside is what matters. It is the *ikar*.

The outside and the inside have different functions. So have men and women. They look different. And the inside and outside of the *Kiddush* cup have even slightly different measurements. You cannot hold on to the wine without the outside, but the wine would never be there in the first place without the inside... because both are one. Both belong together. Bais Yaakov is the *pnimiyus* — the interior beauty of *Klal Yisrael*.

We have two *mitzvos* that deal with lights: kindling *Shabbos* lights and kindling Chanukah lights. These *mitzvos* are commanded to both men and women alike; yet when it comes to *Shabbos* lights, which illuminate the inside — the key to *Shalom Bayis* — men delegate the *mitzvah* to the women. When it comes to Chanukah lights, which are meant to shine outward, into the street, to convey *pirsuma nisah*, publicizing the miracle, the women delegate their *mitzvah* to the men. Both *pnimiyus* and *chitzoniyus* — inward experience and outward expression — the Torah addresses both, together.

G-d's service, and His service alone — can really be quite a simple place. Sarah Schenirer tapped into this simplicity, trod the path that G-d had laid so clearly before her. There were no detours, no false turns. This, then, was her simplicity, a simplicity so profound it is difficult for most of us — still searching for that one clear road — to comprehend.

Her students recall a time when she picked up stones pitched at her by those antagonistic to her, turned to her students and told them that the stones would be of help for building a new school building. In these days of public relations and "hype" running rampant, one might praise her instincts as a showman. It certainly makes for good copy. But one would be wrong. She did not see the incident as an opportunity for a *bon mot*, a memorable line. Those stones were merely stones that would help her build, help her to further what G-d desired of her; and if He had chosen to have them cast at her in such a manner, *gam zu l'tovah*, this too, was for the best.

Her *pashtus* was enhanced by her *tzinius*, her modesty. When the cornerstone for a new and commodious building for the Bais Yaakov Seminary in Cracow was laid, Frau Schenirer, the visionary who could take credit for having begun the entire movement, sat with her students in the audience, allowing others to take the stage. The *tznius* of that moment, the modesty of that woman, resounds to this very day with a clear, clarion sound! What a lesson this life was!

✺ Lessons in Dedication, Lessons in Love

I recently had the privilege of spending a few pleasant hours with a group of Sarah Schenirer's former students. A notable group it was, a room full of our generation's top educators, women who were pioneers in the world of Torah education for American girls, women whose dedication and selflessness have set examples for hundreds of their students.

What struck me most about the group was the change that came over all of them as we began to discuss their beloved teacher. Somber eyes, which had viewed the destruction of European Jewry, began to sparkle; stern features, which had set many a student quaking, softened visibly. The stories gushed forth; the smiles grew more wistful. Suddenly I found myself in the presence of children, children whose enthusiasm and energy cannot be contained, children speaking of a truly beloved mother or friend. The unquenchable brightness of a child's eyes was there, illuminating the faces of each of these righteous women.

What could it have been, I mused afterwards, that could have such an astounding effect over half a century later? What quality of Sarah Schenirer's could evoke such openly expressed emotion, could tear through the mists of forgetfulness and make her seem so alive to those who had known her and loved her?

Although the full answer still deludes me, I suspect that the key word here is love, an *ahavas Yisrael* that was rare, astonishing both in its depth and breadth. Her love for the *Klal*, for all Jewry, is evidenced by her dedication to its welfare, but this love was sharpened and made all the greater by her love for each and every individual. The tales are endless: Sarah Schenirer toiling over her correspondence each night, not allowing one letter to go unanswered; Sarah Schenirer dancing with her students, her face aglow; Sarah Schenirer's burning eyes, which silently demanded the best of each and every student, and silently assured the student that, yes, the best could be achieved.

Just as she looked at Polish Jewry, saw the potential within its womanhood, and brought it out to full flower, so she looked at each girl and saw, not an unlearned child, but a Jewess with the potential of immeasurable accomplishment. It was this love for the individual that enabled her to take the university-trained German Jewess, the scholarly girl of Lithuania, and the Chassidic Polish students, and mesh them together, meld their talents and strengths into one great, united whole.

The two qualities needed to teach, Sarah Schenirer told one of her students, were love for the Jewish child and *mesiras nefesh*, the dedicated sacrifice of oneself for the Jewish people.

Her life teaches us this lesson even more clearly than her words. Fifty years after her *petirah*, her lesson lives on.

☙ . . . Her Legacy

Dramatic testimony to the continuing vitality of Sarah Schenirer's legacy took place on Sunday, the 24th day of Adar, 5745. It is a long trip from an obscure street in Cracow to the Felt Forum in Madison Square Garden, New York City, but the Bais Yaakov movement somehow managed to span the distance, and span it gracefully.

"Speaking out of Her Eyes"
Rebbetzin Dr. J. Grunfeld

I don't know why they called me over from England. You have such wonderful speakers ... There is only one thing perhaps. I am the only one, alas, who worked side by side with Sarah Schenirer. I am the link. I was already grown up then. My beloved and respected pupils — the Rebbitzens who teach in your seminaries and high schools — they were 15 or 16 at the time, when I was already a teacher. So I am the only one who worked with Sarah Schenirer together. I had the *zchiyah* to be with her morning, noon and night, Yom Tov, Purim, *Shabbos*, Yom Kippur ... I heard her, I listened to her. And I felt — how can I describe it — her *neshamah* speaking out of her eyes. She was not tall; a small woman. She was not very significant looking. She was dressed in a very modest way. But her eyes were alive, darting, speaking.

This past week somebody told me that she was a pupil in Vienna when Sarah Schenirer was in her last stage of illness, and she saw her being carried to the train to take her back to Cracow, because the professors in Vienna found that they could not help her in any way anymore in her fatal last illness. The girls in the school in Vienna were told to go to the station: *Sarah Schenirer is being carried on a stretcher onto the train. She will be taken home to*

I came to the memorial marking the 50th *Yahrzeit* of Sarah Schenirer determined to make an objective report, to observe, as a good reporter should, in a detached and unemotional mood.

I looked around, at the masses of chattering, laughing girls filing in. Add a head covering, a slight thickening of chin and waist, a line or two — they are me. I saw their mothers, their eyes resting proudly upon the students. Add a few more lines, a few more children, a few more years — they are what I will be. I saw my teachers, felt, almost as a reflex, that familiar feeling of nervousness mingled with respect. They, too, are a part of me.

Objectivity? Detachment? Another place, another time, perhaps. This was a gathering uniquely Bais Yaakov, and I was part of it, raised and nurtured and influenced by it. I belonged. There was no place here for staying apart, for a mere observer.

Abandoning the role of impartial observer, I sat back and pre-

> Cracow. *Only Hashem Yisbarach can make a Nes to save her.* The girls went to the station and saw Sarah Schenirer being carried on a stretcher. She was so white; she was so ill. But her eyes were dancing. Her eyes were shining. And she gave a smile to the girls and she tried to give a greeting ... Not long after that she passed away.
>
> Anyone who wants to know the meaning of *"Zochreinu lechayim,* remember us for life," should come here. She is no more — and she is alive. She carries on and you are her *talmidos*. And her *Kaddish* is the light that comes from your presence here ...
>
> Let me finish with one cheerful story. A Bais Yaakov girl organized a Chanukah party in the town hall of one of the Polish villages. She had a rehearsal two days before. Afterwards the manager of the hall came to her, "Well, Miss Singer, are you satisfied?" — he was a Jewish fellow, not *frum*.
>
> She said, "Thank you. I am quite satisfied. Thank you for your help."
>
> He said, "I wish you a successful evening," and stretched his hand out.
>
> She said, "Sorry, I don't want to offend you, but we don't shake hands with gentlemen."
>
> "What! In the 20th century? You must be the only one!"
>
> She replied, "In the 20th century I may be the only one; but in the 21st century there will be many, many more."

pared to learn, to enjoy, to remember, to feel.

The gathering, one sensed, was a tremendous affirmation of life. A few years ago I attended the World Gathering of Holocaust Survivors in Yerushalayim. That, too, was an affirmation, a joyous and tearful announcement that the Jewish people had survived, that we could not be destroyed by the latter-day Amalekites. But this was something more. Yes, we affirmed, we have survived physical destruction, have risen out of the ashes to bear new generations, but we have done even more! Our heritage, our learning, our Torah has survived, survived and flourished. We are Jews whom our martyred grandparents and great-grandparents would have been proud of, we have carried on and treasured their legacy to us.

Within this vital affirmation of life, one motif spun round and round, unmistakable: Sarah Schenirer. Sarah Schenirer and her dream. Sarah Schenirer and Bais Yaakov. Inseparable, unforgettable.

It began, as all Jewish events ought, with prayer. *Tehillim* was recited for two of the foremost *gedolim* of our time. The words of *Tehillim* flowed easily on the tongues of five thousand women and girls. Bais Yaakov has done its job well.

And then, the speeches. There were six of them, each inspiring, each illuminating in its own unique way.

As I listened to the words of Torah, I began to realize that we were not alone, we five thousand women in this large auditorium. In any Torah gathering the Jews are accompanied by their past, and by the hopes of their future.

We were treated to a magnificent Torah insight by Rabbi Shimon Schwab — a message and a theme that Sarah Schenirer had equipped us to absorb. [See box, page 306]

We were taken back to our distant past, to our sages of old, by the words of Rabbi Chaim Dov Keller. Rabbi Keller spoke of the accomplishment of Rabbi Yehoshua ben Gamla, *Kohen Gadol* in the time of the second Temple, who was credited with having saved Torah learning among the people of Israel ... and of Sarah Schenirer.

Our books are the bridges we have with the distant past; the older generations are the living links with more recent years. Two who knew Sarah Schenirer spoke, sharing their memories of this unforgettable woman. There were few in the audience who were not moved by the reminiscences of Rebbetzin Vichna Kaplan, as she spoke of the graduation ceremonies in the Cracow Seminary. [See box, page 313] Who did not see before her the picture of Sarah Schenirer, sitting on a chair surrounded by dancing students, all singing *"Vitaheir libeinu* — singing, singing, and singing more, until the sun slipped over the horizon and a new day dawned. And how moving were the words of Sarah Schenirer's colleague, Rebbetzin Dr. Judith Grunfeld* of London, as she described Frau Schenirer's dark eyes, still burning with an inner fire, even as she was borne by stretcher back to Cracow, where soon her *neshamah* was to take leave of this world. [See box pages, 310-311].

If many of the speeches evoked a feeling for our living past, it was the conclusion of the memorial that bound us to our future. Young girls from eight Bais Yaakov schools, the next generation of

---

* Dr. Grunfeld's biographic appreciation of Sarah Schenirer has been published separately by Bnos Agudath Israel.

mothers in Israel, raised their voices in Yiddish, in Hebrew, in English. Sarah Schenirer would have been proud.

◆§ A Final Note

I read, the next day, of another gathering that had taken place in the New York area that Sunday. A concert of a popular rock group had been held in the Nassau Coliseum. Ten thousand had turned out for tickets, and the wait became a slugfest. Mounted police quelled the mini-riot, but not before three people were arrested and several wounded.

I thought of five thousand Jewesses, calmly and politely making their way into the Forum. I thought of the police who stood by the entrance, bored, with nothing to do but give directions to a passing stranger or two.

Bais Yaakov has done its job well.

The lessons of Sarah Schenirer are still being learned.

Graduation in Cracow
Rebbetzin Vichna Kaplan

It was not at all like a graduation today. Nobody was invited — just the staff and ourselves. The program consisted of a couple of speeches. We ate together, and then spontaneously began to dance with Sarah Schenirer, and we danced all night, literally ... and the *niggun* we sang over and over was the same: *"Vetaheir libeinu le'avdecha be'emes* . . . Purify our hearts to serve You, truly." This was not a planned program. Nobody said we should dance this long or sing this song. But it sang of itself, with Sarah Schenirer in the middle.

This was the *ruach* that dominated in Cracow. We felt the gravity of the great moment when we had to leave Sarah Schenirer and at this time we had a *tefillah* to Hashem: "May we be *zocheh* to be *mechanchos* to the children of Poland, and later of our own children. Give us the *zechus* to have the right *derech*, and give us the opportunity to find the *nekudah* of each Jewish heart." This was Cracow: a preparation for a life of *taharah*.

Rabbi Chaim Dov Keller

Were It Not for Her...

*An appreciation of Sarah Schenirer, ע״ה,
on the occasion of her 50th yahrzeit
March 1985*

I.

After Years — An Historic Perspective

ONE CANNOT JUDGE the significance of an individual in his lifetime or put a movement into its proper historic perspective during its initial stages. Historians, even *Chachamim*, can only evaluate a person, an event or a movement after years, perhaps eras have gone by.

The Gemara (*Bava Basra* 21a) tells us:

אמר ר׳ יהודה אמר רב ברם זכור אותו האיש לטוב
ויהושע בן גמלא שמו שאלמלא הוא נשתכחה תורה מישראל

Rav Yehuda said in the name of Rav: Remember this man for good, Yehoshua ben Gamla was his name; were it not for him, Torah would have been forgotten from Israel. For at first whoever did not have a father (or obviously someone whose father was incapable of teaching him) would not learn Torah.

The *Gemara* then describes earlier attempts at solving this problem...until Yehoshua ben Gamla decreed that teachers should be appointed for children in all parts of the country and that children be brought in to learn at the age of six or seven. This, according to Rav, saved Torah for *Klal Yisroel*.

When did Rav live and when did Yehoshua ben Gamla live?

Yehoshua ben Gamla was a *Kohein Gadol* during the reign of King Yanai, towards the end of the Second Temple,[1] which was destroyed in the year 3828. Rav was a disciple of Rabbeinu HaKodosh — Reb Yehudah Hanassi — the compiler of the *Mishna*, the last of the *Tannaim* and the first of the *Amoraim*. This was approximately 150 years after the destruction of the Temple. And yet Rav was the first to define the historic role that Yehoshua ben Gamla played in the spiritual revival of the Jewish people.

There is an amazing insight to be gained in this. All of those schools set up by Yehoshua ben Gamla in every city in the country were destroyed at the time of the destruction of the *Beis Hamikdash*. The schools were destroyed, the teachers and pupils were slaughtered, but the *takana* of Yehoshua ben Gamla — the revolutionary system that he introduced — remained. There were survivors who had learned Torah in those schools, and after the *Churban*, they reinstituted the system and there ensued a glorious period of Torah scholarship, culminating in the compilation of the *Mishna* — all in a relatively short period after the destruction. Rav understood that this phenomenal growth was the result of the *takana* of Yehoshua ben Gamla, and he put the stamp of his Torah authority on that evaluation, stating definitively: "Were it not for him, Torah would have been forgotten from Israel."

৺ From One Room to a Movement

We now stand 50 years since the passing of Sara Schenirer and 68 years since she started her first one-room Bais Yaakov school with 25 pupils. She was one of very few people privileged to see the fulfillment of a dream in their own lifetime. When she passed away in 1935, that school of 25 girls, founded in 1917, had developed into a powerful movement with over 32,000 students in a network of close to 300 schools, in just about every city and town in Poland, as well as in Lithuania, Hungary and Rumania.

Obviously she did not accomplish all of this single-handedly. In a memoir published in the *Bais Yaakov Journal* in Adar, 5692

---

1. See *Tosefos* on the above-quoted *Gemara* (*Bava Basra* 21a: *Zachor*).

(1932), she writes that when the local Agudas Yisroel was founded in Cracow in 1919, leaders of the organization came to her and offered to assume the financial responsibility for her school. She accepted the offer after consulting with the Bobover Rebbe, Rabbi Ben Zion Halberstam זצ״ל, who gave his approval. ...In 1924, the Central Executive Committee (*Central-Rat*) of the World Agudah movement met in Cracow. After visiting the school, the delegates decided to include the Bais Yaakov in the activities of the Keren HaTorah, the fund-raising arm of the World Agudah for the upbuilding and maintenance of Torah institutions, which was headed by Dr. Shmuel (Leo) Deutschlander.

From then on, Dr. Deutschlander threw himself completely into the work of organizing, expanding and raising financial support for the burgeoning Bais Yaakov movement. This was in addtion to the pedagogical genius that he contributed to the Bais Yaakov Seminaries in Cracow and Vienna. Without this organization and support, the moment could never have attained the dimension of success that it did.

Beyond question, however, the inspiration and the personality of Sara Schenirer and the Divine help that she merited were the decisive factors in the miraculous growth of Bais Yaakov. She was not only the founder, the teacher, the leader, the mother of her *talmidos* whom she called "*Kinder*"; she was the message. It was her qualities of soul, her *emuna* and *bitachon* — her unflagging faith and trust in the Almighty, her love for Torah, her *Yiras Shomayim*, her enthusiasm, her simplicity and her single-minded devotion to the ideal of Bais Yaakov that inspired her *talmidos*. She was the living example of everything she sought to impart to her students.

৺§ Enough Time to Make a Judgment

Now — fifty years after her passing, and almost seventy years from the beginning of her dream — we can perhaps begin to make an attempt to evaluate her significance in the history of Klal Yisroel. Aside from the obvious parallel between the educational reforms of Yehoshua ben Gamla and Sarah Schenirer, there is another striking similarity between the two. Just as the world of Yehoshua ben Gamla and all he had built up was destroyed with the *Churban Beis Hamikdash*, so too was the world of Sara Schenirer, all of her beloved schools, and the vast majority of her precious *talmidos* destroyed in the awesome *churban* of European Jewry. And just as that *takana* of Yehoshua ben Gamla made it possible to reconstruct the world of Torah after the *Churban*, so was it with the *takana* of Sara Schenirer's Bais Yaakov.

Our sages tell us that G-d creates the cure before the injury (*Megilla* 13b). Had Yehoshua Ben Gamla not made that *takana before* the *Churban*, there would have been no way to pick up the shattered pieces of the Torah world after the *Churban*. His was the *zechus* to be the messenger of Divine Providence that Torah not be forgotten. So too in our time, just before the greatest cataclysm that befell the Jewish people since the Destruction of the Second Temple, there had to be a Divinely inspired revolution which would turn the tide and fulfill the Divine promise:

והי׳ כי תמצאן אתו רעות רבות וצרות וענתה השירה הזאת
לפניו לעד כי לא תשכח מפי זרעו (דברים לא:כא).

"And it will come to pass when evils and trouble will come upon them, this song will testify before them... for it shall not be forgotten *from the mouths of their seed...*" (*Devarim* 31:21). At the time when the greatest destruction befalls the Jewish people, the Torah will bear witness to the indestructibility of that people, because precisely at that time there will be a Divinely inspired development to insure that Torah will not be forgotten. The Torah does not say, "It will not be forgotten from the mouths *of their sons,*" but from *all* their children.

From the phenomenal success Sarah Schenirer realized, one can see that she was indeed the Divine instrument for this historic fulfillment, insuring the future of Torah — and not only the future of Torah among girls and women... If you walk into the Beis Midrash in Lakewood or Telz, or Mir, or in hundreds of other Yeshivos and Kollelim in this country and in *Eretz Yisroel*, you will see thousands of young men — Kollel scholars dedicating their lives to Torah. Without wives who share their dedication and are willing to forego many of life's comforts to enable their husbands to learn Torah, these Kollelim could not exist. These heroic young women are the products of Torah revolution begun by Sarah Schenirer.

Now, forty years after the *Churban*, when we have witnessed the miraculous rebirth of Bais Yaakov here, in *Eretz Yisroel*, and in England and Europe through the inspired efforts of a handful of Sarah Schenirer's *talmidos*—now, when we see how this made possible the glorious renaissance of the Torah world, I believe that

Were It Not for Her .../317

we can say, "Remember that Woman for good—her name was Sarah Schenirer — for were it not for her, Torah would have been forgotten from Israel."

II.
Beyond a "Hesped"

The gathering marking her *Yahrzeit* was unequivocally an historic occasion, and we cannot permit it to go by with just a *hesped*. Let us not fall into the trap of making Sarah Schenirer some untouchable saint whose memory we revere. We must understand not only what she meant for her generation, but what her significance and her message is for our and future generations.

The name she chose for her life's work was not just an apt borrowing from the interpretation of the Sages on the verse introducing the Torah to the Jewish people on Mt. Sinai: כה תאמר לבית יעקב..., *"So shall you speak to the House of Jacob"*...(*Shemos* 19:3) — these are the women."...*and say to the sons of Israel"* — these are the men (See *Rashi ibid.*).

The name of *Bais Yaakov* — literally, the House of Jacob — was a statement of the basic purpose of the movement, the rededication and resanctification of the Jewish home.

In one of her letters, she explained why the A-lmighty addressed the women at Sinai before the men: because the Jewish mother would educate the next generation — on her lap, the children will become imbued with a love for Torah and fear of Heaven; thus, they insure the spiritual survival of the Jewish people. But even more, the description of Jewish women as *Bais Yaakov* conveys an idea — not that "a woman's place is in the home," but that the woman *is* the home.

The Torah tells us of the *Kohein Gadol* on Yom Kippur (*Vayikra* 16:6): וכפר בעדו ובעד ביתו, "He shall atone for himself and for his house" — *his house* — that is his wife (*Mishna Yoma* 1:1). Without a wife, the *Kohein Gadol* had no home and was unfit for the Yom Kippur service.

◆§ The Impetus for Action

Sarah Schenirer was first moved to begin her work of bringing Torah to Jewish girls because of the breakup of the Jewish home. Wherever she turned, she saw young girls, bored and uninspired, completely lacking in understanding and appreciation of the beauty of Torah, becoming estranged from their devout mothers and fathers. She felt that she must impart to them the inspiration that she herself felt, which would lead them to understand that the ideal of the Jewish woman was *to be* the Jewish home.

◆§ A Home for the Shechina

The Jewish home is not as simple as all that. The Jewish home is the sanctuary where the *Shechina* rests. When our Father Yitzchak took Rivka as a wife, the Torah tells us: ויבאה יצחק האהלה שרה אמו (בראשית כ״ד:סז), *And Yitzchak brought her into the tent of his mother Sarah* (Bereishis 24:67). The *Baal Haturim* points out that the word האהלה is used in *Tanach* eight times, which is an allusion to the eight places where the Divine Presence rested: The *Mishkan*, Gilgal, Shiloh, Nov, Giveon, the First *Beis Hamikdash*, the Second *Beis Hamikdash*, and the *Beis Hamikdash* of the future — may it be built speedily in our days! These were the communal sanctuaries of the Jewish people where the *Shechina* rested — but the foundation of them all was האהלה שרה אמו, *the tent of Sarah*, that tent which had a ה׳ from the Divine Name before it and another ה׳ after it. The tents of the *Avos* and *Imahos* were the resting place of the Divine Presence.

The *Ramban*, in his introduction to *Shemos*, tells us that the redemption from Egypt was not complete until the Jewish people had come to Sinai, and built the *Mishkan*.

ושב הקב״ה והשרה שכינתו ביניהם אז שבו אל מעלת אבותם
שהיה סוד אלוק עלי אהליהם

"And the Holy One once again caused His *Shechina* to rest among them. Then they had returned to the exalted state of their fathers upon whose tents rested the Divine Presence."

The *Mishkan* on a national collective scale was nothing more than a return to the glory of the individual homes of the Patriarchs, which is hinted at in the words האהלה שרה אמו, *the tent of his mother Sarah.*[1]

---

1. The Matriarchs were so imbued with this ideal of establishing a home for the Divine Presence that their lives had no meaning if this mission was not fulfilled.

ותאמר רבקה אל יצחק קצתי בחיי מפני בנות חת אם לקח יעקב
אשה מבנות חת כאלה מבנות הארץ למה לי חיים (בראשית כז:מו).

And Rivka said to Yitzchok: "My life is unbearable because of the daughters of Chais (Eisav's wives); if Yaakov takes a wife from the daughters of Chais like these...of

This was the ideal of the Jewish home that our latter-day Sarah dreamed to revitalize. Indeed, her *talmidos* also called her "Our Mother Sarah."

III.
Different Battles, Same War

It was Sarah Schenirer's overriding concern to raise generations of Jewish daughters who, with their love of Torah, could withstand the blandishments of modern culture and find their fulfillment in serving Hashem by establishing homes where the *Shechina* could dwell.

The challenges that our generation must face are not the same that Sarah Schenirer faced, but then again they are really not that different.

In an article in the *Bais Yaakov Journal* (#43), following the second convention of Bnos Agudas Yisroel — whose spiritual leader Sara Schenirer was — she wrote of the amazement of irreligious journalists that there are "young girls today who speak not about the cinema and the theater, and not about fashions and luxuries, but about how to organize the battle against the emptiness of modern life."

"The delegates," she continues, "spoke about Torah, *Avoda* and *Gemillus Chassadim*. How great was my joy to have lived to see the children of my spiritual aspirations with such seriousness of purpose, imbued with so much enthusiasm!"

It is no longer necessary to fight for acceptance of the idea that girls should study Torah. That battle was fought and won by Sarah Schenirer, with the encouragement of the Chofetz Chaim and other *Gedolei Yisroel* of that time.

---

what purpose is my life?" (*Bereishis* 27:46). The *Baal Haturim* says the letter ק from the word קצתי is small because she saw that the *Beis Hamikdash* whose height was one hundred cubits (the numerical value of ק) would be destroyed.

Rivka's life had meaning only if the wives of her sons would contribute to the building of the Sanctuary — not ח"ו its destruction, as did the wives of Eisav. For it was the descendants of Eisav who finally destroyed the Second Temple. Rivka, in her prophetic vision, saw that this would be the result of the type of home the wives of Eisav would establish. For the *Shechina* cannot dwell in the *Beis Hamikdash* of the Jewish people if there is no room for it in their individual tents.

We no longer have to worry about the lure of the Polish theater and the Polish novel. But is there really a basic difference between the theater of our day and the theater of Pre-War Poland, between the Polish novel and the American novel? The battleground may have changed, but the enemy is the same — only much more sophisticated. For the enemy has learned how to invade our homes and *coexist* — or what is perhaps worse, *synthesize* — with Torah learning.

A "Visit" From Sarah

What would Sarah Schenirer have to say if she would walk into some of our homes today?

In many she would *shep nachas* — she would shed tears of joy that her spiritual heiresses had set up homes of Torah, *Avoda* and *Gemillus Chassadim*, where the *Shechina* could find its place.

In others, she would walk into the living room and would surely rejoice to see bookshelves heavy with *Shas, Mishnayos, Tanach, Mussar Seforim*, English books and periodicals of Torah thought. But she would see other types of literature, as well. She might pick up one of those books or periodicals, leaf through it and turn pale. She might drop it in revulsion and exclaim: מיר טאר דאס נישט האלטען אין האנד אפילו, "You're not even allowed to hold this in your hand."

She might notice a piece of furniture she had never seen in Cracow — a cabinet-like box with a glass screen in front. She would ask one of the girls of the house, "What's this?"

The girl might answer, a bit uncomfortably, "Oh, that.... That's a new thing which provides us with news and educational programs and a bit of entertainment."

And Sarah Schenirer would say, "*Nu*, let's have a look," and the girl might hesitate a bit. At Sarah Schenirer's urging she would turn it on and the two of them would sit down to watch an hour of prime time T.V. Most probably Sarah Schenirer would not make it to the end of the hour....

We could go on with this little fancy. But is it really necessary?

We no longer have to worry as Sarah Schenirer did of the theater and the movies. *Who of our Bais Yaakov girls would think of going to today's movies?* But what have we done? We have brought the theater and the movies and the whole non-Jewish value system into our living rooms.

Were It Not for Her .../321

Over thirty years ago a husband and wife came before my Rebbe, the late Telshe Roshe Yeshiva, Reb Eliyahu Meir Bloch צז״ל. The woman had a complaint. It seems that the husband had inherited a Sefer Torah and had set it up in a small Aron Kodesh, which he had made for it in their living room. Ever since the Torah had been brought into the house, the couple had suffered one misfortune after another. "How can we have a Sefer Torah in our home," the woman cried to the Rosh Yeshiva, "when we have a television in the same room?"

"You're right," said Reb Elya Meir. "So what do you suggest?"

He was shocked by her answer: "Let him take the Sefer Torah out of the house!"

When the Rosh Yeshiva told this over to us, he was beside himself: "See what we have come to? There is no longer room in a Jewish home for a Sefer Torah! Instead of taking out the T.V., the woman came to a Rav to ask that the Sefer Torah be taken out!"

If the woman is the home, then it is her personality, her priorities, her set of values that will permeate the home. It is she, in most cases, who will make the decisions that will determine whether her home is one into which a *Sefer Torah* can be brought, one in which the *Shechina* can find a resting place.

◆§ The On-Going Revolution

Sarah Schenirer began a revolution. It was not a violent revolution. Hers was quiet revolution of *tznius*, which changed the course of history. Today that revolution has to take the form of a palace *coup* in which our proud Jewish daughters reassert the supremacy of the King of kings and His Torah in their own homes.

They must begin thinking in terms of priorities and values. They must ask themselves:

What is important to me as a person? Is it the latest fashion being worn on the avenue, the latest wig style, which would better fit a movie starlet than an Isha Kasheira? Or is it my personal understanding of what it means to be a Jewish woman, a Jewish wife and mother?

What is important in my home? Is it the furniture and the decor, or is it the atmosphere of Kedusha, which will allow my husband and children to learn Torah, and will make a place for the King? What formulates my outlook on life, my hashkafa, and that of my children? Is it Tanach and the words of the Chachamim? Or is it the moral and cultural pollution which seeps out from even the commercials and ads of the media?

Are business and professional careers means of making a livelihood, as they should be, or have they become goals in life?

If Sarah Schenirer had to give us a message today, I believe it would be the same message she gave her *talmidos* in her lifetime. She would quote the same *p'sukim* which were always on her tongue:

עבדו את ה' בשמחה, *Serve Hashem with simcha*. Sadness, despondency, despair — these have no place in the ranks of our vibrant, dynamic, young girls and women. Joy and gladness? For sure! But let the *simcha* be in serving Hashem, not in the fleeting fancies which the modern world calls good times.

תורת ה' תמימה משיבת נפש, *The Torah of Hashem is perfect, it restores the soul*. Let us realize that all we seek can be found in Torah. The sophistication and self-styled intellectualism of the college campus and of secular literature are very attractive. But they can never approach the perfection of Torah — and they can never affect the inner person — they can never restore the *nefesh* — the soul of man or woman. At this historic occasion of 50 years since the passing of that immortal woman who began it all, let us rededicate ourselves to that sublime ideal of Bais Yaakov and go in the light of Hashem!

Baila bat Rifka

An Overwhelming View

One of the last paragraphs in the history of Sarah Schenirer's Seminary in Cracow, Poland

I sit here (in the Felt Forum), overwhelmed, and I remember —

It was the end of the terrible World War II. We had been deported to Russia from Poland during the war. Now, at the end of the war, there was a citizens' exchange and we found ourselves back in Poland, in the city of Cracow. I was six-and-a-half years old at the time.

We entered a beautiful white building around four stories high. It had a large dining hall and many individual rooms. I did not understand the meaning then, but I remember the whispers and the sighs: "This was Sarah Schenirer's Seminary."

There were less than a handful of mothers or fathers with their children. (I was there with both my parents, שיחיו). As for the rest, there were around two hundred orphan girls.

Sarah, perhaps they were the daughters of your daughters . . .

I would see them and ask myself, "How could a little girl without a mommy smile?" And then I caught them when they turned away ... those eyes, those "sad, sad eyes" — there are no other words for the look in those eyes.

One day, my mother made conversation with one such girl — she must have been ten years old. I was standing there when the young girl said, "I am here because I know I am Jewish. I know I am Jewish because before my mother left me, she said with tears, 'Do not forget that you have a Jewish heart' ..." *That mother, Sarah, might have been one of your Bais Yaakov girls.*

I sit here overwhelmed and I remember. — Looking out of the window from that beautiful white building, a serene beauty unfolded before me, It seemed to me that right in front of this white house was a beautiful lake with a cluster of stars beyond it. I asked my mother, "Why is there such a tight bunch of stars across the lake?' — for the first time in my life, I beheld the sight of a town lit up by electricity. Until the next dawn, it was all a wonder. But not the next night: Darkness brought bullets, fright, terror and lights-out to this beautiful white house. The Polish devils weren't satisfied. They still wanted to bring about "The Final Solution." I couldn't understand then why anyone would want to destroy these precious two hundred innocent orphan girls, and this beautiful house.

Only years later, as a Bais Yaakov student and teacher, did I learn of the horror and *Kiddush Hashem* that your beautiful white building had witnessed, the leap to eternity by thirty-five young girls who jumped from the roof (the same roof that sheltered us) in order not to be defiled by the approaching German soldiers, *yimach sh'mam.*

While I sit here, in Madison Square Garden, with five thousand other Bais Yaakov *talmidos* (only a symbol of the many thousands of Bais Yaakov *talmidos* around the world, *ken tirbenah*) — I am overwhelmed ...

Thanks to you, *Sarah Imeinu,* we can listen to and understand a speech with a *d'var Torah.* Thanks to you, we can teach a *d'var Torah.* Thanks to you, we can try to live a life of Torah. And thanks to you, thousands of our daughters are being given the same opportunities. You have indeed saved *Klal Yisrael.*

But I am overwhelmed: for my memory is dipped in the past, and overflows with tears — for those orphan girls, for your daughters and their children, for your white house, symbol of hope and future.

I sit here overwhelmed, and desperately try to pull together one single image from the unbearable tragedy of the past, the fulfillment of the present, and the hope of the future.

A glistening jewel emerges. Let me share it with my sisters.

I see
Tears glistening from Sarah Schenirer,
Tears of fulfillment,
Thousands of daughters under one roof,
    under one banner.
Thousands, wishing to live a Torah life.

I see
Tears of sorrow,
Thousands of Bais Yaakov daughters
In tachrichim, glowing in the light of Kiddush Hashem.

I see
Sarah standing with Rachel Imeinu,
Crying for the past,
Crying for the future.
    Rachel weeps for her children
    And Sarah weeps for her daughters.
Oh, mothers of Israel,
Cry for your children
To be spared the trials of Gog and Magog,
Wail, for we had more than enough!
Cry, mothers, cry,
For the speedy Techiyas Hameisim
Of all your children
Crying with you.

Dear Morah,

Accompanying this letter you will find a child. She's mine. Let me tell you all about her. She's one of six children קע"ה, the second from the top. She's well-behaved and polite, but can be stubborn and rebellious when punished. She's too shy, not outgoing like her sister, and doesn't always get the appreciation she deserves. Of course, she's very bright, but she needs to be drawn out.

I want to tell you more about her — or should I wait until you ask? Please ask. I do hope that our common interest will give us the empathy to do our best, together. Like many mothers, I've gone the route through teachers' seminary, but it's not in the smugness of that knowledge that I approach, but with deference and humility, offering advice from the grass roots — things we never learned in Methodology I.

My respect for you is real, not only the lingering sentiment of the me that was a student sitting in a small desk facing the big one, but a genuine esteem for your dedication, your sacrifice in teaching, and your effective handling of a room full of restless children. (How do you ever do it?) But my potential as a parent to help you is also very real. She's your student but she's my child.

We agree about the importance of the "parent-teacher relationship," yet there's a tendency to reduce it to twice-yearly PTA meetings, and those endless teas. We're familiar with the flowery language of Yeshiva mailings about the "partnership of the school and the home"; by the closing greetings, however, it is clear the partnership seldom gets beyond the school taking care of all educational matters and parents taking care of all the finances.

I'm sorry, Morah. I'm not ready to settle for a back seat. You see that little girl? I raised her from infancy, through her toddler stage, and into her childhood. I'm not about to hand her over now with no questions asked, like so much laundry to be washed, starched and pressed, then delivered home.

I know my child too well. Use me, Morah. Supplement your educational expertise with my homegrown instincts and my specific knowledge of my child. True, I see her through the myopic lens of a mother's prejudice, but there are some things I know that you cannot. Test me. See whether your observations lead you to concur with my conclusions. And then tell me more. Have confidence in me. Share *your* insights in my daughter with me. I'm sure that you see things that somehow evade me, things that would help me in being a better mother. Together we can get closer to discovering the *real* little girl inside my daughter.

As I said, I realize that you deal with a classroom full of children, and you have to think in terms of group dynamics. Nonetheless, next time you have an opportunity, look at my daughter, and stop. Think about her alone.... And do the same for the other mothers' daughters that make up your class. Remember the father, blessed with many children, who was asked, "How many do you have?" He answered, "One," and explained. "One Chani, one Yanky, one Gittle...." Your class is a kaleidoscope of brightly colored fragments and personalities. Over the first weeks they seem at first ever-changing, but eventually one pattern emerges with some colors predominating, and some fading into the background. Remember to shake up the kaleidoscope to realize all the potential beauty in its variations of colors.

As you know, each child is different. This one is mine. Please don't compare her to her peers or her predecessors or even her sisters and cousins. There might be much ground for comparison, but oh what dissimilarities! Like the five fingers of one hand, no two are quite the same. Each is unique and serves a unique purpose, excelling and contributing in its own way.

Please let my child excel. She looks to you innocently. You will guide and educate her, but she doesn't know that. She isn't waiting to be guided or educated or molded. She's only waiting for your approval, your OK, your special smile just for her. She's waiting to be liked by you, even to be loved by you.

I know you need to discipline, to keep control, to criticize and punish. I'll try to always remember that a class as a whole needs an extra measure of control. But please — you, too, bear in mind the hurt and pain and shame that it is your potential to inflict. Think of your own feelings when you are publicly humiliated by a rude saleswoman, or when your silly (and quite human) errors are noticed and commented upon. Multiply it by the sensitivity of a child and remember the dangerous edge of sharp words. How much safer a tool praise is!

I know what you're thinking, Morah. The tables can be turned, and my words applied very appropriately towards myself. True. Every day I also walk the tightrope of discipline, striving for the balance between sternness and forgiveness, preserving my authority and allowing for flexibility. And I appreciate the difficulties, through my own frequent stumbles. But my job is still easier than yours. Time and nature are on my side. My brusqueness in the morning rush can be tempered with a bedtime kiss, and the love between myself and my child is already strong, whereas you have to work to create an affection from ground zero.

Is it too much I'm demanding, or too much demanded from me? Let's think of the privileges that come along with our awesome responsibilities. The enormity of the task is equal to its importance. The street cleaner who is careless on the job is hardly worth berating, the effect is so inconsequential. But from brain surgeons and airplane pilots we demand clear thinking and constant effort. Our lives depend on it. From out teachers and our parents, we demand perfection. Our *neshamos* depend on it.

So, let's see sincere praise flowing in all directions — to the children, and towards you. Don't brush it aside when it comes your way. I want to be a comfortable telling you I appreciate your work. I want to tell you without self-consciousness or apple-polishing motives. I want to write you notes of hurrahs and thank yous, not just tight-lipped messages of polite disagreement.

So count on me. I'll see that your assignments are completed, that your tests are seen and signed. Let's work together.

Accompanying this letter *please* find the child. She's ours.

Mrs. Ita Grinblat

Dear Mother,

I read your letter sympathetically and with a feeling of gratitude. I will rally to your side to champion the personal needs of our children. I will join you in your campaign to insist that the "P" of PTA have a right to participate in our children's education. As a mother of young yeshiva children I advocate the undeniable right of the mother to remind the teacher: *This child is a human being; treat him as an individual, please.*

Yet I would like to straddle the fence in this discussion — for you see, I am both a mother *and* a Morah of primary school children. I play the role of both the "P" and the "T." Even while I staunchly champion your concern for your child's well-being and growth, I find myself swiveling to the other side of the desk, to the Morah's seat. I realize that just as the mother looks to Dear Morah to help her in bringing up Yisrael, Yehuda, and Aryeh, the Morah looks to Dear Mother to do her part. Not only am I unable to do my job without you, there are many things *only* you, the mother, can do.

I would like to explain, but first let me tell you why I'm here in the first place. If I had chosen to work in this field for financial reasons only, I'd be bitter by now. The monetary rewards do not, by any stretch of the imagination, compensate for hours of after-hour work related to the job. When the dismissal bell rings, the school day is over by the time clock, but I cannot discard the title "Morah." It stays with me, it *is* me, constantly. My personal time is an extension of schooltime. How often have I been interrupted during supper at home by phone calls from school parents? I run PTA at my cousin's Bar Mitzva and at my sister's wedding. No, the salary does not cover the time and energy put into teaching.

Obviously, I'm not teaching just for the monetary reward. I also teach for the rewarding feeling of accomplishment when a student says: "Morah, I'll pick up all the crayons from the floor for you so a new *malach* can be born." It is for the *nachas* I feel when a child apologizes for breaking his classmates' block castle and then offers to help rebuild it. It's for the feeling of pride while watching our future *Bnei Torah* say the *Shema* correctly. I also teach for the occasional appreciative note written by a mother, thanking me for my efforts, one of which I quote: "My reaction to my son's behavior these last few days is שכרה הרבה מאוד. I always am a bit envious of teachers. I know parents are teachers too, but the idea of twenty seven boys going to their individual homes, repeating and practicing the Torah you teach them — well, the idea just leaves me in awe... I can never properly thank you, but I'm sure part of your reward lies in knowing that these children think and do *al pi Torah* because you taught them so." For this rare note I teach. For this I will continue to work along with you to strengthen these *Yiddishe neshamos*.

Dear Mother, I'm open to talk,...I'll listen to you, never turn a deaf ear to you, even when you call me at home. (So you forgot about the note sent to you in the beginning of the year that said to leave a message in the office for me, so I can return your call at my convenience...I usually do.) I'll listen to you and discuss all with you willingly. You say that behind that quiet facade there is a wonderful child just waiting to be drawn out? I love a challenge! I'll happily give him extra time, a moment out for a little *shmuess* between just the two of us. I'll give him that extra smile and wink. I'll give him an extra chance to read a flash card. It's a large class and I appreciate the reminder saying: "Hey, that's my child entrusted in your care! He's my son, his *Zeide's ainekel*, his *Bubby's nachas*."

You ask me to give your child extra attention, to make him feel loved and wanted. I sincerely want to. I'll juggle my limited moments about and take time to discuss his new baby brother with him, between setting up tables and serving lunch. If you expect much of me, and set high standards for my performance, fine. I, too, demand the most of myself. I want to be goaded and guided in my role as Morah.

But, please remember. It's not simply a matter of "getting your money's worth." It's a matter of knowing I'm doing my best for your child — our child. Shouldn't I be able to have the same expectations from you? You are surely no less dedicated to "our" little boy. Yet, how often do I clench my fists in frustration when a child excuses himself for not bringing *tzeddakah* and says, "My mother had no time to give me a penny. It was too late and the bus was coming." No time to help your child practice the *mitzvah* of *tzeddakah*, which can *only* be done with parental help — or, when a student says, "Morah, I did a big *chessed* yesterday. I picked up a tissue from the floor so that my mother would not have to bend... I didn't bring a '*midah* note' to school about it because my mother had no time to write it. She was talking on the phone and said she'd write it later." Please bear in mind, Mother: In class there is no *later*. We are working in a designated and limited time span. Our goal is to regulate our time and energies realistically.

It's oft been said, the school is an extension of the home. I'll accept that. But by no means should the school be a *substitute* for the home. You entrusted your child to my care, to guide and educate, but — please — don't abuse my role by burdening me with yours: "Morah, can you please tell my son to listen to me when I tell him to go to bed? He always finds a reason to procrastinate." "Morah, could you please tell my son, maybe through a story, to kiss his *Bubby* when she visits?" So I'm Mother and Morah, doing your job and mine simultaneously. I wash *negal vasser* for half the class. I teach children their full names, phone numbers, and addresses. I teach table manners and cleanliness. These are basic concepts that the home is required to teach. I must keep tabs on hats without names, mateless mittens, and unlabeled boots — even though you've received note after note almost pleading with you to put nametapes on your child's belongings. Then I receive a note: "Chaim's missing a red hat, a blue knapsack and a green scarf. Please make sure my son brings home all his belongings." I do my best to reinforce good character traits, but it's unrealistic to expect me to initiate them. A child's education begins at home. In fact, it should begin far back, at the cradle, before there was a school or a Morah in his life.

Mothering a school-aged child is a two-way system: It's a sensitive system that should not be abused. Of course you have the right to inform the teacher — and be informed by her — about your child's status in class. Just as you wrote me in your letter. I'd like you to keep in mind, though, that as Morah — and not simply an extension of you behind the desk — I have broader responsibilities. I sit up and listen when a mother requests a front seat for her Chaim'l. She does so with concern for her son as her only priority, but I've got to think beyond Chaim: Is the request being made because Chaim has a vision problem and cannot read the board from his seat? Or is the change important because her Chaim'l is "privileged"? Please don't forget — I have obligations to the rest of my students and I must try to discern the nature of her motives.

At the same time, it's worth reminding you that this two-way system is applicable to the Morah as well. I too have the right to inform and be informed. And, how I wish I would be informed! We could have avoided many an unhappy morning if the mother of my student had written a note explaining her son's irritability as being caused by his father's absence on a business trip, or his lack of sleep. Let me know about the trip to Florida, the impending move to a new home, or anything upsetting his routine. This information helps relieve anxieties and maintain the pleasant and warm environment we aim to foster.

School and home — both sources of knowledge and experience. Mother and Morah — both teachers and molders of personalities. We want to be instrumental in the child's growth. Let us work together.

Mrs. (Morah Breindy) Leizerson

Helene Ribowsky, M.S.

R=I: A Dangerous Equation

"Ruchel, I'm not taking him to shul. He can't read and he'll have nothing to do there. He'll sit like a goilem. What should I take him for? So the whole shul can know he's dumb? So they'll know we're cursed with a stupid child? He's not going with me if he can't read and if he can't read, there's something wrong with him."

❈ ❈ ❈

YOSSIE ENTERED Pre-1-A. His parent were confident that he would be at the top of his class, for Yossie — their oldest — has been the darling of the entire family — quick, witty, amusing, highly verbal, agile and curious. He did well in kindergarten — though he was somewhat slower in learning to identify letters of the *Aleph-Bais*.

Three months into Yossie's Pre-1-A year, Ruchel, Yossie's mother, wonders with dismay why Yossie is having such difficulty with his reading. The other children in the class are readying for *Siddur*, but Yossie is still stumbling over even single letters and vowels. He can read all the letters with *one* vowel in alphabetical order but he just cannot switch from one vowel to another. Also, he makes errors even on letters he knows on certain days while not on others.

Ruchel speaks to Chaim, her husband; they are desperately concerned about Yossie's poor reading performance. After all, he is such a bright child — and it is terribly painful to see that "reading look" of defeat, sadness and a tinge of anger clouding Yossie's face each evening as the *Aleph-Bais* text is reluctantly dragged from the briefcase. The text is no longer new; its binding is crumbling, its pages are ripped here and there, with dried teardrops staining the once-white margins. Idle scribble marks obliterate some of the letters.

Yossie slams the text on the table. His lips are set in a thin, tight line.

❊ ❊ ❊

"What can we do, Rebbe B.? What's wrong with our Yossie? You kept assuring us he would read — but it's January, and all the other children are reading beautifully. What does he do in class while the other kids read?"

"To tell you the truth, it *is* getting difficult. He's smart enough to see the difference between *his* reading and the other children's. I wish I had more time: I wish I could work with him alone, but I have thirty boys in my class. He's not the only problem I have, by the way. Two other boys are also having serious reading problems — not as bad as Yossie's, but they are also in trouble. Believe me, I'm torn apart by this. I *did* think he would read — after all, he seems bright."

❊ ❊ ❊

The year is over. Yossie has developed a set pattern of responses to anything that has to do with reading. He refuses to go near an *Aleph-Bais* text; he closes his eyes and sits very still as his parents or Rebbe plead with him to try to read. If forced to read, he has crying tantrums, and so, ultimately, he does not read. Yossie lives for the moment that the nightly reading ritual — for him torturous and bewildering — is over, when he can play outside. He is wonderfully agile — the fastest bike-rider on the block. He is the hero of his peers who live on his street; he saved a wounded bird that had fallen out of a tree and nursed it back to health.

Yossie is five and a half years old; he will be six in November — but he already knows the bitter, bitter taste of failure. He cannot read.

❊ ❊ ❊

"You can't hold him back in Pre-1-A again, Ruchel. People will think he's stupid."

"But, Ma, he can't read. What am I supposed to do with him?"

"Let him sit in class and let his Rebbe teach him a half hour a day extra — alone — not with the other children. This way, he can go on with the other children. He'll feel stupid if you leave him back."

"*Feel* stupid? Let's face it. There *is* something wrong. What does it mean when a child can't read? Chaim, don't you think that a child who reads the way Yossie does has a serious problem ... I mean with his general intelligence? I'm afraid to even say what I'm thinking...."

"Ruchel, I've been thinking the same thing lately. Everyone is talking in circles — everyone is saying he's bright. How can a kid be bright and be stupid in school? How can you be smart and not read? Ruchel, I'm not taking him to *shul* anymore. He can't read and he'll have nothing to do there. He'll sit like a *goilem*. What should I take him for? So the whole *shul* can know he's dumb? So they'll know we're cursed with a stupid child? He's not going with me if he can't read and if he can't read, there's something wrong with him. It must mean that there's something mental..."

It Takes a Brain to Read...

MENTAL! Whispers...euphemisms...catch phrases...but actually, the most dangerous misunderstanding of what it means to have a reading problem. For it is just at this point — the point at which an insidious equation is made — the point at which *Reading = Intelligence* (R=I) becomes an emotional and an intellectual formula — it is at *this* point that the Yossies of our world begin to "lose" IQ points, begin to metamorphose into children with **intelligence** problems instead of **reading** problems.

This equation is probably one of the most destructive imaginable. The $E=mc^2$ equation unleashed a massive force that triggered a social reaction against the end product: Ban the bomb! R=I is a formula that has catalytically caused *educational* destruction of megaton magnitude — but has hardly stirred a social reaction. There are no "ban the R=I equation" groups; there are no debates and there is no outcry because its dangers are hardly perceived. The equation has become a fact of life. Few even realize that there *can* be debate, that accepting a reading problem as proof of or as synonymous with a lower level of intelligence is a gross misunderstanding — that the formula is inaccurate and that, quite to the contrary, a child or adult may have a severe reading problem and have intact intelligence — even superior intelligence.

"Oh, if you're talking about *dyslexia*, I know you can have that and be smart. After all, Vice President Nelson Rockefeller was dyslexic and *he* was smart," says the voice of public opinion.

"But if a boy in Yeshiva can't read, that's different. That's not dyslexia — that's a *mental* problem, and that means he just doesn't have the intelligence. After all, it takes a *brain* to read, doesn't it?"

...to Play Tennis, to Draw

Yes, it takes "a brain." It takes a brain functioning in a particular way to achieve reading — to achieve everything, in fact. If person A cannot carry a tune, is there something wrong with his intelligence? After all, it takes "a brain" to carry a tune. If person B cannot hit a tennis ball more than once in every 25 attempts, is there something wrong with his intelligence? After all, it takes "a brain" to hit a tennis ball. If person C cannot calculate mentally, but can do so quite well with pencil and paper, is he to be relabeled cognitively deficient? If person D — aged 30 — cannot copy an intricate architectural design, should he realize that he simply lacks the same intelligence level that the 20-year-old architect possesses? After all, it takes "a brain" to copy designs.

What should be apparent is that it takes "a brain" to do *everything*; every motion, act and even emotion we create or possess represents a specific function of our brain. What should be equally apparent is that we can possess a high degree of intelligence and still not be able to accomplish a particular task.

Some of us may learn to carry a tune with ease. Some of us will learn to play tennis in twenty lessons (some of us will need years). It is quite possible for most of us to learn to copy intricate architectural designs. Clearly, an altogether different level and type of instruction will be necessary for some of us.

Try "L=I"

Of vital importance is the realization that we can be *taught* that which we do not know. The amount of time needed and the quality of instruction will both be variables in the equation of learning — but, ultimately, learning will occur. There are many professionals in the field of social science, in fact, who will feel quite comfortable with the equation of *learning = intelligence*.

We are, furthermore, under the false assumption that *everyone* learns to read with ease. We do not establish this false expectation for music, sports, art and design and even mathematics. It is almost completely acceptable — is it not? — for us to admit finding geometry or trigonometry totally incomprehensible, and still miraculously manage to maintain our intact levels of intelligence. Only with reading do we almost totally lose perspective. It is reading — a task that requires the integration of unbelievably numerous and complex subskill tasks — that we have bonded to intelligence in an irrevocably proportional relationship.

Why? Probably because of the importance which we have attached to it, in addition to its central role in school learning.

Even now, in the age of alternative pathways to information absorption, we rely very strongly on the skill of reading as a means of information intake. A fascinating socio-psychological investigation might be made, in fact, into the reluctance on the part of disabled readers and their families to abandon the written word as absolutely mandatory when it is clear that the disabled reader could advance far more rapidly through auditory presentation of material.

This is an especially interesting phenomenon in the *frum* world — where *writing down the Oral Law* represented an accommodation to *lessening* skills, and where *Torah she'b'al peh* in its original spoken form had represented the pinnacle of transmission.

⇜§ Trade in Tension for Tranquility

The equation of R=I would make little difference if it resided — quietly and ponderously — in unused texts gathering dust in musky libraries. The problem is that it is a volatile and ubiquitous fact of everyday life — with a potential for destruction at worst and neglect at best. If one believes that intelligence is impaired or absent because reading does not immediately occur, then the possibility exists of resultant behaviors such as anger, frustration, avoidance, neglect, hopelessness, shame, inaction, tension, and, above all, energy expended to hide the problem.

If, on the other hand, non-reading is equated simply with a skill that may be difficult for a particular child or adult, but one that simply requires specialized instruction — then resultant behaviors can include hope, tranquility, practical searching for proper education, relaxed attitudes, candidness, lack of tension, joy in learning.

There are too many victims. Far too many children are hurt and emotionally maimed for life as a result of the terrible destruction of R=I. Who can know, too, how many future generations can be affected by the "fallout" of children who grow to adulthood without self-esteem.

It never helps children when we use *blame* and *anger* because we ourselves perceive hopelessness. It becomes absurd, however, when we perceive hopelessness without cause.

Children who appeared to possess average intelligence prior to failure in reading are *not* automatically stripped of this intelligence *because* of that failure. They need specialized instruction — but they usually *can* be taught.

To rob the Yossies of the yeshivah world — to rob blameless but aching children of their very intelligence because they cannot read — to steal their futures by condemning them through prejudice, fear and a shocking lack of understanding and compassion — to shatter their emotional selves is to make us all guilty of *needless* destruction.

Simply stated — a child can have a severe reading problem and still be smart!

Foolish to Hope?

Is it foolish to hope that societal awareness of this fact will translate itself into happier Yossies who are better understood and for whom suitable education is obtained? Is it futile to hope that we will learn to accept reading problems as just reading problems, and not penalize our non-readers by stripping them — in our minds — of their intellectual capacity for meaningful thought and future learning?

Each person *is* society; each is responsible for his or her own share of the cumulative attitudinal structure. Each of us must decide if Yossie can live in our hearts and minds as a fully franchised member of society — or if he is to be cast aside as a lesser child because he reads poorly.

Rebecca Amster

Teaching the Learning Disabled Student

Recognition is Half the Solution

"It's a terrible thing when you know something is wrong with your child and you don't know what to do for him. Dovid could finish a puzzle in a minute, and he was good at math. We knew he was a bright boy. But he couldn't learn the Aleph Bais, and then he couldn't put the letters together when the other children were doing it."

I.

What Exactly Is Wrong?

READING AND writing are the basis of all our academic subjects: "Read the chapter in Social Studies"; "Find the capital of Ohio"; "Label the parts of the animal's body"; and, of course, "Read the next *pasuk*." Unable to read, a child gets bewildered, lost, and more lost.

Do you recall that in your school years every class had one or two kids who were the 'dummies'? Since first grade they couldn't keep up and they became the class clowns, the butt of jokes, or the ones the teacher sent out for chalk.

Yet some of them, if you spoke to them at recess, didn't seem like dummies. A perceptive teacher might have told you that such a student was intelligent, maybe more creative than his older sister, but he seemed to have missed something somewhere along the line.

"My son was just bumming around. The principal promised to help, but all Dovid did was sit in the office most of the day even though, incredibly, he didn't disturb in class. He just sat quietly and patiently even though he couldn't follow what was going on."

✡ Peaks and Valleys

Dyslexia — an impairment in one's ability to read — is only the best-known form of a broad range of problems that fall under the category of Learning Disabilities. Dyslexics see letters backwards, in a reversed order, or skip some altogether.

An impairment can also affect a person's ability to speak, to concentrate, or to understand number concepts. One youngster, for example, could name the months of the year and could count up to twenty but couldn't relate the two and tell you how many months there are in a year.

Some learning disabled people have trouble memorizing material. This is especially problematic for students in a yeshiva where much early learning is by rote. They're likely to forget an errand or an assignment if they're told to do more than one thing at a time.

Occasionally a child will also experience problems with gross or fine motor coordination which, for example, would affect his handwriting.

Many of the disabilities seem related to difficulties in orienting time and space. "Which letter came first?" "What day of the week is it?" "Which is your right hand?" "Where do you put the *nekudos?*" These can be perplexing questions for some people.

A learning disabled person can experience difficulty in one isolated area or have a combination of problems; its effect can range from mild to severe.

Learning disabilities themselves are usually invisible. Sometimes, though, a problem such as poor organization can manifest itself in a sloppy appearance. And the same problem that makes a child confuse written signals can cause him to miss social cues such as an expression that indicates you wish to start or end a conversation.

❦ What Happens to the 5%?

Recent studies claim that 15% of the population has some learning disability. Let's assume that these statistics are inflated with people whose disabilities are relatively minor. Let's say that 5% of students can't compensate on their own. What becomes of these students? Particularly, what is done for the 5% (and any *rebbe* or *morah* will assure you, we do have our share) in the yeshiva population?

Special Education is a relatively recent entry in the professional vocabulary. It came as part of the new awareness that not everyone fit the mold, which earlier spawned the bilingual education movement. With the passage in 1975 of the Education for all Handicapped Children Act, government-mandated education for learning disabled children came of age in the nation's public school systems. Testing centers, reading programs, and the like sprang up in hospitals, universities, and in the private sector.

Meanwhile, yeshiva students with learning disabilities (if they were accepted at all in schools crowded enough to be choosy) were just passed from grade to grade, from teacher to overburdened teacher. Perhaps they were tutored, but there's not much extra time at home after a long day in yeshiva, and if you take a student out of class to be tutored, he misses new material. If tutoring did not suffice, a student could graduate virtually illiterate in English and barely able to *daven*. Alternatively, such a child was transferred to a public school where he could get help.

"My son was going to learn — and in a yeshiva. I would not accept that he couldn't."

Thus began a saga of awesome determination. Dovid was tested — the first step as soon as parents suspect their youngster (some feel even a pre-schooler) has a learning problem. The results confirmed that Dovid had a profound perception problem but a normal IQ. Peaks and valleys, scoring high in some areas and low in others, is the identifying characteristic of learning disabilities.

For the next six years Dovid remained in yeshiva, but in name only.

"Every morning I shlepped him to a reading center. In the afternoon he was tutored in Chumash *and* Dinim *in the school library. In the evening I took him for eye exercises. It all helped, but the child never had a normal day of school. He never belonged anywhere. We drove him* meshugga."

When he was ready to enter high school, Dovid finally found his place in the newly created P'TACH program.

II.

P'TACH

Eight years ago another parent of a bright, handsome boy who *shuckled* next to his father in *shul*, but couldn't *daven*, could not find a yeshiva high school for his son.

He, together with another parent and an educational psychologist, had only recently forged the nucleus of a self-help group to cope with learning disabilities. They named it P'TACH, an acronym for Parents for Torah for All Children. The name also refers to the *pasuk* "V'at P'TACH lo" (lit. You shall open up for him), which is the Torah's advice for reaching a child who cannot ask questions on his own.

Then they appealed to yeshiva high schools for help. Yeshiva University agreed to accept their pilot program — two self-contained high school classes for 13 boys.

Learning disabilities, say the experts, cannot be cured. Instead a student can be taught to compensate. Either he can circumvent the area in which he is weak by using a different skill to learn the same thing, or he can be taught some strategy that will alleviate his weakness. A strategy can be something as simple as pointing as one reads or learning memory keys.

The field of Special Education draws direction from the *pasuk* "Chanoch lanaar al pi darko." More than with any other group, the key to success in dealing with special children lies in teaching every student on his own level.

After a child is evaluated and his precise strengths and weaknesses are understood, a custom-tailored curriculum is drawn up for him. In P'TACH's self-contained elementary and high school programs, students are divided into three levels roughly corresponding to their grade, but also to their functioning ability. Teaching here can't be accomplished by the usual "frontal" method, where a teacher lectures to a whole class. Here every lesson is a multi-sensory experience. There's something for every student to absorb; they can see a picture, feel a shape, or hear a song. "There's never too much positive reinforcement," said a *Gemara* teacher.

At Bais Yaakov D'Rav Meir in Flatbush, where P'TACH runs a self-contained elementary program just for girls, seven girls in the intermediate level learn in a classroom subdivided into three areas. In one area four girls practice math with the teacher's aide and then are read a story. In a second, one child works with a speech therapist. In the third, two girls continue in their workbooks, building skills in reading, spelling and penmanship under the master teacher's guidance. They have a myriad of questions, and every one receives a patient reply.

The teachers' obvious attention and respect for what each of their students has to say is noticed by students of other classes too. Girls regularly stop P'TACH teachers in the hall and tell them about a problem or share other tidbits with them. They've learned that these teachers care even more than others.

P'TACH's aim is to return every child to the mainstream. Its self-contained classes basically follow the academic curriculum of the other classes in the school. P'TACH helps students develop the skills they need to succeed 'on the outside'; then, as soon as progress and scheduling allow, students enter their parallel class.

At first a child may join his peers for one or two subjects while continuing the rest of the day in his P'TACH class. When a student is mainstreamed, a P'TACH teacher follows his progress, works with his new teacher, and will arrange for support to back him up if necessary.

Some students are able to enter the mainstream after only a few years of specialized help. Others are never able to function well in a traditional setting, and they might remain in a self-contained program throughout high school. The sole consideration is where the child will do best.

✺§ "Here I'm Learning"

"Generally after one month the children are happier here than they've ever been," says Mrs. Ethel Salomon, coordinator of P'TACH at the Bais Yaakov.

Eliezer, an eighth grader who came to P'TACH at Chaim Berlin after third grade, explained, "Here, I'm learning. In a regular class with 32 kids, how is a *rebbe* supposed to stay with one kid until he understands? Now my teacher is always here to answer any question. If I don't understand something, they spend more time on it."

Ironically, today Eliezer feels *more* like an equal with his peers. They play punchball together, *daven* together, go to camp together and now he is mainstreamed for *Chumash*. In his previous yeshiva he sensed he was different.

Even a third grader knows when he's not succeeding. His friends are doing work he can't understand. His teachers either seem angry at him because he's "not listening" or have given up on him. He feels his parents' disappointment in him and hears them fighting over what to do with Yankel who keeps bringing home D's. The frustration can build up in such a child to devastating proportions.

"I always ask a parent 'What does your child think of himself?' " said Rabbi Burton Jaffa, P'TACH's director.

" 'Not very much,' is invariably the answer."

This poor self-image usually creates overlaying emotional problems that make the child appear more disabled than he really is.

"Often we have to spend the first year or so just rebuilding the child's self-esteem." says Mrs. Salomon. "We concentrate on those activities at which the child can succeed."

✎§ To Go out of Business

Crucial to P'TACH's philosophy is that all their students participate with the rest of the schoolchildren in *davening*, lunch and any special activities in which they will be able to perform equally well.

In Bais Yaakov, the girls wear the maroon and gray school uniform and, running around together, they are indistinguishable from the rest of the student body. P'TACH children are considered, and consider themselves, students of Chaim Berlin, or Bais Yaakov, or Manhattan Day School. They have *their* own class just as another sixth grader has *his*. They are taught at a level at which they can learn. They belong and can succeed as Dovid could not.

"Our goal," says Rabbi Jaffa, "is to go out of business." P'TACH was originally envisioned as an organization to help schools set up their own Special Education programs. "Teaching the learning disabled is every yeshiva's problem, not P'TACH's," Rabbi Jaffa says emphatically.

He feels that every school should serve the needs of its entire prospective student body. Three students will not function well as one of 30 girls in Mrs. Stern's grade in room 401, so those three girls should be able to go to a resource room teacher or they should be taught *Chumash* by Miss Stein in room 102. The proper education of all those students who could possibly function within the framework of a regular yeshiva would thus be a routine responsibility of every school.

III.

The Special School

Not all students are best served by a program within a yeshiva that is geared to mainstreaming, Yeshivas Limudei Hashem (YLH) — or Chush, as it is commonly known — pioneered Jewish Special Education when it opened its doors about eleven years ago.

About 65 learning disabled children learn there today in a maze of classrooms in a converted brewery on Brooklyn's Williamsburg waterfront.

Having its own facilities is a big advantage for Chush. It allows space for a gym, a computer room, and an art room — which are essentials, not extras, for these children. Classrooms are spacious enough for young boys who aren't expected to remain at their desks. It is not a lack of space that constrains Chush from accepting more children.

Most of YLH's students have more complex learning problems than the children served by P'TACH. They may have severely underdeveloped speech, be hyperactive, or have a hearing loss, which makes learning as part of a large group difficult. Others have a combination of learning disabilities, and some are on the lower end of the range of a normal IQ — so it's harder for them to pick up the strategies they need to compensate.

"Without a special program," explained Rabbi A. H. Fried, founder of Chush, "these students would not be getting C's and D's; they probably would not be able to function in a yeshiva at all."

For them, YLH offers the advantage of an holistic approach. The staff emphasizes a team effort so its teachers, director, psychologists, therapists, and even secretaries concern themselves with the child as a whole — emotionally, physically, and academically.

Psychological support is particularly critical for children who enter special programs late in their school careers, after having failed in regular programs. Says YLH principal Joan Meyer, "We work to build confidence in the children. We've found that a child who has confidence will cope much better than another, inherently less disabled student, who has none."

Maintaining a child's self esteem also means that he must find acceptance at home. Many of Chush's students come from Chassidic families where Yiddish is spoken and *Chumash* is learned through the Yiddish *teitch*. To feel normal, they have to join their brothers and sisters at the *Shabbos* table and contribute what they've learned about the *parsha* in Yiddish. YLH's *rebbes* are Chassidic and the classes are divided not only by level, but culturally as well. Thus Chassidic and non-Chassidic children are taught *Limudei Kodesh* separately and in the language they are most comfortable with.

How do the children feel about being in a "special school"? Said one teacher simply, "As with everything else, it depends on the kid. But he knows that *here* he's learning and *there* he wasn't."

In one large room, between four and six boys may be learning. One six-year-old may be working with a teacher's aide on number concepts, the master teacher coaxes two boys to find the incongruities in illogical sentences, and one boy who can't concentrate on the lesson is invited to work privately with yet another teacher.

Each student concentrates on the curriculum tailored to his learning profile. About half of YLH's students eventually gain enough from this intensive guidance to be able to transfer to a regular yeshiva— some after only a year or two. As a transition,

> **"A man may study 400 blatt Gemara in one year and yet if he is capable of studying 500 blatt, he is derelict in his obligation. Should the child whose capacity is limited to mastering one Mishna a year actually study that Mishna, then he has fulfilled his charge. The bracha that we recite on Torah study is la'asok — to labor in Torah, and the slower child has done just that."**
>
> *Dr. Abraham Twerski*

Teaching the Learning Disabled Student / 347

Chush might direct a student to a school that has a resource room so that he can continue to receive extra support.

In all classes, learning skills are emphasized over pure academics. Because many learning disabled children miss certain concepts other children seem to pick up by osmosis, skills are broken down into their components. Before a teacher can teach youngsters how to tell time, for example, she has to make sure they understand the concept of the clockwise direction, the concept of time itself, and that they can count by fives. When all this is known, the task of telling time itself is a breeze to grasp; with a piece missing, it's impossible.

New subject matter is also taught with a careful eye toward its component skills. In a simple lesson at YLH, an enlargement was made of a *pasuk* from a *Chumash* with linear translation. Underneath were the "skill questions": *Who said this? What did Avraham do first?* — so the student really grasped the details and the sequence.

There is a plethora of instructional materials on the market for the secular subjects, but for *Limudei Kodesh*, Special Education teachers usually have to design their own materials. The technique of task analysis is really basic to all learning, and teachers in regular schools are welcoming the new materials into their own classrooms.

Several years ago, Sarah Schenirer Seminary (in Boro Park) launched a program to train Special Education teachers. Many of their students now are the teacher's aides at Chush, P'TACH and similar programs around the city. Even those who will eventually lead regular classes will be better teachers because they understand the learning process and are attuned to individual students' abilities.

IV.

The Rest of Us

✌ The Parents' Role

Parents of a learning disabled student are expected to be highly involved partners in their child's education. Beginning at the time of screening for admission to a program and continuing on a yearly basis, the staffs hold conferences with the parents to assess progress and plan for the future.

In between, teachers are constantly in contact with parents, pointing out problems or triumphs. "I prefer a parent who calls me every day to ask how her daughter is doing to one who is apathetic," says Mrs. Salomon, "because support from home is a key factor to a child's success and well-being."

Parents join in deciding when and if their child is to be mainstreamed. Their goals for the child's future also guide the school. A student who, with his family, has aspirations to continue in college or a *yeshiva gedola* will follow a more academically oriented program. For those who are more interested in a vocation, P'TACH, for example, arranges for courses to be taken at an appropriate vocational school. P'TACH's graduates have, in fact, gone on to yeshivos, colleges, and successful jobs.

◆§ The Stigma

"Today Dovid is learning in a yeshiva in *Eretz Yisroel*. Before P'TACH I couldn't dream of such a thing. *Baruch Hashem* for P'TACH! They made a *mentch* out of him."

Dovid's mother's appreciation knows no bounds. Today this mother of four spends every spare minute working for P'TACH.

There are many parents, though, who are reluctant to acknowledge a problem with their offspring, afraid of the stigma of having an "abnormal" child. And, deep down, a couple with toddlers worries about *shidduchim* — for the affected child and for his siblings. If a "defect" can be hidden, they'd rather hide it.

Rabbi Fried is all too familiar with that approach. The parents of one of his students would not greet him when he visited their *shul* for fear of having their secret found out. But people know when a problem exists. Other members of the *shul* whispered to him, "You know there is a little boy here who would probably benefit from your school."

"It's not the help that brings the stigma," Rabbi Fried explains, "it's the problem."

The proud father of a P'TACH student who recently read the *haftorah* flawlessly at his *bar mitzva* goes further: "They saved my son's *Yiddishkeit*. Moshe couldn't have survived yeshiva. Eventually we would have had to put him in public school. With all the negative experience associated with yeshiva, he never would have remained *frum*."

◆§ The Community

The fear of the stigma is a direct reflection of a misguided attitude on the part of the Jewish community. Primarily, the attitude stems from a lack of understanding.

The organic cause of learning disabilities isn't known. Experts only observe that there is a disturbance between the reception and processing of information in the brain. Thus, few people understand that the child who suffers from learning disabilities is probably of at least normal intelligence. The parents of a child who could conceal the problem but wish to acknowledge it in order to get help run the risk of having their child mistakenly labeled retarded.

For centuries, defects have been routinely covered up. There is a prevalent belief that Jews don't have "these kinds of" problems. Our family certainly doesn't, and therefore others don't either. In its infancy, Chush founders had to move mountains to dispel this myth and gain acceptance of their project.

Explains a P'TACH parent, "People don't look at P'TACH as they do Hatzala. They figure, "Them I may need someday. Learning disabilities will never happen to me.' " So the parents of a learning disabled child are left to deal with the burden alone.

"Why should one parent have to pay $7,000 to educated a child with a learning disability?" he asked. Some programs have five applicants for each available spot; and desperate parents have hired private Special Education teachers to tutor their child for up to $50 an hour. The community at large, they feel, should be covering the cost of educating also those who can't learn best in a traditional classroom setting.

◆§ The Yeshivos

If the community is not sufficiently educated about learning disabilities, its lack of initiative to deal with the problem is reflected in the yeshivos. As yet, the yeshivos have not made a commitment to educate all the children. To be sure, there are many reasons, and they are generally the same reasons as mentioned above because, as service institutions, the yeshivos reflect the desires of their constituents.

P'TACH estimates that it costs them $10,000 a year to educate a child. For Chush, with its own facilities, the cost is even higher. Few schools feel able to afford the luxury of hiring one or two teachers plus a support staff of speech therapists and the like to teach five students, or even to hire one or two teachers to staff a resource room. (Here there is no problem of "over-identification" of the learning disabled as in the public schools system. Under state law, public schools receive larger sums to educate students who are labeled learning disabled.)

Also, because many of the good schools today are ב"ה quite crowded, providing classroom space at six students per room creates an unwelcome strain on their tight quarters. Some schools can't even find space for a resource room, and its teacher has to wander from room to office in search of an unoccupied corner.

And then the stigma.

Only a few schools have remedial programs, so those programs that exist are in tremendous demand. Pupils come to P'TACH's two self-contained non-coed programs in Brooklyn, for example, from throughout the tri-state region and as far off as England and Israel.

Aside from the space consideration, a school is naturally concerned with maintaining its image as a good school. Accepting so many problem children risks altering the character of its student body and they fear that it would jeopardize its image and decrease the enrollment.

V.

Hope For the Future

But there is a wind of change in the air. "Parents are getting more sophisticated," a physician commented to Rabbi Jaffa recently. "No longer are they going to allow their children to be destroyed."

Increasingly, as parents perceive the need, yeshivos across the country and abroad are beginning to set up remedial programs. Many turn to Chush and P'TACH for guidance and support. P'TACH today guides 20 programs in the New York area, serving about 500 students. In fact, two Chinuch Atzmai schools in Israel joined the P'TACH network this year as the first in the country to offer Special Education programs within a regular yeshiva, and Bnos Zion of Bobov welcomed the first self-contained P'TACH class in Boro Park this fall.

A few schools, most notably Yeshiva Darchei Torah of Far Rockaway, have established resource rooms independently. A resource room teacher takes a child with a learning disability out of class periodically and works with him on the skills he is deficient in. Unlike tutoring in a particular subject, which is like a crutch, the help a student receives from a resource room should enable him to function better overall.

Ideally, a resource room teacher works closely with the child's regular classroom teacher and helps her incorporate special education techniques in all her lessons. A teacher also should be able to turn to a resource room teacher for guidance in dealing with any student having difficulties, even one who does not need private instruction.

Every student in the school benefits in another way, too. As the resource room becomes more widespread, says one Special Education expert, the attitude of all the children in the school changes. They may once have considered learning disabled children weird, but as they see the attention and effort the staff gives to the needs of an individual student, they develop a new sensitivity and a desire to help too.

More parents are also seeking help earlier — before a child falls behind and before he ever experiences failure. YLH has a pre-school program geared to language stimulation. They are so succesful at nipping problems in the bud that most of the program's graduates continue in regular schools.

And more parents are voicing an attitude similar to Dovid's mother.

"Today Dovid is a lovely, intelligent boy. You can talk to him about any subject. I have no reason to be ashamed and every reason to be proud."

Says Eliezer's father, "We are all disabled in some way. I can't play piano. You can't draw. My son couldn't add the way I do. But P'TACH provided him with the ultimate resource room and he learned to compensate beautifully. He has confidence that he can deal with anything. He's going to be more successful than most mainstream kids."

And, increasingly, the Jewish community at large is beginning to appreciate that whether they be geniuses, average, learning disabled, retarded, or physically handicapped, they are all our children. As Rabbi Yaakov Perlow (the Novominsker Rebbe) said in an address several years ago, every Jewish child is entitled to the privilege of sharing in his birthright and absorbing Torah and *Yiddishkeit* — each to the extent that he is able. And if the challenge of educating certain children holds more pain than *nachas*, the task is no less a *mitzva*.

Here we speak of children who, with proper guidance, *can* be a source of *nachas*. Their feelings and aspirations are no different from our other children's. Last spring, a composition posted on a bulletin board in Chush read: "For *afikomen* I asked for a set of *Mishnayos* and a 3-speed bike."

Malky Brailofsky

In Search of Chavie

৵ It Doesn't Pay to Bother

THE GENERAL SYSTEM of education used in our *yeshivos* and Bais Yaakovs today is probably as good as it will ever be. Teachers strive to abide by it, principals aim to enforce it, and parents may, at times, try to fight it. Sometimes, though, a lack of sufficient resources may force Torah schools to sidestep some painful situations, even though they are mandated to deal with them. Sometimes, a wise, more-experienced member of the administration may advise a novice teacher to budget her time and effort in a way that seems to deprive a student of some desperately needed attention. A student like Chavie. Fortunately, I didn't listen.

"It really doesn't pay to bother yourself with Chavie. She has never participated in any type of schoolwork whatsoever. I'm afraid that she will never be a student. Just let her be; it would prove a wasted effort to try to get her to cooperate — nothing has ever worked."

As I watched my elementary school class *daven*, these words, spoken to me by the principal at a private meeting, echoed round and round in my mind. How true they seemed!

Most of my students were pointing at the proper places in their *Siddurim*, chanting the words of "*Ashrei*" with vitality. Admittedly, two were examining the cracks in their desks, and one was fingering her new bracelet. Chavie, though, sat in a world of her own.

An onlooker would surely have concluded that Chavie was deaf. Or dumb. Or both. But she was none of these! She sat low in her chair, her thin hands resting limply in her lap. Her *Siddur* was still open to "*Adon olam*"; she hardly bothered turning the pages. Her head was bent so that it was nearly parallel to her desk. Sad dark eyes stared blankly at the pages. Her lips mumbled inaudibly; not a sound escaped them.

I thought of the sketchy details that I knew. Not as lucky as most Jewish children, who come home each day to a loving, happy home. Chavie's home was ravaged by marital strife. The oldest of the brood of children, she bore the brunt of most of the household chores. And unlike most children, who receive a cheery, "Thank you, darling, the laundry was folded beautifully," and then later, "Good night, you were a very good girl today," Chavie merited none of these. Bitter, unhappy parents either could not or would not tell her.

Is it a wonder, then, I mused, that Chavie behaves as she does? She probably imagines herself trapped in a cage, with the world one big prison around her. Good for duties, good for tasks, but for little else. Why should she smile? Why should she raise her hand? Why should she study? *No one cares, no one needs me. No one thinks I am important.*

The girls were *davening Shemoneh Esrei* by now. Chavie stood motionless near her desk, her *Siddur* lying limply in her hands. A fresh wave of pity washed over me, and my heart ached for her. Maybe I *could* do something.

The principal's words crept back into my mind. "Just let her be — it really doesn't pay." I fought a quick inner battle, and one more glance at Chavie told me who had won.

"I'll show them," I thought fiercely. "We're going to take this Chavie and replace her with a new one. A happy one. A caring one. A loved one, and a loving one."

◆§ The Long, Long "Quickest Route"

The quickest route to success, I concluded, was an outpouring of love. I was so sure that once Chavie sensed that I truly cared for her and that I had confidence in her abilities, she would shine.

A story that Avi Shulman once told in a lecture strengthened me in my resolve. He described a poor beggar who sat on a broken crate on a street corner selling shoelaces. All day, as passersby approached his corner, he would call out, begging them to make a purchase.

One day, the bank president from the next block passed by our friend. He had often observed him while riding in his shiny black limousine, and now he approached with a gait so sure and certain. The seller held his breath as the entrepreneur edged closer to the broken crate.

"Please, kind sir," he whispered. "Would you care to buy a pair of new black shoelaces?"

"Well," the president bent down to examine the wares. "You know that I only deal with merchandise that is of the finest quality. Are these laces the best that money can buy? Hmmm...Yes, they look quite elegant. I will take two pairs. Thank you very much, and good luck."

The beggar stared at his customer as he tucked his purchase into his smart leather case and strode quickly on.

"Did you hear what he said?" he asked himself. "He said that these laces are top quality. That's quite nice. If I can sell merchandise to please the bank president himself, then maybe I can get a decent job and earn a decent salary. You never know."

In time, this poor, seemingly worthless man has worked his way up the economic ladder, occupying an enviable position in a local firm.

As the girls closed their *Siddurim,* I reflected that Chavie was very much like this man. She had no aspirations, simply because she felt that she would never succeed. Well, I resolved, I will give Chavie a taste of success. And I'm going to make it taste so good that she will want to lick the spoon over and over again.

But how can I show a student success when the pages of her notebook are consistently blank? How could I possibly show her that she could earn a passing grade when every test paper is handed in mostly blank?

Forget it, I told myself. Forget the scholastic part of Chavie. Worry first about Chavie, the starving Jewish child. Worry about Chavie, the student, later. Just love her, and show her that you do. The rest will follow naturally.

← Finding The Tools Of Love

So here I was. I had a goal. I had a dream. But I had the backing of no one. And I did not know which tools to use to achieve my goal. I just knew that it had to be achieved. And nothing was going to come between me and my goal. Nothing.

I began walking up and down the rows more often during *davening*. As I passed Chavie's desk, I would pat her back gently. Repeatedly, I would place her finger at the proper word in the *Siddur*, stroking her cheek as my hand moved back.

At recess one day, I complimented her on how pretty her hair looked. But she didn't even acknowledge my words; just looked sadly right past me, as if I wasn't there. I knew that she had heard, but she did not know how to handle kind words. Yet.

I thought of how to get Chavie to participate more in the lessons. Her notebook was a collection of papers, most of them bent and blank, a few covered with illegible markings. She literally never raised her hand in class, neither to ask a question, nor to answer one.

Before the *Chumash* lesson the next day, I approached Chavie quietly, and urged her to attempt to write notes.

"Just write the hard words in every *pasuk*," I coaxed. "This way, you'll be able to say the *pasuk* for me tomorrow."

She didn't even look up as I spoke. Her eyes glued to her desk, she simply shrugged, ending the conversation.

"This is going to be a slow go," I decided, "if it's going to go at all."

A week later, the class took a *Chumash* test on two *perakim*. As usual, ninety percent of Chavie's paper was blank. Some questions had scribbles on the appropriate blanks. On impulse, I filled in the answers near some of the questions that she had left empty. Then I made big red checks near those numbers. Every scribble that she had made was neatly crossed out, and I printed the correct responses neatly nearby. These questions, too, were awarded bright checks. With a flourish, I marked a big 75 on the paper. Under the mark, I wrote "Chavie, I see that you have done beautiful work. You have made me truly proud. Let's see if you can keep on making me so happy. I am sure that you could!"

When I presented the tests to the principal, as was the rule, she looked at me in surprise when she hit Chavie's 75. Her questioning glance demanded an explanation.

"I am trying a new method," I explained. "No, of course she did not deserve this mark. I gave it to her as a present. I think I know what I am doing. Just have patience, and we might see fantastic results."

I received a frown and a this-is-a-bit-ridiculous look. Undaunted, I hurried to the classroom to return the papers.

Was I in for a disappointment. Chavie didn't even smile when she saw her grade! I expected at least some sign of satisfaction. But I received none. I bit my lip in despair. Perhaps there truly was no way to reach Chavie?

The days turned into weeks. I constantly tried, by subtle movements, to convey to Chavie that I loved her and was proud of her, and wanted to be even prouder. Fellow teachers took notice of my campaign, and as Chavie had several sisters in the school with similar problems, they asked me how I was going about it. I related the method that I used to mark her last test as an example of what I felt was the primary goal: reaching the *neshama* inside, not the scholastic ability.

"That's insane. How can you give a 75 when she deserves a 0?"

"How?" I replied grimly. "With a pen."

The Pages Were Covered With Sentences

One day, I glanced at Chavie's notebook. The pages were covered with neatly written sentences. How beautiful her handwriting actually was! Each letter was perfectly formed, as if she had been writing this way since first grade. Her lonely eyes lit up like a lantern as I told her so.

She slowly began raising her hand in class. At first, even when she spoke to me, she would still stare down at her desk. But as she got used to speaking and being spoken to, she would look straight at me as we conversed.

The English principal was waiting for me as I left the school building one day.

"I want to tell you that Chavie is improving tremendously in her studies. I was told that you were working on her, and so I thought you would be interested to know. She has begun showing great interest in all aspects of the program."

I thanked her politely, noting silently that had I showed her that test paper crowned with a 75, she would surely have berated me for my foolishness.

I looked forward to the following week with trepidation. I had scheduled a major *Chumash* test on an entire *parsha*. I wondered what Chavie would show. The day before, I called her aside, reminding her again to study as well as she could because I expected big things from her tomorrow.

The tension in the class was palpable. The girls quickly turned over the test papers and began working. It was a challenging exam, and they worked feverishly. At the clang of the recess bell, many had still not finished. Chavie, too, was still writing.

Finally, the papers were collected. I stole a quick glance at Chavie's. Every blank was filled in!

I marked her paper the moment I arrived home. Chavie had truly earned a 96! I read and reread her answers in disbelief. So this was the girl that would never succeed in school! This was the girl who should not even be bothered with!

P.S.

I live at present only a couple of blocks away from Chavie. Often, I pass her on the street, walking alone or with friends. The other day, I saw her conversing with two classmates on the corner. Her happy face and animated way of speaking bespoke true joy and confidence. I tried to compare her with the Chavie who sat low in her seat, eyes never once looking upon me. I could not. There was simply no comparison. That first Chavie was gone. A new one had come instead.

～§What She Learns From Adversity

Building a Ghetto of Our Own
The Out-of-Towners
Letters in Response
Commuting on the Right Track
The Call Unanswered
Of Peace. And Pieces
"I Know"

Edith Krohn

Building a Ghetto of Our Own

WHAT DOES THE word *ghetto* suggest? An old-time, self-contained *shtetel*? Chinatown? Little Italy? Boro Park? Monsey? Scarsdale? An enclave where an appreciable number of the same type of people live together, whether by decree or by choice? This is the way a "ghetto" is usually understood.

But there is another type of ghetto. Self-imposed, self-reliant, indestructible: The ghetto of the mind. A ghetto that the outside world can touch but not infiltrate; where concepts and strength come from within, and do not rely on the "without."

Succinctly and briefly, the concept of the ghetto of the mind is the barrier the Jew erects between his Jewishness and the secular values of the outside world. This does not mean that he hibernates or becomes a recluse. Rather, having learned a pattern of living spanning from the hour he awakes until the hour he goes to sleep, he knows what he may or may not do, what he can or cannot do. He builds an inner defense. If the defense is honest and effective, one can hope that there will be no crack in the barrier.

٭ Long Ago, Not So Far Away

Long ago but not far away, there was a tiny group of people who lived in Philadelphia... a lovely city — genteel and gentile. The parents were *frum* and they could not conceive that their children should be anything but *frum* — even as they were, and their parents in Europe before them. Having distanced themselves from Czarist Russia, the Revolution and its aftermath of destruction, they were grateful for America and its freedom and energy. But first and foremost they were *frum* Jews.

All children went to public school, America's great contribution of free and compulsory education to civilization. Among these children was a fourteen-year-old lad in the first year of high school. The transition from elementary to high school is heady and traumatic, changing from a child to a fledgling adult in one step. Hershel had to contend not only with a new curriculum, a lunchroom where everything was *treif*, but also with Mr. Classon, a gym instructor who encouraged potential athletic stars to try out for the various sports. Hershel, a boy with a slow and an unusually quiet approach to everything, was tall and solidly built for his age, and a candidate for the instructor's campaign.

The gym outfit was short pants and a white T-shirt. Hershel's problem was how should he wear his *tzitzis* — under the shirt or over the shirt? Obviously not *over* the shirt. But then again, his father had told him that *tzitzis* must not be worn against the skin — only over an undershirt. Hershel solved the problem by wearing a sleeveless undershirt, his *tzitzis*, then the gym-shirt and shorts. All would have been well had the *tzitzis* not had the tendency to skip out of his pants with the fringes hanging over the sides.

After gym class, Mr. Classon called Hershel over and asked him, "What are those strings hanging over your pants?"

"These are *tzitzis*," he said. "Jewish boys wear them under their top shirts."

"What are *tzitzis*? And why do you wear them?" asked Mr. Classon.

Slightly taken aback, Hershel said, "They are a part of our religion. We wear them all the time."

"There are a lot of Jewish boys here," Mr. Classon said kindly, "but I never saw anybody wear them. Anyway, next class, don't put them on when you change for gym. The gym outfit is pants and gym shirt. Nothing else." He put his hand on Hershel's shoulder and smiled. He really liked the boy.

✥ A Note, Ball, and Pins

That night, Hershel told his father about his dilemma. "I'll write your Mr. Classon a note," Hershel's father said. "I think it will be all right."

It wasn't. Mr. Classon read Hershel's note: "Please allow

Harry to wear his *tzitzis* under his gym shirt. It is a Jewish law and I don't think it will interfere with Harry's gym work."

Mr. Classon was not pleased. "You will have to see the principal, Mr. Lettinger, Harry. You cannot be different than any of the other boys. And if you wear those fringes, I can't let you try out for the track team. And I think you can make it."

Mr. Lettinger was strait laced, proper and lived by the rules. He would not bend. The note became a ball pitched from Mr. Lettinger to Mr. Classon to Hershel's father and back again, round and round. After two weeks of note-pitching, Hershel's father said to him, "There is a way out of this, Hershel, if you want to take it. If you don't wear a *begged* (garment) with four corners, you are *pattur* (exempt) from *tzitzis*. So if it really means so much to you — well, don't wear them while in gym." Hershel's father searched his son's eyes.

"Pop, I just don't feel like a *Yid* without wearing *tzitzis*." Hershel said. Then he smiled gently, "*Nu*, so I won't be a track star."

Mr. Classon was not happy when Hershel told him he would not be trying out for the track team. "Is your father a rabbi?" he asked.

"No sir, he works in a factory."

"Well, keep those fringes pinned up inside the shirt. I don't want to see them flying around." He paused a moment, "I don't know anything about Jewish law, but I do know a fine boy when I see him." He smiled and walked away.

At fourteen, Hershel had begun to build his own intellectual ghetto...

✺ Sweet Abstinence

Philadelphia was not noteworthy for Jewish publications. There was *The Morning Journal*, to be sure, and *the Forward*, the Socialist, anti-religious daily. And then one day out of the fabled city of New York we received THE JEWISH LIGHT (*Der Yiddische Licht*) and it had a section in English. Glory be! Mother read the Yiddish and we kids read the English. It passed from one to another until in a week it was dog eared.

While it was not considered holy, we could nevertheless identify with what it said. And then one day, there was a pronouncement in the *Yiddische Licht* that all candy was *treif!*

One could not tell what was in it except by chemical analysis. The children were dumbfounded. *No candy?* All *Olam Hazeh* was suddenly gone. *No candy?* Schoolyard? Two recesses a day? The Sunday walk to the candy store? The world was suddenly bereft. Why for a nickel you could get — 1 Tootsie Roll, 1 Jawbreaker, a large hunk of chocolate, a nice lollipop — any color, and two licorice sticks. A nickel could keep you going for three or four days.

It was a measure of our parents' strength that the children could be imbued with such character that not one child touched a piece of candy for years, until much later, when another pronouncement came out that Hershey's Chocolate Bar was kosher.

Meantime, after the first shock of deprivation, a kind of silly numbness came over us. If we couldn't eat it, we could at least talk about it. And talk was all we did because talk was not *treif*. Then it was Valentine's Day. Valentine's Day in the early grades of public school was mindboggling. It was equated with candy and cards. All the children sent each other Valentine cards and notes. These were all put into a makeshift mail box on the teacher's desk. Two children would then deliver the cards to all the others in the class. (Every year I got two cards — one from the teacher and one that I had addressed to myself.)

The teacher gave out small bags of candy hearts and other candy goodies. *Candy, candy, candy.* There is a special fragrance in a room filled with candy. Everybody tasted, ate, munched, and chewed candy. Only the Creator Himself could have given us the courage not to touch a single piece of candy on Valentine's Day in school.

We didn't know it, but we were already building our own ghettos of the mind.

◆§ The Greek Disconnection

Public schools had names that a child identified with: John Hartranft, Joseph C. Ferguson, John Welch. No numbers, P. S. 16, P. S. 127 would come a generation later. Nor were there Bais Yaakovs or Yeshivos yet. No yellow buses ferrying children around. You walked to your public school, with books tied up with a strap and slung over the shoulder. There was something invitingly jaunty about it.

In school children were taught the basics — not only for reading, writing and 'rithmetic, but the basics of patriotism, public weal and the political system. We learned early on that it was a privilege to be educated for free. It followed, then, that the Library was the next door to open. Teachers and parents advocated the Library. They wanted the children to learn. The children wanted entertainment. The Library had everything, from Plato to *Winnie-the-Pooh* to the Pyramids; from history to novels, sports and the study of the honeybee.

One day, my beloved Uncle Kalman, a *talmid chacham*, came to our house. My school and library books were stacked neatly on the dining room table, the homework area. Idly he looked at some titles: *Marcus Aurelius, Essays.* Plato's *The Republic. Stories of Greek Mythology.* "What are those books about?"

"About Greeks," I answered promptly.

"Greeks? *Hellenisten!*" he thundered. "Does you mother know?"

On the *Shabbos* following my Uncle Kalman's outrage at my "Greek" books, after Mother had read to me the *Parsha* in the *Tzenah Rehna*, she closed the *sefer* and placed one hand over the other, as it rested on her lap. She leaned back in her wooden rocker and asked, "What kind of books do you take from the library?"

"Oh, I like everything. I used to read fairy tales, stories that were not for real, but now I like fiction books that are about things that could be, but are not, really; and biographies, books about people and the times when they lived."

"What were the books about that made Uncle Kalman so upset?"

"I don't know. We're learning Greek history in school so I got some books about Greeks. There's something called Greek Mythology, about nutty things like a horse with wings (Pegasus) and statues of stone that are supposed to be man-gods and lady-gods. Nobody believes that stuff, anyway. Then I got a book on Plato. He was a big man in law and philosophy as they understood it at that time — but I don't really understand all of it. In a way, though, I think he believed in *Hashem* because he said that there was a Higher Being Who created everything and kept it going according to a system that He created."

"Did you get any other books?"

"On the way out, I picked up one of *Marcus Aurelius.* It was on the same shelf. He was called a Stoic. I couldn't figure out what that is. He said he was a man of peace and he was called a Peaceful

Emperor, but he was in a lot of wars anyway. He didn't like Christians so he threw them to the lions. I don't know what Uncle Kalman was excited about."

My mother smiled, "I think you're right. You don't know what the books are about. Maybe they are too old for you. But anyway, did you know that when the Greeks were in *Eretz Yisrael* they were responsible for a lot of young *Yiddishe kinder* (young people) to *schmad* (convert)?

"They introduced ways of living that were against the Torah and lots of *Yidden* followed them. They, the Greeks, became the beginning of the second *churban*. Uncle Kalman is a big *talmid chacham*, he knows a great deal about our history. Maybe he does not want you to be influenced by their writings."

I thought about if for a while and then said, "If you and Pop teach us what's right in *Yiddishkeit*, then we will understand what is wrong, and we will be able to judge for ourselves."

Mother thought for a while. "I think you'll be all right," she said quietly. "But take those books back on Monday. They are too old for you."

✢§ Stand-Off at Valley Forge

One day, one of my brothers announced, "Teacher is taking the class to Valley Forge. I wanna go. I need a dollar for bus fare."

Said another brother, "I was there two years ago. The whole class went into a church. Teacher said that that was where George Washington prayed when the Revolutionary War was not going so good."

"Did you go in?" I asked.

"Almost," he said carefully. "Then I said, 'We're only allowed to go into synagogues, not churches. I'll wait right here by the steps.' "

"What did your teacher say?" Mother asked.

He hesitated a moment. Then, "Nothing. She just said, 'In America there are no ghettos. You're free to go where you want to go.' "

This was heresy. We looked from Simon to Mother and back to Simon. "What's a ghetto, Mom?"

Mother turned from the food counter where she was always busy, drew herself up to her regal 5'2", and said slowly, "People think a ghetto is where Jews had to live when they were not allowed to live in the rest of a city. Many cities in Europe did have ghettos, and your teacher is right; in America there are no ghettos. But your teacher does not really understand a ghetto. It can be a place where a large group of people live together by choice because they don't want to mingle with others, or it can be a ghetto of the mind, whereby a *Yid* can live anywhere and still be his own person."

"So, if in America we don't have to live in a ghetto, doesn't that mean that we are free?" Simon expressed the question as though he were stating a fact that he understood.

Mother looked at us intensely. "We are free, but we are not free," she said quietly. "To remain a *frum Yid*, you have to make for yourself your own ghetto. The ghetto of your mind. Because we live in such a good country, where we are free to live and work where we want to, a *Yid* must remember that he is never free to join everyone else. He is bound by the laws of the Torah and Tradition, and must live by them."

"Then we are not free," Simon said in a kind of anger. "You can't be free and not free."

I had a sense of fear. I think Mother also had a sense of something inexplicable, something I couldn't quite grasp. We exchanged a glance. Then Mother looked squarely at Simon. "You are free to leave this house. Do you want to?" she said softly but firmly. *Why is she saying that?* I thought wildly. *He might!*

Simon replied, "Of course not, why should I?"

"You don't want to because you feel safe here. You are secure. The Torah and its laws are our security. We are free when we live by those laws. If we go away from them, when we join and try to be like the rest of the world, we have no security and we can be pulled into a current of disaster." She spoke in a rich Yiddish. *Where did she get those big words?* I wondered.

"The ghetto of our mind builds a line of defense against the outside world. We can be *with* them, but not *of* them. We can do what they do, but only up to where our laws of *frumkeit* allow. Then we draw a line. We cannot go further with them."

"I don't understand you, Mom," Simon said in a strange kind of anguish. "Suppose I would have walked into that church. What would have happened?" *He walked in,* I guessed fiercely. *He walked in.*

"*Mein kindt* (my child), from the outside, nothing. From the inside, you would have made the first break of your sacredness as a

Jew, your holiness, your dignity, your difference from any other boy on the 'street'."

Simon stared at Mother. His face was tight and his eyes glittered with a hint of tears. "A small cut is nothing," Mother said nonchalantly. "It's easily mended. The ghetto of the mind is a whole system of lines, where we may and may not go, what we may and may not do. And the mind is the window of the *neshama*."

"Mom," Velvel broke in, "if I don't go to Valley Forge, can I have the dollar for myself?"

Everyone laughed. Mom took down the cookie jar and brought out a glass quart of milk. We fell to it hungrily. No more tension. We ate happily.

Years later, I asked Mother if she had ever asked Simon whether he had indeed gone into that church. Mother smiled enigmatically. "Did you?" she asked.

Simon was one of the first to leave Philadelphia and go to a New York yeshiva. The lines in the ghetto of his mind held fast. He was more stringent in his observance than many a young man who had the advantage of an elementary yeshivah *chinuch*, but not the *chinuch* of adversity.

Emmy Stark Zitter

The Out-of-Towners: A Personal Narrative

On a gray and windy autumn day five years ago, my family and I moved from Brooklyn to Rochester, New York. My son stood at the airport clutching his teddy bear, and I envied him his portable security. The things that made me secure — a close-knit family, a vibrant Bais Yaakov education, a wholly frum environment — were not so easily moved. Going out on our own, into a largely non-Jewish milieu — what might we expect? What might we gain? And what, what did we risk losing?

LONG, LONG AGO, in my high school days, my friends and I had only one clear idea about life "out of town." Susie had gone to visit with relatives in a suburb of Cleveland one summer, and she'd returned with the slight twang she has kept to this day and an image of out-of-town life which impressed us all. "On *Shabbos*," she told us repeatedly, "people whom you don't know say '*Gut Shabbos*' and everybody smiles and answers!" We born-and-bred Boro Parkers were delighted.

Several years later my then-*chassan* and I had a long talk concerning his future. He had to choose between a career in the Rabbinate or in law. We chose the latter, largely because we knew that as a pulpit Rabbi he would almost certainly have to move "out of town." Stories of smiling strangers are nice to while away a long Boro Park *Shabbos* afternoon, I thought to myself, but for *us* to live "out of town?" Unthinkable!

Well, "*a mensch tracht und G-tt lacht*," as my father used to say, and after three years of law school my husband received his best job offer from a firm 350 miles away from "town." Rochester, New York? All I knew about it was that it was further from Brooklyn than Woodbourne was, and that it was home to the Mayo Clinic and to mountains of snow. (Actually, I was wrong about the Mayo Clinic, which is in Rochester, Minnesota; unfortunately, though, I was right about the snow.) We found out from cousins who had lived there that Rochester Yiddishkeit consisted of five Orthodox synagogues (but are there any *shuls*? I asked, in a moment of panic), a small *mikveh*, and the Talmudical Institute, a branch of the Chofetz Chaim Yeshivah. For a person who'd grown up in a neighborhood where five *shuls*, a *mikveh*, and a *yeshivah*, all on one *block* was not unheard of, it did not sound promising. Nevertheless, we decided to go — just for one year, of course, two the most, after which we would promptly return home from out-of-town *galus*.

∾ After 500 Inches of Snow — A New Perspective

Five years and some five hundred inches of snow have come and gone since our arrival in Rochester the day after *Simchas Torah* 1980, and well — here we are still. My husband has become president of our synagogue, which celebrated this year its centennial as a *frum shul*, and my whole family is more involved than I ever dreamed possible with the Rochester Orthodox community in its every aspect. We've learned that the difficulties of "out-of-town" life go much further than the lack of a kosher pizza shop or Meal Mart, but we've also seen that in addition to the problems and, yes, occasional perils of living far from an Orthodox community like Brooklyn, there are tremendous possibilities and rewards to our lives here. Life "out of town" has given us a new perspective, both about ourselves and about other Jews.

One million people live in the Greater Rochester area. Twenty thousand of these people are Jews; of the Jews, approximately one thousand consider themselves Orthodox. All these statistics boil down to two important facts about out-of-town life. The first of these is that when one leaves the major Orthodox population centers, one cannot continue to ignore the fact that the overwhelming majority of Jews are not *Shomer Torah U'mitzvos*, that most American Jews today have completely lost their way. The second fact of out-of-town living is that, though it is a vast and sometimes frightening task, an individual can do something to help these lost Jews find their way back out of the emptiness which characterizes the religious lives of most American Jews today. Out of town, every Orthodox Jew counts in the community, in a way unparalleled in my experience in New York.

~§ Challah for Saturday

In Boro Park, of course, we knew such a thing as non-Orthodox Jews existed. We'd heard of Reform Jews, Conservative Jews, unaffiliated Jews, but we pictured these things in our minds in much the same way that a child pictures the trolls and dragons of fairy tales, as things far away and vaguely threatening, but not as something that need concern us day by day. The first week that we arrived in Rochester, however, my views changed with a jolt. On my first day out strolling with my child on strange streets, a young woman had introduced herself as a neighbor and urged me to drop by. The next day, my son had a slight accident — he cut his lip while climbing on a mountain of unopened *seforim* boxes in our living room — and when the bleeding stopped I suddenly felt terribly alone. Swallowing my xenophobic New York fears, I took a chance and called on that neighbor. Imagine my delight when I spotted a *mezuzah* on her door and entered into a kitchen that smelled of freshly baked *challah*! You're *frum*! I called out, in amazed relief. Actually, no, she answered gently, I'm really a Reform Jew, adding with some pride that her home was strictly kosher — and hers was the only family to walk to Temple on *Shabbos*. At that moment, the culture shock set in.

In Rochester, one inevitably comes to meet the non-Orthodox Jews, becoming their acquaintances and sometimes even their good friends. The problem of *kashrus* can be a complicated one, requiring great tact and delicacy, as you decide by whom you will eat and by whom you will not. But the *kashrus* issue can be solved. There are those who simply make it a policy not to eat at anyone's house but their own, and there are those who will eat at some homes and not at others and try to explain this with honesty and politeness. In my experience, at least, nobody has yet taken offense at either policy. No, the real question is a much tougher one to solve. When one become friends with non-Orthodox Jews is there a danger of being influenced by them and their ideas?

What happens to children who know by the time they reach nursery school that there are homes where they may play but where they may not eat and that most of their classmates ride to Temple on Shabbos, if they attend service at all?

✌ Constantly Explaining Myself

With all these questions swirling about you like December snowflakes you begin to examine the *halachos* and *minhagim* which you've always taken for granted and which have caused the differences so starkly underlined between you and the vast majority around you. All your actions take on additional meaning. What we must always fear in out-of-town life is that we will be influenced by those less observant than we are, for without a doubt our need to be like others is a severe temptation; but what we must never fear are the sincere questions we ask ourselves about our way of life, for the answers will surely glow with the logic, truth, and beauty of Torah.

✌ ... To Myself

When you are constantly surrounded by people questioning what you do, you stop taking things for granted, doing things by rote, and start finding for yourself reasons and answers. Moreover, those who ask the questions generally ask them with real interest, and your honest answers and persistent example will often come to influence them. Many of the Jews in Rochester have had no prior experience with *frum* people; in many cases, you are their only model of Torah-true Judaism. One Rochesterian, a concert violinist and ham radio operator, found his interest in Judaism piqued when he picked up a learning group, "Mesivta D'Rakia," on his radio. He became friendly with some of the Orthodox Jews here, and he and his entire family eventually became *ba'alei teshuvah*. Now he proudly wears his *kipah*, with the words "Mesivta D'Rakia" knitted on it, to concerts as well as to *shul*. There is another *ba'al teshuvah* here whose *kipah* attests to his unusual background — I suspect that his is the only dark-green *kipah* in existence with the "U.S. Army Reserve" crocheted on it, and, in fact, the officers of his reserve unit actually allow him to wear it instead of a conventional lieutenant's cap.

Rochester has an unusually high number of *ba'alei teshuvah*, and most of these people returned because of their personal contact with individual members of the Orthodox community. Even in less dramatic cases, there is no telling what the small influence of a single Orthodox Jew here might effect. Perhaps a family will keep their children in the day school for an extra year, perhaps a woman will stop buying pork for her kitchen, perhaps a child will grow up and decide to marry within the faith, because they've met you, a "normal" person who is proud of a Torah heritage and has been willing to explain and to share it.

What About Our Own Children?

But while we rejoice in influencing those who have lost the way, the question of our own children remains. When we first moved out of town, our son Nachum was just a year old, and we felt that a year or two away in the "wilds" at that age could certainly not hurt him. But he is in first grade now, and with my born-in-Rochester daughters entering nursery school, the question of raising children out of town has become urgent. When he was three years old, my son came home from school crying one day; he'd seen Christmas lights on the local fire station and he'd assumed that this meant that Jews could not be firemen, his great ambition at the time. I was naturally upset, seeing my son hurt because he lived among the non-Jews out of town, but I was also quite proud of a little boy who understood better than most adults that we are a people apart. In New York, the lines are not as clearly drawn; the danger in Boro Park is that we might forget that we *are* different, and that even if Christmas garlands no longer hang over Thirteenth Avenue as they did when I was a child, that Brooklyn still is *Galus* and we ought not get too comfortable there.

In Rochester, the Jewish community is large enough and vibrant enough to fill most of our needs, so aside from the annual problem of Christmas pageantry, our children don't run into too many conflicts with the Gentile culture around us — just enough to remind them of who they are. The issue of less religious or non-religious Jews, though, is another question, and one which is constantly with us. Even in our *shul* there are many levels of observance, and the children meet people in school from every stratum of Judaism. While I don't know what this will mean to them when they are older, right now they haven't suffered from this exposure. Kids are remarkable perceptive and can adjust to difficult situations with great finesse. Sure, they ask questions, but if you answer them honestly and in terms they can understand, and if you back up your words with your actions, they will accept what you have to say.

We've tried to keep our children from feeling arrogant or superior about their observance, while at the same time instilling in them a sense of great pride in what they have and gratitude for having it. We've also tried to teach them that while we may hate the sins of the irreligious Jews, we love and pity those Jews themselves. Perhaps the best part about answering our children's questions simply is that it forces us to confront these problems and clarify them for ourselves. This lesson about *Ahavas Yisrael* is one which I, for one, needed badly after a lifetime spent in the rarefied Boro Park environment. And it is a lesson which I think our children are learning, too. Last year my son's kindergarten class went on a "*Succah* hop," visiting the *succos* of the three children in the class whose families had built them. I shall never forget the look on his face as he showed his *succah* to his friends, explaining the significance of the *s'chach*, pointing to the pictures of the *Ushpizin*, sharing with a glow his pride in his Jewish life.

✺§ Every One Counts

My son knows it, his younger sisters are learning it, and I have found it out too: When you live out of town, every action you take, every *mitzvah* you perform, every work of Torah you learn can have a profound effect on the entire community. I attend a *Chumash* study group every Monday night, and many of the women who participate have ventured out to learn until midnight through snowstorms which would have closed down New York for days. Each of us feels a responsibility for the others' study. If one of us didn't come because of the weather perhaps the other might have second thoughts, and the class could be canceled; the loss of three hours of Torah study for ourselves and for the community would be too great.

My husband attends *minyan* more faithfully here than he ever did in New York. Perhaps he will be the tenth for the *minyan*, maybe they'll need him to *lain*, or there might just be somebody there who will benefit from seeing a young man who goes to *shul* and still makes it to work on time.

Where there is a *bris* in the community (as there was, incidentally, on the morning that I am writing this), I will wake up the children two hours before they need to get up so that they too can celebrate the arrival of this new Jew in our community and get a share in the *mitzvah* of *bris milah*. In New York I could have gone to numerous *brissim*, but I rarely bothered.

In Rochester, I will prepare *Shabbos* classes, where in New York I would only occasionally even attend them. My husband will "hear out" *bar mitzvah* boys learning to *lain* their first *parashah*, and he will help them to understand what it is they are saying and not just teach them to perform it. The list could go on and on. In Rochester, there is no hiding behind a group; if something needs to be done, chances are you will be the only one who can do it — and if you don't, the whole community will suffer.

✥ Things I Still Worry About

Sure there are things I still worry about because I live out of town. I spoke to a prominent *Rav*, who has lived most of his life away from the New York area, about my worries concerning my children's *chinuch*. He admitted that the New York schools were generally more demanding in their Jewish curriculum than out-of-town community schools, but he assured me too that parents' involvement in teaching their own children what might be lacking in the classroom not only would fill the gap but would add a new dimension to the closeness of the family. Still, will I be up to such a challenge? And what about my daughters? Right now, the girls' yeshivah high school, opened under the auspices of the Chofetz Chaim Yeshivah two years ago, is experiencing all the problems and joys of a newly founded institution. In nine years it will be a thriving school, like the yeshivah itself, or will I have to consider sending a little thirteen-year-old girl "out of town" — back to New York — to give her the kind of Jewish education my parents insisted on for me? And, though it seems light years away now, what will happen when the children are ready for *shidduchim*? Will there be anybody here for them in Rochester? Will their out-of-town backgrounds help or hinder them if they move back to New York?

I discussed many of these concerns with another transplanted New Yorker, a friend who has two teenage daughters of her own, and I found her answers both stimulating and encouraging. She told me that she often compared her daughter's upbringing with that of the children whom she knew in New York City. In

Rochester, she noted, the parents are much more involved with their children's *chinuch*, not necessarily in formal teaching, but in carefully watching and advising them in matters of friendship, of *middos*, and of a developing sense of responsibility. Her girls know that to the non-*frum* and non-Jewish world around them, their actions are seen as representing our whole way of life. It is, she admitted, sometimes a heavy responsibility for young girls, but her careful nurturing has helped them learn to bear it. Her friends in New York City, she added, had a more *laissez faire* method of educating their children, depending as they do on the school and the general environment to help take care of their children.

So here I am, five years now in Rochester, with some of my early questions answered and new ones coming up all the time. As for the future — who knows? When I see some of the fine young people that Rochester has already produced, my fears are somewhat allayed. If, however, I find in some years that we have to return to a larger Orthodox community for the sake of the children, though — well, so be it. Meanwhile, I'm enjoying my life here, learning a new feeling of responsibility for my fellow Jews, trying to look inside at myself and outwards at others, and growing with a growing Jewish community. Oh, and yes — I *have* learned to smile at strangers on *Shabbos*. And to invite them in for *Kiddush* and a meal as well.

Letters in Response

◆§ Out-Of-Town Expatriates in the Big City

To the Editor:

When I read Mrs. Zitter's recollections of her friend who was impressed by the way strangers wished her *"Gut Shabbos"* ("The Out-of-Towners" — Oct. '85) it brought back memories of my own childhood out of town. A friend of mine once spent *Shabbos* in Orthodox Brooklyn and upon her return she related to us how she had wished people on the street *"Gut Shabbos,"* and often the return *"Gut Shabbos"* was accompanied by a look of, "Do I know you?" This was *our* view of New York.

Mrs. Zitter portrays very vividly the life in a smaller Jewish community, and her comments and views are very inspiring. I have heard many positive reactions to the article — all from New Yorkers. As a born-and-bred out-of-towner, I would like to make a few comments from the opposite vantage point.

As teenagers we were all very glad that we were raised in a smaller community where life was safer and people friendlier. We were certain that we would all marry and remain out of town. For if we could remain *frum* having gone to day schools, so could our children! Today most of those girls who married *Bnei Torah* are settled in the New York area or in Israel.

I don't think that this was just a result of whom each particular girl happened to marry. Most of the girls married out-of-towners, and they decided to settle in an all-*frum* community. As parents, their outlook changed.

In her article, Mrs. Zitter writes that *chinuch* in the home can make up for what the school is lacking. Not only is this true, but it is also ideal for the parent to teach his own child. She does question whether she will be up to the challenge, but I wonder if she realized how enormous that challenge is. When the father is working, and the mother is, if not also working, taking care of an expanding family, can the parent always be assured of having enough time to fill the gap for each child? Moreover, when mothers bore exclusive responsibility for their daughters' Jewish education, the girls did not attend school. Today, when a girl gets home from school at 4:00, will she willingly give up her playtime to continue her studies?

Mrs. Zitter also mentions in many places the idea that the *chinuch* at home can overcome outside influences, and hold the child true to his parents' values. This is often true. As a child grows older, however, he is more open to peer pressure, less willing to be "different." When the whole class goes to a movie, it is hard for a child to stay home. It may be difficult for a child to miss his friends' get-togethers because of the radio music or the *kashrus* problems. Will the parent sometimes be tempted to give in?

We see in the Torah that everything a person experiences, both physically and spiritually, affects him. *Pirkei Avos* relates of the refusal of Rabbi Yosi ben Kisma to accept the equivalent of a vast sum of money to live in a community without Torah (VI:9).

Chinuch from the home is a very strong influence. But so is the influence of one's peers. Can we take such risks with our own children?

Mrs. E. Bloch
Jerusalem, Israel

◆§ Out-Of-Town in Brooklyn

To the Editor:

I read with delight Emmy Stark Zitter's article about the advantages and drawbacks of living out of town. As a fifth generation New Yorker, I have always agonized over this phenomenon. That is why, when we began our married life many years ago, my husband and I decided that our long-term goal — challenge — would be to bring up our children as out-of-towners in the midst of the New York *frum* community. Not only as out-of-towners, but as *baalei teshuvah* as well — i.e., to cherish their *Yiddishkeit* and love each *mitzvah* — not to get drawn into the quicksand of *mitzvas anoshim melumadah* (performance of *mitzvos* by rote, lacking real feeling and sincerity).

With a tremendous amount of *Siyata Dishmaya* (help from Above), many tears and lots of courage and determination, I can say, with trepidation, that we have had much *hatzlachah* — and we pray to *Hashem* for the help we need for many more years to come.

True, the level of learning in our Torah institutions in New York is far superior to that of out-of-town (mostly), but many New York *menahalim* shed real live tears over their seemingly futile efforts to get across certain facets of *chinuch* that produce a real *eved Hashem* (servant of G-d).

And so, when we accompany our daughters to the *chupah* without the help of a professional make-up artist, when *Hashem* gives us such wonderful daughters-in-law and sons-in-law that I am ever humbled with love and appreciation (and I must admit that they are almost all out-of-towners), I say: Thank You *Hashem* — a million times over — and *please* help us survive New York.

Name Withheld by Request

Bat Sheva Menucha

Commuting on the Right Track

HOMEBOUND. The train rolled on like any other train carrying its load of passengers to or from the working world. Its cars were filled with a sea of faces. Some stared into space, others amused themselves by reading the newspaper, while a few engaged in animated conversation. These commuters and their predecessors have been riding this train, and others like it, staring into space or reading the newspapers, for years. For the moment, they were people trapped in a capsule of emptiness. Once off the train, the setting would change, but the pursuits would be equally trivial. . .in front of their T.V.'s, reading frivolous stories, and playing pointless games. I wanted to disengage myself from this speeding trap, if only possible.

Suddenly I was struck by the sight of a young man boarding the train. He hurriedly found himself a little space in the crowd. Hanging onto a commuter's strap with one hand, he deftly held the pages of his *Gemara* open with the other. Soon he was deeply engrossed in his learning. His knitted brow and grin of satisfaction told it all — joy in what he was doing, with complete oblivion to his surroundings. I studied him and thought: "Why not me?" I, too, would try to be indifferent to those who might ridicule me when I was doing what I knew to be right.

Several mornings later, I was on the train, with a new project of my own: saying my daily chapters of *Tehillim*. Much as I tried,

I could not ignore the gaze of the man sitting beside me. His sidelong glances at my *Tehillim* were making me squirm. "Forget him, and continue with your *Tehillim*," I told myself. "No reason to be ashamed for doing what's right. People think you're doing something unusual? So what! It's not your job to impress these people. They're not authorities on what's important in life. Chances are you'll never see them again, anyway. It's your own approval you need, not some stranger's."

Having put my perspectives in order, I continued to squirm. I just couldn't help but be aware of the stare. My conscience made another bold attempt: "What better thing could you be doing than reciting *Tehillim?* So the man watching you sees you reading from a small book — not too unusual... well, perhaps a bit unusual, but you're entitled to pray." No go.

Finally, I closed the *sefer* in defeat, with more than a tinge of guilt. Immediately, my neighbor asked me, "Excuse me, was that *Tehillim* that you were reading?"

I answered with ill-contained surprise, "Yes, it was! How did you know?"

"I am originally from Israel," he replied. "It's been so many years since I've seen a *Tehillim*. I remember studying it in school. It was very beautiful, very sweet and very strong," he said wistfully. "It's nice to see someone saying *Tehillim*. I really should get back to it myself...."

Bat Sheva Menucha

The Call Unanswered

AN AIR OF PEACE prevailed in our home. All thoughts of the week's drama were forgotten as we focused on the *zemiros* of *Shabbos*. We felt uplifted, as my father spoke of the weekly *sedrah*; uplifted to a special world to which only the chosen few may enter.

Suddenly, the shrill ringing telephone took us by surprise. No one spoke as the phone continued to ring for quite some time. Finally it stopped, only to begin again a moment later. All eyes turned to my father who was clearly determined to remain calm. "We will not interrupt our *Shabbos* meal! One may not worry on *Shabbos*. I'm sure the phone's ringing is just a test for us ..."

The meal resumed, and though it ended a bit more quickly than usual, we tried to enjoy each moment. After we finished *bentching* we all began to walk towards the hospital, about a mile away, where my grandmother was under care. Even as we walked my father spoke calmly, not discussing any fears.

We arrived at the hospital and were very pleased to find my grandmother sleeping peacefully. "You see, it was the *Yetzer Hara* (temptation) calling, not the hospital!" We all sighed with relief.

As we were about to leave the hospital we met one of the nurses. It pained us to see her working on *Shabbos*, especially since we knew that she had been brought up in an Orthodox home. "What brings you here at this time of night?" she inquired. We explained to her how the phone had been ringing and we didn't wish to disturb our *Shabbos*, but we walked over to see if our grandmother was all right.

The nurse had a faraway look in her eyes as she seemed to be recalling a *Shabbos* meal. Suddenly her face tightened and she seemed to be justifying her position as she said, "When I was young I recall the phone ringing on *Shabbos*. My parents didn't want to answer it, but they were so curious to know who was calling that they asked me to answer the phone. Of course, it was always a wrong number."

She turned and walked back to her world of work and we returned to our world of *Shabbos*.

I come not to condemn or even to judge. I thank *Hashem* for giving us the greatest gifts in life. I cry for those who don't know and for those who come to choose not to know. I pray that parents may be able to convey true sincerity in Torah practice, so that their children will never rebel, but will follow with love.

Faygie Borchardt

Of Peace. And Pieces

PEACE. POETS EXTOL it, soldiers fight for it, painters portray it in oils, sculptors in marble. And our people pray for it every day.

People dream of peace ... we yearn for it ... and its elusive quality makes it more precious than time ... disappearing rainbow to pursue on a gray morning.

The other day, I heard a woman talking. A child, really. She was a captive child, a prisoner of history; an unfortunate who walks darkly with a rosy veil on her face.

"Why do they care about details?" she wanted to know. "Why can't they tolerate differences? One commandment less, one ritual omitted .... There are so many ways to be part of a people. Live and let live. Let there be peace. The traditional Jews have no monopoly on observance. Why the fire? Why the outrage? Let them be silent — and then there'll be peace."

I approached the woman and told her, "Our fight is not with you. We wish to be at peace with all of you, we're members of the same family. But can we be in harmony with your ideas — with bits of broken pottery? Torah is not a plaything, raw clay to sculpt into what-you-will. You ask, 'Why the fire? Why the outrage?' If you had an exquisite china vase in your home and I smashed it, wouldn't you protest? If I harassed your family, would you ignore me? When someone — completely unintentionally — tampers with our most sacred treasures, it's impossible to conceal our shudder.

"We cry out — not against people, but against the fragments of china unwittingly shattered. What *you* hear from the distance as 'War!' is really a cry of, 'Danger, Careful — keep away!' "

∽§ Why Do I Struggle?

If peace is so good, why do I get involved in a struggle? Impulse versus knowledge; comfort versus fulfillment; apathy versus compassion. Wild creature caged within me — fighting to overpower me — struggle-conflict-war. And regarding this inner struggle, G-d said, "And it is *very* good." (See *Ramban, Bereishis* 1:31) " 'Very good' — this is the evil inclination."

But what of peace, which we dream of and pray for? I don't want a battlefield! I want a lovely garden. I don't want to challenge, and overcome mighty forces. I want to pluck succulent peaches from dark-green foliage and drink from gentle streams.

If peace is good and desirable, G-d must want it for us. What is it? Peace is *shalom* — related to *shaleim* — complete, whole. When am I at peace? Not when I attempt to still the raging forces, but when I accept their presence and walk on, beyond them, unafraid. Not when I walk tranquilly on broken shard: I'll only cut myself if I ignore its hazards.

Peace is when I help to bandage cuts so they can heal; when I stitch together the raw pieces within me and help mend the fragments without — to bring about שלמות and שלום, *shleimus* and *shalom*.

Peace is achieved when we are with our Creator, when there is harmony between heaven and earth, and between people. When I peacefully look away from my friend in trouble — that is war. When I struggle against joining a gossip session — that is peace. When I see brazenness replace respect, and I peacefully go along — that is war. When I fight my laziness, my anger, my apathy — that can only bring me greater peace.

How can I know? What wisdom instructs me when to protest, and when to be still... when to break, and when to build?

There's only one way to know.

"*Shviti*... Sit in the House of Hashem all my days to see the sweetness of G-d...." With that awareness from that perspective, I can come closer to knowing.

Of Peace. And Pieces. / 387

Aharon Amir

"I Know"

Aharon Amir is an anti-religious writer for the Israeli daily *Yediot Acharonot*. He reported the following conversation between himself and his small daughter, following the Six Day War.

"G-d is looking after us."
"G-d?"
"Yes."
I was utterly astonished. I thought for a moment and then asked another question.
"Who told you? Nadav?"
Nadav is my older son; he's nine and in grade three.
"Yes," the child answered.
I cross-examined my son and told him of my conversation with his baby-sister, and the triumphant retort that she had attributed to his wisdom.
"You told her that G-d is looking after us?"
"Yes," he answered.
"And who told you — the teacher?"
"No. No one."
"Then who told you?"
"No one. Just myself."
"How do you know?"
"I know."

~§How to Be a Jewish Mother

To the Rabbi's Wife

Cholent — Food for Thought

The Credit is Yours

A Prayer

The Oheiv Yisrael — A Profile

Bracha Druss Goetz

To the Rabbi's Wife

Just what did you do?
I bet you never knew.
How did you do more
Than anyone before?

Well, we walked for hours on that cloudy day,
You let me spill out thoughts — I could never say.
Winding on and on through all the narrow streets.
Yerushalayim's hills carried our feet.

A cynic scared to feel
Can't believe G-d is real.
I'm fine. I'm A.O.K.
Then nervous laughter gave me away.

I've seen enough psychologists — but oh, they never heard.
And with all my T.M. chanting — I said just one word.
But you were listening to me so I began to talk.
I first used my real voice on that long, long, walk.

Just what did you do?
It wasn't what you said.
You did not tell me.
You let me tell myself instead.

Brought up to the surface, my doubts didn't seem so black.
After I had let them out — I didn't ever want them back.

You saw me start to trust, you saw me lift my veil.
This frozen heart melts more than a fairytale's.
I never thanked you all these years
But now I've got the chance.
You took the time to let me think
And that's made all the difference.

You really listened — that's what's hard.
You didn't let me just go by.
You held the sky, I spread my wings.
Cocoon to butterfly.

Anna Gotlieb

Cholent — Food for Thought

IT WAS A DREARY Friday morning in winter.
The phone rang.
I answered.
"How do you make cholent?" she wanted to know.
And the question brought tears to my eyes.
"Mazel Tov," I responded and proceeded to give her the recipe, both of us aware, of course, that the precise measurement of beans had little to do with the dish. It was what would lie beneath the food that counted.

You see, this, her first cholent, would symbolize her decision to embrace the *Shomer Shabbos* world. With this pot of beans, she would say to herself she would no longer light a fire on *Shabbos* — that she needed a recipe for a meal that would cook all night because she had taken this significant step...

And she wanted to let me know.

Just as I had wanted to let someone else know when I was ready for a pot of cholent. Back then, some four years ago, in that time before the classes and the courses, before the conversations, the study and the practice, back when I leaned heavily on someone else, I, too, called for recipes. And there was someone who answered. There was a woman who understood more than my surface questions, an individual who led me gently through the maze of rituals who gave me confidence. There was one woman in particular who introduced me to *blechs* and *benchers*, to the concept of *Shabbos*. And it was she who gave me my first taste of cholent.

So... I cried when I received the call. I cried with joy at the evidence of continuity — at a heritage that dates back 3,000 years. I smiled as I gave her my recipe and listened while she thanked me profusely, just as I had thanked someone else four years ago.

Then I heard her ask how she could repay me for the help she thought I'd given — just as I'd wanted to repay another. And I answered with the answer that was given to me. I told her that her call was my reward. She said she did not understand.

"You will," I promised, "some day soon, when, on a dreary winter morning, your phone rings with someone wanting to know your recipe for cholent."

F.H.

The Credit Is Yours

You stare at me
I look different,
I feel different,
I am different.

I used to be *frum*
I used to care
I was more serious
But now no more.

Remember when I was alone
With no one to confide in
When I wished for a friendly shake,
But none came my way?

I tried and attempted
To sit near you at lunch
I even offered you goodies
But you refused.

I invited you, cordially
To spend an afternoon together.
I wanted to share a word with you,
But you looked at me with disdain.

I felt out of place
In the environment I was in,
So I chose one which seemed better...

And then, I thought I liked it.

So now you understand
My emotions then
And why I followed
The way I chose.

Remember when I was alone,
When you looked at me with disdain?
You could have changed my mind —
Well ... you certainly did.
The credit is yours.

Devorah Gershon

A Prayer

Chessed is a sacrifice,
it is an offering
which opens the prison
of the lonely self.
It is the stretching forth
of a helping hand,
the building of bridges
between two souls.
It is the beginning
of love,
a human expression
of the Divine.

But to love
is to be vulnerable
and susceptible to pain.
And *chessed*
is often hard
to sustain.

Give me strength,
Source of All strengths,

to be vulnerable.
Give me strength
to reach out,
to sacrifice,
to build bridges of *chessed* and love,
to march in the footsteps
of the Divine.

Give me strength,
lest I remain alone,
an imperfect creature,
forever apart,
locked behind the doors
of its lonely self.

Rabbi Zelig Pliskin

The Oheiv Yisrael: A Profile

Loving one's fellow Jew is a central Torah command, having its own body of halachic guidelines and ethical ramifications.

⋘ "Ahavas Yisrael" and the Mandate to Rebuke

FROM MY PLACE at the back of the line in a Jerusalem hardware store, I could clearly hear the fellow boomingly extol the virtues of *Ahavas Yisrael* while denouncing those who admonish through shouting. Another bystander asked him why he was so emphatic. He told the following: "For many years I was far from being an observant Jew. I once inadvertently attempted to drive my car through Me'ah She'arim on *Shabbos* and found myself stopped by a roadblock. This infuriated me and I started a weekly practice of driving through religious neighborhoods to antagonize the people there. One *Shabbos*, as I was attempting to move aside a roadblock, a passerby stopped me and with a smile asked me for my name and address. After *Shabbos*, I was startled when this new acquaintance paid a visit to my home. For two full hours I heard about the wonderful benefits of Torah observance, told to me with obvious consideration and love. Those hours were a high point in my life and really changed me."

After the story-teller left the store, the proprietor vouched for the veracity of the tale, adding that before he became observant, this man had earned his living delivering non-kosher meat. Now his sons have *payos* and are learning in one of the foremost yeshivos in *Eretz Yisrael*.

The fellow who changed the defiant driver's life was a true *Oheiv Yisrael* — a person who does not avert his gaze when confronted with wrongdoing. He sees a blaze that threatens to devour his fellow man, and is impelled to act out of compassion. This gives rise to the only meaningful rebuke — one that stems from a heart overflowing with kindness. And the person on the receiving end can sense the source of the words. It has been said that a pat on the back, though only a few vertebrae removed from a kick in the pants, is miles ahead in results.

This incident and its implications inspired me to search out the sources of *Ahavas Yisrael*, its imperatives and its limitations; in short, to sketch a profile of the *Oheiv Yisrael*.

⇜ The Torah's Source

"Love your neighbor as yourself" — the Torah source for *Ahavas Yisrael* — is but one of 613 *mitzvos*, but as Hillel said, it is an all-inclusive ruling. It must thus be a factor in all other *mitzvos*. Love begins with consideration of others, and the main criterion for such consideration is one's own feelings: Hillel advised, "What is hateful to you do not do to others." The Rambam exhorted us to prevent loss to others in the same way that we would safeguard our own dignity and property. And as the Chofetz Chaim said, "If we indeed did love others as much as ourselves, we would never gossip about their misdeeds or slander them. And just as we each draw upon an endless supply of rationalizations to excuse our own misconduct, so should we utilize this stockpile for the vindication of others."

⇜ Emunah as a Base for Love

Ahavas Yisrael devoid of *emunah* is doomed to failure — for without belief, on what should love be based? Man's stature in relationship to the universe is so puny as to be non-existent. After all, what is man, but one of several billion inhabitants on a planet, which is but one speck of matter circling another speck in a vastness of space that extends out beyond for billions of light-years (a light-year is approximately six trillion miles) — leaving the individual lost in an immensity that is beyond all imagination.

From the same secular viewpoint, one man is merely a bundle of bones, nerves, muscles, and blood that happens to function in an orderly fashion. Does this mass deserve more attention and sympathies than similar commodities in the form of a cow or horse?

But taking into account that man is fashioned in the image of the Almighty, he is transformed from an inconsequential being into one that is without parallel. Although small in stature, he is the end-purpose of all creation, and as such is awe-inspiring. Add to this the awareness that all *neshamos* share the same source, as part of Hashem Himself — and one can advance from awe to love.

◆§ Of People and Stones

The special status of man is expanded upon in a well-known Midrash quoted by Rashi in *Shemos:* "The stones of the *mizbe'ach* are inanimate objects lacking feeling. Yet, the approach to the *mizbe'ach* was so constructed as to avoid mounting it in any way that would imply disrespect. How much more considerate must we be in our dealings with a human being who is created in the image of our Maker and experiences suffering when he is abused..." (The practical implications are obvious to anyone who has witnessed people jostling to get on a crowded bus to the *Kosel*.)

This argument speaks volumes on the Torah attitude towards man.

◆§ Another Prerequisite: Trust

In addition to a strong feeling of *emunah* (faith), true *Ahavas Yisrael* also requires *bitachon* (trust). This attitude comes into play when one feels that others have unjustly taken advantage of him. Reacting with *bitachon*, one is fully aware that others cannot successfully cause him harm unless by Divine decree. Then, even when he takes proper action, he will be free from animosity and rancor, for he understands that he suffers only because G-d has willed it.

But *emunah* and *bitachon* as requisites for *Ahavas Yisrael* go beyond this. When beset by misfortunes, even slight ones, one is easily vexed and irritable. To be able to deal decently with others at all times calls for an imperturbability that is rare.

Avraham *Avinu* exemplified this trait when, after Sarah's passing, he engaged in a prolonged transaction to acquire a fitting burial site for her. The task called for delicate diplomacy, and Avraham was able to handle it in spite of the fresh loss of his irreplaceable partner, only because he had the equanimity supplied by *emunah* and *betachon*.

◆§ The Tools of Love: Speech

The saintly Chofetz Chaim זצ״ל was celebrated for his caution in speech. Yet, he exhorted us in *Chovos Hashmirah* to be as expansive in speech as necessary to cheer up a fellow in despair. For a cheerful word has healing powers for both those in mental and physical distress. Moreover, Reb Yochanan ben Zakai, who was singular in his restraint from idle chatter, was always first to greet whomever he would meet. To emulate him with a free and easy "Good Morning" takes minimal effort, but can have boundless results. The six Divine blessings bestowed upon whoever gives charity are increased when one adds a kind word to the act.

Our everyday contacts with numerous people are all fruitful opportunities for word-charity, for in this respect who is not needy?

◆§ The Best of All Tongues

Aside from avoiding invectives and insults, an *Oheiv Yisrael* must exercise extreme discretion in his choice of words.

The Midrash relates that *Rabbeinu Hakadosh* served tongue at a feast he hosted for his disciples. He noticed how each one selected a tender slice, leaving over the tougher pieces. He used the opportunity to point out to his disciples that one must always choose a soft word, leaving over those that are harsh.

Horav Yoseif Dov Soloveitchik of Brisk זצ״ל added that all the tongues that were served were surely palatable; nonetheless, as long as there was a variation in tenderness, one favors the more delectable one. This is the Midrash's point: Not only are outright derogatory words proscribed, but as long as there is a discernible difference between two expressions, one must select the most pleasant one.

People are sensitive, and comments meant as light banter can cause untold anguish. An *Oheiv Yisrael* realizes the consequences of every statement and is continuously on guard.

◆§ Chessed — For Whose Sake?

The Chazon Ish זצ״ל wrote about a truly pious man who one Friday joyfully announced to his family that they would entertain a guest that *Shabbos*. The entire family treasured the opportunity to be helpful to a fellow Jew. After the *tefillos*, through some misunderstanding the stranger went to another home. The would-be host came home with his usual *Shabbos* radiance, but without a guest. He noticed that his family was deeply disappointed, so he explained: "Our concern must be that all should have a meal, but it shouldn't matter if we are the Almighty's agent or if someone else is."

"Similarly," the Chazon Ish said, "a true *Oheiv Yisrael* performs acts of kindness for the benefit of others, not simply to indulge in his personal pleasure of doing charitable deeds."

◆§ Love, Tolerance . . .

Fusses, feuds and fights — all are breaches of peace, and all are anathema to an *Oheiv Yisrael*. These usually begin as differences of opinion and a lack of tolerance for the other fellow's views. Reb Mendel Kotzker offered guidance in avoiding this trap with his interpretation of Talmudic adage: "Just as two people can never have identical facial features, so do they never have a similar faculty of thought." — No one is ever disturbed that others do not have an exact replica of his facial features. In fact, variety and individuality have a host of benefits. In the same vein, we should accept that no two people will ever concur on all matters.

◆§ . . . And the Limits of Tolerance

Not everything must be tolerated. Harav Elchonan Wasserman זצ"ל wrote that the Torah only uses "*kano*" (vindictive) as a descriptive term for the Almighty in connection with idolatry. Since the Torah considers atheism a graver offense than idol worship, one can assume that in both cases the Torah would expect us not to show tolerance.

To be sure, there are those who preach: "We must be tolerant of everybody." As an old saw has it, professional tolerance-teachers harbor foxes in their bosoms that devour anyone who disagrees with them. Tolerance without the foundation of a Divine command is an edifice that will topple at the first entry of personal interests, no matter how petty. And by the same token, those who tolerate atheism find it a simple task because they do not equate an attack on Torah with a threat to their person.

But *kana'us* (vindictiveness) is a highly potent toxin that must be applied with maximum care. Properly used, it can eradicate cancerous growths and elevate the dispenser. — Pinchas serves as the prime example of the *kanai* in action (*Bamidbar* 25). But not everyone is competent to perform such an operation.

Harav Chaim Shmulevitz זצ״ל, the Mirrer Rosh HaYeshiva, constantly stressed that the Torah traces Pinchas's lineage to Aharon Hacohen, the prototype *Oheiv Yisrael*, to impress upon us that only one who is a true *Oheiv Yisrael* is fit to be a *kanai*. Only he can be entirely free from any personal motivation.

← A Tale of Two Eyes

Another facet of *Ahavas Yisrael*, the Chazon Ish wrote, involves control over a seeming paradox: One must be hypersensitive to one's own minor foibles, but overlook even the most obvious faults of others.

As Reb Yisrael Salanter זצ״ל put it, we were given two eyes: one for microscopic introspection ... the other myopic, for viewing others. Only, too often we switch their functions.

When mastered, this ability is passed on to others, as the following anecdote illustrates: Toward the end of W.W.II, Simon Wiesenthal, the renowned tracer of Nazi criminals, was in a concentration camp. A new arrival had smuggled in a *Siddur* and Wiesenthal admired his courage, for by risking discovery he was risking death. His feelings soon changed when he found that the courageous smuggler was bartering fifteen minutes' rental of the *Siddur* in exchange for one fourth of a day's meager rations. The inmates were emaciated, but willingly made the exchange. In time, the *Siddur*-owner died before anyone else ... for the huge quantities of soup he ingested were too much for his shriveled system.

After the war, Harav Eliezer Silver זצ״ל visited the D.P. camps on behalf of the Vaad Hatzala. He arranged *tefillos* and addressed words of encouragement to the survivors. After noticing that Wiesenthal did not come to the *shul*, Harav Silver decided to visit him.

As Mr. Wiesenthal recorded it:

> That night Rabbi Silver came to see me. He was a small man who wore an American army uniform without insignia. He had a small white beard, and his bright eyes shone with great kindness. He must have been at least 75, but his mind was sharp and his voice was youthful.

He put his hand on my shoulder. "So they tell me you are angry with G-d," he said in Yiddish and he smiled at me.

I said, "Not with G-d, but with one of his servants," and told him what had happened.

He kept smiling, "And that's all you have to tell me?"

"Isn't that enough, Rabbi?" I asked.

"*Du dummer* (you silly man)," he said. "So you look only at the bad man who took something from the good one. Why don't you look instead at the good man who gave something to the bad one?" He touched me with his outstretched palm and left.

I went to the services the next day. Ever since I have tried to remember that there are two sides to every problem.

from THE MURDERERS AMONG US, S. Wiesenthal, Heinemann Pub., London 1967, pp. 249-250.

Reb Eliezer Silver did not focus his attention on the proper act. He only took note of the valor of starving people who gave away vital food for the opportunity to feel closer to the Almighty.

◆§ The Portrait Is Complete

Our portrait of an *Oheiv Yisrael* is now complete. He possesses a cheerful disposition fortified by *emunah* and *betachon*, and his company is always a pleasure. Never heard to utter an unkind word, his friendly greetings are a source of encouragement to all. He goes out of his way to save others from any possible loss, financial or emotional, and praise for others is always on his lips. He finds joy in doing a *chessed*, and enhancing his beneficiary's welfare is his only motivation. He is tolerant of the views of others, but within the limits specified by the Torah. While he never seeks out the faults of others, he will not shirk his duty to rectify that which can be rectified.

Recall: We lost the second *Bais Hamikdash* because of *sinas chinam* — groundless hatred. By strengthening *Ahavas Yisrael*, we can be worthy of redemption and the rebuilding of the *Bais Hamikdash* in our days.

~§Home Sweet Home

Women at the Western Wall
Post-Blizzard Musings
The Road Home
Teshuvah
Three Cheers for Turbulence
The Traveler and the Princess

Arleen Naomi Habshush

Women at the Western Wall

Kotel stones of white or gray or mottled,
Stones of cool strength — smooth stones, rough stones, scarred stones...
Some adorned with glistening granite or wild greenery.
Wild greenery adorned with dove at rest...
Deep cracks overflowing with paper scraps.
Paper scraps overflowing with written hopes...
Scraps filling small round punctures, scratches, miniature crevices;
Ready to receive hot tears slowly rolling down and slipping inside.

Tears of gladness, of sadness, of hope, of despair,
Accompanied by quiet sobs, distraught wailing, or silence...
Tears that seep out, trickle steadily, or gush forth.
Tears of the blossoming young, the wise old, and the worn older than old.
Tears that belong to those created in the image of G-d,
    "According to His will."
Tears of women

...Early morning, a new day in Jerusalem,
A day of crisp, cool air and a clean, blue sky
To which these women of the Wall have awakened
and in which they
Have walked to the Kotel where they now stand in supplication.

The woman with a tight black kerchief and black stockings,
Crying for generations long gone, and the Messiah yet to come.
A tourist with camera, whose smiling portrait turns to
grief, as she suddenly mourns the years she did not
know where or to whom to cry.

The woman with the plaid jumper and the huge tummy,
asking for the safe arrival, in a good hour, of the
miracle within her.
The tears of the woman whose body produces no new life,
seep far into the Wall to beg for the Almighty's attention.
Hand in stone, one on prayer book, the woman in sweater and
skirt, recites each word with care, as tears rebound off letters
and onto stone.
Did not G-d Himself ordain a life partner for each soul, and the
right time for each joyful union?
Yet, no tears flow faster than those of the bereaved mother, who
will never be completely consoled over the loss of a
handsome young man.
Obviously quite ill, one woman pleads here for the success of care,
to be given there, in the white sterile rooms and corridors of a
hospital.
Other women give no sign of what is hidden in their
hearts; for they wear masks, much the same as some
Kotel stones — masks of green.

Heads pressed to the Wall of varying stones, all seek comfort,
Miraculously, exchanged for tears...lots of tears...a flood of
tears...
Tears that glide to the cracks and crevices and holes of the stones.
Tears that mingle with those of other women who have
stood here before,
And with those of other women who will stand here later
in the day...
Tears that will mingle with my tears,
For I, too, have come here to cry.
I have cried often, in other places, for so many reasons.
But, this is the place, the only place, where the Almighty will dry
my eyes
with a soft cloth woven of mercy and understanding and
consolation.

Faygie Borchardt

Post-Blizzard Musings

SNOWED IN. Awesome words. It had been predicted. And yet it caught us by surprise.

It's funny how living in a world of remote control, skyscrapers and silicon chips can make us feel at once threatened and protected. Threatened — by the seeming obscurity of the individual. But also powerful, somehow. As though man is en route to conquering the elements; heart monitors, satellites, mechanical spies...and, of course, weather predictors. Accu, compu, and so on.

A fragile, delicate, old-fashioned snowflake. Threatening? Ha.

Well, being able to foresee it can't make us control it. It comes, seemingly, with a will of its own. And then its joined by its hundreds-thousands-millions of wispy fairy cousins. A loyal lot they are, uniting in enviable togetherness on the strong, tough streets of the unconquerable city.

We are conquered. We are vulnerable. We cannot press a button and trap the workings of the sky. But it can trap us. We are vulnerable. The blizzard reminds us.

How sad this all sounds. But is it really? Is happiness a result of conquering one's limits, breaking the barriers that quietly restrain us?

I think not. Hacking away at the Alps or Everglades with a man-made chisel would be mildly frustrating, I'd imagine. Isn't wisdom the knowledge of which barriers must be crossed, and which we must work within?

So many cry, *if only the natural wouldn't exist; if only I were richer...handsomer...wittier.... If only I had different parents...neighbors...talents. If only it weren't snowing, I'd be free to pursue my dreams.*

We can spend our lives hacking at mountains, and weeping when all that breaks is the chisel. Or we can realize that reality is not what we have, that we are as we do.

There is beauty and joy in some kinds of passivity. How hard the destroyer within us works, to conceal that concept. Who knows more contentment — the woman who boldly states that no man or child will chain her — or the mother who has climbed her mountain? Who will know better the exhilaration of gloriously, breathlessly, reaching the top, to be rewarded with the rays of a smile, a gurgle, a laugh, from the miracle beside her?

There is beauty and joy in assertive passivity. It's a paradox that demands great strength, and trust in the Creator of our boundaries. Who knows more joy — the man who fears and rejects Torah study, because of the challenge it presents, the toil it involves, and the sacrifice it demands? Or the student who pursues it, through varying moods of wariness and confidence, struggle and peace — to achieve that inner peak only a *Ben Torah* can know?

There is beauty and joy in active passivity. The snow is magnificent. It is serene. And it implores us — *be serene with me. Find joy in my solitude. Stop your rushing and hurrying. Walk through the high white paths and delight in your barriers.*

He who feels he must always be in control can never be happy.

Prepare for the snow — or any natural eventuality. We are exhorted to prepare for heat, cold, adversity, and the day of death. But we can only succeed if we accept these entities and attempt to work *within* them, rather than think that we can batter them down.

When G-d displays the manifold manifestations of his great power, respect them. Rejoice in that you are a part of His Plan. You are safely in the hands of the One Who knows what is best for us all.

The word is not yours to control. Embrace limitation and you will find freedom.

Leah Kohn

The Road Home: A Woman's Perspective

THE LIFE OF A *baal teshuva* — a "returnee" to Judaism — is as a rule filled with beauty and fulfillment, but this richly rewarding stage is only arrived at after overcoming the many barriers erected by his or her past. While *The Jewish Observer* on several occasions has examined the struggles of men who are *baalei teshuva* (JO, April '86, for instance), I would like to focus on some of the special hardships encountered by women returning to Judaism. We have much to learn from their struggles, and much to offer in helping them succeed.

৽ Fighting the Negative Image

The greatest hurdle in kindling interest in *Yiddishkeit* in a non-religious woman is overcoming the surprisingly unappealing image of the Jewish woman in the secular world. For example, at an Ivy League university where I was invited to speak on the topic of "Women in Judaism," I began the session with: "Imagine a Jewish woman. What is the first picture that comes to mind?" [If the same question would be put to a group born to religious families, the answers would likely be, "A warm, loving individual who guides her children, implanting the love of Torah within their hearts, and providing a happy atmosphere for them to thrive in."]

The replies that I received from the college students were dismaying: "An old decrepit grandmother."

"An apron-clad woman who spends most of here day toiling over a hot stove."

"A woman hidden behind a thick curtain."

"Somebody that men thank G-d every day for not being!"

Many women completely rule out becoming involved with Judaism because they personally perceive the woman's role as demanding. There is a hope, however, that through meeting a religious woman, and seeing her actions and words as negating the ugly stereotype, an unaffiliated girl might consider re-evaluating Judaism as a personal choice. Personal contact with religious women, then, is a crucial first step in winning an uncommitted Jewish woman to Torah. This is something we can all offer on an individual basis.

✥ The "Shul" Hang-up

The very nature of Orthodox Judaism can raise further difficulties for the struggling *baalas teshuva*. Those who stem from Conservative or Reform backgrounds associate their main Jewish activities with the synagogue. Even their social lives revolve around mixers and socials sponsored by the synagogue. So they are shocked to discover that the synagogue is not the central point in the life of an Orthodox woman. Furthermore, she is not counted toward a *minyan*, does not receive an *aliya*, and certainly harbors no aspirations to become a rabbi. Even the Bat Mitzva, as a feminine version of the Bar Mitzva, is non-existent in the Torah world. With time, through lectures and firsthand exposure, it become clear to her the lack of focus on "Synagogue Judaism" in Orthodoxy is because its primary emphasis is on the home as the setting of Jewish life and a prime medium for transmission of Torah values. Taking this into account, the woman's involvement in the home puts her into a more crucial position than one might ordinarily assume,and relegates synagogue to a secondary place in her religious life.

Many women are still particularly disappointed to learn that the obligation for Torah-study as such devolves exclusively upon men, and that women do not learn Talmud. This disenchantment was particularly evident when several young women had returned from their first *Simchas Torah* in an Orthodox *shul* in Monsey, completely up-in-arms. "I don't know what I'm doing here!" cried one of them.

"Back where I come from, I'm as good as any man. I have a prestigious job and earn more than many of my male friends. Out there I really count!" asserted the second.

"We actually sat in that synagogue, and just watched the men dancing and singing, celebrating the joy of completing the Torah, as if it were some kind of spectator sport. I don't know what I'm doing here in Monsey!"

"Think for a moment," I countered. "Why do you remain here in our school? Why haven't you left?"

After some thought, one of the girls responded, "I guess it's because we see that it works. Intellectually I still can't accept it, but it seems that this system of yours works for the women. Judaism is quite new to me, but I have spent several *Shabbosos* with religious families and I am really impressed!"

Many of us who grew up Orthodox cannot relate to the changes that returning women must undergo; nor can we properly verbalize our own satisfaction with our place in Jewish society. This inability to communicate can be a source of frustration to many newcomers to *Yiddishkeit*. We *can*, however, be instrumental in encouraging their efforts by serving as "models of fulfillment," as mentioned. Once the struggling neophyte has encountered several such women, she will be more emotionally attuned to accepting the intellectual explanations that she receives from rabbis and teachers.

ಅಕ್ಕ Obstacles, Real and Imagined

Even after a woman has overcome the negative images described at the outset, after she has been educated in Torah life and values, and she is basically willing to accept her truly significant role within Judaism, she is still bound to hit upon a number of obstacles.

Many young women exploring Judaism are successful and accomplished individuals, whose careers play an important role in their lives. Before long, they discover how difficult it is to combine the roles of career woman and co-head of a household.

Technically, the duties of a housewife are numerous and never ending, while the successful professional woman's schedule is also grueling and demanding. It is virtually impossible for one woman to give both jobs her "all." The family must not suffer due to the demands of a career.... And yet, it would be a great sacrifice on the part of a woman to abort a successful career in favor of her family.

While there *are* individual women who work full-time and still maintain a household, this is not physically or emotionally feasible for most of us. There is some comfort in that even those "super Moms" who can handle a double workload certainly would choose their home life if a decision between the two had to be made.

Persisting Image Problems

Considerations of competing allegiances aside, problems of negative image persist even after a woman has chosen to lead a religious life. Many women of secular background regard someone who is not pursuing a career as "merely a housewife" — an unskilled drudge, with no interests or activities aside from scrubbing floors and changing diapers. Unfortunately, this negative view has to some extent invaded the established Jewish world, as well.

In my teaching and counseling, I ask the women to conjure up a vision of a prominent psychiatrist: After many years of schooling and sundry degrees earned, the doctor of psychiatry launches his/her illustrious career, treating hundreds of individuals suffering from various mental illnesses. Very impressive.

Now picture a Jewish mother: She provides support, love, encouragement and advice to her children. She becomes quite an expert in child development in terms of physical, intellectual, emotional, and social growth. Her career spans several decades, and her clients admire her and emulate her as they grow and mature. When she succeeds, she has created normal, productive, G-d-fearing human beings — no mean accomplishment in today's troubled, confused world.

Why, then, is the first job considered so much more prominent than the second? Is it because the psychiatrist treats an ongoing parade of complete strangers with whom he shares no true bond, while the mother deals with her very own flesh and blood, the same faces, day-in, day-out, year-in, year-out? Is it because the psychiatrist's professional standing earns him social status and financial reward, while a mother earns her pay in smiles and tears, in *nachas* from her children, and in the reward awaiting her in the World-to-Come?

Once the *baalas teshuva* recognizes the genuine significance of her life as a Jewish woman, charged with the future of our nation by cultivating her children's appreciation for Torah and *mitzvos*, her priorities will eventually change, with family and home easily topping the list. Moreover, her commitment will be stronger, for it is born of weighing the options and making an intelligent, deliberate choice.

Non-Assertiveness Training

Another point for women growing up in the throes of E.R.A. and feminism is the expected demeanor of women in the religious world. From childhood, girls in the secular world are groomed to be assertive. They are encouraged to do all the things men do (only *better*), for therein lies their road to equality. Upon entering the Torah-observant world, women are instructed to disregard these ideas, to assume the demeanor of an *isha tzenua*. This is a formidable task, especially since many of them resent being assigned to what they view as the "back seat" in Jewish life.

I am constantly searching for analogies to illustrate for the returning woman, that the importance of women in Judaism is in no way reflected in her low profile. The C.I.A.'s role in the U.S. government certainly demonstrates that high visibility is not necessarily an indicator of how crucial a role is to the functioning and security of a nation.

"If the woman's input is so important," demanded one student, "why does the husband have the last word? That sounds like dictatorship to me!"

My reply: Two people can never really share a partnership equally. In either-or confrontations, one of them must prevail. But this type of face-off should be rare in Jewish family life. Similar to viable business partnerships, a successful family usually entails a division of labor and responsibility. The husband, as a *ben Torah*, should be sufficiently proficient in his Torah studies to refer to halachic guidelines and Torah values in his decision-making. Moreover, a good husband (and wife) must always try to take his (and her) partner's opinion into account. Possessing final authority does not have to mean being authoritarian.

Radical Changes in Midstream

Even after they have accepted a basic Torah outlook on life, many *baalos teshuva* find difficulty in accepting many details of life as a Jewish woman. Their new commitment to a Torah life often forces them to abort lifelong dreams or abandon chosen would-be professions because they would violate Torah laws. Dancers, opera singers, athletes and rabbinical students are forced to channel their talents and skills into other directions and relinquish what they have toiled so long to achieve.

Also, marriage looms prominently on the horizon of young religious women. The newly *frum* are shocked by the idea of marrying young, before one has had a chance to "see the world," "find one's self," or further one's career. And at at time when 1.2 children is the norm, a family of seven is unimaginable. Many women question how it is possible that the Torah, as sensitive as it is to the needs of the individual, has seemingly overtaxed the woman in this manner. All of these issues must be dealt with and discussed in depth to assuage all doubts that may arise.

At the opposite extreme, *baalos teshuva* who have come to appreciate Jewish family life often tend to idealize the institution as utopian. Their exposure to religious families, for the most part, occurs when everyone is on his and her very best behavior — during a *Shabbos* meal, or at a *simcha*. This may promote unrealistically high expectations in terms of looking for a spouse and raising a family. The women must realize that marriage and raising a family are formidable struggles; the results are usually very rewarding, but never perfect. Forewarned, these future wives and mothers can deal with the situation more realistically and sensibly.

The "Shidduch" Game

Now that these young women have accepted the idea of imminent marriage, they must embark on *"shidduchim."* To them, the term *"shadchan"* calls to mind Yenta the Matchmaker from *Fiddler on the Roof*, and provokes dismay, to say the least: "How can someone who barely knows me suggest who my partner-in-life should be?" True, the results speak for themselves, but not without difficulties along the way.

The process of investigating the background and character traits of a young man prior to accepting a *shidduch* suggestion and risking emotional involvement is totally foreign to these women. Intellectually, they realize that this is the best possible means of avoiding problems later on, but many of them balk at the idea of actually participating in this process.

In addition, a woman discovering her Jewish identity embarks upon a path of constant growth. She meets a young man who is at a similar stage in his progress, but who is to stay that they will continue to grow at the same pace and choose the same direction within Judaism? The final decision to join together as partners-in-life becomes an especially frightening one in terms of what the future may hold.

The answers to her problems lie in dedicated interest, concern, timely advice, and a dash of humor from those of us who have already established our Jewish homes.

◆§ The Quandaries of Married Life

Engaged and ready to marry, for a life of Torah and *mitzvos*, the problems have not yet disappeared.

Before marriage, many young women become confused by the variety of customs they observe as guests in different homes. They lack a specific tradition of their own. On top of that, it is often difficult for them to discriminate between a law and a custom. The women must be directed to follow *one* rabbinical authority as a source of guidance. They should be taught to distinguish between a *din* and a *minhag*, and to understand the halachic implications of each.

Women who grew up *frum* are accustomed to the practice of covering one's hair. The wig is considered an essential component of a child's costume when dressing up like Mommy, and most of the married women whom these children associate with do cover their hair. The sight of a wig is so commonplace to them that donning one does not constitute a traumatic change as a new wife.

By the contrast, countless *baalos teshuva* have related to me their first experience at the *sheitel macher* — many cried and others were dismayed by the artificial look of the wigs. Hats, berets, and scarves are definitely favored, as they are common attire in the secular world.

A painful situation common to the *baalas teshuva* is the rift between herself and her family that often results from her change in ideology. Family bonds may have been strong and sure. Yet, when the main focus of a person's life — *Yiddishkeit*, in this case — is in direct conflict with the life-style and ideals of her family, an unavoidable breach often results. In addition, many women travel hundreds of miles to study Judaism. The physical distance compounded by the growing emotional gap can be very taxing to the searching woman, and leaves her with no psychological support as she takes this major step forward and embraces *Yiddishkeit*.

Family help is often lacking in many practical areas, as well. For example, many girls are forced to make all of the arrangements for their own weddings entirely unaided (save for the help of concerned friends or teachers). Once married, they have no parents or in-laws to visit for *Shabbos* or *Yom Tov*; and should they risk the visit, they find it a mine field of emotional, halachic, and ideological traps. In times of stress — after a birth or during a *simcha* — the couple usually has to "go it on their own." Thus, every invitation and every extension of courtesy and concern that they receive from neighbors or friends is cherished.

⋅ A Task for Us All

My purpose in examining the trials and tribulations involved in a woman's transition to *Yiddishkeit* is not to inspire pity for them. Their lives are filled with beauty and meaning, as they uncover new revelations of wisdom in their day-to-day encounters with Torah. Without a great deal of *Siyata diShmaya* (Divine assistance) and the support of families and friends, however, the entire process of return would surely be a formidable task, beyond ordinary folks. Our families bear a special responsibility to serve as role models for those returning to *Yiddishkeit*, while they point out for us the way toward a deeper involvement in Torah through constant struggle for self-improvement.

Marsha Shine

Teshuvah

The realization happened in a moment
Yet the transition took many years.

I can't remember exactly when
I discovered Hashem within me.

I didn't know He was there all along...
Waiting...
Hoping for me to open the right door.

Three Cheers for Turbulence Le-Shem Shomayim!

Dear Editor:

Upon reading the exchange correspondence in the September, 1982, J.O., I thought I would contribute my two cents' worth on the subject, too.

> *"Ba'alei teshuvah come out of disillusionment, out of despair. Some simply cannot face the world, their lives are in shambles, and they suffer emotional problems, physical addictions and failure in their endeavors."*
>
> —D. Gottlieb, *Planting Seeds of Return*,
> J.O., March, 1982

Are these words necessarily derogatory and insulting? Perhaps it depends upon how they are viewed. I feel qualified to speak on this subject, as I have been part of the *"teshuvah* movement" ever since my conversion to Judaism ten years ago.

⋺ Turbulence Le-Shem Shomayim

In my forty-eight years in *Olam HaZeh* I have known periods of calm, and periods of turbulence. The calm periods, seen from the inside, were ones of boredom, emptiness, inanity. The turbulent one started when I left my George Jensen-appointed apartment in Paris, my sports car and my successful lawyer husband of twenty years' standing to come to Israel with a suitcase in one hand, a one-way ticket in the other, and the firm intention to become Jewish in head and heart.

Yes, I "came out of disillusionment" with the vapid members of the jet set whom I faced so frequently over *escargots a l'aille* (snails in garlic sauce) at the city's best restaurants. I suffered from "failure in my endeavors" to adapt to the *tumah* in the street in front of our building (and upstairs, and next door, and nearly everywhere I turned). This was "simply a world I did not want to face" any more. Thus a period of "calm" came to an end... and then it really hit the fan.

Imagine what it would be like. Picture to yourself, as if in a technicolor movie:

☐ going to a new country, where the word "foreign" as a description is the understatement of the year;

☐ a new language, completely unlike anything you have ever seen or heard before;

☐ new ways of dressing and eating;

☐ a collection of different kinds of people from all over the world, living on top of one another, each with his different mentality, reaction patterns, likes and dislikes and national customs;

☐ an economic situation where many single women cannot earn enough to afford both rent and food — with the result that you cut down on food and, after a few years, your health cuts down on *you* (complicated by the problem of finding a full-time job where modesty can be safe-guarded);

☐ a complete reupholstery job in the idea-and-attitude department: Everything you thought, took for granted from childhood, gets questioned, subjected to a spiritual roto-rooter, and replaced by new concepts... ditto for *midos* (character);

☐ a change of identity entailing not only a new, unfamiliar name on an identity card, but a highly uncomfortable feeling, somewhere in the subterranean caverns of the *neshamah*, of not knowing really who you are after forty years of thinking you did.
6.5

Now, set the electric mixer dial at "high," stir, and fold in a wrench for good measure. Then imagine all this coming at you at once, from all sides. And all alone, initially, no family, no familiar circle to run to for encouragement and advice.

Turbulence? Yes, ma'am.

"... and they suffer from emotional problems." If someone

Three Cheers for Turbulence Le-Shem Shomayim! / 421

caught up in the throes of the foregoing did not suffer from emotional problems, he probably should see a shrink, fast.

I admit there were times, in the middle of the above-mentioned entanglement, when I was ashamed of my mess. I looked at the quiet, serene, ordered, predictable daily lives of my neighbors, and then looked at me. Ugh! "Convert" was not a word I liked to think about in those days, and when someone tried to cheer me up with the story of Ruth, I would answer: "But *she* had a *family* (Naomi) and a *roof* over her head."

I believe this sensitivity and feeling of shame may be natural to many going through the turbulence of the major life change involved in *teshuvah*. However, seen from one angle, these feelings can be a stimulus to the hard work, learning and prayer needed to straighten things out.

And now the good news: IT DOESN'T LAST FOREVER.

Like the automatic washing machine's cycle, the spiritual wash, spin, rinse and wring comes to an end and you are left with much cleaner, brighter *midos* and attitudes than when you started.

◆§ The Task: Finding My Niche

It appears to me that the central task confronting the newcomer to Judaism is finding his/her own niche in *Am Yisrael*. First of all, I want to establish what I do *not* mean by finding one's own niche. I do not mean passing for an FFB as life's goal; I do not mean marrying into a family of prestigious lineage and living merrily ever after; nor becoming "one of the crowd" in the Rolls-Royce owners' club. I am speaking of something that has to do with making a unique, personal contribution to the Jewish People and the discovery and development of a one-of-a-kind set of talents in the process.

After ten years I am finding my niche. Somewhere, back toward the beginning of the Turbulence, I started to become interested in a rather specialized field, one which has very few exponents in the religious community and not anyone I had ever heard of that spoke English. Out of love and fascination with the subject, I read everything I could get my hands on about it, and it was not long before I started writing thereon. (I had never written before.) Seven years, a sheaf of articles and one book later, I was invited to lecture on my subject at a seminary for *ba'alos teshuvah*.

I am currently lecturing at two seminaries and give an occasional *shi'ur* in my neighborhood in Hebrew.

৸ On the Surface: Domestic Tranquility

But more important is my job as Jewish homemaker. I am married to a man who shares my interest in this specialty, and who studies full time in a small yeshivah. We are far from rich; my wardrobe mostly consists of creations off the racks of used clothing stores, and hand-me-downs. We live in a poor neighborhood which is largely irreligious, although there is a steadily growing, strong religious nucleus. We chose this neighborhood because we feel we can be an influence for *Kiddush Hashem* here. A weekly women's *shi'ur* meets in our home; very few *Shabbosim* go by that we do not have *ba'alos teshuvah* from the seminaries as guests. The house is open to anyone in need of a meal, companionship over a cup of tea, or help in finding a room, job, or *shidduch*. I enjoy cooking yet another traditional Jewish dish for *Shabbos* and baking my own *challos* as much as I relish writing.

This is the "outside view," the surface. Simultaneously, on the inside, I note the blossoming of new attitudes. For one, I am at peace with myself as a convert. Rabbi Gottlieb, in his letter to the editor in the September, 1982, JO, writes:

"In many areas of life, a ba'al teshuvah never stops being a ba'al teshuvah."

This is quite true. But I have found now that instead of being a stumbling block, it has become an asset, both in my neighborhood and in the classroom. Actually, I hardly think of it any more. I feel at home.

But, the question may arise: "Were there any instances when you were not accepted?" No, never. There *were* occasions, however, when, without rejecting me as a Jew, my choice of *poseik*, *Siddur*, and the customs I decided to follow were rejected loudly and clearly, pressure being brought to change my approach to Judaism to conform to various molds that did not fit my basic inner structure. And this, as luck would have it, just at the spin-and-wring cycle, when sensitivity and vulnerability were at their zenith. (It was an experience, I believe, that I could have done without at that particular epoch in my history!)

Now, firmly rooted in my own little patch, such occasions pass me by with as little effect as the dulcet tones of a grumpy bus driver. Truth to tell, they rarely happen these days. Time is probably a vital factor.

Dealing With Criticism

Suspicion of a newcomer is a natural, deeply rooted instinct, usually unconscious. But if the newcomer sticks it out, quietly and persistently, going about his business over a long period of time, the uncomfortable feelings of those individuals seem to evaporate as it is seen and felt that the new person is not a threat to security, even with his differences in custom. The formula appears to be Time-plus-Perseverance.

To newcomers I would say: "Recognize that there are two kinds of criticism: that which can be useful as an educational tool (regarding, for example, lengths of hemline and neckline, the finer points of *kashrus*, etc.) and that which comes from a disquieting feeling within the critic himself when faced with a kind of person he has never seen before in his life, and who perhaps also voices ideas which, although 120% kosher, are nonetheless also completely outside the critic's ken. Learn to know the difference, in spite of how you might feel at the moment you receive the criticism."

When confronted with a more-brusque-than-necessary *tochachah*, ask yourself:

"Is this true? *Is* my hemline too high?" Or, "Is this statement on the *halachah* of *kashrus* accurate?" If in doubt, ask a *she'eilah*. If you know you are right and the other person is wrong, it is best not to argue. Best response is: "You may be right; maybe I should look into it." This answer, accompanied by an outwardly calm, smiling manner, is recommended in assertiveness training courses and doeth much to gentle down even the roughest of conversation partners.

If pressured to follow a particular rebbe or *poseik* which you do not feel is "your thing" or to wear a wig instead of a kerchief, for instance — a good answer, respectively, is: "Yes, I am sure *Rav* so-and-so has many merits," or, "You're right, wigs *are* attractive"...and then continue doing what you know to be best for you. I stress again, in these instances time is on your side.

Advice to the Born-Religious

To the born-religious, I would like to offer a suggestion when dealing with a *ba'al teshuvah* or convert. If you have an uncomfortable feeling when you are with a certain person, ask yourself: "Why do I feel this way? What about him/her makes me tense? Could what I am about to say hurt this person?"

I can't recommend gentleness too highly when speaking to a newcomer to Judaism.

If a convert or *ba'al teshuvah* comes to you for advice or help, and you are not able to be of assistance — you believe you do not have the time, or you feel that his personality is not compatible with yours — instead of a preemptory dismissal you might try:

"I really can't help you, but I know someone who may be able to. Why don't you try this address?"

I assure you that you will be remembered with a blessing.

Keep in mind that, willingly or involuntarily, you are providing an example for the newcomer, an impression that will stick with him in his new life. This, I believe, is one of the meanings of the phrase "*Kiddush Hashem.*"

In answer to the possible question: "What's the matter, you oversensitive or something?" The answer (as I wrote once) is:

"Yes, we are generally a sort of sensitive crowd (with exceptions, of course); and there are periods and circumstances when we are more so than usual. People who are attracted to Judaism are usually above average in intelligence and sensitivity. Abstract questions regarding Truth, Justice, Human Behavior and its causes and effects, Meaning, etc., rarely enter the mind of the less perceptive individual, while the insensitive and coarse are not likely to notice such things in their environment as emptiness, moral decay, lies, corruption, cruelty, and the suffering they breed. These types accept such conditions as "natural," feel at home where they are, and have no reason to search for anything else. Perhaps this is the reason the *mitzvah* relating to converts appears so many times in the *Chumash*.

ৰ্ড Aids Along the Way

I believe that finding one's particular niche is a pure gift from *Hashem*. To be sure, efforts on our part are necessary — but someone could make all the efforts in his power and not find his place; or conversely, he could suddenly become aware of an open door where there was none yesterday and *voila!* he finds himself rooted in his own little patch.

Prayer is perhaps the most important of my *hishtadlut* activities. One great scholar said that *Hashem* often puts us into certain circumstances for the purpose of chasing us under the wings of the *Shechinah*. The tribulations of the *teshuvah* reconstruction period are guaranteed to do just that, if nothing else.

Again I want to emphasize *persistence*. It is written that nothing stands in the way of the will. This means keeping the will up-and-at-'em day after day after day, especially during stretches of desert where it seemed no progress was being made, or when the treadmill appeared to be going backwards.

I don't see how it is possible to do all this alone — perhaps for some extraordinary souls, it is. But I found Rabbi Gottlieb accurate in his statement:

"*Ba'alei teshuvah*"] (and most converts)[1] have very unique needs — specialized *shi'urim*, sensitive counseling and *psak halachah*. (Among other things)... At each stage in life the *ba'al teshuvah* (or convert) is trying to live according to a life-style of which he had no personal experience until adulthood. It is our experience to help him fill that gap, not only one year after he makes his commitment, but throughout the rest of his life — even after he can pass for an FFB through his dress and Torah knowledge."

I received this kind of support (and still do) all along the way, and I am deeply indebted to all those in the community who are my "family." It is not only their advice and concrete assistance, but their *example* — when the tumult dies down and one is over the hump, it is the example that endures.

Although I did say that membership in the "in" crowd was not my cup of tea, far be it from me to disparage aristocracy. On the contrary: I am all for it — *aristocracy* that is *nobility of the spirit*. This has nothing to do with family lineage and possessions, or even knowledge in some cases. This nobility concerns *midos*, particularly those touching on *ve'ahavta l're'acha ka'mocha*; and it can be had by those on all social strata and income levels, by the unlettered as well as by PhDs. Thus I have friends in all these categories, who in addition represent a cross-section of all the different national origins and approaches to Judaism in the country. True aristocracy is not snobbish, and I found this confirmed when one of the scions of an American "prestigious lineage" family married a hitherto unknown *ba'alas teshuvah* not long ago.

---

1. Parentheses mine.

◈§ Three Cheers

I do not see disillusionment, failure in endeavors, emotional problems, and inability to face the world as necessarily derogatory terms. Wouldn't it make sense to look coolly at what someone is disillusioned about? And exactly which endeavors did he fail in? What was the world like that he was unable to face? What is causing his emotional problems, and what is he doing about them? And, isn't it written that Torah, *Eretz Yisrael* and the Next World are won by suffering?

I say, "Three cheers for turbulence *le shem shomayim*."

Sincerely,

S. Bat Abraham
Jerusalem

Libby Lazewnik

The Traveler and the Princess

(Or Lament Of An F.F.B)

Discontented sat the Princess on her golden chair.
Then they brought a traveler in. She sat up with a stare.
"Tell me," she beseeched the traveler, radiant of face.
"Tell me of your bitter journey back to this, your place."

Wistfully she listened to the tales poured in her ear.
"Tell me of your joy," she begged, "now that you've made it here!"
Shifting shadows played upon her features as he spoke
And when he'd done, she murmured in a voice that sadly broke:

"Not for me the frozen march across the windswept waste
Nor the bliss of seizing what so very long I've chased!
Here I sit in cozy splendor, fed from silver spoons.
Not for me the lonely baying under silver moons;

"Not for me exquisite warming at a newfound fire
Soaring up on brand-new wings, high and ever higher;
How I envy you, dear traveler, fresh from wind and frost
Hugging to yourself the joy of finding what you've lost!

"Never will I stand upon a long-awaited shore
Knowing that I've reached at last the home I'd left before.
An uncut diamond, how you've worked to free your inner glow!
Something I — a gem in velvet box — will never know."

The traveler seemed astonished, his brow creased in thought.
"You've never known real cold, it's true, although you think you
    ought.
The freezing trek is strange to you, the ice that takes its toll —
But Princess, have you never felt a chill upon the soul?

"You haven't hunted wary miles, of that I will be bound.
But tell me, have you never strained to gain a little ground?
And have you never felt the longing, just as I have done,
To draw a little closer to the Ineffable One?

"You've never felt the bliss of toasting at a newborn flame
But Princess, doesn't aged fire warm you just the same?
Soaring high on brand-new wings is what you yearn to do
But don't you know the joy already? Haven't you flown, too?

"Finding something that was lost is splendid, I'll admit,
But you, dear Princess, haven't known the pain of losing it!
Coming home is quite a thrill, back from a distant shore —
But don't you fell the same, each time you step inside your door?"

The Princess bowed her lovely head. "How right you are!" she
    cried.
"The way you feel today is how I've always felt inside.
I have always known and cherished that which you've just found.
We two are but a pair of jewels adorning the same Crown.

"In my quiet way I've made my journeys, just like you
And if your tales are more exciting — mine are special, too.
Two travelers are we, indeed, for no one stands quite still:
We both are striding down one road, to satisfy one Will."

The Traveler and the Princess / 429

This volume is part of
THE ARTSCROLL SERIES®
an ongoing project of
translations, commentaries and expositions
on Scripture, Mishnah, Talmud, Halachah,
liturgy, history and the classic Rabbinic writings;
and biographies, and thought.

For a brochure of current publications
visit your local Hebrew bookseller
or contact the publisher:

Mesorah Publications, ltd

4401 Second Avenue
Brooklyn, New York 11232
(718) 921-9000